T0202900

Communications
in Computer and Information Science 1982

Rationale

The CCIS series is devoted to the publication of proceedings of computer science conferences. Its aim is to efficiently disseminate original research results in informatics in printed and electronic form. While the focus is on publication of peer-reviewed full papers presenting mature work, inclusion of reviewed short papers reporting on work in progress is welcome, too. Besides globally relevant meetings with internationally representative program committees guaranteeing a strict peer-reviewing and paper selection process, conferences run by societies or of high regional or national relevance are also considered for publication.

Topics

The topical scope of CCIS spans the entire spectrum of informatics ranging from foundational topics in the theory of computing to information and communications science and technology and a broad variety of interdisciplinary application fields.

Information for Volume Editors and Authors

Publication in CCIS is free of charge. No royalties are paid, however, we offer registered conference participants temporary free access to the online version of the conference proceedings on SpringerLink (http://link.springer.com) by means of an http referrer from the conference website and/or a number of complimentary printed copies, as specified in the official acceptance email of the event.

CCIS proceedings can be published in time for distribution at conferences or as post-proceedings, and delivered in the form of printed books and/or electronically as USBs and/or e-content licenses for accessing proceedings at SpringerLink. Furthermore, CCIS proceedings are included in the CCIS electronic book series hosted in the SpringerLink digital library at http://link.springer.com/bookseries/7899. Conferences publishing in CCIS are allowed to use Online Conference Service (OCS) for managing the whole proceedings lifecycle (from submission and reviewing to preparing for publication) free of charge.

Publication process

The language of publication is exclusively English. Authors publishing in CCIS have to sign the Springer CCIS copyright transfer form, however, they are free to use their material published in CCIS for substantially changed, more elaborate subsequent publications elsewhere. For the preparation of the camera-ready papers/files, authors have to strictly adhere to the Springer CCIS Authors' Instructions and are strongly encouraged to use the CCIS LaTeX style files or templates.

Abstracting/Indexing

CCIS is abstracted/indexed in DBLP, Google Scholar, EI-Compendex, Mathematical Reviews, SCImago, Scopus. CCIS volumes are also submitted for the inclusion in ISI Proceedings.

How to start

To start the evaluation of your proposal for inclusion in the CCIS series, please send an e-mail to ccis@springer.com.

Ana I. Pereira · Armando Mendes ·
Florbela P. Fernandes · Maria F. Pacheco ·
João P. Coelho · José Lima
Editors

Optimization, Learning Algorithms and Applications

Third International Conference, OL2A 2023
Ponta Delgada, Portugal, September 27–29, 2023
Revised Selected Papers, Part II

 Springer

Editors
Ana I. Pereira (iD)
Instituto Politécnico de Bragança
Bragança, Portugal

Armando Mendes (iD)
University of Azores
Ponta Delgada, Portugal

Florbela P. Fernandes (iD)
Instituto Politécnico de Bragança
Bragança, Portugal

Maria F. Pacheco (iD)
Instituto Politécnico de Bragança
Bragança, Portugal

João P. Coelho (iD)
Instituto Politécnico de Bragança
Bragança, Portugal

José Lima (iD)
Instituto Politécnico de Bragança
Bragança, Portugal

ISSN 1865-0929   ISSN 1865-0937 (electronic)
Communications in Computer and Information Science
ISBN 978-3-031-53035-7   ISBN 978-3-031-53036-4 (eBook)
https://doi.org/10.1007/978-3-031-53036-4

This Springer imprint is published by the registered company Springer Nature Switzerland AG
The registered company address is: Gewerbestrasse 11, 6330 Cham, Switzerland

Paper in this product is recyclable.

Preface

The volumes CCIS 1981 and 1982 contains the refereed proceedings of the III International Conference on Optimization, Learning Algorithms and Applications (OL2A 2023), a hybrid event held on September 27–29.

OL2A provided a space for the research community in optimization and learning to get together and share the latest developments, trends and techniques as well as develop new paths and collaborations. OL2A had the participation of more than four hundred participants in an online and face-to-face environment throughout three days, discussing topics associated with areas such as optimization and learning and state-of-the-art applications related to multi-objective optimization, optimization for machine learning, robotics, health informatics, data analysis, optimization and learning under uncertainty and 4th industrial revolution.

Six special sessions were organized under the topics Learning Algorithms in Engineering Education, Optimization in the SDG context, Optimization in Control Systems Design, Computer Vision Based on Learning Algorithms, Machine Learning and AI in Robotics and Machine Learning and Data Analysis in Internet of Things. The event had 66 accepted papers. All papers were carefully reviewed and selected from 172 submissions. All the reviews were carefully carried out by a scientific committee of 115 PhD researchers from 23 countries.

The OL2A 2023 volume editors,

September 2023

Ana I. Pereira
Armando Mendes
Florbela P. Fernandes
Maria F. Pacheco
João P. Coelho
José Lima

Organization

General Chairs

Ana I. Pereira   Polytechnic Institute of Bragança, Portugal
Armando Mendes   University of the Azores, Portugal

Program Committee Chairs

Florbela P. Fernandes   Polytechnic Institute of Bragança, Portugal
M. Fátima Pacheco   Polytechnic Institute of Bragança, Portugal
João P. Coelho   Polytechnic Institute of Bragança, Portugal
José Lima   Polytechnic Institute of Bragança, Portugal

Special Session Chairs

João P. Teixeira   Polytechnic Institute of Bragança, Portugal
José Cascalho   University of the Azores, Portugal

Technology Chairs

Paulo Medeiros   University of the Azores, Portugal
Rui Pedro Lopes   Polytechnic Institute of Bragança, Portugal

Program Committee

Ana Isabel Pereira   Polytechnic Institute of Bragança, Portugal
Abeer Alsadoon   Charles Sturt University, Australia
Ala' Khalifeh   German Jordanian University, Jordan
Alberto Nakano   Federal University of Technology – Paraná, Brazil
Alexandre Douplik   Ryerson University, Canada
Ana Maria A. C. Rocha   University of Minho, Portugal
Ana Paula Teixeira   University of Trás-os-Montes and Alto Douro, Portugal
André Pinz Borges   Federal University of Technology – Paraná, Brazil

André Rodrigues da Cruz	Federal Center for Technological Education of Minas Gerais, Brazil
Andrej Košir	University of Ljubljana, Slovenia
António José Sánchez-Salmerón	Universitat Politècnica de València, Spain
António Valente	University of Trás-os-Montes and Alto Douro, Portugal
Armando Mendes	University of the Azores, Portugal
Arnaldo Cândido Júnior	Federal Technological University – Paraná, Brazil
B. Rajesh Kanna	Vellore Institute of Technology, India
Bilal Ahmad	University of Warwick, UK
Bruno Bispo	Federal University of Santa Catarina, Brazil
C. Sweetlin Hemalatha	Vellore Institute of Technology, India
Carlos Henrique Alves	CEFET - Rio de Janeiro, Brazil
Carmen Galé	University of Zaragoza, Spain
Carolina Gil Marcelino	Federal University of Rio de Janeiro, Brazil
Christopher Expósito Izquierdo	University of Laguna, Spain
Clara Vaz	Polytechnic Institute of Bragança, Portugal
Damir Vrančić	Jožef Stefan Institute, Slovenia
Dhiah Abou-Tair	German Jordanian University, Jordan
Diamantino Silva Freitas	University of Porto, Portugal
Diego Brandão	CEFET - Rio de Janeiro, Brazil
Dimitris Glotsos	University of West Attica, Greece
Eduardo Vinicius Kuhn	Federal Technological University – Paraná, Brazil
Elaine Mosconi	Université de Sherbrooke, Canada
Eligius M. T. Hendrix	Malaga University, Spain
Elizabeth Fialho Wanner	Federal Center for Technological Education of Minas Gerais, Brazil
Felipe Nascimento Martins	Hanze University of Applied Sciences, The Netherlands
Florbela P. Fernandes	Polytechnic Institute of Bragança, Portugal
Florentino Fernández Riverola	University of Vigo, Spain
Francisco Sedano	University of León, Spain
Fredrik Danielsson	University West, Sweden
Gaukhar Muratova	Dulaty University, Kazakhstan
Gediminas Daukšys	Kauno Technikos Kolegija, Lithuania
Gianluigi Ferrari	University of Parma, Italy
Glaucia Maria Bressan	Federal University of Technology – Paraná, Brazil
Glotsos Dimitris	University of West Attica, Greece
Humberto Rocha	University of Coimbra, Portugal
João Paulo Carmo	University of São Paulo, Brazil
João Paulo Coelho	Polytechnic Institute of Bragança, Portugal
João Paulo Teixeira	Polytechnic Institute of Bragança, Portugal

Jorge Igual	Universitat Politécnica de Valencia, Spain
Jorge Ribeiro	Polytechnic Institute of Viana do Castelo, Portugal
José Boaventura-Cunha	University of Trás-os-Montes and Alto Douro, Portugal
José Cascalho	University of the Azores, Portugal
José Lima	Polytechnic Institute of Bragança, Portugal
José Ramos	Nova University Lisbon, Portugal
Joseane Pontes	Federal University of Technology – Ponta Grossa, Brazil
Josip Musić	University of Split, Croatia
Juan A. Méndez Pérez	University of Laguna, Spain
Juan Alberto García Esteban	University de Salamanca, Spain
Júlio Cesar Nievola	Pontifícia Universidade Católica do Paraná, Brazil
Kristina Sutiene	Kaunas University of Technology, Lithuania
Laura Belli	University of Parma, Italy
Lidia Sánchez	University of León, Spain
Lino Costa	University of Minho, Portugal
Luca Davoli	University of Parma, Italy
Luca Oneto	University of Genoa, Italy
Luca Spalazzi	Marche Polytechnical University, Italy
Luis Antonio De Santa-Eulalia	Université de Sherbrooke, Canada
Luís Coelho	Polytechnic Institute of Porto, Portugal
M. Fátima Pacheco	Polytechnic Institute of Bragança, Portugal
Mahmood Reza Khabbazi	University West, Sweden
Manuel Castejón Limas	University of León, Spain
Marc Jungers	Université de Lorraine, France
Marco Aurélio Wehrmeister	Federal University of Technology – Paraná, Brazil
Marek Nowakowski	Military Institute of Armoured and Automotive Technology in Sulejowek, Poland
Maria do Rosário de Pinho	University of Porto, Portugal
Martin Hering-Bertram	Hochschule Bremen, Germany
Matthias Funk	University of the Azores, Portugal
Mattias Bennulf	University West, Sweden
Michał Podpora	Opole University of Technology, Poland
Miguel Ángel Prada	University of León, Spain
Mikulas Huba	Slovak University of Technology in Bratislava, Slovakia
Milena Pinto	Federal Center of Technological Education Celso Suckow da Fonseca, Brazil
Miroslav Kulich	Czech Technical University Prague, Czech Republic
Nicolae Cleju	Technical University of Iasi, Romania

Paulo Alves	Polytechnic Institute of Bragança, Portugal
Paulo Leitão	Polytechnic Institute of Bragança, Portugal
Paulo Lopes dos Santos	University of Porto, Portugal
Paulo Medeiros	University of the Azores, Portugal
Paulo Moura Oliveira	University of Trás-os-Montes and Alto Douro, Portugal
Pavel Pakshin	Nizhny Novgorod State Tech University, Russia
Pedro Luiz de Paula Filho	Federal Technological University – Paraná, Brazil
Pedro Miguel Rodrigues	Catholic University of Portugal, Portugal
Pedro Morais	Polytechnic Institute of Cávado e Ave, Portugal
Pedro Pinto	Polytechnic Institute of Viana do Castelo, Portugal
Roberto Molina de Souza	Federal University of Technology – Paraná, Brazil
Rui Pedro Lopes	Polytechnic Institute of Bragança, Portugal
Sabrina Šuman	Polytechnic of Rijeka, Croatia
Sancho Salcedo Sanz	Alcalá University, Spain
Sandro Dias	Federal Center for Technological Education of Minas Gerais, Brazil
Sani Rutz da Silva	Federal Technological University – Paraná, Brazil
Santiago Torres Álvarez	University of Laguna, Spain
Sara Paiva	Polytechnic Institute of Viana do Castelo, Portugal
Shridhar Devamane	Global Academy of Technology, India
Sławomir Stępień	Poznań University of Technology, Poland
Sofia Rodrigues	Polytechnic Institute of Viana do Castelo, Portugal
Sudha Ramasamy	University West, Sweden
Teresa Paula Perdicoulis	University of Trás-os-Montes and Alto Douro, Portugal
Toma Rancevic	University of Split, Croatia
Uta Bohnebeck	Hochschule Bremen, Germany
Virginia Castillo	University of León, Spain
Vítor Duarte dos Santos	Nova University Lisbon, Portugal
Vitor Pinto	University of Porto, Portugal
Vivian Cremer Kalempa	State University of Santa Catarina, Brazil
Wojciech Giernacki	Poznań University of Technology, Poland
Wojciech Paszke	University of Zielona Gora, Poland
Wynand Alkema	Hanze University of Applied Sciences, The Netherlands
Zahia Guessoum	University of Reims Champagne-Ardenne, France

Contents – Part II

Machine Learning and AI in Robotics

Contents – Part I

Learning Algorithms in Engineering Education

Machine Learning and Data Analysis in Internet of Things

Optimization

Optimization in the SDG Context

Computer Vision Based on Learning Algorithms

Assessing the Reliability of AI-Based Angle Detection for Shoulder and Elbow Rehabilitation

Luan C. Klein[1,2(✉)], Arezki Abderrahim Chellal[2,4], Vinicius Grilo[2],
José Gonçalves[2,3], Maria F. Pacheco[2,3], Florbela P. Fernandes[2,3],
Fernando C. Monteiro[2,3], and José Lima[2,3]

[1] Universidade Tecnológica Federal do Paraná, Campus Curitiba, UTFPR/PR,
Curitiba, Brazil
[2] Research Centre in Digitalization and Intelligent Robotics (CeDRI), Instituto
Politécnico de Bragança, Bragança, Portugal
{luanklein,arezki,viniciusgrilo,goncalves,pacheco,fflor,
monteiro,jllima}@ipb.pt
[3] Laboratório Associado para a Sustentabilidade e Tecnologia em Regiões de
Montanha (SusTEC), Instituto Politécnico de Bragança, Bragança, Portugal
[4] Universidade de Trás-os-Montes e Alto Douro UTAD, 5000-801 Vila Real, Portugal

Abstract. Angle assessment is crucial in rehabilitation and significantly
influences physiotherapists' decision-making. Although visual inspection
is commonly used, it is known to be approximate. This work aims to
be a preliminary study about using the AI image-based to assess upper
limb joint angles. Two main frameworks were evaluated: MediaPipe and
Yolo v7. The study was performed with 28 participants performing four
upper limb movements. The results showed that Yolo v7 achieved greater
estimation accuracy than Mediapipe, with MAEs of around $5°$ and $17°$,
respectively. However, even with better results, Yolo v7 showed some
limitations, including the point of detection in only a 2D plane, the
higher computational power required to enable detection, and the difficulty of performing movements requiring more than one degree of Freedom (DOF). Nevertheless, this study highlights the detection capabilities of AI approaches, showing be a promising approach for measuring
angles in rehabilitation activities, representing a cost-effective and easy-
to-implement solution.

Keywords: Join Angle Measurement · Artificial Intelligence · Motion
Capture · Robotic Rehabilitation

1 Introduction

The general movements of the human arm are obtained by combining the movements of the shoulder, elbow, and arm. Tracking the rate at which these angles
change during rehabilitation sessions can provide therapists with useful information about how patients respond to rehabilitation treatments.

© The Author(s), under exclusive license to Springer Nature Switzerland AG 2024
A. I. Pereira et al. (Eds.): OL2A 2023, CCIS 1982, pp. 3–18, 2024.
https://doi.org/10.1007/978-3-031-53036-4_1

Several research teams have extensively studied the kinematics of the human arm in the last few years [1–3]. Understanding the kinematics of the human arm is crucial in several fields, including biomechanics, sport, and rehabilitation. By defining the patient's limits at the outset of rehabilitation sessions, it is possible, thanks to the application of human arm kinematics, to calculate the entire workspace accessible to the patient, i.e., the patient's range of movement (ROM) [4]. Figure 1 presents the general structure of the human arm motion kinematics, highlighting the different screw axes R_A, R_F, R_R, R_7, most suitable for this study.

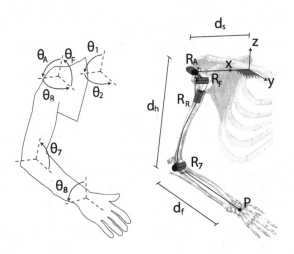

Fig. 1. (Left) principal motions of the human arm. (Right) the human arm motion kinematics representation is investigated in this study.

The shoulder joint is a complex joint composed of external and internal parts. The external shoulder joint constitutes a spherical joint, which is represented by three rotations (R_A, R_F, R_R); these rotations are related to the following movements: abduction and adduction, flexion and extension, and external and internal rotation, respectively. This spherical joint is connected to the rest of the body by a translation of $[d_s\ 0\ 0]^T$, representing the shoulder size. It is followed by a single rotation joint labeled R_7, translated with a distance of $[0\ 0\ -d_h]^T$, representing the humerus (the main bone of the arm). This rotation is equivalent to the flexion and extension movements. In addition, it is essential to point out the existence of the supination and pronation movements performed with the rotation θ_8, translated by the forearm with $[0\ d_F\ 0]^T$, that will not be considered in this study.

The reference frame is located at the internal shoulder joint. It is important to note that the torso possesses additional rotation joints in the internal shoulder region (θ_1 and θ_2). While these rotations have been neglected for this preliminary study and general upper limb rehabilitation, it is essential to consider them in specific cases such as frozen shoulder rehabilitation, where addressing these internal shoulder joint rotations becomes crucial [5].

Motor deficits in the arm are commonly observed following a stroke, with studies suggesting that approximately 55% to 75% of patients experience such deficits at 3 and 6 months post-stroke [6]. These consequences can be treated or minimized with rehabilitation techniques, but, in general, rehabilitation requires a professional to perform repetitive movements of the affected limb [7]. Robotic-assisted rehabilitation processes show promise as solutions, providing precise and constant movements to speed up the recovery process and other technological tools [8]. This technology offers the advantage of monitoring and recording accurate data on patient progress, allowing for an evidence-based approach and continuous treatment adaptation. But for this process to be successful, a good patient sensing system is required.

The procedure for assessing angles, based on visual inspection in the rehabilitation community, is approximate and further complicated by the dynamic nature of patient mobility throughout the rehabilitation process [9]. Studies have shown that this visual examination is subject to errors of up to 10° [10]. The integration of technology and artificial intelligence (AI) into the assessment process seems the most appropriate.

This work is a preliminary study to verify and validate the possibility of using AI image-based for joint angle estimation in rehabilitation. An approach that applies a camera coupled with an AI-based algorithm compares two state-of-the-art frameworks for pose detection: MediaPipe and Yolo v7. These two frameworks have already been developed and subsequently trained by other research teams, the objectives being solely to validate the possibility of using AI-based approaches. In addition, this study aims to provide a more accurate and consistent assessment method during rehabilitation sessions, facilitated by a robotic arm and controlled by the SmartHealth software. The presented results aim to assess the effectiveness and reliability of AI applications in robotic rehabilitation and their limitations.

In addition to this Introduction, this paper is structured as follows: Sect. 2 describes state of the art in angle detection using automatic and intelligent methods and the added value of AI in rehabilitation robotics. Section 3 describes the methodology to incorporate the MediaPipe and Yolo v7 techniques into the angle detection algorithm of the SmartHealth software. Section 4 highlights the obtained results and offers some details for additional discussion. Finally, Sect. 5 provides a general conclusion about the work and the proposition of future developments that will enhance this study.

2 State of the Art

The use of AI and robotics is transforming the health ecosystems [11]. Machine learning and robotics focused on rehabilitation is an interesting field and has been the object of increasing attention. An interesting review of several approaches, including wearable devices, virtual and augmented reality, physical and socially assistive, and other aspects, was developed in [12]. A review focused on cognitive rehabilitation training was also developed in [13].

Another interesting review was performed in [14]; it summarizes AI approaches used to estimate the error trajectory function, joint angular velocity, and others. AI and robotics were also explored in rehabilitating children and youth [15].

Besides the use of AI in rehabilitation robotics, vision-based detection techniques are also an interesting approach used in several areas, such as rehabilitation. A variety of approaches can be used for motion detection to support rehabilitation, such as computer vision, haptic devices [16], approaches using Inertial Measurement Units (IMUs) [17], and others [18]. Vision-based approaches are interesting in practical terms since attaching devices to the patient is unnecessary, increasing the freedom of movement and not requiring additional equipment.

In work presented in [19], a hand tracking system can be visualized to improve hand and arm sensitivity for accident recovery or cognitive disabilities. The application incorporates exercises that encompass diverse shapes, each varying in complexity. Users' performance is logged and stored to effectively evaluate the progress of the rehabilitation process compared with predefined curves. Using a remote interface, the medical staff can remotely access each user's exercise databases, allowing progress to be assessed by analyzing numerical and graphical results. A similar solution is shown in [20], but an interaction is added between the patient and the graphical interface to provide visual feedback on the movement to be performed.

In [21], an application to detect the upper joints of the human body to calculate the compensations needed in the process of robot rehabilitation is presented. An RGB image is used to estimate the position of each body part in a 2D space. A spatial mapping relationship is established to calculate the 3D coordinates of joints. Then it calculates the transformation matrices to transform the pixel coordinates into a real reference system. The patient's pose calculates the positions of a collaborative robot UR5 that assists the rehabilitation process.

The work developed in [10] studied the use of the Microsoft Kinect V2 device to detect body movement and to monitor the execution of rehabilitation exercises involving lower limb pathologies. The methodology was validated using two simultaneous motion capture systems, the Vicon MX3, composed of 14 infrared cameras, and the Microsoft Kinect system, consisting of an RGB camera and a 3D depth sensor. In conclusion, it was verified that the evaluation of joint angles and positions with the Kinect showed poor to good reliability, especially in movements with low amplitude, when compared to the Vicon MX3 system, which showed less variability. Another interesting discussion suggested that joint angles and positions were only assessed at the beginning of the movement and at maximum excursion, but that assessment throughout the movement would provide better conclusions about the systems.

3   Methodology

The methodology section is divided into two main parts. The first focuses on the theoretical background, explaining the MediaPipe and Yolo v7 functionality.

The second part is related to the implementation, how the approaches were used to calculate the angles, and how the AI was integrated into the pre-existent software for rehabilitation.

3.1   Theoretical Background

Machine Learning (ML) is a computer technique that learns from a set of data without specific instruction and draws inferences based on the patterns found in the data. There are three main types of learning: unsupervised, supervised, and reinforcement learning [22]. Several libraries are available to help in the implementation use of AI applications, for instance, the Scikit-Learn[1], PyTorch[2], TensorFlow[3] and others. Other interesting frameworks have already been developed, which provide techniques ready to use, i.e., pre-trained models. Yolo v7[4] and MediaPipe[5] are examples of such frameworks. Since these, both already have pose tracking (the detection of the key points of the person) implemented and ready to use. They are part of the current state-of-the-art in this kind of application. These two approaches were selected to validate the possibility of the use in the application to calculate the angles in the context of the SmartHealth project. It is important to emphasize that the models were already trained, i.e., the models already learned from several datasets, and the focus of this preliminary study is to check the feasibility of the use.

MediaPipe. MediaPipe framework was developed by Google as an open-source, cross-platform aiming to help the development of pipelines for performing inference over various types of sensory data. It enables the construction of a perceptual pipeline as a network of interchangeable elements, such as model inference, media processing algorithms, data transformations, etc. Perceived descriptions such as object-localization and facial landmark streams leave the graph while sensory data such as audio and video streams enter the graph [23].

The Mediapipe has several solutions available that have already been previously trained for use with different inputs; for vision: object detection, image classification, hand landmark, face landmark detection, pose detection, and others; for text: text classification, text embedding; and language detection; and finally for audio: audio classification and audio embedding.

The MediaPipe framework comprises three main concepts: Packets, Graphs, and Calculators. The pipeline is a graph of components, each being a calculator, where they communicate using Packets. Besides that, the graph is run using a Graph object. Further details about the MediaPipe, its structure, and how it learns are available in [23].

---

[1] https://scikit-learn.org/stable/index.html.
[2] https://pytorch.org/.
[3] https://www.tensorflow.org/.
[4] https://github.com/WongKinYiu/yolov7.
[5] https://developers.google.com/mediapipe.

One of the features of MediaPipe is the Pose, a single-person pose estimation framework used in this work. It is a variant of the BlazePose [24, 25], and it can estimate an individual's full 3D body pose through videos or images.

Yolo V7. You only look once (YOLO), presented in [26], is an approach first developed to object detection in images and video. In summary, instead of using multiple steps to extract and classify regions of interest, Yolo performs object detection and classification in a single step. Several versions of Yolo have been developed (including non-official versions), aiming to improve the quality of the predictions [26].

In this work, version 7 of Yolo was used [27, 28]. In this version, a specific task called pose detection is specialized in pose tracking. It was trained using the well-known COCO dataset[6], which contains 17 landmarks in the body. The pre-trained model with the weights used in this work is called *yolov7-w6-pose.pt*[7].

3.2 Implementation

The AI system was implemented based on the MediaPipe Hollistic and Yolo v7, as previously explained. The system's input is an image (in the present case, captured using the OpenCV library[8]). To capture the images, a camera is positioned in front of the patient during the execution of the exercises, and as a restriction of this work, only the patient should be presented in the image captured by the camera.

The execution of MediaPipe and Yolo v7 occurred at different moments. The structure and execution of the software were the same for both techniques. The main difference is regarding the hardware used to execute: while MediaPipe could execute in CPU, the Yolo was executed in GPU. This difference is due to the development of the libraries and the respective necessary computational powerful.

The respective processing function of each technique was called for each image. The function results are different landmarks of the human body. For the MediaPipe, three different aspects were returned: points on the face, hand points, and key points of body position. The key points were given in 3D, according to the image size (in pixels or real-world coordinates), where the zero is below the stomach. On the other side, Yolo v7 only returns the 2D key points related to the image size.

Then, considering the key points of the body returned (in the MediaPipe case, the points related to the real world), it is possible to calculate the body angles using three different joints of the human body. The following equation gives the formula to calculate the angle among three points (A, B, and C) in 3D:

$$\theta = \arccos\left(\frac{\mathbf{BA} \cdot \mathbf{BC}}{\|\mathbf{BA}\| \cdot \|\mathbf{BC}\|}\right), \tag{1}$$

---

[6] https://cocodataset.org/#home.
[7] https://github.com/WongKinYiu/yolov7.
[8] https://pypi.org/project/opencv-python/.

where $\mathbf{BA} = (x_a - x_b, y_a - y_b, z_a - z_b)$ is the vector with endpoints points A and B, and $\mathbf{BC} = (x_c - x_b, y_c - y_b, z_c - z_b)$ is the vector whose endpoints are C and B. In the case of the 2D points returned by Yolo, the third dimension (z) of all the points was considered 0.

In this study, the default parameters and settings of Yolo v7 were used without modification. For the MediaPipe approach, the following settings were applied: *static_image_mode = True, model_complexity = 2, enable_segmentation = True*, and *min_detection_confidence = 0.5*. These settings were chosen to ensure optimal performance and accuracy for the MediaPipe framework in the study context.

Figure 2 presents the flow of the AI, i.e., the process to obtain the angle values. The same flow was followed by the two techniques used in this work. The initial step is the image capturing (using a camera positioned in front of the patient), followed by library processing, which returns the landmarks. The next step is the definition of the key points used to calculate each angle, and finally, the value of the respective angle is generated using the equation previously presented.

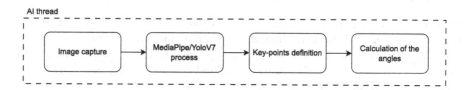

Fig. 2. Flow of the AI execution.

The AI-driven angle detection algorithm mentioned above has been incorporated into the developed software designed to control a UR3 robotic arm to conduct a rehabilitation procedure. As this paper focuses on the implementation details of this specific feature, it is unnecessary to dwell on an overview of the software. Nevertheless, interested readers can consult [29,30] for more information. The workflow can be summarised as follows.

Upon user interaction with the settings tab, relevant information and option concerning the rehabilitation session are displayed. Additionally, the camera is initialized. After a brief initialization period, an independent thread called *"AI_thread"* is launched to execute the AI function. As previously described, the AI algorithm identifies the joint and calculates the angles within this thread. Concurrently, two other threads, named *"reading_thread"* and *"control_thread"*, gather the acquired data (including patient force, robot position, patient's muscle activity, and joint angle) and control the robot, respectively.

A dedicated subroutine named *"update_video"* in the main thread ensures the software's video display is refreshed at ten milliseconds. Furthermore, an animate function is responsible for real-time plotting of the parameters gathered in the *"reading_thread"*. These visualizations are presented within two separate graphics components within the software interface. Figure 3 presents the integration insight of the proposed algorithm within the SmartHealth software.

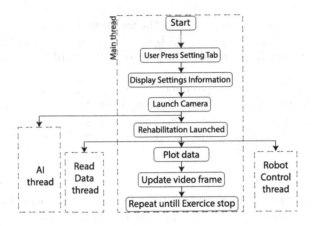

Fig. 3. General Implementation Flowchart.

3.3 Participants and Procedure

Twenty-eight (28) participants (23 males, 5 females) took part in this study. The average height of the participants was 177 cm, with the shortest participant measuring 162 cm and the tallest measuring 198 cm. The average arm length was 29 cm, ranging from 22.50 cm to 36 cm, and the average forearm length was 26 cm, ranging from 22 cm to 30 cm.

The study was divided into two parts to assess the performance of the MediaPipe and Yolo v7, for angle detection. For the experimental evaluation, the participants were assigned to three distinct groups. The first group consisted of 11 individuals who exclusively underwent tests using the MediaPipe framework. Similarly, the second group comprised 11 individuals who exclusively underwent tests using the Yolo v7 framework. Additionally, a subset of 6 participants completed tests involving both the MediaPipe and Yolo v7 frameworks, allowing for comparative analysis. Therefore, the distribution of participants in the groups was 11 + 6 for the MediaPipe evaluations and 11 + 6 for the Yolo v7 evaluations. In addition, only the assessment of the left upper limbs was carried out.

Angle assessments were not performed when the participant's arm was in continuous motion. Instead, a controlled approach was used, in which patients were asked to move their arms to specific predetermined points and maintain the posture for a short period. During this idle state, the AI-based algorithm detects the joints and calculates the target angle. The participant is then invited to move their arm again to another specified point. This deliberate strategy of interrupting movement at specific points was intended to determine the highest precision and accuracy that these algorithms could achieve, minimizing the potential variability introduced by continuous movement. In addition, this procedure also allows reliable comparison between participants by standardizing data collection and reducing fluctuations between participants.

The predetermined points, which the participants were instructed to aim for varied depending on the exercise, for instance, the shoulder abduction exercise had six evaluation angles (minimum angle (min), 40°, 60°, 70°, 90°, and maximum angle (max)), while the shoulder flexion exercise had five (min, 40°, 60°, 90°, and max). Similarly, the external shoulder rotation exercise had five evaluation angles (min, 30°, 60°, 90°, and max), and the elbow extension exercise had five angles (min, 60°, 90°, 120°, and max). The selection of these angles was done to cover the full ROM for each exercise. Despite this standardization, variations have been encountered among participants, due to variations in body structure between individuals and levels of flexibility, leading to differences in the measured angle during the study, especially at the ROM's limits.

However, in the case of the external shoulder rotation exercise, there was a slight difference in the number of targeted angles between the two groups. This variation occurred due to the exercise's unique characteristics and the dynamic nature of the participants' movements during the assessment. Specifically, the Mediapipe approach targeted four evaluation angles, while the Yolo v7 approach included five.

The white protractor fixed to the wall is a basic reference, allowing straightforward reading of the patient's angles. However, it is imperative to recognize the inherent limitations and potential sources of measurement error associated with this approach. As this method relies on manual readings by human observers, the possibility of human error introduces slight inaccuracies in angle measurements. Despite this, the judicious and consistent use of the protractor provides valuable and meaningful comparative data. It serves as a reliable reference for evaluating the performance of the AI-based angle estimation system, facilitating clear and direct comparisons between estimated and actual angles.

4   Results and Discussion

The results section can be divided into two main parts. The first one is related to the procedure applied, where some pictures and examples are presented. The second part considers the results collected from all participants, the Mean Absolute Error (MAE) of the approaches, and discussions about the results.

The MediaPipe-based algorithm was executed on a CPU with an 11th Gen Intel(R) Core(TM) i7-11375H processor running at 3.30 GHz. On the other hand, the Yolo v7 algorithm was executed on a GPU with an NVIDIA GeForce RTX 3060 Laptop GPU.

The choice of using the GPU for the Yolo v7 algorithm was motivated by the high computational demands of this approach. The powerful GPU allowed efficient processing of the complex Yolo v7 algorithm, improving performance. Specifically, the Yolo v7 algorithm achieved a frame rate of 12 Frames per Second (FPS) due to the enhanced computing power provided by the GPU. In contrast, the MediaPipe algorithm, running on the CPU, achieved a frame rate of 30 FPS.

Shoulder Abduction/Adduction (R_A)

Figure 4 showcases real-time angle computation of the shoulder complex, using the R_A rotation as a specific example.

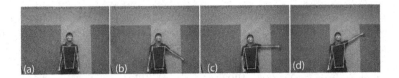

Fig. 4. Real-time Angle Computation for the Shoulder Complex: R_A.

The four images captured the subject's arm movement in 1 DOF, focusing on the R_A rotation. The AI system detects the targeted joints and estimates the angle. The participants faced the camera in the same way in both approaches.

Shoulder Flexion/Extension (R_F)

The subsequent test also affects the shoulder complex but is based on the flexion exercise, i.e., a movement related to the R_F rotation angle. Some samples for real-time computation for the shoulder complex applying both the Mediapipe and Yolo v7 approach are shown in Fig. 5.

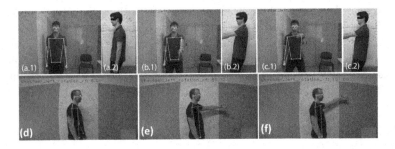

Fig. 5. Real-time Angle Computation for the Shoulder Complex: R_F. **(a, b, c)** with MediaPipe. **(d, e, f)** with Yolo v7.

As the flexion movement is a straightening movement that increases the angle between body parts forward, it would be difficult for the user to assess the viability of the angle detection. Thus, to provide a comprehensive analysis, the results presented in Fig. 5.a, 5.b, and 5.c highlight two sets of images for each frame, distinguished by index 1 and index 2. The pictures with index 1 represent screenshots taken from the AI perspectives, showing the angle estimation made by the system. On the other hand, the index 2 images are captured from different angles, allowing for a clear visualization of the actual angle at which the arm is positioned.

Furthermore, it is important to note that the Yolo v7 approach operates planarly, which means it cannot accurately detect arm length in three-dimensional space. This limitation is inherent to the Yolo v7 algorithm, which primarily focuses on object detection and localization within a two-dimensional image. Consequently, when applying the Yolo v7 approach to angle estimation, it is crucial to consider the potential implications of this planar constraint and to position the camera as shown in Fig. 5.d, 5.e, and 5.f.

Shoulder Internal/External Rotation (R_R)

The last shoulder-related test is external shoulder rotation, equivalent to R_R rotation, which can be seen in Fig. 1. The results of this test follow the same procedure as those described above and are summarised in Fig. 6, which highlights once again the difference in camera positioning between both techniques.

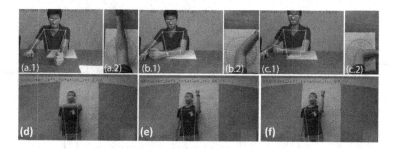

Fig. 6. Real-time Angle Computation for the Shoulder Complex: R_R. (**a, b, c**) with MediaPipe. (**d, e, f**) with Yolo v7.

The internal shoulder rotation test faces a similar pattern as the previous test involving flexion movement. The MediaPipe-based AI algorithm again encounters challenges when the arm faces the camera, resulting in discrepancies between the AI-guessed and observed angles. While the Yolo v7-based AI algorithm also requires the movement to be performed in front of the camera.

Elbow Flexion/Extension Rotation (R_7)

The last exercise performed was the elbow extension movement, equivalent to rotation along the R_7 axis. The tests were performed similarly for both the Mediapipe and Yolo v7. The results of this test are shown in Fig. 7.

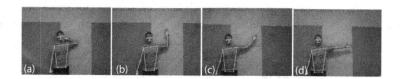

Fig. 7. Real-time Angle Computation for the Elbow Joint: R_7.

Figure 8 provides a comprehensive overview of the test results conducted by the participants, illustrating the outcomes obtained for each technique employed. In this visual representation, each data point shown in the figure corresponds to a single measurement of the error relative to the real value achieved by a participant. The top row displays the results of the Mediapipe approach, involving 17 participants, while the bottom row, corresponds to Yolo v7, also with 17 participants. Furthermore, each column in the figure corresponds to a specific exercise performed: R_A, R_F, R_R, and R_7.

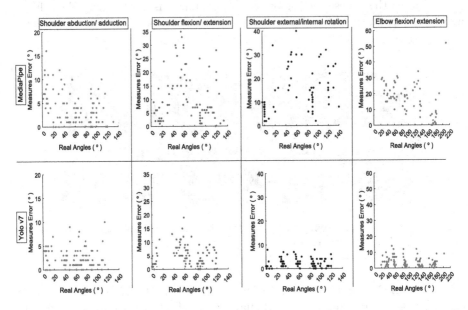

Fig. 8. Descriptive data on the absolute estimation error between the real angle and AI estimation as a function of the real angle, for both Mediapipe and Yolo v7.

The MAE is a measure that quantifies the average magnitude between all the gathered data between the real and estimated angles. Table 1 presents the MAE of each approach in each exercise. It is interesting to notice that all the MAE in the Yolo v7 were lower than 6°, while in the MediaPipe, this value changed considerably, achieving 17.39°.

Table 1. MAE of the results collected in the four exercises with the two approaches.

	R_A	R_F	R_R	R_7
MediaPipe	4.32°	10.98°	15.53°	17.39°
Yolo v7	2.43°	5.16°	2.36°	2.66°

In order to capture the overall trend of each approach while mitigating the impact of individual variations, a k-means clustering technique has been employed. This method enabled to group the measurements into clusters based on their proximity to the targeted angle. The number of clusters was determined based on the number of measurements performed. Figure 9 provides a graphical representation of the different local averages, highlighting the clusters' behavior.

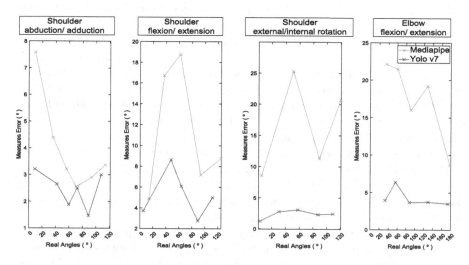

Fig. 9. Local averages comparison for MediaPipe and Yolo v7.

Analyzing the results, it is possible to notice that using the MediaPipe approach, the best estimation was the R_A, with the other rotations presenting considerably higher errors. On the other hand, the Yolo v7 presents a similar error pattern for the four exercises. Analyzing the results, it is possible to notice that for R_A, the results obtained for both approaches were relatively similar, even in the behavior and average. However, for the R_F, R_R, and R_7, the Yolo v7 presented results notably better than MediaPipe, as demonstrated by Fig. 9 and Table 1. In addition, by observing Fig. 8, it is possible to notice that the MediaPipe results have more dispersion than the Yolo v7.

Another interesting result to be noticed is regarded to the Yolo v7. The worse result in this approach was obtained in the R_F. This is due to the patient's position (facing to the right), where the left arm was hidden during some parts of the test, contributing to a decrease in the quality of the estimations.

The difference in the angles estimations quality in different exercises has also been noticed in a similar study presented in [10], dealing with the Lower limb joint, where the approach worked for some exercises. However, that study only considered the ROM's limit angles, i.e., it did not perform a complete follow-up assessment, as done in this work.

5   Conclusion

This preliminary study aimed to investigate the feasibility of implementing two different approaches, Mediapipe and Yolo v7, for estimating the angles of different human body joints for therapeutic and rehabilitative use. Tests carried out on 17 participants demonstrated the low reliability of using Mediapipe as such a tool. On the other hand, a second analysis carried out on 17 participants for AI estimation based on Yolo v7 offered surprising results with a few degrees of error. Using AI in such a low-cost, low-bulk method for patients can considerably improve rehabilitation sessions and help them function properly. The performance of this AI tool on the evaluated angles proves the possibility of their application for different tests such as SLAP Lesion, Impingement Syndrome, and Chronic Rotator Cuff Tendinopathy.

It was possible to notice an interesting trade-off between the two techniques used; MediaPipe presented lower computational power consumption and more available features. The Yolo v7, on the other hand, was much more accurate but could only detect movement with a single DOF, given that the algorithm's detection capability was limited to a 2D plane.

The results of the preliminary work put forward the possibility of applying AI-based images as a powerful tool used by physiotherapists to improve patients' treatment. However, it's important to note that even if an AI-guided system provides valuable insights into movement analysis, it still provides some limitations; since the estimation of the depth in the image is either not available or offers poor estimation accuracy, it excludes its usage for exercise requiring multiple rotations at the same time. Shoulder and arm diseases often require a multi-faceted approach involving physical examinations, imaging studies, medical history, and specialized assessments conducted by healthcare professionals. It is crucial to integrate the theoretical findings with clinical expertise and other diagnostic modalities for a comprehensive evaluation of the patient's condition.

In future works, it is considered to implement the angle calculation for other body rotation joints, as well as exploring other possibilities for AI approaches based on the camera's images and pose tracking, such as OpenPose[9]. In addition, it is necessary to investigate and understand the effect of some variables of the environment in the AI human identification, such as luminosity, color of the clothes, and background. Also, other approaches can be explored using alternative methods, such as applying a 3D Light Detection and Ranging (LiDar) sensor, which can provide high precision of the movements and identify the position of the subject's body.

Acknowledgements. This work has been supported by SmartHealth - Inteligência Artificial para Cuidados de Saúde Personalizados ao Longo da Vida, under the project ref. NORTE-01-0145-FEDER-000045. The authors are grateful to the Foundation for Science and Technology (FCT) for financial support under ref. FCT/MCTES (PIDDAC) to CeDRI (UIDB/05757/2020 and UIDP/05757/2020) and SusTEC (LA/P/0007/2021). Arezki A. Chellal is grateful to the FCT Foundation for its support through the FCT PhD scholarship with ref. UI/BD/154484/2022.

---

[9] https://github.com/CMU-Perceptual-Computing-Lab/openpose.

References

1. Klopčar, N., Lenarčič, J.: Kinematic model for determination of human arm reachable workspace. Meccanica **40**, 203–219 (2005)
2. Liu, L., et al.: Kinematics analysis of arms in synchronized canoeing with wearable inertial measurement unit. IEEE Sens. J. (2023)
3. Liu, R., Liu, C.: Human motion prediction using adaptable recurrent neural networks and inverse kinematics. IEEE Control Syst. Lett. **5**(5), 1651–1656 (2020)
4. O'Sullivan, S.B., Schmitz, T.J.: Physical Rehabilitation. 5th edn (2007)
5. Kelley, M.J., Mcclure, P.W., Leggin, B.G.: Frozen shoulder: evidence and a proposed model guiding rehabilitation. J. Orthopaedic Sports Phys. Therapy **39**(2), 135–148 (2009)
6. Olsen, T.S.: Arm and leg paresis as outcome predictors in stroke rehabilitation. Stroke **21**(2), 247–251 (1990)
7. Qassim, H.M., Hasan, W.Z.W.: A review on upper limb rehabilitation robots. Appl. Sci. **10**(19), 6976 (2020)
8. Krebs, H.I., Volpe, B.T.: Chapter 23 - Rehabilitation robotics. In: Barnes, M.P., Good, D.C. (eds.) Neurological Rehabilitation. Handbook of Clinical Neurology, vol. 110, pp. 283–294. Elsevier, Amsterdam (2013)
9. Argent, R., Drummond, S., Remus, A., O'Reilly, M., Caulfield, B.: Evaluating the use of machine learning in the assessment of joint angle using a single inertial sensor. J. Rehabil. Assist. Technol. Eng. **6** (2019)
10. Wochatz, M., et al.: Reliability and validity of the kinect v2 for the assessment of lower extremity rehabilitation exercises. Gait Posture **70**, 330–335 (2019)
11. Denecke, K., Baudoin, C.R.: A review of artificial intelligence and robotics in transformed health ecosystems. Front. Med. **9** (2022)
12. Luxton, D.D., Riek, L.D.: Artificial intelligence and robotics in rehabilitation (2019)
13. Yuan, F., Klavon, E., Liu, Z., Lopez, R.P., Zhao, X.: A systematic review of robotic rehabilitation for cognitive training. Front. Robot. AI **8** (2021)
14. Phan, G.H., Solanki, V.K., Quang, N.H.: Artificial intelligence in rehabilitation evaluation-based robotic exoskeletons: a review. In: Bio-inspired Motor Control Strategies for Redundant and Flexible Manipulator with Application to Tooling Tasks. SAST, pp. 79–91. Springer, Singapore (2022). https://doi.org/10.1007/978-981-16-9551-3_6
15. Kaelin, V.C., Valizadeh, M., Salgado, Z., Parde, N., Khetani, M.A.: Artificial intelligence in rehabilitation targeting the participation of children and youth with disabilities: scoping review. J. Med. Internet Res. **23**(11), e25745 (2021)
16. Bermejo, C., Pan, H.: A survey on haptic technologies for mobile augmented reality. ACM Comput. Surv. **54**(9), 1–35 (2022)
17. Leardini, A., Lullini, G., Giannini, S., Berti, L., Ortolani, M., Caravaggi, P.: Validation of the angular measurements of a new inertial-measurement-unit based rehabilitation system: comparison with state-of-the-art gait analysis. J. Neuroeng. Rehabil. **11**(1), 1–7 (2014)
18. Daponte, P., De Vito, L., Riccio, M., Sementa, C.: Design and validation of a motion-tracking system for rom measurements in home rehabilitation. Measurement **55**, 82–96 (2014)
19. Boato, G., Conci, N., Daldoss, M., De Natale, F.G.B., Piotto, N.: Hand tracking and trajectory analysis for physical rehabilitation. In: 2009 IEEE International Workshop on Multimedia Signal Processing, pp. 1–6 (2009)

20. Zestas, O.N., Soumis, D.N., Kyriakou, K.D., et al.: A computer-vision based hand rehabilitation assessment suite. AEU - Int. J. Electron. Commun. **169**, 154762 (2023)
21. Lin, G., Wu, W., Lin, C., Song, Y., Xie, L., Cai, S.: A vision-based compensation detection approach during robotic stroke rehabilitation therapy. In: 3rd International Academic Exchange Conference on Science and Technology Innovation, IAECST 2021, pp. 768–771 (2021)
22. Russell, S.J.: Artificial Intelligence a Modern Approach. Pearson Education Inc, London (2010)
23. Lugaresi, C., et al.: Mediapipe: a framework for building perception pipelines. arXiv preprint arXiv:1906.08172 (2019)
24. Bazarevsky, V., Grishchenko, I., Raveendran, K., Zhu, T., Zhang, F., Grundmann, M.: Blazepose: on-device real-time body pose tracking. arXiv preprint arXiv:2006.10204 (2020)
25. Bazarevsky, I., Grishchenko, V.: On-device, real-time body pose tracking with mediapipe blazepose, June 2023. https://ai.googleblog.com/2020/08/on-device-real-time-body-pose-tracking.html
26. Redmon, J., Divvala, S.K., Girshick, R.B., Farhadi, A.: You only look once: unified, real-time object detection. CoRR, abs/1506.02640 (2015)
27. Wang, C.-Y., Bochkovskiy, A., Liao, H.-Y.M.: YOLOv7: trainable bag-of-freebies sets new state-of-the-art for real-time object detectors. arXiv preprint arXiv:2207.02696 (2022)
28. Wang, C.-Y., Liao, H.-Y.M., Yeh, I.-H.: Designing network design strategies through gradient path analysis. arXiv preprint arXiv:2211.04800 (2022)
29. Chellal, A.A., et al.: Smarthealth: a robotic control software for upper limb rehabilitation. In: Brito Palma, L., Neves-Silva, R., Gomes, L. (eds.) CONTROLO 2022. LNNE, vol. 930, pp. 667–676. Springer, Cham (2022)
30. Chellal, A.A., et al.: Robot-assisted rehabilitation architecture supported by a distributed data acquisition system. Sensors **22**(23), 9532 (2022)

Movement Pattern Recognition in Boxing Using Raw Inertial Measurements

Radosław Puchalski🆔 and Wojciech Giernacki$^{(\boxtimes)}$🆔

Poznan University of Technology, Poznan, Poland
radoslaw.puchalski@doctorate.put.poznan.pl,
wojciech.giernacki@put.poznan.pl
http://www.uav.put.poznan.pl

Abstract. In the paper, a new machine-learning technique is proposed to recognize movement patterns. The efficient system designed for this purpose uses an artificial neural network (ANN) model implemented on a microcontroller to classify boxing punches. Artificial intelligence (AI) enables the processing of sophisticated and complex patterns, and the X-CUBE-AI package allows the use of these possibilities in portable micro-processor systems. The input data to the network are linear accelerations and angular velocities read from the sensor mounted on the boxer's wrist. By using simple time-domain measurements without extracting signal features, the classification is performed in real-time. An extensive experiment was carried out for two groups with different levels of boxing skills. The developed model demonstrated high efficiency in the identification of individual types of blows.

Keywords: activity recognition · artificial intelligence · artificial neural networks · edge computing · microcontrollers

1 Introduction

The knowledge of movement patterns in boxing may give a coach a lot of useful information about their effectiveness, repeatability, strength, and individual profile. On the basis of the above, it is possible to build computer-aided, effective, individualized training plans recording the repeatability of performed exercises, especially in a group. The present study aims to analyze the movement patterns of boxers at different skill levels using artificial neural networks (ANNs). The recognition of a movement pattern is a process that, based on measurement data, is able to assign a motion to a specific class. It is the type of common Human Activity Recognition (HAR) problem [35]. Since tiny inertial sensors made in microelectromechanical system (MEMS) technology have become popular, the range of their applications has increased. Currently, they are standard equipment for the most commercially available smartphones [9], smartwatches [32], and devices designed for athletes [25]. HAR is increasingly used to study everyday human activity, including the elderly and the sick. It enables continuous

© The Author(s), under exclusive license to Springer Nature Switzerland AG 2024
A. I. Pereira et al. (Eds.): OL2A 2023, CCIS 1982, pp. 19–34, 2024.
https://doi.org/10.1007/978-3-031-53036-4_2

monitoring of human behavior based on compact sensors. They are the basis for the so-called Internet of Healthcare Things (IoHT) [31]. Another large group of applications is predefined systems for sports. They test various parameters used in individual disciplines and activities of a sports and recreational nature [20].

Recently, methods and procedures for recognizing movement patterns have been widely studied. Signal analysis forms [26], quaternions [15], and artificial neural networks [31] are the most widely implemented. Until now, the possibility of using advanced machine learning (ML) solutions and extensive numerical algorithms were usually associated with efficient stationary equipment, which allowed for complex mathematical calculations [31], or the processing was performed in the cloud [26].

There is a trend for complex calculations to be performed directly by microcontrollers, without involving additional devices and cloud computing [33]. So far, a few scientific articles on the use of artificial neural networks in 32-bit microcontrollers have been published [8,14,23,27]. It turns out that solutions based on microcontroller units (MCUs) are able to perform complex tasks, such as image processing [5]. Artificial intelligence allows the identification of intricate and difficult-to-interpret signals but requires complex floating-point calculations. To take full advantage of the potential of machine learning, while maintaining the energy efficiency and compactness of the devices used, it was decided to test the capabilities of the X-CUBE-AI package [29] in cooperation with the STM32 microcontroller.

In this study, a Nucleo board with an ARM Cortex M7 processor was used as the computing unit. The compact inertial sensor enables the collection of motion data. An artificial neural network model implemented directly in the microcontroller was used. Our solution processes the input data in real-time and performs classification on the fly. Three basic types of boxing punches were chosen as the movement pattern. The novelty compared to existing solutions is the data processing method, which is done continuously. The moments when each punch starts and ends are not distinguished at all. The main contribution of the paper is to show that sequential raw sensor readings can be used for processing. No extraction of frequency features or transformation of readings beyond simple normalization of values has been performed. This reduces the time required for data processing. The effectiveness of the proposed method has been proven in online and recorded data tests.

The article's Sect. 2 presents the artificial neural networks and their use in a microcontroller. Section 3 describes the method of preparing the proposed system. The experimental evaluation of system effectiveness is discussed in Sect. 4. Finally, Sect. 5 gives a short summary of the work.

2   Artificial Neural Networks in Pattern Recognition

The artificial neural network works in a similar way to the central nervous system of a living organism [1]. To acquire new skills, training is necessary. The artificial model must also be provided with training data to have "learning" material. The principle here is intuitive: the more material we have, the better the network will work. Therefore, first of all, it is necessary to collect data from the sensors during physical activities, which are assigned to specific classes.

In general, artificial neural networks have three types of layers (see Fig. 1):

- input – provides raw data entered into the network,
- hidden – determined by the inputs and weights,
- output – function depends on the activity and weight of the hidden unit [7].

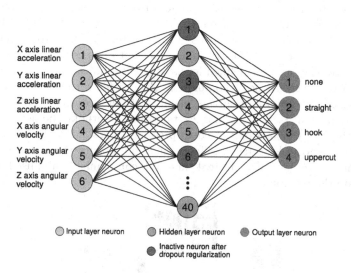

Fig. 1. General structure of an artificial neural network.

Thanks to the X-CUBE-AI package, it is possible to use ANNs implemented in STM microcontrollers. This add-on directly supports various frameworks such as Keras, TensorFlow Lite, Caffe, and others. It also offers 8-bit network quantization. As far as the structure of the network is concerned, both fully-connected, convolutional, or recurrent-type layers (such as gated recurrent unit (GRU) or long short-term memory (LSTM)) can be used. The only limitation is basically the size of the MCU memory. However, it is possible to adapt larger networks, whose weights are stored in external flash memory and activation buffers in external RAM [30].

3   ANN System Design

In order to test the effectiveness of the recognition of movement patterns, it is proposed to develop a system that, based on the readings of the IMU sensor, correctly classifies boxing blows. It is expected to perform both the acquisition and classification of movement patterns without introducing significant changes to the hardware and software configuration. The same program that runs in the microcontroller simultaneously categorizes the movements performed according to the learned patterns and collects new data for further model training, making it more effective.

3.1   General Concept of System Operation

Preparing the system for pattern recognition takes place in two stages. The first one, artificial neural network training, is performed once on the basis of training data collected from inertial sensors and a keyboard used to mark individual activities. Sensory data are sent from the microcontroller through the Bluetooth (BT) protocol to the PC, where the *.csv* file is created. It is used to train and validate ANN. Of course, the model training process itself is usually repeated many times until satisfactory user-defined levels of quality indicators such as *accuracy* and *loss* are achieved. After its completion, the *.h5* file with the network model is prepared. It is the most important element of microcontroller software. The pattern recognition itself, stage no. 2 - takes place without the active participation of the PC, which is only used to present the results of the classification (naturally, it is possible to use a different method, not using another computer at all). This stage takes place in real-time. BT communication is used again to demonstrate the results.

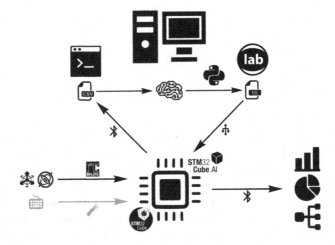

Fig. 2. General concept of the system. The upper part shows the ANN model preparation stage, while the lower part shows the data flow during the blows.

Figure 2 includes both the stage of preparation of the artificial neural network model that takes place on a PC (upper part) and the data flow in the phase of operation of the system to recognize movement patterns (lower part). The matrix keyboard, which is placed next to the inertial sensors, is actually only used at the point of network training, and it does not take an active part in the identification itself.

Graphs of sensor sample readings collected during the execution of various blows by one of the study participants are presented in Fig. 3 (see video at collecting_data).

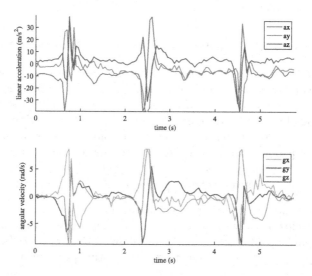

Fig. 3. Accelerometer and gyroscope data during 3 different blows: straight (left), hook (middle), uppercut (right).

3.2   Hardware Used in the Project

A 32-bit microcontroller with a Cortex-M core is used as a computing unit. These STM32 MCUs, both with M4, M7, and M33 processors, provide fast numerical calculations support [21, 22]. Due to the high performance and easy access to the I/O ports, the STM32F746ZG chip on the Nucleo-144 board is proposed, since the platform offers floating point unit (FPU), real-time accelerator, and digital signal processing (DSP) instructions.

The use of specific sensors gives a lot of freedom of choice, limited in principle only to the compatibility of the supply voltage (+3.3 V) and the communication interface used (I^2C). The MPU9250 system is used to measure linear accelerations and angular velocities, which include a 3-axis accelerometer and a 3-axis gyroscope. The following configuration parameters in the research presented in the article are utilized: data are collected from the IMU sensor, and the measuring ranges are set at ±4 g for the accelerometer and ±500 dps for the gyroscope, the data acquisition rate is set at 20 Hz, which is a sufficient value to identify human motor activities [18]. Data from the three axes of the accelerometer and the three axes of the gyroscope are saved in a .csv file every 50 ms.

The system is equipped with an independent power bank with a capacity of 2200 mAh, a universal shield with a Bluetooth module for wireless communication, and 4-pin connectors for connecting sensors via the I^{2}C bus. The numeric keyboard is linked to the GPIO ports of the microcontroller, led out to the connectors of the shield used.

3.3 The Process of Collecting Measurement Data for ANN

Preparation of the input data for network training is one of the most important and time-consuming stages of building the ANN model. To prepare a universal neural network, data was collected from several dozen volunteers with various levels of boxing ability. 32 participants were examined, half of whom were people who had trained or practiced boxing or other combat sports in the past. The other half were people who were not related to any martial arts. 3 people from each group were randomly chosen to test the prepared models, with their data excluded from neural network training. This resulted in 4 separate groups:

- novice participants competing in all phases (group *novice*),
- novice participants only competing in the testing phase (group *novice**),
- advanced participants competing in all phases (group *advanced*),
- advanced participants only competing in the testing phase (group *advanced**).

The establishment of groups marked with asterisks will determine the effectiveness of the models for people whose data were not involved in the preparation of the network.

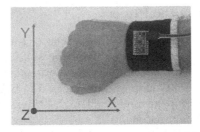

Fig. 4. MPU9250 sensor mounted on the wrist. On the left side, there is a mark for the orientation of the accelerometer and gyroscope axes.

All study members were asked to wear a wristband with an attached MPU9250 sensor to their right hand (Fig. 4) and perform at least 30 movements of each of 3 types of blows:

- cross strokes (straight) – inflicted in a straight line,
- hooks – strike inflicted in an arc, the hand works in a horizontal plane,
- chin strokes (uppercut) – delivered from the bottom up.

The duration of individual experiments ranged from 148 to 343 s. The collected data has been preprocessed (already in the microcontroller) by scaling to the range $[-1, +1]$. Unnecessary and redundant data was deleted. In the dataset taken from each participant, only 30 blows of each type were left, with no long pauses of inactivity between blows or idle data. Data prepared in this way were divided 60%—20%—20% into training, validation, and test datasets, respectively.

3.4   Preparation of the ANN Model

For the purposes of the research, artificial neural network models were made from scratch. The reads processed from the inertial sensor are the input to the network. The main intention was to use the sensor readings themselves in the least processed form possible. The extraction of any signal features was abandoned. More sensor samples were fed into the network. The number of readings from every sensor axis used, included in each vector, is set to 32. For this value of the length of the measurement window, the model offers the best parameters *validation accuracy* and *validation loss* parameters. Thus, the length of the measurement window was 1.6 s. This is the time sufficient to perform each type of blow tested, taking into account all phases of its execution. Each input vector consists of 192 elements that include data from the axes of the MPU9250 chip. The structure of prepared vectors conforms to the formula:

$$
\begin{aligned}
in_{0...n-1} = [&ax_0, ax_1, ..., ax_{n-1}, \quad ay_0, ay_1, ..., ay_{n-1}, \\
&az_0, az_1, ..., az_{n-1}, \quad gx_0, gx_1, ..., gx_{n-1}, , \\
&gy_0, gy_1, ..., gy_{n-1}, \quad gz_0, gz_1, ..., gz_{n-1}]
\end{aligned} \tag{1}
$$

where ax, ay, az are accelerometer readings along the X, Y, Z axes, gx, gy, gz are gyroscope readings around the same three axes, n is the measurement window length (number of samples of every sensor axis).

The input tensor contains individual vectors sequentially shifted by a sample. Its construction is shown below:

$$
input = [in_{0...n-1}, \ in_{1...n}, \ in_{2...n+1}, ...]. \tag{2}
$$

As (2) shows, the overlap is very large. In the subsequent iteration, only one specimen is replaced by a new one, so the processing is continuous. This approach allows us to skip the stage of recognizing the start of the blow execution. Its volume depends on the size of the training data file. When collecting data for boxing shots, information about the type of punch is also added after each shot using the numeric keyboard.

When designing the neural network model, common feed-forward units were chosen to reduce memory consumption and computational complexity. Fully connected layers, despite their simple structure, ensure good efficiency [3,19]. Similarly to the authors of [24], these types of layers were used to build the network. Feed-forward networks are a relevant type of artificial neural network because, when combined with a sufficient number of neurons and the appropriate activation functions, they are able to achieve any accuracy for any problem. They are widely used in many areas, such as modeling, control, and image processing [7,28].

When preparing the network, the best values of the selected indicator were obtained by the models with only 1 hidden layer with 40 neurons, a dropout parameter of 0.4, and L2 regularization at the level of 0.01. The batch size is set at 1000 and training takes place during 175 epochs. All tested models are prepared in a similar way to make it easier to compare them with each other.

In prepared models, the following functions are used: *softmax* for the last-layer activation, rectified linear unit (*ReLU*) as the activation function for the other layers, and *categorical_crossentropy* as the loss function.

The main task of the *ReLU* activation function is to reset negative values. It does not change positive ones [4]. This function only applies to the last layer.

In the previous layers (regardless of their number) a kind of logistic function is proposed. The softmax function, which is used for multiclass, single-label classification tasks [4], is a generalization of the logistic sigmoidal function (3):

$$\sigma(x) = \frac{1}{1 + exp(-a \cdot x)}, \tag{3}$$

where a is the logistic growth rate. Softmax activation function works with real-valued $\mathbf{x}$ vectors. It converts values to scalars ranging from 0 to 1, whose sum is always 1.0. Thus, the results can be interpreted as the probability of a given class. This function is commonly defined in the literature [2,6,10,16,17,36] as (4):

$$softmax(x_i) = \frac{exp(x_i)}{\sum\limits_{j=1}^{n} exp(x_j)}. \tag{4}$$

For the network to learn efficiently, it needs feedback from the weight tensors. The goal is to minimize the loss function [4]. Typically, for multiclass projects, the categorical cross-entropy loss function (5) is used [11,37]:

$$\mathcal{L}_{CCE} = -\frac{1}{M} \sum_{k=1}^{K} \sum_{m=1}^{M} y_m^k \times \log\left(h_\theta(x_m, k)\right), \tag{5}$$

where:

M number of training datasets,

K number of predefined classes,

y_m^k target label for training dataset m for class k,

x_m input for training dataset m,

h_θ model with calculated neural network weights θ

This function calculates the distance between the probability distributions obtained by the network and the real ones, which allows to increase the efficiency of pattern recognition.

Using the mentioned parameters, structure, and appropriate activation and loss functions, 3 models of the artificial neural network were prepared:

- model prepared with 13 *novice* users dataset (*AMA*),
- model prepared with 13 *advanced* users dataset (*PRO*),
- model prepared with 26 *novice* and *advanced* users dataset (*MIX*).

Models for the novice group and the advanced group were trained separately. This way seems to be more appropriate if it is known which athletes the system will work with. However, to show the effectiveness of the neural network, a single universal model was also prepared, including data collected from both groups of boxers.

The specifications of the prepared models are summarized in Table 1. Note that all models have the same size, computational complexity, and memory consumption. The selection of the best values is based on the criterion of the lowest possible rate of the *validation loss* parameter of the *PRO* model. The loss and accuracy parameter charts during the training of individual models are shown in Fig. 5. After obtaining the appropriate accuracy and a small error of the network, its model is saved to a *.h5* file.

Table 1. Properties of used ANN models

Properties	Model AMA	Model PRO	Model MIX
File size [kB]	80	80	80
Complexity [MACC]	13850	13850	13850
Flash [kB]	53.88	53.88	53.88
RAM [kB]	1.05	1.05	1.05
Training loss	0.2808	0.2748	0.3103
Training accuracy	0.8992	0.9057	0.8874
Validation loss	0.3652	0.2811	0.3430
Validation accuracy	0.8770	0.8987	0.8773

MACC - *Multiply-and-accumulate complexity* is a unity that indicates the complexity of a deep learning model from a processing standpoint [30]

3.5   X-CUBE-AI Package

X-CUBE-AI is an add-on to STMicroelectronics software and supports systems with Cortex-M4/M7/M33 cores [30]. It allows an extension of the capabilities of STM32 CubeMX with the automatic conversion of a pre-trained neural network and its integration into the user's project. On the basis of the prepared model, it generates a library optimized to the capabilities of the processor used. In the case of the tested STM32F746ZG, the flash memory limit of 1024 kB must

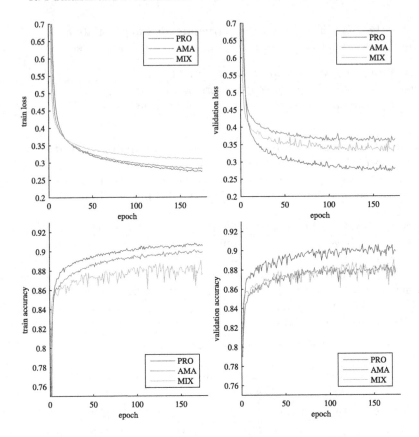

Fig. 5. Loss and accuracy functions during training and validation steps.

be respected [22]. It is possible to use the compression procedure in STM32 CubeMX for larger models, but this method was not used during the experiment.

After generating the project using STM32CubeMX, the program code is written. It is worth mentioning that the part responsible for the AI module is in the *app_x-cube-ai.c* file. Inside the file, the *void MX_X_CUBE_AI_Process (void)* function should be modified. Sensor data should be entered into the *nn_input[]* array in accordance with the scheme of the input tensor used to train the network. The *nn_output[]* array returns the probability of detection for each of the predetermined classes to which each movement pattern is to be assigned. Therefore, the sum of the individual values of this array is 1.0. Reading the value of the *nn_output[]* array allows for checking the assignment of the tested movement patterns to the appropriate classes. In the project described in the paper, the function responsible for machine learning calculations is called in a timer interrupt activated every 50 ms.

The prepared program processes data with values that the network used in the training stage. Thus, data from the range $[-1, +1]$ are sent to the function that handles ML tasks. This function returns an array of values corresponding to the probability of each of the 4 defined activity classes (0 – no blow, 1 – straight, 2 – hook, 3 – uppercut). This allows for an unambiguous determination to which class a given hit is assigned and checking whether the classification is done correctly.

4   Experimental Results

In order to investigate the possibility of using deep learning techniques in STM32 microcontrollers, 3 models of artificial neural networks were prepared. During the collection of training, validation, and testing data, blows were executed with the right hand at head height. The starting posture was the position with the left leg in front. As the `online_test` video shows, classification is done in real-time, and the system recognizes blows immediately after they are taken.

To compare the effectiveness of the ANN model, the quality indicator is used in the form of the *Acc* parameter, calculated according to the formula (6):

$$Acc = \frac{Pos}{Pos + Neg} \, , \tag{6}$$

where *Pos* is the number of correct classifications, and *Neg* is the number of incorrect classifications.

The labels assigned to each blow at the stage of collecting measurement data are used to determine the correctness of the punch classification. If the neural network assigned only one activity class a value ≥ 0.5 and it corresponded to the class marked with the keyboard, the classification is considered correct. In all other cases (value < 0.5; value ≥ 0.5 for two or more classes) the classification is incorrect.

The effectiveness of individual models in relation to different groups of participants and different blows is presented in tabular form (Tables 2 and 3). A comparison of the performance of different ANN models when testing a single dataset from one of the study participants is presented in the video: `recorded_data_test`.

The battery life with a capacity of 2200 mAh during continuous pattern recognition and sending results via BT transmission is approximately 4 h 25 min. The effect of network size, model compression, and placement of weights and activation buffers in external memory on the processing speed of movement patterns has not been studied, but close to real-time, such action would be redundant.

4.1   Discussion

The most similar to our study is [14], which also uses the X-CUBE-AI package to recognize boxing punches. The author has developed a complex ANN model consisting of 4 hidden layers with a total number of 940 neurons. He accessed a high classification efficiency (in the best model 95.33 ± 2.51%). However, to obtain such results, it took many days of collecting large amounts of data (a

Table 2. Accuracy for groups of participants

Model	Group of participants			
	novice	advanced	novice*	advanced*
Model AMA	96.15%	91.03%	75.93%	98.15%
Model PRO	85.04%	98.72%	72.22%	98.15%
Model MIX	94.02%	97.44%	75.93%	98.15%
Average	91.74%	95.73%	74.69%	98.15%

Table 3. Accuracy of blows detection depending on the used ANN model

Model	Type of blow			Overall
	straight	hook	uppercut	
Model AMA	95.83%	88.54%	92.71%	92.36%
Model PRO	99.48%	80.21%	92.19%	90.63%
Model MIX	97.40%	87.50%	97.40%	94.10%
Average	97.64%	85.42%	94.10%	92.36%

total of 210,000 hits) and 10-min network training. In our project, the dataset was smaller, the model was much simpler, the effectiveness of punch recognition was comparable, and the training process (on a PC with worse parameters) took about 18 s. Thanks to this, our solution can be easily and quickly adapted to various applications, to the needs of various activities, and to a specific group of users. Real-time punch recognition allows one to monitor whether the training is progressing successfully, determine the correctness and repeatability of the strokes, and immediately react to mistakes.

Another work that can be compared to ours is [34]. A person participated in the described study, and the dataset collected for 5 boxing punches is much smaller (332 punches in total). Two sensor mounting configurations were tested. In the system with 2 sensors mounted on the wrists (each equipped with an accelerometer, gyroscope, and magnetometer), an ANN model with 3 hidden layers, 8 nodes in each, was used as one of the methods. The results were at the level of 90% and 84% for the untuned and tuned network parameters, respectively. Although other methods obtained better results, our models proved to be more effective in the case of artificial neural networks.

In [32], the authors use a smartwatch with a built-in 3-axis accelerometer to classify 3 boxing blows, the hand that delivers the punch, and the athlete's name. A database of more than 7,600 blows was collected from 8 participants in the study. Various machine-learning models were tested. The effectiveness of punch classification was 98.68%.

In the study [25], Omcirk et al. tested several commercial punch trackers to detect six different punches. It turned out that their effectiveness is highly debatable and for some types of punches, it is below 50%. This shows that universal solutions that cannot be personalized for a specific user do not always produce satisfactory results.

Completely different ways of classifying blows are solutions based on the overhead depth imaginary. In [12,13] the authors use a camera suspended at a height of about 5 m. They use an SVM classifier to detect 6 types of blows. In both studies, the best models achieved 96% and 97.3% efficiency, respectively.

The research results presented in the article confirmed that even deep learning can be used in portable equipment. High classification efficiency enables the use of the potential of ANN in a wide range of applications. The most recognizable blow was the straight and the weakest was the hook. The efficiency of all models was similar and ranged from 90.63% for the *PRO* model to 94.10% for the *MIX* model. The lowest effectiveness of punch detection was recorded – as expected – in the group of amateurs, who did not participate in the training phase. The highest effectiveness was achieved for the advanced group who did not participate in the training stage, which was unexpected. It is also surprising that the *advanced** group achieved the same overall effectiveness for each of the tested models. This is due to the fact that a chin stroke from the test dataset was performed in a manner similar to the hook blow and was recognized as such. All other blows performed by this group were correctly classified.

In fact, only the *novice** group achieved significantly lower efficacy results (74.69% on average). It is caused by a very different way of blowing. The straight hit scored a surprisingly high score in this group, whereas the hook was usually incorrectly classified. However, for the *novice* group, whose data was involved in the network training process, the same blow was more than twice as effective. This shows the potential of such a simple ANN structure, which after providing training data from a specific group of users (or one user who will use such a system for his training) will recognize all types of punches with high efficiency.

5   Conclusions

The number and range of applications for microcontrollers and microcomputers have grown significantly in the last decade. Thanks to the increasing computing power of these small devices, it becomes possible to transfer some or all of the calculations from external devices or solutions based on cloud computing to systems equipped with the MCU. Even recently, artificial intelligence techniques unavailable to them, which were associated rather with powerful stationary workstations, can now be used in wearable technology. Such a migration allows for faster processing of data that does not need to be sent to other devices. This minimizes time and costs and increases operational reliability, the weak link of which is often communication, especially wireless. This approach also enables the use of advanced deep learning methods wherever, for various reasons, sufficiently fast and reliable communication is not available, or where there are limitations in the supply of energy. The new high-performance microcontrollers are energy-efficient, making battery power possible.

The proposed method's solution can build a small system for boxing training, especially for beginners, indicating accurate hits. Advanced boxers can utilize it to collect statistics on frequently performed punches in sparring fights.

For the purpose of movement patterns, boxing blows were selected (as a representative example). Their parameters were read with simple inertial sensors. There is nothing to prevent these possibilities from being used to recognize other movement patterns. When the motion sensor is changed to another, or when using other types of data, the only limitation to the use of microcontrollers with ANN is the size of the memory of devices and the imagination of the creators and users of these technologies.

An important observation from the study is that sophisticated data processing methods are not needed for effective recognition of repetitive patterns. If the classification method has been trained for a specific user, ordinary time-domain inertial data are sufficient even for 100% detection of movement patterns.

Future research in this study will focus mainly on the use of other types of artificial neural network layers. There are also plans to design a more compact device that can be worn continuously. After proper training of the neural network, such a system will be able to detect dangerous events to which elderly people and people with motor impairment are exposed.

Acknowledgment. This research was financially supported as a statutory work of Poznan University of Technology (grant no. 0214/SBAD/0241). The Authors thank Dr. Tomasz Marciniak for the idea and help in carrying out the research and all participants who willingly agreed to conduct the tests.

References

1. Abiodun, O.I., Jantan, A., Omolara, A.E., Dada, K.V., Mohamed, N.A., Arshad, H.: State-of-the-art in artificial neural network applications: a survey. Heliyon **4**(11), e00938 (2018). https://doi.org/10.1016/j.heliyon.2018.e00938
2. Bin, L., Liang, W., Guosheng, Y.: A graph total variation regularized softmax for text generation (2021). https://arxiv.org/abs/2101.00153
3. Chen, M., Li, Y., Luo, X., Wang, W., Wang, L., Zhao, W.: A novel human activity recognition scheme for smart health using multilayer extreme learning machine. IEEE Internet Things J. **6**(2), 1410–1418 (2018)
4. Chollet, F.: Deep Learning with Python, 1st edn. Manning Publications Co., USA (2017)
5. de Vita, F., Nocera, G., Bruneo, D., Tomaselli, V., Giacalone, D., Das, S.K.: Quantitative analysis of deep leaf: a plant disease detector on the smart edge. In: 2020 IEEE International Conference on Smart Computing (SMARTCOMP), pp. 49–56 (2020). https://doi.org/10.1109/SMARTCOMP50058.2020.00027
6. Dukhan, M., Ablavatski, A.: Two-pass softmax algorithm. In: 2020 IEEE International Parallel and Distributed Processing Symposium Workshops (IPDPSW), pp. 386–395 (2020)
7. El Jerjawi, N.S., Abu-Naser, S.S.: Diabetes prediction using artificial neural network. J. Adv. Sci. **124**, 1–10 (2018)

8. Falbo, V., et al.: Analyzing machine learning on mainstream microcontrollers. In: Saponara, S., De Gloria, A. (eds.) ApplePies 2019. LNEE, vol. 627, pp. 103–108. Springer, Cham (2020). https://doi.org/10.1007/978-3-030-37277-4_12

9. Fisher, E., Ivry, A., Alimi, R., Weiss, E.: Smartphone based indoor localization using permanent magnets and artificial intelligence for pattern recognition. AIP Adv. **11**(1), 015122 (2021). https://doi.org/10.1063/9.0000076

10. Gao, B., Pavel, L.: On the properties of the softmax function with application in game theory and reinforcement learning. http://arxiv.org/abs/1704.00805

11. Ho, Y., Wookey, S.: The real-world-weight cross-entropy loss function: modeling the costs of mislabeling. IEEE Access **8**, 4806–4813 (2020). https://doi.org/10.1109/ACCESS.2019.2962617

12. Kasiri, S., Fookes, C., Sridharan, S., Morgan, S.: Fine-grained action recognition of boxing punches from depth imagery. Comput. Vis. Image Underst. **159**, 143–153 (2017)

13. Kasiri-Bidhendi, S., Fookes, C., Morgan, S., Martin, D.T., Sridharan, S.: Combat sports analytics: boxing punch classification using overhead depthimagery. In: 2015 IEEE International Conference on Image Processing, pp. 4545–4549. IEEE (2015)

14. Khasanshin, I.: Application of an artificial neural network to automate the measurement of kinematic characteristics of punches in boxing. Appl. Sci. **11**(3), 1223 (2021)

15. Kico, I., Liarokapis, F.: Comparison of trajectories and quaternions of folk dance movements using dynamic time warping. In: 2019 11th International Conference on Virtual Worlds and Games for Serious Applications (VS-Games), pp. 1–4 (2019). https://doi.org/10.1109/VS-Games.2019.8864604

16. Kouretas, I., Paliouras, V.: Hardware implementation of a softmax-like function for deep learning. Technologies **8**(3) (2020). https://doi.org/10.3390/technologies8030046

17. Kusner, M.J., Hernández-Lobato, J.M.: Gans for sequences of discrete elements with the gumbel-softmax distribution (2016)

18. Lara, O.D., Labrador, M.A.: A survey on human activity recognition using wearable sensors. IEEE Commun. Surv. Tutor. **15**(3), 1192–1209 (2013). https://doi.org/10.1109/SURV.2012.110112.00192

19. Magno, M., Pritz, M., Mayer, P., Benini, L.: Deepemote: towards multi-layer neural networks in a low power wearable multi-sensors bracelet. In: 2017 7th IEEE International Workshop on Advances in Sensors and Interfaces, pp. 32–37 (2017)

20. Malawski, F.: Depth versus inertial sensors in real-time sports analysis: a case study on fencing. IEEE Sens. J. **21**(4), 5133–5142 (2021). https://doi.org/10.1109/JSEN.2020.3036436

21. Marciniak, T., Dabrowski, A., Puchalski, R., Dratwiak, D., Marciniak, W.: Application of STM32F410 microcontroller for presentation of digital signal processing. Przeglad Elektrotechniczny (Electr. Rev.) **95**(10), 118–120 (2019). https://doi.org/10.15199/48.2019.10.26. (in Polish)

22. Matusiak, M., Ostalczyk, P.: Problems in solving fractional differential equations in a microcontroller implementation of an FOPID controller. Arch. Electr. Eng. **68**(3), 565–577 (2019). https://doi.org/10.24425/aee.2019.129342

23. Merenda, M., Porcaro, C., Iero, D.: Edge machine learning for AI-enabled IoT devices: a review. Sensors **20**(9) (2020). https://doi.org/10.3390/s20092533

24. Mundt, M., et al.: Estimation of gait mechanics based on simulated and measured IMU data using an artificial neural network. Front. Bioeng. Biotechnol. **8** (2020)

25. Omcirk, D., Vetrovsky, T., Padecky, J., Vanbelle, S., Malecek, J., Tufano, J.J.: Punch trackers: correct recognition depends on punch type and training experience. Sensors **21**(9) (2021). https://doi.org/10.3390/s21092968, https://www.mdpi.com/1424-8220/21/9/2968

26. O'Brien, M.K., et al.: Augmenting clinical outcome measures of gait and balance with a single inertial sensor in age-ranged healthy adults. Sensors **19**(20) (2019). https://doi.org/10.3390/s19204537

27. Puchalski, R., Bondyra, A., Giernacki, W., Zhang, Y.: Actuator fault detection and isolation system for multirotor unmanned aerial vehicles. In: 2022 26th International Conference on Methods and Models in Automation and Robotics (MMAR), pp. 364–369 (2022). https://doi.org/10.1109/MMAR55195.2022.9874283

28. Qiao, J., Li, F., Han, H., Li, W.: Constructive algorithm for fully connected cascade feedforward neural networks. Neurocomputing **182**, 154–164 (2016)

29. STMicroelectronics: DB3788, X-CUBE-AI, Data brief, Artificial Intelligence (AI) software expansion for STM32Cube Rev 6 (2020). https://www.st.com/en/embedded-software/x-cube-ai.html#documentation

30. STMicroelectronics: UM2526, User manual, Getting started with X-CUBE-AI expansion package for artificial intelligence (AI) Rev 6 (2020). https://www.st.com/en/embedded-software/x-cube-ai.html#documentation

31. Uddin, M.Z., Hassan, M.M., Alsanad, A., Savaglio, C.: A body sensor data fusion and deep recurrent neural network-based behavior recognition approach for robust healthcare. Inf. Fusion **55**, 105–115 (2020). https://doi.org/10.1016/j.inffus.2019.08.004

32. Wagner, T., Jäger, J., Wolff, V., Fricke-Neuderth, K.: A machine learning driven approach for multivariate timeseries classification of box punches using smartwatch accelerometer sensordata. In: 2019 Innovations in Intelligent Systems and Applications Conference (ASYU), pp. 1–6. IEEE (2019)

33. Wang, X., Magno, M., Cavigelli, L., Benini, L.: FANN-on-MCU: an open-source toolkit for energy-efficient neural network inference at the edge of the internet of things. IEEE Internet Things J. **7**(5), 4403–4417 (2020). https://doi.org/10.1109/JIOT.2020.2976702

34. Worsey, M.T.O., Espinosa, H.G., Shepherd, J.B., Thiel, D.V.: An evaluation of wearable inertial sensor configuration and supervised machine learning models for automatic punch classification in boxing. IoT **1**(2), 360–381 (2020). https://doi.org/10.3390/iot1020021, https://www.mdpi.com/2624-831X/1/2/21

35. Yang, J., Nguyen, M.N., San, P.P., Li, X., Krishnaswamy, S.: Deep convolutional neural networks on multichannel time series for human activity recognition. In: IJCAI, vol. 15, pp. 3995–4001. Buenos Aires, Argentina (2015)

36. Ye, M., Shen, J., Zhang, X., Yuen, P.C., Chang, S.F.: Augmentation invariant and instance spreading feature for softmax embedding. IEEE Trans. Pattern Anal. Mach. Intell. 1–16 (2020). https://doi.org/10.1109/TPAMI.2020.3013379

37. Zhang, Z., Sabuncu, M.R.: Generalized cross entropy loss for training deep neural networks with noisy labels (2018)

An Evaluation of Image Preprocessing in Skin Lesions Detection

Giuliana M. Silva[1,2]($\boxtimes$) (iD), André E. Lazzaretti[2] (iD),
and Fernando C. Monteiro[1] (iD)

[1] Research Centre in Digitalization and Intelligent Robotics (CeDRI),
Laboratório para a Sustentabilidade e Tecnologia em Regiões de Montanha
(SusTEC), Instituto Politécnico de Bragança, Campus de Santa Apolónia,
5300-253 Bragança, Portugal
monteiro@ipb.pt
[2] Federal University of Technology - Paraná, Curitiba 80230-901, Brazil
giusil@alunos.utfpr.edu.br, lazzaretti@utfpr.edu.br
https://cedri.ipb.pt

Abstract. This study aims to evaluate the impact of image preprocessing techniques on the performance of Convolutional Neural Networks (CNNs) in the task of skin lesion classification. The study is made on the ISIC 2017 dataset, a widely used resource in skin cancer diagnosis research. Thirteen popular CNN models were trained using transfer learning. An ensemble strategy was also employed to generate a final diagnosis based on the classifications of different models. The results indicate that image preprocessing can significantly enhance the performance of CNN models in skin lesion classification tasks. Our best model obtained a balanced accuracy of 0.7879.

Keywords: Skin Lesion Classification · Convolutional Neural Networks · Deep Learning · Image Preprocessing

1 Introduction

Skin cancer, a prevalent global health concern, is categorized into malignant melanoma and non-melanoma types, which include basal and squamous cell carcinoma. Malignant melanoma, in particular, is a lethal form of skin cancer that necessitates early detection and treatment to prevent a fatality [1]. According to the Global Cancer Observatory, melanoma was the 19th most common cancer worldwide in 2020, with an estimated 324,635 new cases. The incidence of this cancer type was notably high in Oceania, North America, and Europe [2].

The initial diagnosis of pigmented skin lesions is typically based on the ABCD criteria, a diagnostic evaluation that dermatologists use to assess four key characteristics of the lesion: asymmetry (A), border irregularity (B), color variation (C), and diameter greater than 6 mm (D) [3] and, in Fig. 1, we present examples for each of them. However, the accuracy of this observational diagnosis method is restricted by the dermatologist's experience. Dermatologists with extensive experience can achieve diagnostic accuracy rates of up to 80%, while those with less experience may only obtain accuracy rates between 56% and 62% [4].

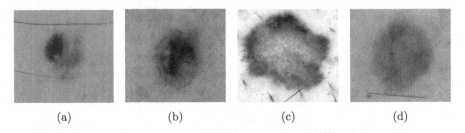

(a)   (b)   (c)   (d)

Fig. 1. Examples of lesions presenting each of the characteristics evaluated in ABCD criteria: (a) asymmetry; (b) border irregularity; (c) color variation and (d) diameter greater than 6 mm.

In addition to the ABCD criteria, other diagnostic methods have been developed to facilitate the diagnosis of melanocytic lesions, such as the 7-point checklist, the 3-point checklist, the Menzies method, chaos and clues, and CASH. These methods aim to quantify the overall organization of a lesion by assessing features such as symmetry, architectural disorder, border sharpness, and heterogeneity in colors and structures [5].

These methods are usually allied to dermoscopy, a non-invasive technique that enables visualization of the skin's subcutaneous structures. However, studies indicate that dermatologists trained in this technique can enhance their diagnostic capabilities, but those who are not prepared may misclassify the samples [5,6]. A biopsy may be performed to corroborate the diagnosis, wherein a skin lesion sample is excised and analyzed.

In recent years, the advent of computer-aided diagnosis (CAD) methods has brought about a significant transformation in the field of dermatology. These methods, which are currently being researched, developed, and commercialized, leverage deep learning (DL) techniques to detect and classify skin lesions automatically. Deep learning is a subset of machine learning that uses artificial neural networks with multiple layers [7].

A deep neural network (DNN) is a type of neural network characterized by multiple layers. This characteristic allows the DNN to learn complex patterns, extract features and classify data based on these features [8]. Convolutional neural networks (CNN), a specific type of DNN, are utilized in computer vision tasks to recognize and classify different elements. They can extract significant representations from input data, making them ideal for image-related tasks. A CNN is composed of multiple layers of convolutions and activations, with pooling layers strategically placed between various convolution layers [7].

In dermatology, these CNNs can be used to analyze images of skin lesions and classify them based on their characteristics. They can potentially improve the accuracy and efficiency of skin lesion diagnosis allied with dermatologists' expertise, making it a promising area of research and application.

One major challenge when classifying skin lesions is the presence of artifacts in dermoscopic images that can affect the model's accuracy. These artifacts include air bubbles, hair, pen marks, and light reflection. Additionally, lighting differences between the images can occur due to the different devices used to acquire the images. In order to improve the images before feeding them into the deep learning model, image preprocessing can be done as the first step. Techniques such as noise reduction, contrast enhancement, and normalization can help highlight the essential features of the skin lesions and minimize the impact of unwanted variations in the images, leading to a significant improvement in the model's performance [9,10]. Therefore, integrating image preprocessing techniques into computer-aided diagnosis systems for skin lesion classification can significantly enhance diagnostic accuracy and efficiency.

In addition, ensemble techniques have been a popular approach to achieve higher classification accuracy in the skin lesion classification task, as observed in the last two Melanoma Classification Challenges organized by the International Skin Imaging Collaboration Challenges [11].

In this paper, we address the impacts of different image preprocessing combinations on several pre-trained CNNs and evaluate whether the performance was positively impacted. We also evaluate the performance of different models' ensemble techniques with and without image preprocessing and choose the best one. In conclusion, we will assess the effects of preprocessing and different ensemble techniques on the models' performance, which will inform future research in this field. This paper is organized as follows. In Sect. 2, we present an overview of the recent work related to this subject. In Sect. 3, we describe the details of the proposed method. The experiments performed and results are explained in Sect. 4, and the analysis of the results are shown in Sect. 5, and finally, in Sect. 6, we conclude the work.

2 Related Work

In recent literature, several Computer-Aided Diagnosis (CAD) systems based on Convolutional Neural Networks (CNNs) have been proposed for skin lesion detection and classification. Skin lesion challenges, such as those organized by the International Skin Imaging Collaboration (ISIC), have been a great place to test and refine these systems. The ISIC has provided a substantial, publicly accessible dataset of skin images, which has been a critical resource for advancing research in this area [12].

These challenges are a great resource to check the popular techniques applied for skin lesion classification and segmentation tasks, and it is common to find solutions using image prepreprocessing techniques as one of the first steps to enhance the quality of images before they are used for further analysis. These techniques aim to remove noise and artifacts, correct lighting issues, enhance contrast, and adapt the input data by resizing and cropping the images.

One popular technique is the Shades of Grays method [13], a color constancy algorithm that aims to provide a better perception of the colors in the image by reducing the impact of the light in the image; it was used in three of the top-ranked methods in the ISIC 2019 Challenge [14,15] and the first place solution of ISIC 2017 Challenge [16].

Other authors utilize techniques to reduce the presence of artifacts in skin lesion images. Khouloud et al. [17] employed a Gaussian filter as a preprocessing step, and Akram et al. [18] used software that performs bilinear interpolation to locate hair, erase it, and employ a median filter to smooth the erased region.

Image enhancement can help to the features of the image. Afza et al. [19] used both local and global contrast enhancement. Khan et al. [20] applied an artificial bee colony algorithm to enhance contrast and improve the image's content.

Sakar et al. [21] used a combination of algorithms consisting of (1) non-local means filter to remove the noise, (2) CLAHE-DWT to enhance the image, (3) merging RGB color space with the saturation channel, b* channel from CIELAB color space and the inverted grayscale channel, and (4) normalization of the intensity and image resizing.

In this work, we aim to evaluate the use of different types image preprocessing techniques for the skin lesion classification task using different CNN models, transfer learning, and different ensemble methods.

3 Method Details

To implement a network model that can classify the skin lesions between 3 diagnoses, we decided to train 13 popular models of 7 different architectures used by the leaderboard models of ISIC Challenge 2019 and SIIM-ISIC Challenge 2020. The used architectures were EfficientNet0-6, PNASNet, SEResNeXt101, ResNeXt101, ResNeSt101, VGG19, and DenseNet121.

The goal is to employ the transfer learning technique to train models on the ISIC 2017 dataset using diverse image preprocessing methods. The image preprocessing techniques can improve image quality and help to extract relevant information, and reduce variations in illumination and contrast, leading to better accuracy and generalization of deep learning models [22].

Subsequently, an ensemble strategy is proposed to generate a final diagnosis based on the final classification of different models. A model ensemble can help to reduce variance and bias, capturing complementary information from different sources, and mitigating the weaknesses of individual models. Sections 3.2, 3.3, and 3.4 provide a detailed explanation of image preprocessing, the transfer learning technique, and the models' ensemble technique, respectively.

Since the data in ISIC 2017 dataset is imbalanced, the evaluation metric used to choose the best configuration was the balanced accuracy, as it provides a more accurate measure of the model's performance and ensures that the model is not biased towards the majority class.

3.1   Dataset

In this work, we used the ISIC 2017 dataset. The ISIC 2017 dataset is widely used in research and competitions related to skin cancer diagnosis and classification [23]. The unique aspect of this dataset is its clear partitioning into three subsets: train, validation, and test. This clear separation creates a fair and balanced environment for comparing different models that use the same dataset. By keeping data quality consistent across all models, the only variable becomes the training process and the model itself, allowing for a fair comparison. This dataset contains dermoscopic images of skin lesions classified into three classes: melanoma, seborrheic keratosis, and common nevi. Figure 2 presents some examples of the images included in the dataset.

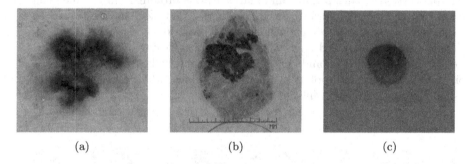

(a)   (b)   (c)

Fig. 2. Examples of dermoscopic skin lesion images from ISIC 2017 dataset: (a) melanoma; (b) seborrheich kerastosis; and (c) common nevi.

3.2   Image Preprocessing

For this work, we consistently applied the same normalization technique as used in the initial training of the models on the ImageNet dataset to ensure that the input data for the pre-trained network is in a similar format as what the network initially expected.

Image resizing was applied systematically on all images to ensure that their height and width conform to the input dimensions required by the pre-trained model. This step was consistently applied across all experimental iterations to maintain compatibility between the image data and the model's processing and analysis requirements.

Image cropping was performed to eliminate irrelevant regions of the image. A centered square cropping technique was chosen as the preferred method because a significant number of images contained lesions in the center. The cropping was done with respect to the smaller dimension of the image, typically the height. Thus, an image with 600×400 dimensions would be cropped to 400×400 after this procedure. This approach effectively removed unnecessary skin information unrelated to the lesion in most images and mitigated potential distortions after image resizing while preserving the original format of the lesion.

We used the CLAHE (Contrast Limited Adaptive Histogram Equalization) technique to enhance contrast, a variation of the adaptive HE (Histogram Equalization) method, where the image or volume is divided into smaller blocks and applied independently to each block. This technique allows for local contrast enhancement, as it adapts the amplification of contrast to the characteristics of each block, preventing over-enhancement or amplification of noise [24].

Some ISIC Challenge leaderboard models commonly use color constancy algorithms [14,15] to decrease the disparity of illumination and color due to the different environments and acquisition devices. This method consists of normalizing images' color, minimizing the color and illumination differences [25]. For this work, we used the color constancy Shades of Gray algorithm [13].

Some artifacts, such as hairs and marks, can be prominent in specific images, impacting the model's performance. Therefore, we utilized the DullRazor algorithm to address this issue. The algorithm identifies dark regions corresponding to hair using a generalized grayscale morphological closing operation and checks for the characteristic thin and long structure of hair pixels. It replaces the verified pixels with bilinear interpolation. Finally, the replaced hair pixels are smoothed using an adaptive median filter [26].

Figure 3 illustrates the image preprocessing techniques used in this work.

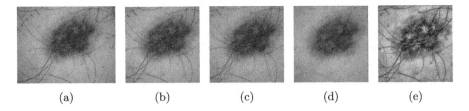

    (a)   (b)   (c)   (d)   (e)

Fig. 3. Examples of preprocessing techniques applied to an image: (a) original image; (b) center crop; (c) color constancy; (d) hair removal; and (e) CLAHE.

3.3 Transfer Learning

In machine learning, transfer learning is the practice of using a previously developed model for one task as the foundation for a new model for a different task. This technique is used when a limited amount of data is available for training. It works as a "knowledge transfer" that use the model learned from the area with lots of data to improve the results in the area with fewer data [27].

In our work, we used pre-trained models trained for the ImageNet dataset. To customize these models to our particular dataset, we replaced the fully convolutional (FC) layer with a new one with the same number of neurons as the number of classes in our dataset. We conducted another training round on the models, including the CNN part, to finetune them with the skin lesion dataset.

3.3.1 Pre-trained Models

In our work, we used 13 models of 7 different architectures. They were chosen based on the leaderboard approaches of the last two ISIC Challenges.

- EfficientNet (B0-B6): EfficientNet [28] is a family of CNNs that employs a scaling strategy to balance the network's depth, width, and resolution for optimal performance. This is accomplished through a compound scaling method that uniformly scales these dimensions using a compound coefficient. The scaling levels B0, B1, B2, etc., represent different base model versions. Each version is progressively larger, potentially offering higher accuracy and requiring more computational resources.
- PNASNet5: Progressive Neural Architecture Search (PNASNet) [29] is a model that employs a sequential model-based optimization strategy. This approach uses a search strategy that starts with simple cells and gradually increases complexity by adding more blocks.
- ResNeSt101: ResNeSt101 [30] is a variant of the ResNet model. The feature called "Split-Attention" block allows attention to be spread over various groups of feature maps. In our work, we used the ResNeSt101, which consists of 101 layers. The ResNeSt architecture maintains the residual connections that help mitigate the vanishing gradient problem, allowing for the training of very deep networks.
- ResNeXt101: ResNeXt101 [31] is a variant of the ResNet model that introduces a new "cardinality" dimension which refers to the number of independent paths in the network. This addition allows the model to effectively increase its capacity and performance without significantly increasing computational cost. Like the ResNeSt, the architecture of ResNeXt maintains the residual connections of ResNet. Our work used the ResNeXt101, which consists of 101 layers.
- SEResNeXt101: SEResNeXt [32] is a variant of the ResNeXt model that incorporates Squeeze-and-Excitation (SE) blocks. These SE blocks adaptively recalibrate channel-wise feature responses by explicitly modeling the interdependencies between the channels of the convolutional features. This allows the model to emphasize informative features and suppress less useful ones, enhancing the representational power of the network. Our work used the SEResNext101 model, which consists of 101 layers.
- DenseNet121: Dense Convolutional Network (DenseNet) [33] is a type of CNN where each layer is connected to all other deeper layers in the network. Unlike traditional CNNs, in DenseNet, each layer acquires the feature maps of all previous layers as inputs, and its feature maps are used as inputs into all successive layers. This dense connectivity pattern facilitates feature reuse throughout the network, significantly reduces the number of parameters, and

improves the flow of information and gradients throughout the network, making it easier to train. In our work, we used a DenseNet with 121 layers.

- VGG19: Visual Geometry Group (VGG) model [34] is a CNN characterized by its architecture uniformity. All hidden layers are convolutional, using a minimal receptive field. To maintain spatial resolution after convolution, the convolution stride remains fixed at 1 pixel. The network follows this with a max-pooling step with a 2×2 pixel window and stride 2. In our work, we used the VGG model composed of 19 layers.

3.4 Ensemble Techniques

In recent years, the ensemble technique has been explored by several works for classifying skin lesions [14,15,35], indicating that the ensemble of several classification models is a suitable mechanism to obtain a better accuracy for skin lesion analysis [36]. In our work, we compare the results of three different ensemble techniques described as follows:

- Average ensemble: The final classification is given by the average of the predictions from all models.
- Average of 3: The final classification is given by the average of the predictions from three models. The models are exhaustively combined 3 by 3, and the best ensemble combination is selected.
- Voting: The final classification is the one with more votes from each model, i.e., each model will classify the skin lesion with a class, and the class that appears the most is chosen.

3.5 Training Process

For the training process, we utilized the Cross-Entropy as the loss function for all the models, as it is commonly used in classification tasks. To account for class imbalance in the dataset, we assigned weights to different classes in the loss function, allowing the model to be more sensitive to the minority class and learn from both majority and minority classes equally, thus addressing the class imbalance issue.

The hyperparameters such as optimizer, initial learning rate, and batch size were selected based on experiments to identify the optimal settings for each model. In addition, a learning rate scheduler was implemented to dynamically adjust the learning rate during training based on the observed plateauing of the validation loss, aiming to enhance convergence and overall performance potentially. Specifically, a patience number of 10 epochs, a minimum learning rate of 1×10^{-6}, and a reduction factor of 0.1 were set for the learning rate scheduler. If the loss does not improve within ten epochs, the learning rate will be reduced by a factor of 0.1 until it reaches the minimum threshold of 1×10^{-6}. This approach aims to ensure that the model's learning rate is appropriately adjusted during training to facilitate better convergence and performance.

Furthermore, we incorporated an early stop condition, where the training process is terminated if the balanced accuracy does not improve for a specified number of epochs. The number of epochs for early stop varies depending on the experiment. Finally, the best epoch model is saved based on balanced accuracy to prevent overfitting and obtain the optimal performance of the model.

4   Experiments and Results

The first steps to achieve the optimal model configuration involved determining the most suitable hyperparameters for each model. To accomplish this, we conducted experiments utilizing the SGD, Adam, and AdamW optimizers, employing initial learning rates of 1×10^{-3} and 1×10^{-4}. Furthermore, we tested batch sizes ranging from 4 to 64, considering the GPU constraints for each model. We trained each model for 100 epochs, implementing an early stopping criterion after 15 epochs. Finally, we evaluated the optimal hyperparameters for every model by analyzing the balanced accuracy metrics on the test data. Table 1 presents the final hyperparameter configuration used in each model.

Table 1. Model performance with different hyperparameters

Model	Batchsize	Initial learning rate	Optimizer
EfficientNet-B0	8	0.001	AdamW
EfficientNet-B1	8	0.001	AdamW
EfficientNet-B2	8	0.001	Adam
EfficientNet-B3	32	0.001	Adam
EfficientNet-B4	16	0.001	AdamW
EfficientNet-B5	8	0.0001	AdamW
EfficientNet-B6	4	0.0001	AdamW
ResNest101	8	0.0001	AdamW
SEResNeXt101	32	0.0001	Adam
VGG19	8	0.001	SGD
DenseNet121	32	0.0001	Adam
ResNext101	8	0.001	SGD
PNASNet5	8	0.0001	Adam

The next step was to evaluate the performance of each model when employing preprocessing techniques. For a better understanding, each preprocessing algorithm is associated with a letter as follows:

- A: Contrast Enhancement
- B: Color Constancy
- C: Hair Removal
- D: Center Crop

Table 2 presents the balanced accuracy for each experiment combining the different preprocessing techniques.

Table 2. Experiments Results for each model

Model	No PP	A	B	C	D	BC	ABC	BCD	ABCD
EfficientNet-B0	**0.7073**	0.6871	0.6529	0.6960	0.6623	0.6968	0.6304	0.6645	0.6096
EfficientNet-B1	0.6654	0.6716	0.6840	0.6601	0.6880	**0.7016**	0.6440	0.6255	0.6944
EfficientNet-B2	0.6993	0.6957	0.6445	**0.7091**	0.6572	0.6833	0.6600	0.6928	0.6262
EfficientNet-B3	0.6767	0.7120	0.6982	0.7248	0.6830	0.7010	0.6612	**0.7278**	0.7260
EfficientNet-B4	0.7216	0.6944	0.7039	0.7093	0.6734	**0.7317**	0.6493	0.7284	0.6470
EfficientNet-B5	0.6976	0.7113	0.6522	0.7099	**0.7250**	0.6816	0.6814	0.6846	0.6958
EfficientNet-B6	0.6874	0.6943	**0.7395**	0.7213	0.6735	0.7139	0.7057	0.6953	0.6856
ResNest101	0.7344	0.7104	**0.7620**	0.7447	0.6993	0.7083	0.6706	0.7070	0.7306
SEResNeXt101	0.7310	0.7032	**0.7481**	0.6863	0.7117	0.7165	0.6650	0.6939	0.6634
VGG19	**0.6922**	0.6011	0.6450	0.6606	0.6121	0.6506	0.6546	0.6142	0.6532
DenseNet121	0.6753	0.6716	0.6923	**0.7176**	0.6974	0.6282	0.6092	0.6534	0.6330
ResNext101	0.6828	0.6731	**0.7281**	0.6957	0.7194	0.7253	0.6535	0.6967	0.6950
PNASNet5	0.7406	0.6718	0.7271	0.7398	**0.7522**	0.7123	0.6963	0.6871	0.6783

Next, ensemble techniques were applied for each experiment, and we obtained the results presented in Table 3. Each row represents the balanced accuracy score of the ensembling techniques for each preprocessing configuration.

Table 3. Ensemble Results

Ensemble	No PP	A	B	C	D	BC	ABC	BCD	ABCD
Average	0.7547	0.7674	0.7685	0.7713	0.7690	**0.7769**	0.7146	0.7570	0.7657
Average of 3	0.7671	0.7620	0.7846	**0.7879**	0.7703	0.7798	0.7565	0.7697	0.7808
Voting	0.7371	0.7617	**0.7718**	0.7693	0.7647	0.7709	0.7166	0.7493	0.7591

5 Analysis

Initially, by analyzing the performance of each model without preprocessing, we notice that some models such as EfficientNet-B0, EfficientNet-B2, EfficientNet-B4, EfficientNet-B5, ResNest101, and PNASNet5 demonstrate balanced accuracy values exceeding 0.7, indicating their potential effectiveness in this classification task. Furthermore, PNASNet5 achieves the highest balanced accuracy score of 0.7406, suggesting its superior performance. On the other hand, models such as EfficientNet-B1, EfficientNet-B3, EfficientNet-B6, SEResNeXt101, VGG19, DenseNet121, and ResNext101 exhibit relatively lower balanced accuracy values below 0.7, indicating the need for further improvement. These results are shown in Fig. 4.

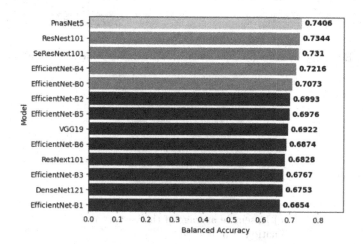

Fig. 4. Balanced accuracy of all models without PP.

By analyzing the results of the image preprocessing experiments performed on each model presented in Table 2, we notice that the performance of all models, except for EfficientNet-B0 and VGG19, was improved with the implementation of preprocessing steps. The impact of each preprocessing, however, varied significantly between models and the different image preprocessing configurations. Seven of the thirteen models achieved the highest performance using the Color Constancy technique; four used only this technique, two combined with Hair Removal, and one combined with Hair Removal and Center Crop. Nevertheless, the experiments that included Contrast Enhancement did not outperform the other configurations, indicating that adding this technique to these models did not help improve the performance.

In the ensemble results presented in Table 3, we observe that the highest score achieved was for the "Average of 3" ensemble with the C configuration, corresponding to the employment of the Hair Removal. Next, the "Average" ensemble with the application of Color Constancy and Hair Removal, followed by the "Voting" ensemble with Color Constancy.

In Fig. 5, we notice that the ensemble of the models performs better than the models individually. These results indicate that combining the predictions of multiple models can be beneficial by providing diverse perspectives and combining the strengths of each model. Furthermore, the ensemble technique takes advantage of the diversity of the models and can reduce the impact of individual model weaknesses or errors.

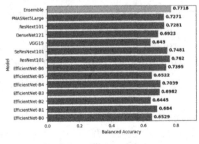

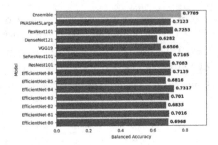

(a) Ensemble by voting.   (b) Ensemble average of all models.

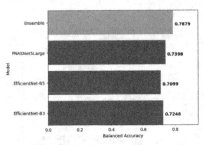

(c) Ensemble average of the best combination of 3 models.

Fig. 5. Comparison of the results between the ensembles and each model.

Figure 6 presents the best ensemble results for each experiment performed. By analyzing those results, we notice that the application of image preprocessing techniques improved the performance of the ensemble of models compared to the ensemble of the models trained with the raw data.

Overall, the best-performing ensemble method was the "Average of 3" with the "C" configuration, which employed Hair Removal and resulted in a balanced accuracy of 0.7879. This model is the average of the PNASNet5, EfficientNet-B3, and EfficientNet-B5 results.

Other works of the ISIC 2017 Challenge leaderboard [16,37,38] obtained better performance than our best-performing method. However, it is important to mention that the goal study isn't to propose an outstanding model but to evaluate how image preprocessing techniques impact a model's performance and the use of ensemble techniques.

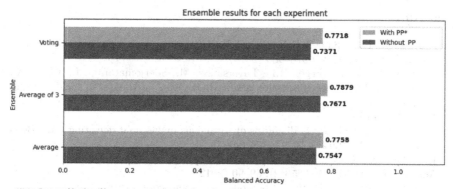

Fig. 6. Ensemble results for each experiment.

6   Conclusion

The work presented in this paper evaluated the combination of image preprocessing allied with deep learning techniques and ensemble techniques for the
classification of skin lesions, specifically melanoma and seborrheic keratosis. We
evaluated the use of different image preprocessing techniques, including contrast
enhancement, color constancy, hair removal, and center cropping. Our goal was
to assess the effects of these techniques on performance, setting the groundwork
for future research.

Finally, the result suggests that the image preprocessing technique can
improve the skin lesion classification task performance. In our experiments with
the individual models, we notice that different CNN models can benefit more
or less from the different combinations of image preprocessing techniques. This
indicates that it is crucial to evaluate the use of different image preprocessing
techniques to select a final combination.

Although the results indicate that the use of image preprocessing and ensemble techniques can improve performance, it is important to notice that it also
increases the complexity of the models, and the training of different models can
be time-consuming.

In addition, three ensemble techniques were tested, and the best one was
the ensemble of PNASNet5, EfficientNet-B3, and EfficientNet-B5 models with a
balanced accuracy of 0.7879.

One limitation of this study is the use of few image preprocessing algorithms
with low complexity. For future work, it is possible to evaluate the results for
a higher number of techniques and more complex algorithms, such as lesion
segmentation. Also, it is possible to apply data augmentation allied to the techniques presented in this paper and evaluate the results.

Acknowledgments. The authors are grateful to the Foundation for Science and Technology (FCT, Portugal) for financial support through national funds FCT/MCTES to
CeDRI (UIDB/05757/2020 and UIDP/05757/2020) and SusTEC (LA/P/0007/2021).

References

1. Narayanan, D.L., Saladi, R.N., Fox, J.L.: Ultraviolet radiation and skin cancer. Int. J. Dermatol. **49**(9), 978–986 (2010)
2. Sung, H., Ferlay, J., Siegel, R.L., Laversanne, M., Soerjomataram, I., Jemal, A., Bray, F.: Global Cancer Statistics 2020: GLOBOCAN estimates of incidence and mortality worldwide for 36 cancers in 185 Countries. CA: A Cancer J. Clinicians **71**, 209–249 (2021)
3. Abbasi, N.R., et al.: Early diagnosis of cutaneous melanoma: revisiting the ABCD criteria. JAMA **292**(22), 2771–2776 (2004)
4. Korotkov, K., Garcia, R.: Computerized analysis of pigmented skin lesions: a review. Artif. Intell. Med. **56**(2), 69–90 (2012)
5. Carrera, C., et al.: Validity and reliability of dermoscopic criteria used to differentiate nevi from melanoma. JAMA Dermatol. 152(7), 798 (2016)
6. Cazzaniga, S., et al.: Agreement on classification of clinical photographs of pigmentary lesions: exercise after a training course with young dermatologists. In: Dermatol. Reports 15(1), 9500 (2023)
7. Li, H., Pan, Y., Zhao, J., Zhang, L.: Skin disease diagnosis with deep learning: a review. Neurocomputing **464**, 364–393 (2021)
8. LeCun, Y., Bengio, Y., Hinton, G.: Deep learning. Nature **521**(7553), 436–444 (2015)
9. Silva, G.M., Lazzaretti, A.E., Monteiro, F.C.: Deep learning techniques applied to skin lesion classification: a review. In: 2022 International Conference on Machine Learning, Control, and Robotics (MLCR). Suzhou, China: IEEE, October 2022
10. Salvi, M., Acharya, U.R., Molinari, F., Meiburger, K.M.: The impact of pre- and post-image processing techniques on deep learning frameworks: a comprehensive review for digital pathology image analysis. Comput. Biol. Med. **128**, 104129 (2021)
11. ISIC Challenge — challenge.isic-archive.com. https://challenge.isicarchive.com/. Accessed 12 Jun 2023
12. Finnane, A., et al.: Proposed technical guidelines for the acquisition of clinical images of skin-related conditions. JAMA Dermatol. **153**(5), 453–457 (2017)
13. Finlayson, G.D., Trezzi, E.: Shades of gray and colour constancy. In: Color and Imaging Conference, vol. 2004. 1. Society for Imaging Science and Technology, pp. 37–41 (2004)
14. Gessert, N., Nielsen, M., Shaikh, M., Werner, R., Schlaefer, A.: Skin lesion classification using ensembles of multi-resolution EfficientNets with meta data. MethodsX **7**(100864), 100864 (2020)
15. Pacheco, A.G.C., et al.: PAD-UFES-20: A skin lesion dataset composed of patient data and clinical images collected from smartphones. Data Brief **32**, 106221 (2020)
16. Matsunaga, K., Hamada, A., Minagawa, A., Koga, H.: Image Classification of Melanoma, Nevus and Seborrheic Keratosis by Deep Neural Network Ensemble (2017). arXiv: 1703.03108 [cs.CV]
17. Khouloud, S., Ahlem, M., Fadel, T., Amel, S.: W-net and inception residual network for skin lesion segmentation and classification. Appl. Intell. **52**(4), 3976–3994 (2021)
18. Akram, T., et al.: A multilevel features selection framework for skin lesion classification. In: Human-centric Comp. and Information Sciences 10.1 (2020)
19. Afza, F., Sharif, M., Mittal, M., Khan, M.A., Jude Hemanth, D.: A hierarchical three-step superpixels and deep learning framework for skin lesion classification. In: Methods 202 (2022). Machine Learning Methods for Bio-Medical Img. and Sig. Processing: Recent Advances, pp. 88–102

20. Khan, M.A., Sharif, M., Akram, T., Bukhari, S.A.C., Nayak, R.S.: eveloped Newton-Raphson based deep features selection framework for skin lesion recognition. Pattern Rec. Lett. **129**, 293–303 (2020)

21. Sarkar, R., Chatterjee, C., Hazra, A.: Diagnosis of melanoma from dermoscopic images using a deep depthwise separable residual convolutional network. IET Image Processing 13 (2019)

22. Hoshyar, A.N., Al-Jumaily, A., Hoshyar, A.N.: The beneficial techniques in preprocessing step of skin cancer detection system comparing. Procedia Comput. Sci. **42**, 25–31 (2014)

23. Codella, N.C.F., et al.: Skin lesion analysis toward melanoma detection: a challenge at the 2017 international symposium on biomedical imaging (ISBI), hosted by the international skin imaging collaboration (ISIC) (2017)

24. Lucknavalai, K., Schulze, J.P.: Real-time contrast enhancement for 3D medical images using histogram equalization. In: Advances in Visual Computing. Lecture notes in computer science. Springer International Publishing, pp. 224–235 (2020)

25. Barata, C., Celebi, M.E., Marques, J.S.: Improving dermoscopy image classification using color constancy. IEEE J. Biomed. Health Inform. **19**(3), 1146–1152 (2015)

26. Lee, T., Ng, V., Gallagher, R., Coldman, A., McLean, D.: DullRazor: a software approach to hair removal from images. Comput. Biol. Med. **27**(6), 533–543 (1997)

27. Weiss, K., Khoshgoftaar, T.M., Wang, D.: A survey of transfer learning. J. Big Data **3**(1) (2016)

28. Tan, M., Le, Q.: Efficientnet: rethinking model scaling for convolutional neural networks. In: International Conference on Machine Learning. PMLR, pp. 6105–6114 (2019)

29. Liu, C., et al.: Progressive neural architecture search. In: Proceedings of the European Conference on Computer Vision (ECCV), pp. 19–34 (2018)

30. Zhang, H., et al.: Resnest: split-attention networks. In: Proceedings of the IEEE/CVF Conference on Computer Vision and Pattern Recognition, pp. 2736–2746 (2022)

31. Xie, S., Girshick, R., Dollár, P., Tu, Z., He, K.: Aggregated residual transformations for deep neural networks (2016)

32. Hu, J., Shen, L., Sun, G.: Squeeze-and-excitation networks. In: Proceedings of the IEEE Conference on Computer Vision and Pattern Recognition, pp. 7132–7141 (2018)

33. Huang, G., Liu, Z., Van Der Maaten, L., Weinberger, K.Q.: Densely connected convolutional networks. In: Proceedings of the IEEE Conference on Computer Vision and Pattern Recognition, pp. 4700–4708 (2017)

34. Simonyan, K., Zisserman, A.: Very deep convolutional networks for large-scale image recognition. In: arXiv preprint arXiv:1409.1556 (2014)

35. Ha, Q., Liu, B., Liu, F.: Identifying melanoma images using EfficientNet ensemble: Winning solution to the SIMM-ISIC Melanoma Classification Challenge. In: arXiv preprint arXiv:2010.05351 (2020)

36. Perez, F., Avila, S., Valle, E.: Solo or Ensemble? Choosing a CNN architecture for melanoma classification. In: Proceedings of the IEEE/CVF Conference on Computer Vision and Pattern Recognition Workshops (2019)

37. Díaz, I.G.: Incorporating the Knowledge of Dermatologists to Convolutional Neural Networks for the Diagnosis of Skin Lesions (2017). arXiv: 1703.01976 [cs.CV]

38. Menegola, A., Tavares, J., Fornaciali, M., Li, L.T., Avila, S., Valle, E.: RECOD Titans at ISIC Challenge 2017 (2017). arXiv: 1703.04819 [cs.CV]

Pest Detection in Olive Groves Using YOLOv7 and YOLOv8 Models

Adília Alves[1,2,3,4(✉)] ⓘ, José Pereira[3,4] ⓘ, Salik Khanal[6] ⓘ,
A. Jorge Morais[2,5] ⓘ, and Vitor Filipe[1,5] ⓘ

[1] Universidade de Trás-os-Montes e Alto Douro, 5000-801 Vila Real, Portugal
aidcalves@gmail.com
[2] Universidade Aberta, 1269-001 Lisboa, Portugal
[3] Centro de Investigação de Montanha (CIMO), Instituto Politécnico de Bragança,
Campus de Santa Apolónia, 5300-253 Bragança, Portugal
[4] Laboratório Associado para a Sustentabilidade e Tecnologia em Regiões de
Montanha (SusTEC), Instituto Politécnico de Bragança, Campus de Santa Apolónia,
5300-253 Bragança, Portugal
[5] LIAAD - INESC TEC, 4200-465 Porto, Portugal
[6] Center for Precision and Automated Agricultural Systems, Biological Systems
Engineering, Washington State University, Prosser, WA, USA

Abstract. Modern agriculture faces important challenges for feeding a
fast-growing planet's population in a sustainable way. One of the most
important challenges faced by agriculture is the increasing destruction
caused by pests to important crops. It is very important to control and
manage pests in order to reduce the losses they cause. However, pest
detection and monitoring are very resources consuming tasks. The recent
development of computer vision-based technology has made it possible
to automatize pest detection efficiently.

In Mediterranean olive groves, the olive fly (Bactrocera oleae Rossi)
is considered the key-pest of the crop. This paper presents olive fly
detection using the lightweight YOLO-based model for versions 7 and 8,
respectively, YOLOv7-tiny and YOLOv8n. The proposed object detection models were trained, validated, and tested using two different image
datasets collected in various locations of Portugal and Greece. The
images are constituted by sticky yellow trap photos and by McPhail
trap photos with olive fly exemplars. The performance of the models
was evaluated using precision, recall, and mAP.95. The YOLOV7-tiny
model best performance is 88.3% of precision, 85% of Recall, 90% of
mAP.50, and 53% of mAP.95. The YOLOV8n model best performance
is 85% of precision, 85% of Recall, 90% mAP.50, and 55% of mAP.50
YOLO8n model achieved worst results than YOLOv7-tiny for a dataset
without negative images (images without olive fly exemplars). Aiming at
installing an experimental prototype in the olive grove, the YOLOv8n
model was implemented in a Ubuntu Server 23.04 Raspberry PI 3 microcomputer.

The authors are grateful to the Foundation for Science and Technology (FCT, Portugal) for financial support through national funds FCT/MCTES (PIDDAC) to CIMO
(UIDB/00690/2020 and UIDP/00690/2020) and SusTEC (LA/P/0007/2020).

Keywords: Olives sustainable production · Convolutional Neural Network · Deep Learning · YOLOv7 · YOLOv8

1   Introduction

The olive tree (Olea europaea) is one of the oldest plants and it is widespread in different parts of the world with Mediterranean climate. This crop has great economic, social and cultural impact in the Mediterranean basin, and the olive products (olive oil and table olives) are very appreciated and nutritional balanced. Several pests, pathogens, and nematodes affect olive trees, threatening plant health and production and, consequently, causing annual economic losses. Olive fly (Bactrocera oleae Rossi) is one of the most serious pests that attack olives, being considered a key pest in the producing countries of the Mediterranean region. The olive fly larvae causes important losses that can be, directly, caused by pulp consumption, and indirectly, caused by the decrease in product quality. When attacked, the quality of fruits which are destined to olive oil extraction is affected (e.g., increase of free acidity and peroxide values, decrease of oil stability and organoleptic score). When fruits are destined to table olives, an attack higher than 1–2% makes the production of this product unfeasible.

Nowadays, computer vision-based methods, in particular Deep Learning methods, are revolutionizing agriculture and pest detection pushing toward digital agriculture technology. In recent years, scientists are focusing their research on pest detection and management using computer vision-based models. Ahmad et al. [1], proposed a smartphone-based automated system using an IP-camera to detect insect pests from digital images/videos to reduce farmers' reliance on pesticides. The proposed approach was based on You Only Look Once (YOLO) object detection algorithm including YOLOv5 (n, s, m, l, and x), YOLOv3, YOLO-Lite, and YOLOR. Likewise, Dai et al. [2] proposed an improved YOLOv5m-based model to detect pests in plants. Zu et al. [3] considered three families of detectors to identify and detect pests using Raspberry Pi where the detection of the pest was carried out using faster region-based convolutional neural networks (Faster R-CNN), region-based fully convolutional networks (R-FCN), and single multi-box detectors (SSD). These meta-architectures were combined with deep feature extractors (e.g., VGG nets and ResNet).

Machine Learning/Deep Learning application for automatic pest detection be-came recently, more than an important academic research topic, a broad market application service. Examples of pest detection tools available in the market are Farmesense[1] which counts the prevalence of different insects using its distinctive wing beat sound and RapidAIM[2] which detects different insects using its distinctive behavior (movement and wing beat sound).

The use of electronic and communication devices for monitoring and control of olive plants diseases and pests has made slow progress, mainly in small farms,

---

[1] https://www.farmsense.io/.
[2] https://rapidaim.io/.

mostly due to devices and system cost, climatic limitations (temperature, humidity, solar exposition) in olive crops, and the absence of good communication means, since internet connection, and even GSM system, can be, and often are, unavailable in olive crops. Even though much research and advances have been made in automatic agricultural pest detection regarding deep learning-based object detection, it is always valuable to consider the robustness, reliability, and cost-effectiveness of the system.

Last years, YOLO family models, thanks to its fastness and accuracy performances, have been used with success to detect insects [4]. So, it is relevant to test more recent YOLO family models (YOLOv7 and YOLOv8) in the context of pest detection. The present study evaluated the two more recent YOLO family object detection methods - YOLOv7 and YOLOv8 for olive fly detection in olive groves. In this article, YOLOv7 and YOLOv8 algorithms are compared in object detection mode (training, validation, and detection) with its lightweight models (optimized for inference on edge devices), using the same training, validation, and test datasets, and running the algorithms in the same hardware and software infrastructure. This study is part of a wider project to create a technically feasible system for the detection/prediction of olive fly pest attacks using small, affordable devices (edge devices) to decrease the cost of the olive fly detection system.

YOLOv7 is an anchor-based single-stage object detection algorithm whereas YOLOv8 is a center-based anchor-free single-stage object detection algorithm. In anchor-based object detection algorithms, the process to locate objects begins with the identification/location of potential bounding boxes (anchors), the selection between these bounding boxes of the most promising ones to match objects (the distinction between positives and negatives), and finally slightly movement and resizing of the selected bounding boxes, as necessary, to obtain the best possible fit of the bounding boxes to the objects. Center-based detectors are like anchor-based detectors, as they treat points (instead of anchor boxes) as preset samples. Center-based detectors begin with just one point (center) per object and use spatial and scale constraints to select samples (the distinction between positives and negatives) looking for the best possible fit of the bounding boxes to the objects.

According to Zhang, Chi, Yao, Lei and Li [5], "The essential difference between anchor-based and anchor-free detection is actually how to define positive and negative training samples, which leads to the performance gap between them. If they adopt the same definition of positive and negative samples during training, there is no obvious difference in the final performance, no matter regressing from a box or a point."

The smallest models (YOLOv7-tiny and YOLOv8n) based on the number of deep learning layers and functionality were used for the experiments to maintain the affordable speed in less powerful computing devices. For example, the YOLOv7 neck network, more precisely, its FPN/PAN feature fusion method adds a top-down pathway and lateral connections to the regular bottom-up pathway (normal flow of a convolution layer) allowing the fusion of received features into three feature maps at multiple scales with semantically strong features. According to Li, Xu, and Zhong [6] YOLOv7 utilizes the combination of FPN and PAN for feature fusion, which cannot guarantee detection accuracy in different resolution images, leading to poor performance in detecting objects with varying shapes and sizes. In present study, the olive fly exemplars have similar body size and well-preserved physiognomy.

This paper is divided into the following sections: The second section introduces the datasets, the deep learning models used to detect olive flies exemplars in traps and the metrics used to compare models performance; The third section focuses on the comparative experiments and the obtained experimental results; The fourth section is the conclusion and the direction of subsequent work and improvement.

2   Materials and Methods

2.1   Dataset Description

All the proposed models were trained, validated, and tested using two custom datasets: a) one dataset constituted by yellow sticky trapped insects images collected in Portugal [7], (Dataset-1) and another dataset constituted by three smaller datasets (Dataset-2). Dataset-2 includes Dataset-1 and two other datasets: a dataset of McPhail-type trapped insects images [8] (Greck dataset), and a dataset of yellow sticky trapped insects images without olive fly exemplars [9] (md-121 dataset). Dataset-1 contains 513 RGB images of olive groves captured by mobile phones of diverse brands (e.g. TCL 10 Plus T782H 6 GB/256 GB, HUAWEI P40 LITE JNY-LX1 6 GB/128 GB) in a vineyard located in Vila Real or Bragança districts of Portugal (Trás-os-Montes). The images were collected between September and November 2022. The image resolution is 72ppi (ppi-points per inch) or 96ppi and the image dimension is 2448×3264, 3840×2160 or 4000×3000. In the images, the olive fly exemplars body measures about 60px and are not overlapped (but sometimes very close to one other). All olive fly exemplars captured by trap are roughly the same size and are presented in a lateral or dorsal position. The dataset images have shadow and tilt areas. Almost all the olive fly exemplars have a yellow background with black lines (the look of the yellow sticky trap) (see Fig. 1)

As previously mentioned, Dataset-2 is constituted by three smaller datasets: Dataset-1, Greek dataset and md-121 dataset.

The Greek dataset consists of 542 images with a pixel per inch of 72 ppi with diverse dimensions (450×2015px to 2064×1161px). The olive fly exemplars body measures around 40px. This dataset, according to Kalamatianos et al. [8], was collected from year 2015 to 2017 in various locations of Corfu, Greece. As the images were collected using different devices (smartphones and tablets running the e-Olive app, photo-cameras available at the field during trap inspection, etc.) the images of the dataset are not standardized in terms of resolution and dimension. In the images, the olive fly exemplars' body measures about 60px, is not overlapped and also has a well-preserved physiognomy. All olive flies'

Fig. 1. The images of olive flies collected where the olive flies are trapped in a yellow background trapper. (Color figure online)

exemplars captured by trap are the same size and are presented in a lateral or dorsal position (see Fig. 2).

Fig. 2. The images of olive flies collected with McPhail Traps

The md-121 dataset consists of 283 images of yellow sticky traps that contain insects but no olive fly exemplars. According to Deserno and Briassouli [9] the small size of objects, occlusions, similarity in appearance and other factors are the major characteristics of the images. The images were taken in laboratorial environment, so they have less visual noise (shadow, tilt). All images have the dimension 5184 × 3456px and the resolution 72ppi (see Fig. 3).

2.2   Experimental Design

YOLOv7-tiny v0.1 and YOLOv8n version 8.0.59 were trained in a 12th Gen Intel Core i9-1290K 3.2 GHz CPU with 32.0 Gb RAM and with a NVIDIA GeForce

Fig. 3. Dataset3 collected in laboratorial environment.

RTX 4080 16 GB, using Jupyter Notebooks and GPU in Visual Studio Code 1.77.1, running in Windows 10 (with the CONDA version 4.12.0, programming language Python 3.10.9, and the deep learning framework Pytorch 1.13.1).

All the images were labeled using LabelImg tool by an olive-growing researcher producing a text file in YOLO format (x-top left, y-top left, width, height) for each dataset image. Note that all olive fly exemplars (both male and female) were encoded as 'dracus', so just one class object was considered for YOLO detection and all other insects present in the image were ignored (considered background). All the experiments were carried out on Roboflow platform[3] which requires uploading the labeled dataset to platform. For training, it generates several versions of the original dataset using preprocessing and augmentation operations. After splitting the dataset randomly into the train, test, and validation folders, with respectively 80%, 10% and 10% of images, the dataset was exported into YOLOv7 PyTorch TXT and YOLOv8 formats (which includes a config file with YAML extension and the images and annotations distributed by three folders - train, test and validation) and used in YOLO training and detection. Care has been taken to ensure that the three folders, after randomly division of Dataset-2's images, have images from its three constituent datasets.

Both YOLOv7 and YOLOv8 resized input image maintaining proportions and padding the smaller dimension (width or height), by default, to 640 × 640. As insects are small targets in images and the default initial resize of YOLO model reduces even more the insects size, in this study the input images size is defined as 1280. The input images size is not bigger than 1280px because of the processing and memory limitations of the training system and because of the constraints defined by the device that will capture future images - ESP32-CAM - in the broader system for olive fly's detection in olive groves.

First, several combinations of hyper parameters (e.g. image rotation angle, zoom scale, use or not of mosaic) were used in several trainings and no considerable variation in the results was obtained, meaning that the not so good performance results of YOLOv8n (essentially with Dataset-1) is not in the tuning of these parameters. Thus, the YOLOv8n's worst performance results either

---

[3] https://roboflow.com/.

from the lack of discriminant signal of the dataset (underfitting) or from the adequacy of the YOLOv8's neuronal structure to the olive fly detection in the traps (over-fitting or underfitting).

2.3 Evaluation Metrics

The performance of the object detection models was evaluated using Precision, Recall, mAP and mAP.95. Precision measures the accuracy in positive prediction.

$$Precision = \frac{True\ positive}{True\ positive + False\ positive}$$

Recall measures the proportion of actual positive cases that the model correctly identifies.

$$Recall = \frac{True\ positive}{True\ positive + False\ negative}$$

There is often a trade-off between precision and recall; for example, increasing the number of True Positives (higher recall) can result in more False Positives too (lower precision). To account for this trade-off, the Average Precision (AP) metric and its average over all categories, the Mean Average Precision (mAP) metric incorporate the precision-recall curve that plots precision against recall for different confidence thresholds.

$$AP = \frac{1}{n}\sum_{i=1}^{n} p(\gamma i),$$

where $p(\gamma i)$ is the Precision at each chosen confidence threshold $\gamma 1, \gamma 2, ...$

$$mAP = \frac{1}{N}\sum_{i=1}^{N} p(AP\ i)$$

where APi is the Average Precision for each class.

In present study just a class will be detected (olive fly), so, AP and mAP will have the same value. The mAP.0.5 is the mean average precision at the intersection over union (IoU) threshold of 0.5. The mAP.95 is the average mAP over different IoU thresholds, ranging from 0.5 to 0.95.

$$IoU = \frac{area(gt \cap pd)}{area(gt \cup pd)}$$

where gt is the ground truth and pd is the prediction.

3   Results and Discussion

YOLOv7-tiny performs better than YOLOv8n for Dataset-1 and both models perform similarly for Dataset-2, as can be seen in Table 1. To analyze and understand weaker experimental performance results obtained by YOLOv8n for Dataset-1 changes on the Dataset-1 and on the YOLOv8n model were made, as follows. The number of Backbone layers was reduced for model YOLOv8n (with remotion of the three final layers) to check if YOLOv8 weaker performance results from overfitting introduced by the large YOLOv8 structure relative to the small object detection. Note that the operation of layers' removal in YOLOv8n model obligates to train the model straight from the beginning (ignoring pre-train with COCO dataset). This YOLOv8n training performance did not improve, on the contrary, it got worse (Precision: 0.652; Recall:0.742; mAP.50: 0.707 and mAP.95: 0.331). A larger version of YOLOv8 was tested - YOLOv8s - and the training performance did improve significantly. Analyzing the two previously mentioned YOLOV8 structural changes implemented, we can conclude that the worst performance of YOLOv8n with Dataset-1 results essentially from features' extraction or from definition of positive and negative samples during training. Some recognized problems with the two used datasets are, mainly with Dataset-1, visual noise (shadow and tilt) and small objects.

The difficulty of YOLO family algorithms in small object recognition is identified and reported by literature [5,10]. Some published workarounds to this problem are: to change the detection model or to change the dataset. Feasible options to change the dataset are: a) increase image resolution; b) increase model input resolution; c) tilt the images; d) generate more data augmentation. Table 1

Table 1. Table with training configurations and resulting evaluation metrics.

Model	Dataset	Size (pixels)	Precision	Recall	mAP.50	mAP.95
YOLOv7-tiny	Dataset-1	1280px	0.817	0.872	0.900	0.529
YOLOv7-tiny	**Dataset-2**	**1280px**	**0.8827**	**0.845**	**0.9038**	**0.531**
YOLOv8n	Dataset-1	1280px	0.738	0.712	0.776	0.378
YOLOv8n	Dataset-1 with bounding box augmentation	1280px	0.62144	0.546	0.547	0.178
YOLOv8n with less background layers	Dataset-1	1280px	0.652	0.742	0.707	0.331
YOLOv8s with COCO[3] pre-train	Dataset-1	1280px	0.725	0.727	0.774	0.393
YOLOv8n	**Dataset-2**	**1280px**	**0.854**	**0.854**	**0.905**	**0.55**

[3] The MS COCO (Microsoft Common Objects in Context) dataset is a large-scale object detection, segmentation, key-point detection, and captioning dataset. The dataset consists of 328K images

Results with Higher Resolution Images

This study is part of a wider project to create a technically feasible system for the detection/prediction of olive fly pest's attack using small, affordable devices

- edge devices - to collect and process traps' photos. The tested edge device used to capture photos' traps is the ESP32-CAM module (with video camera OV2640). The maximum resolution captured by this device is 1600×1200px.

The same models were tested with two datasets (Dataset-1 and Dataset-2) at 1280×1280 input resolution and gave the better accuracy for Dataset-2 (a larger and more heterogeneous dataset). Increase YOLO input resolution increases results, however, YOLO input resolution cannot be greater than image input resolution, so, the model's input resolution must be 1280×1280px.

This study augmented the number of images dataset but YOLOv8n model's training results did not be significantly improved. Filtering out extraneous class is not possible for present study because the only labelled class in images is the olive fly. All other insects are considered background because they are not labelled. The Portuguese images' background (outside the trap) was removed, trying to remove false positives. The training results did not improve, so it seems that YOLOv8 features' extraction problem is only in discriminating what is an olive fly exemplar and what is another insect exemplar. In order to increase detection accuracy of images with visual noise (for example, shadow areas and tilt), some authors find ways to automatically detect and remove such visual problems [11,12].

In order to increase detection accuracy of small objects in YOLO family algorithms without loosing the detection accuracy of other objects, some changes to detection models are suggested in literature: improve the Backbone module in order to make the context information saved in the feature extraction process more complete; improve feature fusion method of different scaled feature maps; improve identification/location of potential objects [4,10]. Finally, the inference/detection was performed, using a minimal confidence of 0.25 and the weights (best.pt) obtained in the training phase by 'YOLOv7-tiny with COCO pre-train' for Dataset-2 for three different datasets, described bellow.

A dataset constituted by 11 trap photos captured in the field. Some examples of the resulting inference executed with images of this dataset are presented bellow (see Fig. 4).

A dataset constituted by 12 trap photos captured in the laboratory environment. These photos have exclusively olive fly exemplars. Some examples of the resulting inference executed with images of this dataset are presented bellow Fig. 5. A dataset constituted by 41 trap photos captured in laboratory environment with-out olive fly exemplars. Some examples of the resulting interference executed with images of this dataset are presented bellow (see Fig. 6).

The inference executed in previously described datasets achieved very good results. The probability boxes are positioned around the detected objects with associated confidence, and as can be seen, in Figs. 4, 5 and 6, most of the pests were correctly identified with good confidence. As can be seen in Fig. 6, in a dataset without olive flies no probability box was placed, so, no False Positive was detected.

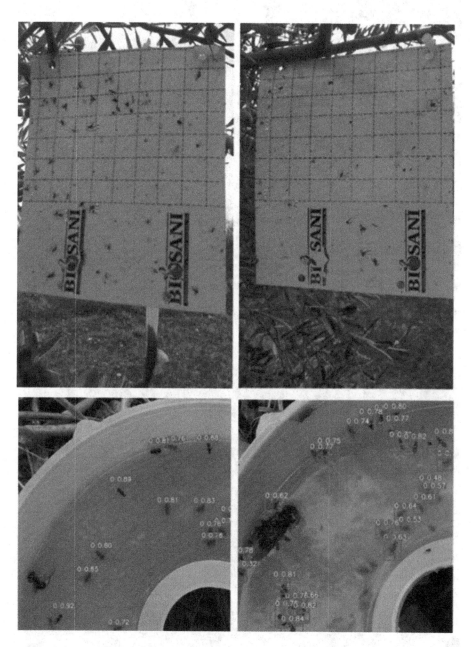

Fig. 4. Result of inference executed for dataset captures in the field (with olive fly exemplars and other insects)

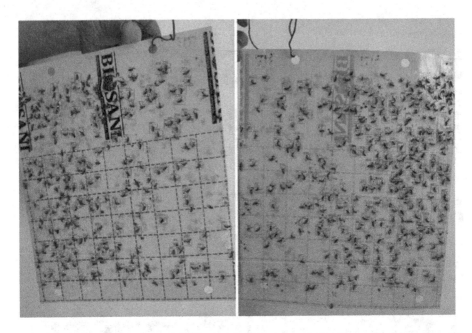

Fig. 5. Result of inference executed for dataset captured in laboratory (with olive fly exemplars).

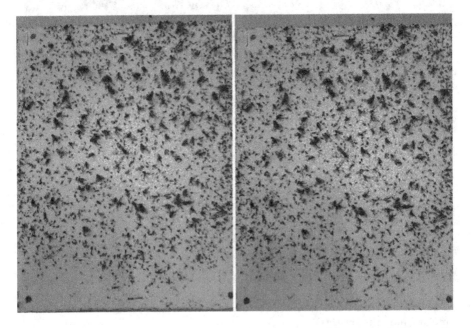

Fig. 6. Result of inference executed for dataset captured in laboratory (without olive fly exemplars).

4   Conclusions and Future Work

YOLOv7-tiny and YOLOv8n models obtained better results for Dataset-2 than for Dataset-1. YOLO8n model achieved slightly better training performance results than YOLOv7-tiny for Dataset-2 and much worst results than YOLOv7-tiny for Dataset-1. Dataset-2 introduced, relatively to Dataset-1, false training samples using md-121 dataset to reduce the false alarm rate (False positives number). YOLOv7-tiny Image segmentation can be perceived as a further extension of object detection because, instead of enclosing each object in the image with a bounding box, it marks each object's pixel through pixel-wise masks. Image segmentation is not necessary for pests detection in photos because the shape of the pest brings no relevant information for the pests detection task. Although YOLO family models give good results for medium to large objects, detection of small objects in messy images performs not so well. As future work: a) improvements must be done to the dataset images (for example with noise remotion and olive fly body preservation) and to the object detection model in order to improve olive fly detection. All traps' photos will be captured in the field, so, some important and urgent steps are: to fix the trap on a fixed structure in such a way as to prevent the trap borders from bending; and use yellow sticky traps that have not printed logotypes and black lines. This will drastically reduce images noise. b) the Raspberry 3 device must receive photos acquired by ESP32 web CAM devices scattered in olive grove using LoRa (Long Range) technology, count the number of detected olive fly exemplars and communicate the counting using a GSM/GPRS module. The images must be sent once a week and the traps must be cleaned once a month.

References

1. Ahmad, I., Yang, Y., Yue, Y., Ye, C., Hassan, M., Cheng, X., Yunzhi, W., Zhang, Y.: Deep learning based detector YOLOv5 for identifying insect pests. Appl. Sci. **12**(19), 10167 (2022)
2. Min Dai, Md., Dorjoy, M.H., Miao, H., Zhang, S.: A new pest detection method based on improved YOLOv5m. Insects **14**(1), 54 (2023)
3. Zhu, D., et al.: Knowledge graph and deep learning based pest detection and identification system for fruit quality. Internet Things **21**, 100649 (2023)
4. Nithin Kumar, N., Flammini, F.: YOLO-based light-weight deep learning models for insect detection system with field adaption. Agriculture **13**(3), 741 (2023)
5. Zhang, S., Chi, C., Yao, Y., Lei, Z., Li, S.Z.: Bridging the gap between anchor-based and anchor-free detection via adaptive training sample selection. In: 2020 IEEE/CVF Conference on Computer Vision and Pattern Recognition (CVPR). IEEE, June 2020
6. Li, B., Chen, Y., Xu, H., Zhong, F.: Fast vehicle detection algorithm based on lightweight yolo7-tiny (2023)
7. Pereira, J.A.: Yellow sticky traps dataset olive fly (Bactrocera Oleae) (2023)
8. Kalamatianos, R., Karydis, I., Doukakis, D., Avlonitis, M.: DIRT: the dacus image recognition toolkit. J. Imaging **4**(11), 129 (2018)

9. (Ard) Nieuwenhuizen, A.T., et al.: Raw data from yellow sticky traps with insects for training of deep learning convolutional neural network for object detection (2019)
10. Lou, H., et al.: DC-YOLOv8: small size object detection algorithm based on camera sensor, April 2023
11. Tatar, N., Saadatseresht, M., Arefi, H., Hadavand, A.: A new object-based framework to detect shodows in high-resolution satellite imagery over urban areas. The International Archives of the Photogrammetry, Remote Sensing and Spatial Information Sciences, XL-1/W5:713–717, December 2015
12. Belde, S.: Noise removal in images using deep learning models, April 2021

An Artificial Intelligence-Based Method to Identify the Stage of Maturation in Olive Oil Mills

João Mendes[1,2,4]([✉]) [ID], José Lima[1,4] [ID], Lino A. Costa[2] [ID], Nuno Rodrigues[3,4] [ID], Paulo Leitão[1,4] [ID], and Ana I. Pereira[1,2,4] [ID]

[1] Research Centre in Digitalization and Intelligent Robotics (CeDRI), Instituto Politécnico de Bragança, 5300-253 Bragança, Portugal
{jllima,pleitao,apereira}@ipb.pt
[2] ALGORITMI Center, University of Minho, 4710-057 Braga, Portugal
joao.cmendes@ipb.pt, lac@dps.uminho.pt
[3] Centro de Investigação de Montanha (CIMO), Instituto Politécnico de Bragança, 5300-253 Bragança, Portugal
nunorodrigues@ipb.pt
[4] Laboratório Associado para a Sustentabilidade e Tecnologia em Regiões de Montanha (SusTEC), Instituto Politécnico de Bragança, Campus de Santa Apolónia, 5300-253 Bragança, Portugal

Abstract. Identifying the maturation stage is an added value for olive oil producers and consumers, whether this is done to predict the best harvest time, give us more information about the olive oil, or even adapt techniques and extraction parameters in the olive oil mill. In this way, the proposed work presents a new method to identify and count the number of olives that enter the mill as well as their stage of maturation. It is based on artificial intelligence (AI) and deep learning algorithms, using the two most recent versions of YOLO, YOLOv7 and YOLOv8. The obtained results demonstrate the possibility of using this type of application in a real environment, managing to obtain a mAP of approximately 79% with YOLOv8 in the five maturation stages, with a processing rate of approximately 16 FPS increasing this with YOLOv7 to 36.5 FPS reaching a 66% mAP.

Keywords: Olive ripening stages · You Only Look Once (YOLO) · Intelligent System · Computer Vision · Precision Agriculture

1 Introduction

For thousands of years, olive oil has been produced and used worldwide. Unlike other vegetable oils, this oil is extracted from a fruit and not from a seed, the olive, which is responsible for the nutritional value and all the characteristics present in the oil. Originally from the Mediterranean basin, it is also here that the largest productions are concentrated and also the largest exports. Moving billions of euros annually, this is a sector in constant development and of great economic importance for all producers. Recognized worldwide as a premium product, it is used in the most varied fields,

A. I. Pereira et al. (Eds.): OL2A 2023, CCIS 1982, pp. 63–77, 2024.
https://doi.org/10.1007/978-3-031-53036-4_5

highly associated with cuisine and the Mediterranean diet, it is also combined with the conservation of foods such as canned fish, used in the textile [22], cosmetics [20] and pharmaceutical industries [15]. Whether as a product or by-product, olive oil obeys several criteria when it comes to its preparation, with its quality depending on several factors, such as the cultivar [14], fruit ripening [12], environmental conditions [4], agronomic factors [2] (e.g., irrigation, fertilization, pest, and diseases incidence), conditions used during oil extraction, storage, etc. Causing this directly impacts the sensory profile, including the aroma and flavor of the oil, making it one of the main factors to consider when harvesting the olive.

This harvest can be carried out at different stages of maturation, according to the farmer and the intended purpose, with harvests at a more immature stage being more linked to high concentrations of phenol, lower amounts of polyunsaturated fatty acids, and more stable oils [21,35]. Evolving these characteristics in opposite way with the ripening of the olive. The amount of oil also tends to increase during this ripening process. However, its quality tends to degenerate considering the increase in acidity, generally speaking, the later the fruit is collected, the greater its production but the worse will be its quality. In this way, it is up to the producer to choose the harvesting stage according to his objectives. It is not always linear since the stages can differ from tree to tree or olive grove to olive grove, even if the environmental factors are similar.

This process of identifying the ripening stage of the olive can be carried out using the most varied techniques, from simpler techniques such as determining the firmness of the fruit with a densimeter or its color with a colorimeter [13] to more advanced techniques such as the use of chlorophyll fluorescence spectroscopy [1], or near infrared spectroscopy (NIR) [16]. One of the methods that are well-accepted by the community for identifying the stage of the olive is the visual ripeness index (RI). This index is determined according to the International Olive Council guidelines [9], observing the color of the skin and pulp of the olive [32] and consists of distributing 100 olives into 8 groups according to the following characteristics:

– Group 0 - bright green bark;
– Group 1 - yellowish-green skin;
– Group 2 - green skin with reddish spots;
– Group 3 - reddish-brown skin;
– Group 4 - black skin with white flesh;
– Group 5 - black skin with <50% purple flesh;
– Group 6 - black skin with pulp >50% purple;
– Group 7 - black skin with 100% purple pulp;

To do this, the technicians have to open and manually separate the olives according to their color and the color of their pulp, identifying the group to which they belong and counting the specimens that are part of it, the final result is given by the formula: $MI = \sum i \times \frac{ni}{100}$, i is the group number, ni is the number of specimens contained in it and MI is the maturation stage. From this, the farmer can make informed decisions, correctly plan the harvest of his fruit or, on the other hand, value his lot, adding this information to the label of the olive. Also for those in charge of the olive oil mill, the maturation index is valuable information considering that it is possible to adjust some extraction parameters like temperatures and mixing times optimizing the extraction process considering the degree of maturation of olives [24]. Maximizing in this way the production and the quality of the oil.

The maturation index is undoubtedly an added value for producers and consumers, however, it is a process that is not available to all of them considering that all these identification processes have some drawbacks, from the need to have some materials such as densimeter or colorimeter, or on the other hand, having to take the samples to laboratories for this index to be estimated, involving associated costs. The visual maturation index also has drawbacks, namely the delay, and subjectivity of the problem, always depending on the opinion and experience of the evaluator, which can be compromised by various environmental factors such as the state of the olive, its appearance and the different lighting conditions.

In this way, and considering the advances in hardware and software that have been presented in recent years, several new techniques using computer vision in conjunction with machine and deep learning algorithms have been studied and applied to facilitate this task. Similarly, this article also presents a new way of identifying the stage of maturation of the olive, having as its main objective the identification of the maturity index in real-time in the oil mill, using for that a state-of-the-art You only look once (YOLO) real-time object detection system. In addition to enhancing the product without any cost associated with the producer, this method will also allow the optimization of parameters in the olive oil extraction process, allowing the adjustment of temperatures and mixing times to obtain maximum yield for the lot to be worked on. To this end, a comprehensive survey of relevant literature was made, encompassing commonly employed techniques for maturation stage identification as well as the learning algorithms utilized for this type of image classification. This survey will be elaborated upon in Sect. 2. Subsequently, Sect. 3 will delve into the proposed methodology. The primary outcomes and their analysis will be presented in Sect. 4, while Sect. 5 will provide a conclusion along with key avenues for future research.

2   Related Works

With technological advances, image analysis and processing capabilities have been efficiently applied to improve the safety and effectiveness of processes related to food production, inspection and classification. By combining advanced algorithms and computational power, Computer Vision allows to quickly identify and evaluate characteristics and anomalies, such as quality [34], maturity [10,23] and food damage [36]. Achieving, with the use of this type of applications, revolutionizing processes in the food and agricultural industry, providing more accurate, efficient and sustainable solutions to guarantee food safety, increase productivity and improve the quality of agricultural products.

As the case of olives was not overlooked in this process, the first articles on the subject of computer vision applied to olive growing appeared in the early 2000s. In 2004, the authors R. Diaz et al. saw their article [11] published which used computer vision techniques for the inspection of table olives. The authors compared three different algorithms to classify the quality of table olives into four categories. From this comparison, encouraging results emerged when a neural network with a hidden layer was used, achieving an accuracy of 90%. This accuracy dropped to 70% when the classification was performed by the other two algorithms least squares discriminant and Mahalanobis distance.

Working on the same issue, the article [28] also presents us with a classification proposal according to external damage to olives. In this case, the authors resort to segmentation techniques, color parameters and morphological characteristics of defects and whole fruits. With the aim of classifying the olives into eight distinct classes according to the degree of damage, the authors present results in the calibration set of 97%, reducing this percentage to 75% in the validation set. It is also highlighted by the authors the difficulty of classifying some of the classes, ranging from 38% to 100% in the validation set.

Still within the field of evaluating the state of the olive, the authors of the article [3] present an online monitoring system, which presents an accuracy rate of around 98%. For this, the authors use two artificial intelligence algorithms, an Artificial Neural Network (ANN) and a Support Vector Machine (SVM) to classify the olives into two categories (olives picked from the ground and from the tree). Two systems for capturing images were set up in a real scenario, one before the washing process and the other after, and the system was validated with 6325 images of 100 different batches. In this validation set, the authors present an accuracy percentage of 98.4 before washing with the SVM algorithm and a percentage of 98.8% after washing with the ANN algorithm.

Also in the field of evaluation of the maturation stage, several works have been developed, using the most varied computer vision techniques. The authors give an example of these applications in the article [5] in this study the authors propose a new method for automatically determining the color scale of fruits to create color scales with the aim of estimating stages of maturation in olives and grapes pits. To do so, they resort to Support Vector Regression algorithms in order to create a multidimensional regression in order to create the color scales. The method was implemented using two different datasets, one consisting of 250 grape seeds and the other with 200 olive samples. Its evaluation was carried out using the K-fold Cross validation method. Based on this, the authors state that the generated scales can be used to establish various phenolic states in the fruit, not just two classes (ripe and immature) as is traditionally done. The authors also highlight the advantages of using this type of method, namely its cost, since this is a simple and inexpensive method to implement compared to other tools such as colorimeters or other equipment associated with this process.

A similar view is presented in the article [17] machine vision techniques are used to classify the ripeness stage, size and weight of olives. In this case, the authors used color-based segmentation algorithms together with edge detection operators. For the evaluation of the system, a comparison was made with the maturation index normally used by the industry based on the subjective visual determination of the color of the skin and pulp of the fruit. The performance demonstrated by the method was quite encouraging, managing even in images with several olive samples to be in agreement with the visually estimated maturation index. Also the results of estimating the weight of the fruits showed good results, achieving an R2 of 0.91. Having presented the results, the authors also point out the possibility of this being a useful method for classifying the olives upon reception at the mill, allowing for better quality control of the production process.

Also thinking about the stage before arriving at the olive press, and as already mentioned, determining the stage of maturation is a fundamental point in harvest planning, and it is on this subject that the paper [18] tells us. In this the authors present a new approach for identifying the maturation stage using computer vision techniques based on artificial intelligence algorithms such as convolutional neural networks (CNN). The system was designed using two distinct varieties of olives in four stages of maturation (immature, green, black and fully ripe). Several CNN's structures were compared as well as several optimizer algorithms. In the end, the authors present an overall accuracy of 91.91%, reaching 100% if only the classification of a certain variety (Zard) in a specific maturation stage (green) was considered. With the results presented, the authors refer to the possibility of using this system in real time considering that it took only 12.64ms to classify an image.

The last document considered for this bibliographical study refers to the article [29], in this, the authors present a system for quality management as well as for the classification of the maturation stage. To this end, a whole simulation system is set up, including a conveyor belt simulating the mill environment, several images are taken using a high resolution RGB camera, two models are trained, the first referring to batches predestined for the production of olive oil (trained with 1500 images), and the second referring to table olives (trained with 930 images). For both models, the objective was to classify between seven categories (black, black dented, green, green dented, middle maturation, middle maturation dented and other). To carry out this classification, the authors resorted to four versions of the YOLO algorithm (YOLOv1, YOLOv2, YOLOv3 and YOLOv3tiny), with the best results presented by the YOLOv3 versions, with a percentage of classification greater than 95% for both sets of data.

As can be seen from the articles presented, the application of computer vision techniques to the detection of the maturation stage as well as the assessment of olive quality is growing, not only in the number of applications but also in the results presented by the models. In this way, the work proposed here will meet this trend, trying to improve some points of previous works such as the application being in a real environment and not in controlled environments and taking advantage of the technological advances felt in recent years. In this way, it is expected that this work will contribute to the state of the art, but also to the modernization of the olive sector.

3   Method and Materials

As the main objective of this work is to develop an artificial intelligence system capable of identifying and counting the number of olives in different stages of maturation, there is a set of steps to be taken and implemented, thus ensuring the correct functioning of the system. Therefore, this section was divided into subsections: Dataset, Classification Models and Evaluation Metrics, and Methodology.

3.1 Dataset

The data set is a key point for any artificial intelligence model, as all learning will be based on these. It is necessary to ensure that is concise, accurate and representative of what the model is intended to learn. Likewise, to build a robust model capable of generalizing to different implementation environments, it is also necessary to guarantee data heterogeneity, considering that each mill will have its own luminosity conditions, thus not being able to provide only specific environment data, this being one of the variations that will need to be taken into account in the process of constructing the dataset. In this way, and taking into account that no data of this type was found available online for use, it was decided by the team that a dataset of its own would be created for identifying the different stages of olive maturation.

According to this objective, several steps were followed, starting with choosing a local oil mill. This one was selected considering the olive varieties with which it works, prioritizing Protected Designation of Origin (PDO), and considering the proximity to the research center. In this way, the mill of Macedo de Cavaleiros, located in the district of Bragança in Portugal, was selected. Once inside the olive mill, it was necessary to choose a strategic location where the conditions for correct identification were met, namely a space with some natural light so that it was not necessary to use artificial lights that could change the color of the olives. The cleaning of the olives was also taken into account, that is, priority was given to areas where the olives were already clean of most contaminating agents such as stones, leaves, and branches of the olive trees, it also needed to be placed where there was no overlapping of the fruits, to ensure that all fruits are classified. In this way, the place chosen is located after the washing process and before entering the olive crushing process was chosen.

Having chosen the location for capturing the images, a digital camera, RGB, was used to capture several images and videos with dimensions of 1920×1080 at a speed of 60 frames per second (FPS). The images were captured during the entire processing of several batches of the Negrinha variety (Monovarietal), on November 18, 2022. After obtaining the images, the pre-processing part was carried out, here simple processes of cutting and Brightness corrections resulted in an image similar to Fig. 1A. The following process consists of annotating the images, this is a laborious process since it is necessary to identify each of the olives present in the image. It was created using the labelimg software [31] and all the images were annotated in YOLO format, creating a text file (.txt) for each of the images with the class information and normalized coordinates for each of the objects in the image, resulting in a fully annotated image similar to the one in Fig. 1B.

Taking into account the experimental and introductory character of this article to the theme of identifying the maturation stage in real-time on the mill, it was decided to carry out two datasets. The first one completely annotated and validated by a technician of the area, of smaller dimensions, emphasizing once again the time needed to annotate each of the images, consists of 38 completely annotated images, with an average of 60 olives in each image, making approximately 2200 objects. The second dataset, in turn, was annotated by an algorithm-assisted labeling process, as shown further in the 3.3 section, and consists of 100 fully annotated images.

Fig. 1. Dataset image example: a) Original; b) Labeled

3.2 Classification Models

In order to carry out this study, and take into account the main objective, which is real-time identification, several types of algorithms were analyzed. It was initially thought to use classification algorithms such as Random forest classifiers, however, given the nature of the problem where in the same frame there can be dozens or hundreds of different objects, this idea was put aside, giving way to the use of convolutional neural networks (CNNs) with object detection frameworks. For this, some of the main algorithms such as YOLO (You Only Look Once) and Faster R-CNN were analyzed.

The choice here was essentially due to the fact that YOLO follows a single-stage approach, where object detection and classification are performed in a single pass through the network. In comparison, Faster R-CNN follows a two-stage approach, where it first generates a set of default bounding boxes and then classifies and refines these boxes in a subsequent pass. This structural difference between the algorithms is essentially reflected in their accuracy and processing time, with Faster R-CNN being more linked to better accuracy and YOLO more linked to high processing speeds [30], which is more in line with the nature of the problem presented since there is a need for the algorithm to work in real-time or very close to it.

Having presented the main factors that led us to choose the YOLO neural network, it was also necessary to choose which version to use, since, until the moment this paper was written, there are eight versions of the algorithm. They all work on the same principle, an end-to-end neural network that predicts bounding boxes class probabilities simultaneously. The first version was introduced by Joseph Redmon et al. in the year 2015 [25] in this original version, the input image is divided into a grid of S × S cells, where each one aims to determine if an object's center is present within it. These cells also make predictions about bounding boxes, which consist of five values: the coordinates of the box's center, its height, width, and a confidence score. These predictions are evaluated using the Intersection over Union (IOU) approach, which helps eliminate less accurate bounding boxes. The architecture of the YOLO detector is based on GoogLeNet, incorporating 24 convolutional layers and two fully connected layers. However, it modifies the inception module by utilizing a 1×1 reduction layer followed by 3×3 convolutional layers. The loss calculation in this detector is based on the sum of squares.

Since the first version that has been optimized, for example, in its second version YOLO9000 or YOLOv2 [26], its structure has been optimized, removing all fully connected layers, thus leaving 19 convolutional layers and five max-pooling layers, as well the size of the training images was increased, going from 224×224 of YOLOv1 to 448×448, in addition to these optimizations, more improvements were made such as the addition of anchor boxes, the utilization of the k-means model to cluster grids for artifacts and multi-scale training that allowed the prediction of the results for different resolutions, reaching 90 FPS rate in low image resolution and 78.6 mAP when high-resolution images are used.

Two years later, the third version of the algorithm appeared, YOLOv3 [27] this presents a new logistic regression cost function concerning the bounding boxes, likewise, the Softmax function was replaced by logistic regression regarding the prediction of classes. As the main change, the architecture of the network started to use a variation of ResNet, Darknet-53.

Also in its fourth version [6] the structure was updated, this time the authors presented a new architecture called CSPNet, also a variation of ResNet but with only 54 convolutional layers managed to achieve several stat-of-art results in several datasets. In addition to the structure, other factors were optimized, such as the introduction of the term "GHM loss", which improved the behavior in unbalanced datasets. Also introduced in this version is the so-called "k-means clustering" to generate the anchor boxes, allowing them to be more closely aligned with the detected objects' size and shape.

With the entry of the new decade, a new version of YOLO was also presented, the YOLOv5 [37]. Presented by the same team that developed the original version, this version brought improvements in terms of accuracy and generalization, achieved through a more complex structure, EfficientDet. The detection of small objects was also considered, presenting optimizations by introducing the "spatial pyramid pooling" concept, a pooling layer to reduce the feature maps' spatial resolution, enabling the algorithm with a view at multiple scales. The generation of anchor boxes was also the target of optimizations, presenting a new method the "dynamic anchor boxes" the process entails employing a clustering algorithm to categorize the ground truth bounding boxes into clusters, instead utilizing the centroids of these clusters as the anchor boxes.

The sixth version [19] of the algorithm arrived in the year 2022 and presented as main improvements the use of a new base architecture, the EfficientNet-L2 structure that presents a smaller number of parameters, however, a greater computational efficiency. Also, a new method to generate anchor boxes was presented in this structure, called "dense anchor boxes". These combinations allowed for achieving state-of-art results in several datasets for object detection.

Still in the year 2022, the seventh version was published [33]. This version features several optimizations starting with the loss function, where a new function called "focal loss" allows better behavior with smaller objects, by reducing the weight of the loss for well-classified examples and placing greater emphasis on challenging examples. Thinking about the same case of detection of smaller objects, the resolution of the images was also changed, processing images of 640×640 pixels. In order to reduce the number of false positives, YOLOv7 now uses nine anchor boxes, this enhancement enables it to detect a broader array of object shapes and sizes in comparison to earlier versions. Another of the great optimizations was the processing rate, according to the authors, the processing capacity is at a rate of 155 frames per second, which makes it capable of being applied in the context of real-time applications, as is the case intended in this study.

The latest version of YOLO available at the time this paper is being written is the eighth. At the moment, the authors have not yet released a scientific article describing the architecture of the model or its performance, however, several improvements have already been announced, namely the ease of training either using the GPU or the CPU. Other main features have already been announced by the authors, such as a new anchor-free detection system, changes in the convolutional blocks used by the model, and even Mosaic augmentation applied during training, turned off before the last 10 epochs.

Having presented all the models and after studying their functioning, the choice fell to version seven of the algorithm, taking into account mainly the speed of the model, however, taking into account the improvements that have been obtained with the updates, it was also taken into account the YOLOv8 model. In this way, these two versions will be used in order to compare their results in the proposed dataset, as will be demonstrated in the methodology used.

To evaluate the performance of the two selected versions, three quantitative metrics will be used, namely precision, recall, and mean average precision (mAP). In a global way, its possible to define precision as the proportion of true positives relative to the total number of predictions generated by the model. The recall, in turn, can be defined as the ratio of the model's total predictions made for a specific class to the total number of existing labels for that class. Recall and precision exhibit a trade-off, which is visualized as a curve by adjusting the classification threshold. The area under the precision-versus-recall curve represents the Average Precision per class achieved by the model. The mAP refers to the average of these values across all classes [7].

3.3   Methodology

The classification process proposed in this paper follows the visual maturation index methodology, however, this had to be adapted since there is no possibility of verifying the color of the olive pulp, thus being limited to five stages. In this way, the classification is divided as suggested in Fig. 2, leaving stage 1 composed of olives with a bright green skin; stage 2 with yellow-green skin; stage 3 composed of olives with green skin with reddish spots; stage 4 with reddish-brown skin and finally stage 5 with completely black skin.

Once the classes were divided, the images were duly annotated by a technician and the first Dataset was formed, as shown in Fig. 3. With the first dataset created, it was

Fig. 2. Maturity stage example from the 1st stage(right) to 5th stage (left).

divided into 75% of data for training and the remaining 25% for validation. This division resulted in 1137 annotations in the training set, divided as follows: 134, 356, 160, 221, and 266 from the 1st Stage to the 5th. Similarly, the validation set comprises 28, 97, 32, 49, and 61 objects from each stage, making a total of 267 objects in its entirety. After the first evaluation of the models, the second part of the test was carried out, the autolabel using the pre-trained algorithms. For this, a new dataset was created with 100 images under which the labels were predicted according to the pre-trained algorithms. Once the new labels were obtained, the algorithms were trained again, keeping the weights from the first training, thus retraining the models with the new images. Finally, the models were validated using the previously presented metrics.

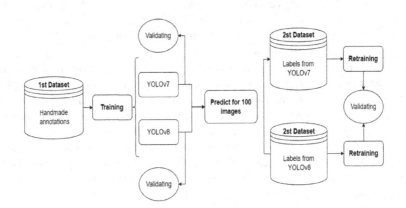

Fig. 3. Applied methodology diagram.

Noting that the training process was similar for the two algorithms, always with an 75/25 division of the datasets, and all hyperparameters were kept in default with the exception of the number of batches which was adjusted to 16, the dimensions of the images were 640×640 and the number of workers was 4. The models were trained for 500 epochs and the best weights were restored, it is important to point out that the YOLOv8 model, even with the default conditions, is already equipped with an early stopping function that allows defining patience given an x number in the function of the chosen evaluation metric. In this case, patience of 50 epochs was adopted if the mAP0.95 did not improve within this interval, the training should stop All the algorithms presented in this work were tested, trained, and implemented in google colab using a Tesla T4 GPU, with CUDA version 12 and using the GitHub of the respective algorithms[1].

Once the models were trained, the part of counting the olives according to their stage was carried out. For this purpose, a code was designed using the OpenCV library [8] in the 4.7.0 version. How it works is quite simple, a loop is created to run through all the frames of the video, and a line is drawn at the desired coordinates, then a classification is made for each frame using the trained YOLO algorithms. This results in the coordinates of each one of the objects, through which it is possible to see if they have already crossed the traced line and in which direction. Counting in this way the number of objects of each class that exceeds the drawn line.

4   Results and Discussion

Following the presented methodology, the algorithms were trained on the first dataset, using 28 training images and were evaluated on the validation set and on the test set, both with five images. Taking into account the reduced dimensions of the validation and test sets, 5-fold cross-validation was used to guarantee the security of the results. Taking into account that YOLOv8 uses some early stopping and adaptive learning rate functions, it was defined that only the results referring to the test set would be used for comparison because in some way, the results of the validation set could provide a biased evaluation since they were used for optimizing the hyperparameters of the network. In this way, the results of the test set of algorithms for the first dataset are presented in Table 1. Observing the results presented by YOLOv7, the low accuracy rate is noticeable, considering that this is the general value for the 5 stages, with the recall being well above it. The mAP presents an average of 65.9%, reaching its maximum in stage 5 with 94.3%. Still, in stage 1 it only reaches 20.3%, emphasizing that the presented values of the mAP are for a threshold of 0.5 of IoU (intersection over Union) in practice, IoU is the ratio of the intersection area between the predicted bounding box and the ground truth bounding box to the union area of the two boxes. An IoU threshold of 0.5 means that a predicted bounding box is considered a true positive if its IoU with the ground truth bounding box is greater than or equal to 0.5. The results of YOLOv8 were more encouraging, reaching a mAP of 78.3%. Still, stage 1 was also the one that most affected its average with a percentage of accuracy of 29.1%, far behind the average of approximately 81% in the other 4 stages. Comparing the two models, it is possible to state that the YOLOv8 model makes more predictions and is more accurate in classifying objects. Due to the time needed to predict an average for each image, YOLOv7 needed approximately 27.4ms for each image while its competitor needed approximately 62.1ms, this processing time allows identification of approximately 16 fps (FPS) in the case of YOLOv8 and about 2.27 times more in the case of YOLOv7 with a rate of 36.5 FPS.

---

[1] https://github.com/WongKinYiu/yolov7 and https://github.com/ultralytics/ultralytics Accessed on June 15, 2023.

Table 1. Comparison of the results obtained by the two versions of YOLO on the two datasets.

	1st Dataset			2nd Dataset		
	Precision	Recall	mAP.5	Precision	Recall	mAP.5
YOLOv7	0.510	0.783	0.659	0.510	0.768	0.659
YOLOv8	0.708	0.819	0.783	0.712	0.822	0.785

Once the results for the first dataset were presented and the model validated, the auto labelling process was carried out to create the second dataset. In the second dataset, the models were retrained, adding the new 100 images to the training set, conserving the learning obtained in the first dataset, and emphasizing that the best weights of the five evaluations carried out (cross-validation) were preserved. Subsequently, they were evaluated again, but this time cross-validation was not used, but the same five test images from the first iteration were used, with the results presented in Table 1. As it is possible to see, the improvements were quite tenuous in the case of YOLOv8, managing to reach 0.2% more in mAP and 0.3% more in recall and precision. In the case of YOLOv7, the mAp and the precision remained constant, while the recall decreased by 0.5%. The prediction times per image remained practically the same, showing differences of only 2 ms.

Analyzing the presented results, it is possible to verify that the improvements of using pseudo-annotated datasets are quite tenuous, this can happen mainly since the initial model was trained with a dataset of reduced dimensions and presented not very satisfactory precision and recall rates, especially in the case of YOLOv7. However, analyzing the accuracies of the initial models, there was a high probability that the classes with lesser precision, as was the case with the first stage, would fade throughout the auto labeling, taking into account that the increment was greater than three times, and the same did not happen thus proving the robustness of the model. Comparing the two models, YOLOv8 showed the best results in all metrics except the forecast time, although it is acceptable for the proposed problem.

Leaving the evaluation metrics aside and thinking about the real application of the problem, the results are quite satisfactory, taking into account that in the example of the video presented (about 5 s), it was possible to count approximately 320 olives and it was practically impossible to distinguish them according to their stage of maturation. In turn, the algorithm (YOLOv8) managed to detect about 275 (85%) and managed to divide them into the different stages of maturation as shown in Fig. 4.

Fig. 4. Example of application in real environment.

5   Conclusion and Future Works

In this study, a new method was proposed to identify and count the number of olives in a real environment. With the main objective of valuing olive oils and optimizing extraction techniques and parameters within the olive oil mill. To this end, the two most recent versions of YOLO were tested and an algorithm to count objects was developed.

The results obtained demonstrate the possibility of using this type of techniques in a real environment, not only due to the classification rate but also due to the processing time that is possible to obtain, noting that on average the v7 version of YOLO allows identifications to be made at a rate of 36.5 FPS. The best classification results were obtained with the latest version of YOLOv8 and it was possible to reach a mAP of approximately 79%. This result is below those achieved in the related works, however, in none of the cases studied was the application in an environment as extreme as the one presented in this study, remembering that in a short video of just 5 s (60FPS) approximately 320 samples were counted in all stages of maturation, making it humanly impossible to count and identify them.

Due to the results presented, its possible to improve the algorithm in terms of precision, this being one of the main future works, to retrain the algorithm with more data in order to improve its generalization, mainly from the initial maturity stages. The identification speed will also be studied, with some work to be done in optimizing the counting algorithms.

Acknowledgements. This work was carried out under the Project "OleaChain: Competências para a sustentabilidade e inovação da cadeia de valor do olival tradicional no Norte Interior de Portugal" (NORTE-06-3559-FSE-000188), an operation to hire highly qualified human resources, funded by NORTE 2020 through the European Social Fund (ESF). The authors are grateful to the Foundation for Science and Technology (FCT, Portugal) for financial support through national funds FCT/MCTES (PIDDAC) to CeDRI (UIDB/05757/2020 and UIDP/05757/2020), ALGO-RITMI (UIDB/00319/2020) and SusTEC (LA /P/0007/2021).

References

1. Agati, G., Pinelli, P., Ebner, S., Romani, A., Cartelat, A., Cerovic, Z.: Nondestructive evaluation of anthocyanins in olive (olea europaea) fruits by in situ chlorophyll fluorescence spectroscopy. J. Agricult. Food Chem. **53**, 1354–1363 (2005). https://doi.org/10.1021/jf048381d
2. Aguilera, M., et al.: Characterisation of virgin olive oil of italian olive cultivars: 'frantoio' and 'leccino', grown in andalusia. Food Chem. **89**, 387–391 (2005). https://doi.org/10.1016/j.foodchem.2004.02.046
3. Aguilera Puerto, D., Cáceres Moreno, Ó., Martínez Gila, D.M., Gómez Ortega, J., Gámez García, J.: Online system for the identification and classification of olive fruits for the olive oil production process. J. Food Measur. Character. **13**(1), 716–727 (2019). https://doi.org/10.1007/s11694-018-9984-0
4. Aparicio, R., Ferreiro, L., Alonso, V.: Effect of clima on the chemical, composition of virgin olive oil. Anal. Chim. Acta **292**(3), 235–241 (1994). https://doi.org/10.1016/0003-2670(94)00065-4
5. Avila, F., Mora, M., Oyarce, M., Zuñiga, A., Fredes, C.: A method to construct fruit maturity color scales based on support machines for regression: application to olives and grape seeds. J. Food Eng. **162**, 9–17 (2015). https://doi.org/10.1016/j.jfoodeng.2015.03.035

6. Bochkovskiy, A., Wang, C.Y., Liao, H.Y.M.: Yolov4: optimal speed and accuracy of object detection (2020)
7. Boyd, K., Costa, V.S., Davis, J., Page, D.: Unachievable region in precision-recall space and its effect on empirical evaluation (2012)
8. Bradski, G.: The OpenCV Library. Dr. Dobb's J. Softw. Tools (2000)
9. Council, I.O.: Guide for the Determination of the Characteristics of Oil-Olives. Technical Document COI/OH/Doc. No. 1, IOC, Madrid (2011)
10. Cárdenas-Pérez, S., et al.: Evaluation of the ripening stages of apple (golden delicious) by means of computer vision system. Biosyst. Eng. **159**, 46–58 (2017). https://doi.org/10.1016/j.biosystemseng.2017.04.009
11. Diaz, R., Gil, L., Serrano, C., Blasco, M., Molto, E., Blasco, J.: Comparison of three algorithms in the classification of table olives by means of computer vision. J. Food Eng. **61**(1), 101–107 (2004). https://doi.org/10.1016/S0260-8774(03)00191-2
12. Garcia, J.M., Seller, S., Perez-Camino, M.C.: Influence of fruit ripening on olive oil quality. J. Agric. Food Chem. **44**(11), 3516–3520 (1996)
13. García, J., Yousfi, K.: Non-destructive and objective methods for the evaluation of the ripening level of olive fruit. Eur. Food Res. Technol. **221**, 538–541 (2005). https://doi.org/10.1007/s00217-005-1180-x
14. Giuffre, A.M.: Influence of harvest year and cultivar on wax composition of olive oils. Eur. J. Lipid Sci. Technol. **115**(5), 549–555 (2013). https://doi.org/10.1002/ejlt.201200235
15. Gorini, I., Iorio, S., Ciliberti, R., Licata, M., Armocida, G.: Olive oil in pharmacological and cosmetic traditions. J. Cosmet. Dermatol. **18**(5), 1575–1579 (2019). https://doi.org/10.1111/jocd.12838
16. Gracia, A., León, L.: Non-destructive assessment of olive fruit ripening by portable near infrared spectroscopy. Grasas Aceites **62**(3), 268–274 (2011). https://doi.org/10.3989/gya.089610
17. Guzmán, E., Baeten, V., Pierna, J., García-Mesa, J.A.: Determination of the olive maturity index of intact fruits using image analysis. J. Food Sci. Technol. **52**, 1462–1470 (2015)
18. Khosravi, H., Saedi, S., Rezaei, M.: Real-time recognition of on-branch olive ripening stages by a deep convolutional neural network. Scientia Horticult. **287**, 110252 (2021). https://doi.org/10.1016/j.scienta.2021.110252
19. Li, C., et al.: Yolov6: a single-stage object detection framework for industrial applications (2022)
20. Lupi, F.R., Gentile, L., Gabriele, D., Mazzulla, S., Baldino, N., de Cindio, B.: Olive oil and hyperthermal water Bigels for cosmetic uses. J. Colloid Interface Sci. **459**, 70–78 (2015). https://doi.org/10.1016/j.jcis.2015.08.013
21. Matos, L., et al.: Chemometric characterization of three varietal olive oils (cvs. cobrançosa, madural and verdeal transmontana) extracted from olives with different maturation indices. Food Chem. **102**, 406–414 (2007). https://doi.org/10.1016/j.foodchem.2005.12.031
22. Meksi, N., Haddar, W., Hammami, S., Mhenni, M.F.: Olive mill wastewater: a potential source of natural dyes for textile dyeing. Indust. Crops Prod. **40**, 103–109 (2012). https://doi.org/10.1016/j.indcrop.2012.03.011
23. Mendoza, F., Aguilera, J.: Application of image analysis for classification of ripening bananas. J. Food Sci. **69**, E471–E477 (2006). https://doi.org/10.1111/j.1365-2621.2004.tb09932.x
24. Monteleone, E., Caporale, G., Carlucci, A., Pagliarini, E.: Optimisation of extra virgin olive oil quality. J. Sci. Food Agric. **77**(1), 31–37 (1998). https://doi.org/10.1002/(SICI)1097-0010(199805)77:1<31::AID-JSFA998>3.0.CO;2-F
25. Redmon, J., Divvala, S., Girshick, R., Farhadi, A.: You only look once: unified, real-time object detection (2016)

26. Redmon, J., Farhadi, A.: Yolo9000: better, faster, stronger (2016)
27. Redmon, J., Farhadi, A.: Yolov3: an incremental improvement (2018)
28. Riquelme, M.T., Barreiro, P., Ruiz-Altisent, M., Valero, C.: Olive classification according to external damage using image analysis. J. Food Eng. **87**(3), 371–379 (2008). https://doi.org/10.1016/j.jfoodeng.2007.12.018
29. Salvucci, G., et al.: Fast olive quality assessment through RGB images and advanced convolutional neural network modeling. Eur. Food Res. Technol. **248**, 1395–1405 (2022). https://doi.org/10.1007/s00217-022-03971-7
30. Tan, L., Huangfu, T., Wu, L., Chen, W.: Comparison of yolo v3, faster r-cnn, and ssd for real-time pill identification (2021)
31. Tzutalin: Labeling. Free Software: MIT License (2015). https://github.com/tzutalin/labelImg
32. Uceda, M., Frias, L.: Harvest dates, evolution of the fruit oil content, oil composition and oil quality. In: Proceedings II, Seminario Oleícola Internacional, COI, Córdoba, pp. 125–128 (1975)
33. Wang, C.Y., Bochkovskiy, A., Liao, H.Y.M.: Yolov7: trainable bag-of-freebies sets new state-of-the-art for real-time object detectors (2022)
34. Wu, D., Sun, D.W.: Colour measurements by computer vision for food quality control - a review. Trends Food Sci. Technol. **29**(1), 5–20 (2013). https://doi.org/10.1016/j.tifs.2012.08.004
35. Yorulmaz, A., Erinç, H., Tekin, A.: Changes in olive and olive oil characteristics during maturation. J. Am. Oil Chem. Soc. **90**, 647–658 (2013). https://doi.org/10.1007/s11746-013-2210-7
36. Zhang, B., et al.: Principles, developments and applications of computer vision for external quality inspection of fruits and vegetables: a review. Food Res. Int. **62**, 326–343 (2014). https://doi.org/10.1016/j.foodres.2014.03.012
37. Zhu, X., Lyu, S., Wang, X., Zhao, Q.: Tph-yolov5: improved yolov5 based on transformer prediction head for object detection on drone-captured scenarios (2021)

Enhancing Forest Fire Detection and Monitoring Through Satellite Image Recognition: A Comparative Analysis of Classification Algorithms Using Sentinel-2 Data

Thadeu Brito[1,2,3,4](✉) ⓘ, Ana I. Pereira[1,2] ⓘ, Paulo Costa[3,4] ⓘ, and José Lima[1,2,3] ⓘ

[1] Research Centre in Digitalization and Intelligent Robotics (CeDRI), Instituto Politécnico de Bragança, Campus de Santa Apolónia, 5300-253 Bragança, Portugal
{brito,apereira,jllima}@ipb.pt

[2] Laboratório para a Sustentabilidade e Tecnologia em Regiões de Montanha (SusTEC), Instituto Politécnico de Bragança, Campus de Santa Apolónia, 5300-253 Bragança, Portugal

[3] INESC TEC - INESC Technology and Science, Porto, Portugal

[4] Faculty of Engineering of University of Porto, Porto, Portugal
paco@fe.up.pt

Abstract. Worldwide, forests have been harassed by fire in recent years. Either by human intervention or other reasons, the history of the burned area is increasing considerably, harming fauna and flora. It is essential to detect an early ignition for fire-fighting authorities can act quickly, decreasing the impact of forest damage impacts. The proposed system aims to improve nature monitoring and improve the existing surveillance systems through satellite image recognition. The soil recognition via satellite images can determine the sensor modules' best position and provide crucial input information for artificial intelligence-based systems. For this, satellite images from the Sentinel-2 program are used to generate forest density maps as updated as possible. Four classification algorithms make the Tree Cover Density (TCD) map, consisting of the Gaussian Mixture Model (GMM), Random Forest (RF), Support Vector Machine (SVM), and K-Nearest Neighbors (K-NN), which identify zones by training known regions. The results demonstrate a comparison between the algorithms through their performance in recognizing the forest, grass, pavement, and water areas by Sentinel-2 images.

Keywords: Machine Learning · Classification algorithm · Satellite Imagery · Wildfires · Tree Cover Density

1 Introduction

Portugal is currently facing a significant challenge with the highest incidence of vegetation fires in Europe, both in terms of the number and burnt area. This annual ecological

A. I. Pereira et al. (Eds.): OL2A 2023, CCIS 1982, pp. 78–92, 2024.
https://doi.org/10.1007/978-3-031-53036-4_6

disturbance has resulted in substantial social, economic, and environmental damage, as documented in various studies [2, 23]. The historical data indicates that wildfires have been increasingly frequent and severe in recent decades, with the year 2021 witnessing over 7 452 rural fires in Portugal, burning an area close to $271\,km^2$ [15]. In the year 2022 recorded approximately 10 449 rural wildfires, with an area of around $1100\,km^2$ burned, and the Bragança region ranking as the sixth district with the highest burnt area [15].

Based on that, monitoring the forests in Portugal holds immense significance for our future as it enables us to observe and safeguard flora and fauna and anticipate and prevent potential fire outbreaks. In this sense, the Forest Alert Monitoring System (SAFe) project has been initiated to enhance nature monitoring and complement existing surveillance systems. The project deploys innovative sensor modules to detect wildfires and monitor forests, it is installed at the trunk trees in the Serra da Nogueira region of Bragança. However, owing to the forest's unique characteristics, installing these modules throughout the entire area may not be feasible [18]. Therefore, developing a strategy to install them in the most appropriate vegetation type is crucial to ensure optimal coverage and performance.

The selection of sensor placement in forested areas is influenced by a variety of factors that include forest type, historical data, estimation of areas prone to fire, burnt areas, terrain elevation, and forest density. These factors must be considered in conjunction with each other to determine the optimal location for inserting sensor modules. However, as a starting point for the SAFe project to find this point in common, it is essential to acquire the Tree Cover Density (TCD) map [3]. Moreover, the TCD map can be input information for artificial intelligence system based. In this regard, Copernicus [10] provides high-resolution satellite images that may be useful to support the definition of the vegetation amount in a given region by image analysis and recognition techniques.

This work will detail the development of a TCD recognition system utilizing data sourced from the Sentinel-2 program [10]. By implementing recognition and classification algorithms, the system enables the accurate assessment of the current state of the TCD or the most recently available information. The proposed method can provide the SAFe project with detailed maps, which may be utilized to identify the optimal locations for the sensor modules. By adopting this system, the SAFe project can not only employ the yearly maps provided by the "Instituto da Conservação da Natureza e das Florestas" (ICNF) [16] but also have access to the latest information to identify if the Wireless Sensor Networks (WSN) are adequately addressing the risks of forest fires [6, 7].

This paper is organized as follows. After an introduction in Sect. 1, related work about fire detection techniques is presented in Sect. 2. In Sect. 3 SAFe system architecture is described. Next is demonstrated in Sect. 4 the algorithms' concepts. The obtained results are presented in Sect. 5. Finally, Sect. 6 concludes the paper and points some future work direction.

2 Related Work

Wildfires are considered complex events in terms of causes, intensity, behavior, variability, hard to control, size, and severity, their early detection is essential [20,28]. In this context, the maximum time interval from ignition to the alert response of firefighters depends on the detection technique used. In [12], the authors found that a machine learning-based image recognition software and cloud-based workflow can detect smoke from fires usually within 15 min of ignition. In [26], is developed a deep learning-based wildfire event object detection system that can detect wildfires in 4K aerial images acquired by Unmanned Aerial Systems (UAS) with an average inference speed of 7.44 frames per second. The work [4] investigated the potential of Sentinel-1 Synthetic Aperture Radar (SAR) time series with a deep learning framework for near real-time wildfire progression monitoring. It can detect wildfires and capture their temporal progression, as demonstrated by three large and impactful wildfires. On the other hand, according to [9], after reviewing various detection techniques, if a fire is detected within 6 min of its occurrence, it can be easily disposed of before it turns into a large-scale fire.

Regarding the early detection capabilities via satellite imagery, in [1], it shows that Sentinel-2 Multispectral Instrument (MSI) sensors can be applied to discern burnt areas and burning severity using spectral indices and environmental variables. And in [8], it proposes an approach using Sentinel-2 MSI sensors to discern burnt areas and burning severity with the Normalized Burn Ratio (NBR). In [24] describes a workflow for detecting fire-affected areas from satellite imagery using deep semantic segmentation, with the best detection rate achieved by fusing Sentinel-2 and Sentinel-3 data. Moreover, in [25], it is presented a framework for detecting burnt areas using Sentinel-2 imagery and MODerate-resolution Imaging Spectroradiometer (MODIS) land cover product within the Google Earth Engine cloud platform. And in [27], it is proposed an automated active fire detection framework using Sentinel-2 imagery, which can provide dynamic fire detection results of Sentinel-2 inputs with coverage of about $12\,000\,km^2$ in less than 6 min.

In [11], a very high spatial resolution satellite imagery and machine learning methods are used to classify tree species in mixed deciduous forests. Applying Random Forest (RF) was effective in classifying tree species in a mixed deciduous forest using WorldView-3 satellite imagery. In [5], it is presented a global method to identify trees inside and outside of forests with medium-resolution satellite imagery. The proposed method exceeded 75% user's and producer's accuracy in identifying trees in hectares with a low to medium density of canopy cover and 95% user's and producer's accuracy in hectares with dense canopy cover. In [13], an object-oriented approach and RF algorithm are employed to classify urban trees with an overall accuracy of 91.89%. This work also indicates that RF was the best classifier for urban tree classification using UAV multispectral imagery.

It is proposed, in [14], an individual tree extraction method based on transfer learning and Gaussian Mixture Model (GMM) separation to obtain more accurate individual tree extraction results. Based on the experimental results, it has been proven that the proposed method has an average correctness rate of 87.68%. [19] examines the use of a Support Vector Machine (SVM) with Sentinel-2 imagery to map tree cover density. The study was carried out in Poland, using images from different dates and resolutions. The results show high classification accuracy, reaching 99.6%, confirming that the SVM is effective in map tree cover. Also, it defines that the images captured during leaf growth are the best suited for this purpose. In [21] is evaluated using Object-Based Image Analysis (OBIA) and high-resolution imaging to detect and map mixed hardwood and softwood forests. The objective was to quantify the spatial extent of mixed stands on a detailed spatial scale. A segmentation-based classification approach was used, combined with the non-parametric K-Nearest Neighbors (K-NN) method, trained with a dataset independent of validation. The study revealed that 11% of the mapped forest area consisted of mixed forests, with an overall accuracy of 85% and a K index of 0.78. Better levels of accuracy were achieved in stands dominated by conifers and hardwoods (85–93%). The results show that high-resolution images can be reliably used to detect detailed patterns in mixed forests, aiding in the monitoring and managing forest resources at precise spatial scales.

3   Background of SAFe Project

As previously stated, SAFe strives to introduce a series of innovative measures to be implemented in areas with a higher risk of fires. To achieve this goal, SAFe is implemented through an integrated approach that incorporates key tools specific to its objectives. The diagram in Fig. 1 displays the grouping of these tools, defining a target monitoring region that will benefit from the proposed components and applications [3, 6, 7]. The system in question operates on four critical components, namely the monitoring region, sensor modules, communication system, and control center. By leveraging an artificial intelligence-based system, these components work in tandem to facilitate intelligent and efficient data analysis. The result is the generation of hazard alerts that can be promptly communicated to rescue and combat teams, such as fire brigades, civil protection units, or town halls. These alerts will be customized to meet the specific needs of

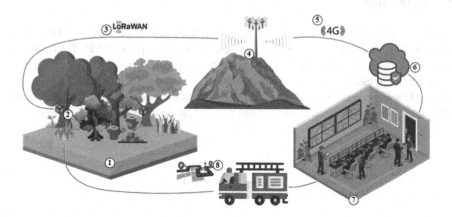

Fig. 1. Illustration of SAFe system architecture. ① The monitoring region, ② Wireless sensor module, ③ Communication via LoRaWAN, ④ LoRaWAN gateway, ⑤ 4G/LTE link, ⑥ Cloud, ⑦ Control center, and ⑧ Accurate positioning to act [6].

each organization involved. The project is structured around eight categories that work together in a coherent and symbiotic manner, as illustrated in Fig. 1.

- The monitoring region (represented by ①) is the region where the wireless sensor modules are placed. In this case, the monitoring region is placed in the Trás-os-Montes area [6,7];
- The wireless sensor modules (represented by ②) are responsible for the data acquisition at the forest in real-time. The coordinates of each node is calculated through an optimization procedure that considers the hazard fire in each coordinate [3];
- The LoRaWAN Gateway (④) receives data from each sensor module (③) and then forward the data through a 4G/LTE link (⑤) (or by Ethernet where available) to a server (represented by ⑥) [6,7];
- The control center (represented by ⑦) analyzes all information and sends alerts for hazardous situations or forest fire ignitions to the surveillance agent in the region. This control center has a cloud (represented by ⑤) that stores all collected data, and perform artificial intelligence procedures; such as local scale real-time fire hazard indexes, availability fuel content, weather data and moisture content of the vegetation [6,7].

The scope of this project will be limited to the generation and identification of TCD maps, with the aim of providing inputs for artificial intelligence. Given the complexity of the task at hand, it is deemed necessary to focus solely on these aspects rather than attempting to describe and develop each of the elements involved. In this way, a discussion is presented about different algorithms that identify forest areas through classification. Therefore, to generate the TCD map, four types of algorithms are implemented: GMM, RF, SVM, and k-NN. All of these concepts are described respectively in the next section.

4   Algorithms

In order to identify forest regions, we implement a set of four algorithms. These algorithms analyze the Sentinel-2 map and generate an output map with TCD. To effectively classify the map, the algorithms require a `shapefile` identifier. The classes for classification are grass, forest, pavement (building), and water. Each class is assigned a unique ID and a corresponding value of twenty pixels for land or vegetation. Additional information regarding these classifications can be found in Fig. 2.

Fig. 2. Shapefile identifier and Sentinel-2 image.

To ensure accurate recognition of the target region by satellite images, we configured the algorithms to classify in a supervised mode. This is due to the high range of pixels involved, which can result in misidentifying. By incorporating labels into the `shapefile` identifier, the algorithms are able to generate accurate TCD maps.

4.1 Gaussian Mixture Model

The GMM technique is commonly used for pattern recognition, where the parametric probability density function represents the weighted sum of the densities of each Gaussian component used. In short, the GMM represents the sum of several Gaussians. In this work, GMM will identify the nearest pixels and, consequently, will add higher weight to the set found. The GMM algorithm used is based on [17], where it is assumed that a given sample x is the realization of the distribution of a random vector:

$$p(x) = \sum_{c=1}^{C} \pi_c p(\mathbf{x}|c) \tag{1}$$

where π_c is the proportion of class c and $p(\mathbf{x}|c)$ is a d-dimensional Gaussian distribution.

Applying the Gaussian parametric model, it is assumed that each f_c is conditioned to c, and then it will become a Gaussian distribution of the parameters $\mu_\mathbf{c}$ and $\Sigma_\mathbf{c}$:

$$p(\mathbf{x}|c) = \frac{1}{2\pi^{\frac{d}{2}}|\Sigma_c|^{\frac{1}{2}}} exp(-\frac{1}{2}(x - \mu_c)^t \Sigma_c^{-1}(x - \mu_c)) \tag{2}$$

Using the Bayes formula, the posterior probability can be written as:

$$p(c|\mathbf{x}) = \frac{\pi_c p(\mathbf{x}|c)}{\Sigma_{k=1}^{C} \pi_k p(\mathbf{x}|k)} \tag{3}$$

The estimator of the model parameters is made by log-likelihood, with the n_c being the number of samples in the class:

$$\hat{\pi} = \frac{n_c}{n} \tag{4}$$

$$\hat{\mu}_c = \frac{1}{n_c} \sum_{i=1}^{n_c} x_i \tag{5}$$

$$\hat{\Sigma}_c = \frac{1}{n_c} \sum_{i=1}^{n_c} (x_i - \hat{\mu}_c)(x_i - \hat{\mu}_c)^t \tag{6}$$

The accuracy of the cross-validation was calculated with the number of folds fixed at 5; this parameter determines the number of times the data entered for analysis will be split. Then, the algorithm does the training through the ratio of the number of dimensions, in this case, the minimum quantity is defined by $\frac{d(d+1)}{2}$.

4.2 Random Forest

This type of supervised machine learning algorithm is based on ensemble learning. Ensemble learning is the result of a process in which several algorithms (whether different or not) form a robust forecasting model. RF is commonly used with several identical algorithms, where they form a network in the shape of a decision tree. The choice to use this algorithm in this work is due to the fact that this algorithm is not biased since there are several branches during the modeling, which is done in a subset of separate data. In other words, the algorithm works in a kind of cluster of opinions of each individual in a crowd.

The RF version used in this work is based on the Skicit-learn library [22], in which the configuration of the estimator is applied with a vector of multiple of three, and the features parameter to consider for the best split is done with a one-third decay of the total of samples that still have to be analyzed. The rest of the settings were left as default.

4.3 Support Vector Machines

The SVM is an algorithm widely used in the field of machine learning, as it has absolute versatility in its mode of operation (its operating cores can be based on linear, polynomial, Gaussian, and others). With this, the SVM tries to adapt in the best possible way to the problem to be solved. The core implemented in this work is the Radial Base Function (RBF), making the support vectors become the samples closest to the separation margin (according to the analyzed class). This type of separation by a margin can be considered with a discriminative classification.

For the identification of forest zones in the Sentinel-2 image, the SVM used is the one provided by the Skicit-learn library [22]. Since the regularization parameter is used to try to avoid noise distortion (there are some pixels mixed in the Sentinel-2 image), it was chosen to enter values less than 1. However, this can cause a variance and low bias. For this reason, the Grid Search technique was used, where a range of C (SVM regularization) and Gamma values are inserted.

4.4 K-Nearest Neighbors

Considered to be one of the main algorithms in the machine learning field, K-NN is simple to apply, versatile, and easy to understand. In this work, K-NN is configured to determine the number of neighbors of a given pixel, and then it will be classified according to the characteristics of its neighbors. Therefore, it is enough to indicate the number of neighbors that the algorithm must check to determine the characteristic of the target pixel. Generally, when the number of classes for identification is an even number, the neighbors (K) value is configured with odd numbers.

5   Results

The proposed system architecture was implemented using Python in Q-GIS software. The data processing and machine learning was performed based on widely used libraries, like NumPy, QGIS core, and Skicit-learn. The image from the Sentinel-2 satellite was extracted using the QGIS SCP plugin, from the Serra da Nogueira region located in the Bragança district, as already mentioned in the previous section. The map used is in raster format, and has a total dimension of 54.10 km in width and height of 30.29 km. Each pixel in this raster is 10 m × 10 m in size. Then, it gives a total of approximately 163 869 pixels to be processed. For the classification, a shapefile was applied with four classes identified manually by regions already known, and each class has a total of 20 values of areas belonging to grass, forest, pavement (building), and water. The experiments were executed by a PC with Windows 10, i7-8750H, 16GB RAM, and GeForce GTX 1050Ti.

5.1   GMM Output Map

The first algorithm to carry out the recognition of the Sentinel-2 satellite image was the GMM. Figure 3 shows the output TCD map generated by this algorithm. It is possible to notice that some areas were classified as regions with water, but they can only be shadows from the height of the relief (mountains). There was a slight disturbance in the classification when the areas of grass, forest, and pavement were mixed. The same method was performed several times (without using the same training and model), and in all the executions the time to finish the classification was 4 seconds.

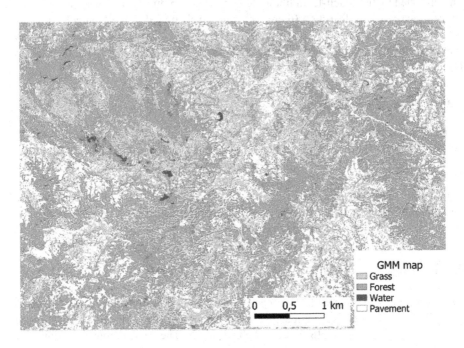

Fig. 3. Map created by output from GMM.

5.2   RF Output Map

Using the RF algorithm, it was also possible to recognize the raster provided by Sentinel-2. The first execution of this method took about 7 s, the second 30 s and the last one obtained the map recognition in 7 s. The TCD map can be seen in Fig. 4, which demonstrates the RF's performance in classifying the terrain. Regions with dense forests were well located, as well as medium-height vegetation. Some pavement areas can also be clearly defined, such as some highways. However, there was recognition of areas with water in high-relief regions; which shows a possible shadow of the mountains in the image.

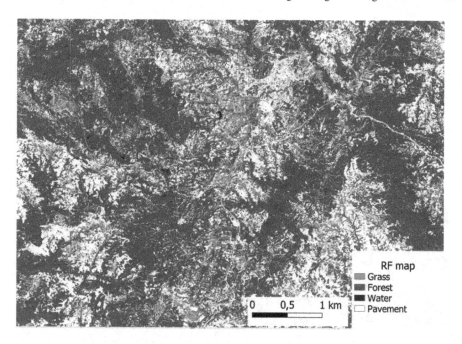

Fig. 4. Map created by output from RF.

5.3 SVM Output Map

During the third test, the SVM algorithm was chosen to identify forest areas in the region of Trás-os-Montes in Bragança. Even after the three runs (with times of 10, 12, and 10 s, respectively), the algorithm was unable to identify grass areas in vast proportions. Therefore, some identified regions appear to go abruptly from the forest to the pavement, as shown in Fig. 5. On the other hand, the output map indicates that there was no false classification of shade as watery regions.

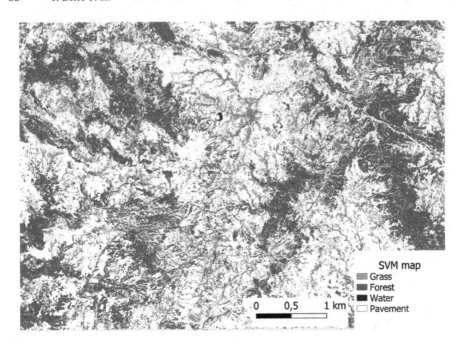

Fig. 5. Map created by output from SVM.

5.4   K-NN Output Map

Finally, the test with the K-NN algorithm was performed in three different attempts. The execution time for the first attempt was 334 s, the second attempt was 346 s, and in the third, the time spent was 338 s. The TCD map demonstrates that this algorithm recognized in greater quantity the regions classified as grass, and the areas of dense forest are identified with excellent clarity. However, parts with possible mountain shadows have been classified as water. The sections with human construction are well defined, as shown in Fig. 6, the highways can be visualized, and the contours of the cities.

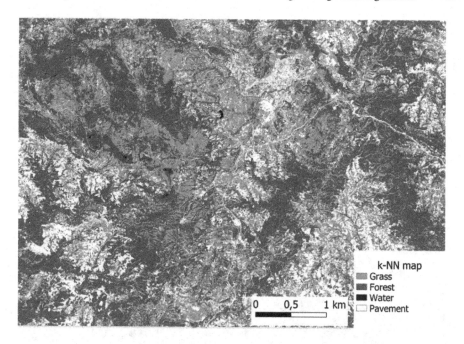

Fig. 6. Map created by output from K-NN.

5.5 Comparison

When comparing the output maps of each algorithm, one can notice the recognition quality of the Sentinel-2 image of each one. In Fig. 7, a region is shown side by side with all four classes inserted in the identifier shapefile. It is possible to notice the complexity of the chosen area with zoom, where there is a small town surrounded by a narrow river and small regions of dense vegetation and grass. Therefore, the difficulty that the GMM had to identify the class of grass is visibly notorious; such difficulty is evidenced as the grass mixes with the pavement. On the other hand, this algorithm was the fastest among the four.

Regarding the smoothness of the identified areas, the SVM was the one that had the highest contrast. In other words, when there is a mixture of forest, grass, and pavement, SVM does not have a high definition. In the lower corner of the SVM image, there is an abrupt identification of the forest to the highway. When the analysis is done in comparison with the Sentinel-2 image, there is transition vegetation. In this way, the two algorithms that had better performance compared to the quality of identification were RF and K-NN. With a small advantage for K-NN. Therefore, when high-quality satellite image recognition is required, the K-NN algorithm is recommended. On the other hand, when image recognition is needed more quickly, the RF algorithm may be the right choice.

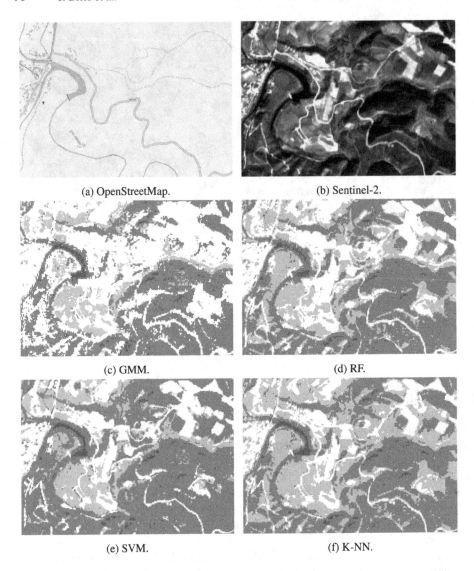

(a) OpenStreetMap.   (b) Sentinel-2.

(c) GMM.   (d) RF.

(e) SVM.   (f) K-NN.

Fig. 7. Comparison between the results with zoom in an area with grass, forest, water and pavement.

6   Conclusions

The Forest Alert Monitoring System (SAFe) project proposes the development of innovative operations to minimize the alert time for forest fire ignitions. This project contributes to real surveillance systems, improving firefighters and civil protection with more details and real-time information. As a basis for this project, the acquisition and communication modules, which are spread across the forest, gather information on various data relevant to the efficient characterization of existing forest conditions. This work presents an approach for classifying the satellite images in the Trás-os-Montes forests. Four algorithms were applied to identify forest areas as updated as possible, providing a solution to the problem of static maps supplied by the ICNF (annual). Preliminary tests indicated that the four algorithms could be used to generate the TCD map. However, when comparing their results, some considerations of time spent and quality of identification emerge during their performances. In the next steps, it is possible to generate a system to run the soil classification in real-time or when the artificial intelligence system requires it. In addition, a computational comparison of these four algorithms could be performed and confront the advantages and disadvantages of each one of them. Besides, other algorithms could be analyzed and discussed, such as Convolutional Neural Network (CNN).

Acknowledgment. The authors are grateful to the Foundation for Science and Technology (FCT, Portugal) for financial support through national funds FCT/MCTES (PIDDAC) to CeDRI (UIDB/05757/2020 and UIDP/05757/2020) and SusTEC (LA/P/0007/2021). Thadeu Brito is supported by FCT PhD Grant Reference SFRH/BD/08598/2020.

References

1. Amos, C., Petropoulos, G.P., Ferentinos, K.P.: Determining the use of sentinel-2A MSI for wildfire burning & severity detection. Int. J. Remote Sens. **40**(3), 905–930 (2019)
2. Amraoui, M., Pereira, M.G., DaCamara, C.C., Calado, T.J.: Atmospheric conditions associated with extreme fire activity in the western mediterranean region. Sci. Total Environ. **524**, 32–39 (2015)
3. Azevedo, B.F., Brito, T., Lima, J., Pereira, A.I.: Optimum sensors allocation for a forest fires monitoring system. Forests **12**(4), 453 (2021)
4. Ban, Y., Zhang, P., Nascetti, A., Bevington, A.R., Wulder, M.A.: Near real-time wildfire progression monitoring with sentinel-1 SAR time series and deep learning. Sci. Rep. **10**(1), 1322 (2020)
5. Brandt, J., Stolle, F.: A global method to identify trees inside and outside of forests with medium-resolution satellite imagery. arXiv preprint abs/2005.08702 (2020)
6. Brito, T., et al.: Data acquisition filtering focused on optimizing transmission in a lorawan network applied to the WSN forest monitoring system. Sensors **23**(3), 1282 (2023)
7. Brito, T., Pereira, A.I., Lima, J., Valente, A.: Wireless sensor network for ignitions detection: an IoT approach. Electronics **9**(6), 893 (2020)
8. Brown, A.R., Petropoulos, G.P., Ferentinos, K.P.: Appraisal of the sentinel-1 & 2 use in a large-scale wildfire assessment: a case study from Portugal's fires of 2017. Appl. Geogr. **100**, 78–89 (2018)
9. Chowdary, V., Gupta, M.K., Singh, R.: A review on forest fire detection techniques: a decadal perspective. Networks **4**, 12 (2018)
10. Copernicus: Europe's eyes on earth (2023). https://www.copernicus.eu
11. Deur, M., Gašparović, M., Balenović, I.: Tree species classification in mixed deciduous forests using very high spatial resolution satellite imagery and machine learning methods. Remote Sens. **12**(23), 3926 (2020)
12. Govil, K., Welch, M.L., Ball, J.T., Pennypacker, C.R.: Preliminary results from a wildfire detection system using deep learning on remote camera images. Remote Sens. **12**(1), 166 (2020)

13. Guo, Q., et al.: Urban tree classification based on object-oriented approach and random forest algorithm using unmanned aerial vehicle (UAV) multispectral imagery. Remote Sens. **14**(16), 3885 (2022)

14. Hui, Z., Jin, S., Li, D., Ziggah, Y.Y., Liu, B.: Individual tree extraction from terrestrial lidar point clouds based on transfer learning and gaussian mixture model separation. Remote Sens. **13**(2), 223 (2021)

15. ICNF: 8.° relatório provisório de incêndios rurais - 2022: 01 de janeiro a 15 de outubro (2023). http://www.icnf.pt/api/file/doc/4e8a66514175d0f7

16. ICNF: Plano nacional de defesa da floresta contra incêndios (2023). https://www.icnf.pt/florestas/gfr/gfrplaneamento/gfrplanos/planonacionalpndfci

17. Lagrange, A., Fauvel, M., Grizonnet, M.: Large-scale feature selection with gaussian mixture models for the classification of high dimensional remote sensing images. IEEE Trans. Comput. Imaging **3**(2), 230–242 (2017)

18. Lloret, J., Garcia, M., Bri, D., Sendra, S.: A wireless sensor network deployment for rural and forest fire detection and verification. Sensors **9**(11), 8722–8747 (2009)

19. Mirończuk, A., Hościło, A.: Mapping tree cover with sentinel-2 data using the support vector machine (SVM). Geoinf. Issues **9**(1), 27–38 (2017)

20. Mohapatra, A., Trinh, T.: Early wildfire detection technologies in practice-a review. Sustainability **14**(19), 12270 (2022)

21. Oreti, L., Giuliarelli, D., Tomao, A., Barbati, A.: Object oriented classification for mapping mixed and pure forest stands using very-high resolution imagery. Remote Sens. **13**(13), 2508 (2021)

22. Pedregosa, F., et al.: Scikit-learn: machine learning in Python. J. Mach. Learn. Res. **12**, 2825–2830 (2011)

23. Pereira, M.G., Calado, T.J., DaCamara, C.C., Calheiros, T.: Effects of regional climate change on rural fires in Portugal. Clim. Res. **57**(3), 187–200 (2013)

24. Rashkovetsky, D., Mauracher, F., Langer, M., Schmitt, M.: Wildfire detection from multisensor satellite imagery using deep semantic segmentation. IEEE J. Sel. Top. Appl. Earth Obs. Remote Sens. **14**, 7001–7016 (2021)

25. Seydi, S.T., Akhoondzadeh, M., Amani, M., Mahdavi, S.: Wildfire damage assessment over Australia using sentinel-2 imagery and MODIS land cover product within the google earth engine cloud platform. Remote Sens. **13**(2), 220 (2021)

26. Tang, Z., Liu, X., Chen, H., Hupy, J., Yang, B.: Deep learning based wildfire event object detection from 4K aerial images acquired by UAS. AI **1**(2), 166–179 (2020)

27. Zhang, Q., Ge, L., Zhang, R., Metternicht, G.I., Liu, C., Du, Z.: Towards a deep-learning-based framework of sentinel-2 imagery for automated active fire detection. Remote Sens. **13**(23), 4790 (2021)

28. Zhao, Y., Ban, Y., Nascetti, A.: Early detection of wildfires with GOES-R time-series and deep GRU network. In: 2021 IEEE International Geoscience and Remote Sensing Symposium IGARSS, pp. 3765–3768. IEEE (2021)

Assessing the 3D Position of a Car with a Single 2D Camera Using Siamese Networks

Youssef Bel Haj Yahia[1], Júlio Castro Lopes[1,3], Eduardo Bezerra[2],
Pedro João Rodrigues[1,3], and Rui Pedro Lopes[1,3(✉)]

[1] Research Center in Digitalization and Intelligent Robotics (CeDRI),
Instituto Politécnico de Bragança, Bragança, Portugal
{youssefyahia,juliolopes,pjsr}@ipb.pt
[2] CEFET/RJ, Rio de Janeiro, Brazil
ebezerra@cefet-rj.br
[3] Laboratório Associado para a Sustentabilidade e Tecnologia em Regiões de
Montanha (SusTEC), Instituto Politécnico de Bragança, Bragança, Portugal
rlopes@ipb.pt

Abstract. Using computer vision for the classification of an object's 3D position using a 2D camera is a topic that has received some attention from researchers over the years. Visual data is interpreted by the computer to recognize the objects found. In addition, it is possible to infer their orientation, evaluating their spatial arrangement, rotation, or alignment in the scene. The work presented in this paper describes the training and selection of a siamese neural network for classifying the 3D orientation of cars using 2D images. The neural network is composed of an initial phase for feature selection through convolutional neural networks followed by a dense layer for embedding generation. For feature selection, four architectures were tested: VGG16, VGG19, ResNet18 and ResNet50. The best result of 95.8% accuracy was obtained with the VGG16 and input images preprocessed for background removal.

Keywords: Computer Vision · Maintenance support · Siamese networks · Object Orientation

1 Introduction

Being able to infer an object's orientation based on a 2D image is a useful feature in several areas and applications [20, 23]. In Industry 4.0, for example, increasing digitalization of processes promises predictive maintenance of machinery, process optimization, simulation towards 'what-if' cases via digital twin, and operator support, among other benefits [16]. Operators start to use smart devices or Virtual Reality/Augmented Reality goggles to assist them in the development of their work, providing constant and up-to-date information in context [6, 21].

The quality control of the assembly process in a car factory is an example of this digital evolution. In this phase, operators measure several points in the

A. I. Pereira et al. (Eds.): OL2A 2023, CCIS 1982, pp. 93–107, 2024.
https://doi.org/10.1007/978-3-031-53036-4_7

assembled car to identify misalignment and incorrect placement of components. The number of points is, sometimes, in the order of several dozens, which requires that the operator remembers which points are already measured and which are still missing.

An Augmented Reality (AR) system can provide valuable assistance to the operator, allowing the visualization of the points that are still missing through virtual indications over the real view of the car [5]. For that, it is essential that the system can perceive the orientation of the car so that the points can be highlighted precisely and that the virtual indications can point to the correct part of the car.

Through computer vision algorithms, where a camera would constantly capture the environment, the system must assess the location and orientation of the car. However, training a model to carry out this task can represent a challenge. The model's responsibility should not only be to detect the object, but also to check the object's orientation to be able to clearly display the zones to be inspected.

This paper describes the use of Siamese Neural Networks [3], using triplet loss learning, to identify the 3D orientation of a car. For that, 16 scenarios are tested, within four dataset transformations and four model configurations.

This paper is structured in 5 sections, starting with this introduction. Section 2 describes, according to the scientific literature, the state of the art and the paper continues in Sect. 3 with the methodology. Section 4 presents some results and the paper ends with some conclusions in Sect. 5.

2   State of the Art

Computer Vision is a field of study within Artificial Intelligence (AI) that aims at providing computers with a high-level understanding of visual data (image/video). It has many areas of applications, such as cyber security [8,33], healthcare [1,17,26], manufacturing [27,32], and much more [2,7,18].

Object detection is a computer vision task that seeks to identify and localize objects in images or videos. By the detection and recognition of these objects, visual data can be then interpreted by the computer and recognize the objects found. In addition to identifying the objects, it is possible to infer their orientation, evaluating their spatial arrangement, rotation, or alignment in the scene [24]. For example, estimating the orientation of vehicles in the context of autonomous driving can aid in determining their heading or direction of movement, which is critical for safe navigation and decision-making [10,15].

The assessment of an object's 3D position using a single 2D camera, in a computer vision context, is a topic that has received some attention from researchers over the years [4,12,14,19,25,30,31,34]. Recently, Hung et al. [11] proposed a low-cost solution for the bin-picking problem by combining a single 2D camera on a robotic arm with deep learning-based models for object classification, detection, and instance segmentation, as well as monocular depth estimation, achieving high grasping accuracy rates and eliminating the need for expensive

3D cameras. Wang et al. [31] presented a machine learning-based system for estimating and tracking surface vehicle 3D position using a mono-camera. The system detects objects using a YOLOv5 neural network, improves accuracy with temporal filtering, and predicts the target's 3D position using a piece-wise projection model.

There have even been applications with a similar purpose to the work described in this paper [13]. Kim et al. method introduces an innovative approach by leveraging inverse perspective mapping to accurately estimate the distance from the image. It comprises two main stages for robust distance estimation. In the first stage, the method utilizes data from an inertial measurement unit to compensate for pitch and roll camera motions, effectively aligning the image to a corrected front view. Subsequently, an inverse perspective mapping technique is employed to project this corrected front view image onto a bird's eye view representation. In the second stage, a convolutional neural network is employed to detect and extract important features such as the position, size, and orientation of vehicles within the transformed bird's eye view.

3   Methodology

This section discusses the different aspects of the methodology used for inferring the 3D position of a car using a single 2D camera, including the data collection and preprocessing, the loss function used to train the models, the model architectures used for feature extraction, as well as the training scenarios.

3.1   Dataset

The dataset used for this task is a public access database containing 20 different sequences of images of cars [22]. Each sequence contains photos of a car placed on a rotating pad at the 2008 Geneva International Motor Show, as it accomplishes rotations of 360° and it is made available by CVLab - EPFL (https://www.epfl. ch/labs/cvlab/data/data-pose-index-php/). Two of the sequences were taken in a tilted pod. The photos were taken every 3 to 4°, with a Nikon D70 camera on a tripod (Fig. 1).

For the purpose of this work, the dataset was manually filtered, selecting the images that correspond to steps of 20°, removing the sequences that were taken in an tilted pod, totaling 18 images for each car (from 0 to 340°). Each image was labeled with the corresponding rotation angle: an image labeled as "180" degrees refers to a car facing towards the camera, while one labeled "0" degrees refers to a car facing away. The final dataset contains a total of 324 images, composed of 18 sequences of 18 images, facing one of the specified angles.

The dataset was used to train a model that could infer the orientation of the car through a single RGB camera. For that, a Siamese Neural Network [3] was developed with a Convolutional Neural Network (CNN) for feature extraction.

Fig. 1. Multi-View Car Dataset

3.2 Siamese Neural Network Model

The Siamese Neural Network architecture is composed of two identical that share the same weights. Each is presented with two different images, and the weights are updated so that the images could be discriminated if different or considered similar otherwise (Fig. 2).

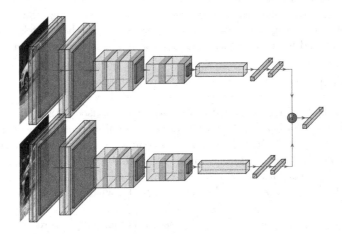

Fig. 2. Representation of a siamese neural network

Since the dataset is composed of images, the siamese network was based on CNNs for feature extraction and a final dense layer for outputing an embedding vector. This embedding vector will depend on the image, so similar orientations will have close vectors and different orientations will have distant vectors.

The network is trained for image similarity estimation with a triplet loss [28]. This concept is based on a triplet of inputs (in this situation, images of car orientations) where each of them correspond to the anchor A (the image we want as input), a positive sample P (an image with the same orientation) and a negative sample N (an image with a different orientation)

The images are then presented to the network simultaneously and the weights are updated according to the triplet loss function. This takes the vectors that represent the embeddings of the anchor (A), the positive (P), and the negative (N) and computes the pairwise Euclidean distance between them. The objective is to make the distance between the anchor and the positive smaller than the distance between the anchor and the negative by a predefined *margin* value that represents the desired separation between positive and negative pairs (Anchor-Positive) (Eq. 1).

$$L(A, P, N) = max(||f(A) - f(P)||^2 - ||f(A) - f(N)||^2 + margin, 0) \quad (1)$$

The total of 324 images were split in train and test sets, with 14 sequences and 4 sequences respectively. The resulting 252 training images were combined into A, P and N images, meaning the current image, another image in the same orientation and another image with a different orientation (Fig. 3).

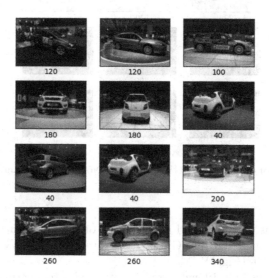

Fig. 3. Set of anchor, positive and negative images

For each A, a randomly chosen P (same orientation) was selected and, for each combination, 17 remaining orientations were selected for N. This means that, for each orientation, a total of $14 * 17 = 238$ samples were built and, this, a total of $18 * 14 * 17 = 4284$ triplets were build. This algorithm was ran twice, so 8568 triplets were used in the training of the siamese network.

With the train and test defined, the process proceeds to find the best structure for the siamese network.

3.3   Approach

The objective of this work was to develop a model for inferring 3D orientation of a car using 2D RGB images. The model should be as accurate as possible and, as such, it was necessary find the best combination of data preprocessing approaches and network architectures.

For the first step, four variations of the dataset were tried: full RGB image, full grayscale image, RGB image without background and grayscale image without background (Fig. 4). The background was removed with `rembg` (https://github.com/danielgatis/rembg).

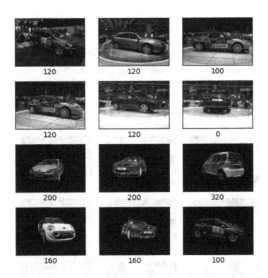

Fig. 4. Variations of the dataset: RGB, Grayscale, No background and Grayscale without background

The model was, as mentioned above, based on siamese neural network with CNN for feature extraction. The CNNs selected were VGG16, VGG19, ResNet18 and ResNet50 [9, 29] (Fig. 5).

The VGG16 and VGG19 encoders are both CNN architectures developed by the Visual Geometry Group (VGG) at the University of Oxford. The VGG16 encoder is renowned for its simplicity and effectiveness in image classification tasks. It consists of 13 convolutional layers with small receptive fields (3×3), followed by ReLU activation functions. Max pooling layers are applied to reduce spatial dimensions. Three fully connected layers with ReLU activation produce a 4096-dimensional feature vector as the final output. On the other hand, VGG19 builds upon the success of VGG16 with a deeper architecture, featuring 19 layers. It includes 16 convolutional layers with ReLU activations, additional convolutional layers for capturing intricate details, and the same fully connected

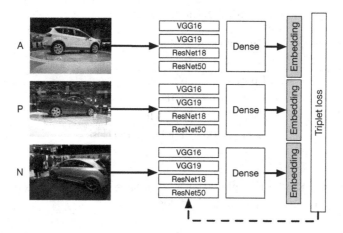

Fig. 5. Combination of CNNs in the car orientation siamese network

layers. Both models assume 224×224-pixel images as input and capture high-level abstract representations of the input images, through their convolutional layers and produce feature vectors for further analysis.

ResNet18 is designed to address the problem of vanishing gradients in deep neural networks. With 18 layers, it incorporates residual connections or skip connections that enable the network to learn residual mappings, making it easier to train very deep architectures. These connections facilitate the propagation of gradients, leading to improved training performance. On the other hand, ResNet50 is a deep CNN architecture that extends the ResNet family. It also tackles the challenge of training deep networks by introducing residual connections. With 50 layers, ResNet50 offers significant capacity for capturing complex features and representations.

In total, the 4 transformations on the dataset and the four CNN models correspond to a set of 16 scenarios (Table 1).

Table 1. Test scenarios

	VGG16	VGG19	Resnet18	Resnet50
RGB with background	S1	S5	S9	S13
RGB without background	S2	S6	S10	S14
Grayscale with background	S3	S7	S11	S15
Grayscale without background	S4	S8	S12	S16

The hyperparameters chosen for the training were kept in all combinations. These include a batch size of 64, 50 training epochs and relied on an Adadelta optimizer, along with a learning rate of 0.01 (Table 2). The training was performed in an NVIDIA GeForce RTX 3090.

Table 2. Model Parameters

Parameter	Value
Batch size	64
Epochs	50
Learning rate	0.01
Optimizer	Adadelta
Loss function	Triplet margin loss

To decide on the best combination within these scenarios, it is necessary to define and apply an evaluation methodology.

3.4 Evaluation

The evaluation is performed on a dataset that contains images not used in the training phase. Each image in the test dataset is considered an anchor (A) and it is compared with 18 images, one from each angle class (T) (Fig. 6). These reference images were taken from the training dataset.

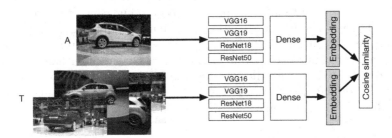

Fig. 6. Testing the siamese network

As a result, each anchor image will go through 18 different comparisons, of which 17 are expected to be negative comparisons and 1 positive comparison. The output will be two embeddings, one for the anchor and the other one for the compared image, which are then used to compute the cosine similarity. After passing all 18 pairs through the network, the pair that obtained the highest score is considered the most similar and, thus, its orientation considered the predicted label. For testing purposes, if the predicted label is equal to the real label, the classification is considered to be 'true' for ground truth predictions, otherwise it is considered 'false'.

The count of 'true' and 'false' predictions leads to the definition of the True Positives (TP), True Negatives (TN), False Positives (FP) and False Negatives (FN) (Table 3).

Table 3. Confusion matrix

	Actual positive	Actual negative
Predicted positive	TP	FP
Predicted negative	FN	TN

Once the predictions of all pairs in every class are determined, the evaluation metrics are computed to assess the performance of each model. The metrics include the accuracy (Acc) of the model, which indicates the percentage of correctly classified car images out of all the classifications (Eq. 2).

$$Acc = \frac{TP + TN}{TP + TN + FP + FN} \tag{2}$$

The next metric is precision, representing the proportion of correctly classified car images for a specific orientation angle out of all the car images predicted to belong to that angle. It provides insight into the model's ability to minimize false positives (Eq. 3).

$$Precision = \frac{TP}{TP + FP} \tag{3}$$

Recall, also known as sensitivity or true positive rate, was also used to measure the models' ability to capture all positive instances. It indicates the proportion of correctly classified car images for a specific orientation angle out of all the car images that actually belong to that angle (Eq. 4).

$$Recall = \frac{TP}{TP + FN} \tag{4}$$

Another metric considered was the F1 score. It is the harmonic mean of precision and recall. It provides a single metric that balances both precision and recall (Eq. 5).

$$F_1 = 2 \times \frac{precision \times recall}{precision + recall} \tag{5}$$

4 Results and Discussion

This section discusses the results obtained in the 16 scenarios to determine whether the approach has yielded interesting results. The test set was composed of 72 images, 4 images of each of the 18 classes. Every model was tested based on the data variation it was trained on.

For each scenario, the confusion matrix was built and the Accuracy, Precision, Recall and F1 was calculated (Table 4).

The top performing model for all data variants was the VGG16 model. It scored an accuracy of 95.83% and an F1 score of 95.76% for RGB images without background and 91.66% and an F1 of 91.71% on RGB images with background.

Table 4. The Evaluation Metrics Values For Each Combination

		Accuracy	Precision	Recall	F1
RGB	VGG16	0.91667	0.93333	0.91667	0.91711
	VGG19	0.81944	0.83333	0.81944	0.81429
	ResNet18	0.59722	0.68426	0.59722	0.57093
	ResNet50	0.26389	0.15355	0.26389	0.18335
Grayscale	VGG16	0.90278	0.92897	0.90278	0.89530
	VGG19	0.80556	0.82156	0.80556	0.79503
	ResNet18	0.68056	0.80073	0.68056	0.66889
	ResNet50	0.25000	0.17417	0.25000	0.19252
RGB no Background	VGG16	**0.95833**	**0.96667**	**0.95833**	**0.95767**
	VGG19	0.88889	0.90278	0.88889	0.88690
	ResNet18	0.76389	0.82765	0.76389	0.74604
	ResNet50	0.43056	0.43735	0.43056	0.39510
Grayscale no Background	VGG16	**0.95833**	**0.96667**	**0.95833**	**0.95767**
	VGG19	0.88889	0.91296	0.88889	0.88474
	ResNet18	0.80556	0.83452	0.80556	0.80332
	ResNet50	0.37500	0.47526	0.37500	0.36827

In the latter scenario, the VGG19 model is the only other model that scored close results to the VGG16 model by a difference of a bit more than 10%. The ResNet models have both performed poorly in this category with scores as low as 59.72% accuracy and 57.09% F1 for the Resnet18 and 26.38% accuracy and 18.33% F1 for the ResNet50. For grayscale images with background, the performance has generally decreased across all metrics for all models across all evaluation metrics but only by 1% to 2%.

A significant improvement across all evaluation metrics can be observed in the next two data categories, which are respectively RGB and grayscale images with the background removed. The VGG16 model's performance have gone up by more than 5% in accuracy and more than 4% in F1, compared to the highest results scored in the previous categories. This improvement was exactly the same in both categories. For the VGG19 model however, the improvement was even more significant reaching a value of more than 7% across all metrics. Even with a higher improvement rate, the VGG19 model did not exceed the VGG16 model which recorded an accuracy of 95.83% and an F1 score of 95.76%. The rest of the models also showed significant improvement. The ResNet18 model recorded 17% increase in both accuracy and F1. For grayscale images it had an even higher improvement rate of 21% in accuracy and 23% in F1 score. Even with its highest scores across different metrics, the ResNet18 model was still surpasseed by both VGG architectures. The ResNet50 model also recorded an improvement across both scenarios. It scored 17% higher accuracy and 21% higher F1 score for the first and 11% increase in accuracy with almost double the F1 score for the second. Nevertheless, the ResNet50 model is still considered ineffective for this approach given that the highest accuracy recorded across all data categories was 43.05% along with an F1 score of 39.51%.

For better visualization, the confusion matrices for the RGB images without background are visualized (Fig. 7). It is to be noted that every class number from 0 to 17 refers to one of the 18 angles we are trying to identify (0 to 340°). According to the results, the best performing VGG16 model performed reasonably well on most angles (Fig. 7a). A slight confusion occurred in identifying the angle 0, 180 and 280.

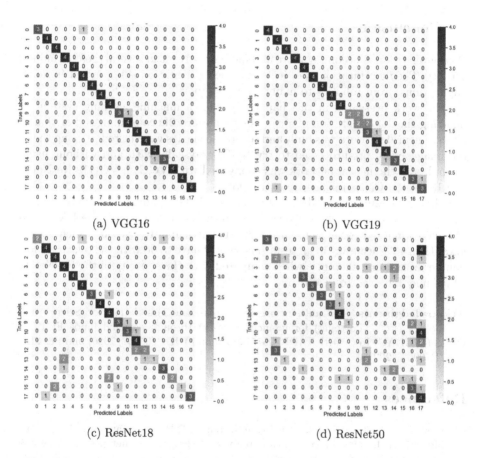

(a) VGG16 (b) VGG19

(c) ResNet18 (d) ResNet50

Fig. 7. Confusion matrices for the RGB without background dataset

Figure 7b describes the performance of VGG19. It performed perfectly in identifying angles from 0 to 160 along with angles 240 and 260. However it had a significant issue with angles 180 and 200 where the model was only able to identify them 50% of the time. The rest of the angles were subject to a slight confusion as well.

The ResNet18 model shown in Fig. 7c also shows good results in identifying 8 of the target angles. However the results are significantly lower than the other concerning the other angles.

In Fig. 7d, the results of the Resnet50 model are displayed. The only two angles this model was able to perfectly identify were 160 and 340°. All the other angles were subject of classification mistakes. The results associated with this model were below the expectations. Nevertheless, the possibility of identifying the orientation of cars opens new possibilities for maintenance support as well as for other areas.

5   Conclusion

Computer vision is becoming more and more important in several areas of human activity. The identification of objects and their orientation is important in many applications, from robotics to maintenance support.

The work presented in this paper describes a machine learning system for inferring the 3D orientation of a car using standard 2D color images. For that, a siamese neural network was built and several scenarios were tested. Among these, the images were pre-processed to try RGB, grayscale, with and without background, and the neural network was configured with VGG16, VGG19 ResNet18 and ResNet50 CNNs for feature extraction.

The best results were obtained with the VGG16 model with RGB images without background, achieving 95.8% accuracy. It is surprising the low values obtained for the ResNet configurations, in particular ResNet50, which scored lower than 43% accuracy in all tests. These may have to do with the relatively low number of training examples when compared with the capacity of the ResNet50, which may have led to overfitting.

Acknowledgments. The authors are grateful to the Foundation for Science and Technology (FCT, Portugal) for financial support through national funds FCT/M-CTES (PIDDAC) to CeDRI (UIDB/05757/2020 and UIDP/05757/2020) and SusTEC (LA/P/0007 /2021).

References

1. Castro Lopes, J., Vieira, J., Van-Deste, I., Lopes, R.P.: An architecture for capturing and synchronizing heart rate and body motion for stress inference. In: Accepted for publication: 11th International Conference on Serious Games and Applications for Health. Athens, Greece (2023)

2. Chatzichristofis, S.A.: Recent advances in educational robotics. Electronics **12**(4), 925 (2023). https://doi.org/10.3390/electronics12040925, https://www.mdpi.com/2079-9292/12/4/925

3. Chicco, D.: Siamese neural networks: an overview. In: Cartwright, H. (ed.) Artificial Neural Networks. MMB, vol. 2190, pp. 73–94. Springer, New York (2021). https://doi.org/10.1007/978-1-0716-0826-5_3

4. Dahlberg, T., Strömberg, V.: Automatic LiDAR-camera calibration: extrinsic calibration for a LiDAR-camera pair using structure from motion and stochastic optimization (2022). https://hdl.handle.net/20.500.12380/304955

5. Dalle Mura, M., Dini, G.: Augmented reality in assembly systems: state of the art and future perspectives. In: Ratchev, S. (ed.) IPAS 2020. IAICT, vol. 620, pp. 3–22. Springer, Cham (2021). https://doi.org/10.1007/978-3-030-72632-4_1

6. Durchon, H., Preda, M., Zaharia, T., Grall, Y.: Challenges in applying deep learning to augmented reality for manufacturing. In: Proceedings of the 27th International Conference on 3D Web Technology. pp. 1–4. Web3D '22, Association for Computing Machinery, New York, NY, USA (2022). https://doi.org/10.1145/3564533.3564572. https://dl.acm.org/doi/10.1145/3564533.3564572

7. Ellinger, A., Woerner, C., Scherer, R.: Automatic segmentation of bulk material heaps using color, texture, and topography from aerial data and deep learning-based computer vision. Remote Sens. **15**(1), 211 (2023). https://doi.org/10.3390/rs15010211, https://www.mdpi.com/2072-4292/15/1/211

8. Hasan, Z., Mohammad, H.R., Jishkariani, M.: Machine learning and data mining methods for cyber security: a survey. Mesopotamian J. CyberSecur. 2022(47–56) (2022). https://doi.org/10.58496/MJCS/2022/006, https://mesopotamian.press/journals/index.php/CyberSecurity/article/view/30

9. He, K., Zhang, X., Ren, S., Sun, J.: Deep residual learning for image recognition (2015). https://doi.org/10.48550/arXiv.1512.03385, http://arxiv.org/abs/1512.03385,arXiv:1512.03385 [cs]

10. Hoque, S., Xu, S., Maiti, A., Wei, Y., Arafat, M.Y.: Deep learning for 6D pose estimation of objects - A case study for autonomous driving. Exp. Syst. Appl. **223**, 119838 (2023). https://doi.org/10.1016/j.eswa.2023.119838, https://www.sciencedirect.com/science/article/pii/S0957417423003391

11. Hung Nguyen, N.D., Nguyen Nguyen, L.H., Pham, P.T., Nguyen, Q.C., Ly, P.T.: Bin-picking solution for industrial robots integrating a 2D vision system. In: 2022 International Conference on High Performance Big Data and Intelligent Systems (HDIS), pp. 266–270 (2022). https://doi.org/10.1109/HDIS56859.2022.9991341

12. Ingberg, B.: Registration of 2D objects in 3D data (2015). https://urn.kb.se/resolve?urn=urn:nbn:se:liu:diva-119338

13. Kim, Y., Kum, D.: Deep learning based vehicle position and orientation estimation via inverse perspective mapping image. In: 2019 IEEE Intelligent Vehicles Symposium (IV), pp. 317–323 (2019). https://doi.org/10.1109/IVS.2019.8814050, iSSN: 2642-7214

14. Kite, D.H., Magee, M.: Determining the 3D position and orientation of a robot camera using 2D monocular vision. Pattern Recogn. **23**(8), 819–831 (1990). https://doi.org/10.1016/0031-3203(90)90129-9, https://www.sciencedirect.com/science/article/pii/0031320390901299

15. Lim, S., Jung, J., Lee, B.H., Choi, J., Kim, S.C.: Radar sensor-based estimation of vehicle orientation for autonomous driving. IEEE Sens. J. **22**(22), 21924–21932 (2022). https://doi.org/10.1109/JSEN.2022.3210579

16. Liu, X., et al.: A pose estimation approach based on keypoints detection for robotic bin-picking application. In: 2021 China Automation Congress (CAC), pp. 3672–3677 (2021). https://doi.org/10.1109/CAC53003.2021.9727987, iSSN: 2688-0938

17. Lopes, R.P., et al.: Digital technologies for innovative mental health rehabilitation. Electronics **10**(18), 2260 (2021). https://doi.org/10.3390/electronics10182260, https://www.mdpi.com/2079-9292/10/18/2260, iF (2021): 2.69 - Q2

18. Mendes-Neves, T., Meireles, L., Mendes-Moreira, J.: A survey of advanced computer vision techniques for sports (2023). https://doi.org/10.48550/arXiv.2301.07583, http://arxiv.org/abs/2301.07583, arXiv:2301.07583 [cs]

19. Miseikis, J., Brijacak, I., Yahyanejad, S., Glette, K., Elle, O.J., Torresen, J.: Multi-objective convolutional neural networks for robot localisation and 3D position estimation in 2D camera images. In: 2018 15th International Conference on Ubiquitous Robots (UR), pp. 597–603 (2018). https://doi.org/10.1109/URAI.2018.8441813

20. Mohan, N., Kumar, M.: Room layout estimation in indoor environment: a review. Multimedia Tools Appl. **81**(2), 1921–1951 (2022). https://doi.org/10.1007/s11042-021-11358-1

21. Mourtzis, D., Angelopoulos, J., Panopoulos, N.: Challenges and opportunities for integrating augmented reality and computational fluid dynamics modeling under the framework of industry 4.0. Procedia CIRP **106**, 215–220 (2022). https://doi.org/10.1016/j.procir.2022.02.181, https://www.sciencedirect.com/science/article/pii/S2212827122001822

22. Ozuysal, M., Lepetit, V., Fua, P.: Pose estimation for category specific multi-view object localization. In: 2009 IEEE Conference on Computer Vision and Pattern Recognition, pp. 778–785. IEEE, Miami, FL (2009). https://doi.org/10.1109/CVPR.2009.5206633, https://ieeexplore.ieee.org/document/5206633/

23. Qi, Q., Zhao, S., Shen, J., Lam, K.M.: Multi-scale capsule attention-based salient object detection with multi-crossed layer connections. In: 2019 IEEE International Conference on Multimedia and Expo (ICME), pp. 1762–1767 (2019). https://doi.org/10.1109/ICME.2019.00303, iSSN: 1945-788X

24. Rao, C., Wang, J., Cheng, G., Xie, X., Han, J.: Learning orientation-aware distances for oriented object detection. IEEE Trans. Geosci. Remote Sens. **61**, 1–11 (2023). https://doi.org/10.1109/TGRS.2023.3278933

25. Ren, J., Orwell, J., Jones, G., Xu, M.: A general framework for 3D soccer ball estimation and tracking. In: 2004 International Conference on Image Processing, 2004. ICIP 2004, vol. 3, pp. 1935–1938 (2004). https://doi.org/10.1109/ICIP.2004.1421458, iSSN: 1522-4880

26. Rodrigues, A.S.F., Lopes, J.C., Lopes, R.P., Teixeira, L.F.: Classification of facial expressions under partial occlusion for vr games. In: Pereira, A.I., Košir, A., Fernandes, F.P., Pacheco, M.F., Teixeira, J.P., Lopes, R.P. (eds.) Optimization, Learning Algorithms and Applications, vol. 1754, pp. 804–819. Springer, Cham (2022). https://doi.org/10.1007/978-3-031-23236-7_55, https://link.springer.com/10.1007/978-3-031-23236-7_55

27. Sagodi, A., Schniertshauer, J., van Giffen, B.: Engineering AI-enabled computer vision systems: lessons from manufacturing. IEEE Softw. **39**(6), 51–57 (2022). https://doi.org/10.1109/MS.2022.3189904

28. Schroff, F., Kalenichenko, D., Philbin, J.: FaceNet: a unified embedding for face recognition and clustering. In: 2015 IEEE Conference on Computer Vision and Pattern Recognition (CVPR), pp. 815–823. IEEE, Boston, MA, USA (2015). https://doi.org/10.1109/CVPR.2015.7298682, http://ieeexplore.ieee.org/document/7298682/

29. Simonyan, K., Zisserman, A.: Very deep convolutional networks for large-scale image recognition (2015), http://arxiv.org/abs/1409.1556, arXiv:1409.1556 [cs]

30. Takahashi, M., Ikeya, K., Kano, M., Ookubo, H., Mishina, T.: Robust volleyball tracking system using multi-view cameras. In: 2016 23rd International Conference on Pattern Recognition (ICPR), pp. 2740–2745 (2016). https://doi.org/10.1109/ICPR.2016.7900050

31. Wang, J., Choi, W., Diaz, J., Trott, C.: The 3D position estimation and tracking of a surface vehicle using a mono-camera and machine learning. Electronics **11**(14), 2141 (Jan 2022). https://doi.org/10.3390/electronics11142141, https://www.mdpi.com/2079-9292/11/14/2141

32. Wang, J., Gao, P., Zhang, J., Lu, C., Shen, B.: Knowledge augmented broad learning system for computer vision based mixed-type defect detection in semiconductor manufacturing. Robot. Comput. Integr. Manuf. **81**, 102513 (2023). https://doi.org/10.1016/j.rcim.2022.102513, https://www.sciencedirect.com/science/article/pii/S0736584522001958

33. Wei, H., et al.: Physical adversarial attack meets computer vision: a decade survey (2022). http://arxiv-export3.library.cornell.edu/abs/2209.15179v1

34. Yan, X., Zhang, H., Li, H.: Computer vision-based recognition of 3D relationship between construction entities for monitoring struck-by accidents. Comput. Aided Civil Infrastruct. Eng. **35**(9), 1023–1038 (2020). https://doi.org/10.1111/mice.12536, https://onlinelibrary.wiley.com/doi/abs/10.1111/mice.12536, https://onlinelibrary.wiley.com/doi/pdf/10.1111/mice.12536

Deep Learning-Based Hip Detection in Pelvic Radiographs

Cátia Loureiro[1], Vítor Filipe[1,2], Pedro Franco-Gonçalo[3,4,5],
Ana Inês Pereira[3,6], Bruno Colaço[4,5,6], Sofia Alves-Pimenta[4,5,6],
Mário Ginja[3,4,5], and Lio Gonçalves[1,2(✉)]

[1] Department of Engineering, University of Trás-os-Montes and Alto Douro (UTAD),
5000-801 Vila Real, Portugal
al67570@utad.eu
[2] Institute for Engineering and Computer Systems, Technology and Science
(INESC-TEC), 4200–465 Porto, Portugal
{vfilipe,lgoncalv}@utad.pt
[3] Department of Veterinary Sciences, University of Trás-os-Montes and Alto Douro
(UTAD), 5000–801 Vila Real, Portugal
{al58040,al51330}@alunos.utad.pt
[4] Animal and Veterinary Research Centre (CECAV), University of Trás-os-Montes
and Alto Douro (UTAD), 5000–801 Vila Real, Portugal
{bcolaco,salves,mginja}@utad.pt
[5] Associate Laboratory for Animal and Veterinary Sciences (AL4AnimalS),
5000–801 Vila Real, Portugal
[6] Department of Animal Science, University of Trás-os-Montes and Alto Douro
(UTAD), 5000–801 Vila Real, Portugal

Abstract. Radiography is the primary modality for diagnosing canine
hip dysplasia (CHD), with visual assessment of radiographic features
sometimes used for accurate diagnosis. However, these features typically constitute small regions of interest (ROI) within the overall image,
yet they hold vital diagnostic information and are crucial for pathological analysis. Consequently, automated detection of ROIs becomes a
critical preprocessing step in classification or segmentation systems. By
correctly extracting the ROIs, the efficiency of retrieval and identification of pathological signs can be significantly improved. In this research
study, we employed the most recent iteration of the YOLO (version 8)
model to detect hip joints in a dataset of 133 pelvic radiographs. The
best-performing model achieved a mean average precision (mAP50:95)
of 0.81, indicating highly accurate detection of hip regions. Importantly,
this model displayed feasibility for training on a relatively small dataset
and exhibited promising potential for various medical applications.

Keywords: Deep learning · Hip detection · Canine hip dysplasia

1 Introduction

Automated detection of regions of interest (ROI) is critical in various medical image applications [1]. In the case of canine hip dysplasia (CHD), accurate

A. I. Pereira et al. (Eds.): OL2A 2023, CCIS 1982, pp. 108–117, 2024.
https://doi.org/10.1007/978-3-031-53036-4_8

and efficient ROI detection can play a crucial role as a preprocessing step in diagnosing and treating this common orthopedic condition. CHD is a complex developmental disease affecting the coxo-femoral joint, commonly observed in dogs [2]. The condition is characterized by joint laxity, resulting in the degeneration of articular cartilage and the eventual development of osteoarthritis [3]. Focusing on the ROI makes the detection process more targeted, allowing for detailed examination and recognition of specific abnormalities associated with CHD, such as joint incongruity and osteophyte formation [4].

This approach can be especially important in artificial intelligence (AI) applications, particularly in computer vision, and has demonstrated successful outcomes in medical imaging [5]. Medical images are densely packed with information and have complex architecture. Extracting the ROI accurately from these images can enhance both retrieval efficiency and the classification of pathological signs. Furthermore, through prioritizing the analysis of ROIs within the image, it has the potential to decrease computational load and effectively manage the exponential expansion of image data [6]. Numerous studies have investigated approaches to harness AI's potential in this field [7,8]. Some have adopted a two-stage methodology involving two distinct stages: (1) detecting specific ROIs and (2) subsequently employing classification, segmentation, or other conventional techniques. Using a two-stage method, researchers can accurately pinpoint and separate important areas within medical images before moving on to other tasks [9]. The two-stage approach offers a distinct advantage by effectively identifying subtle, localized abnormalities.

The main objective of this research is to assess the applicability of the most recent iteration of the YOLO model, namely YOLOv8, in the detection of hip joints in pelvic radiographs. This investigation is specifically carried out on a limited dataset comprising canine X-ray images. The primary purpose of this research is to establish a first-stage pipeline that can be implemented to identify and classify pathological signs associated with CHD. Figure 1 illustrates a pipeline system that focuses on the initial stage of detecting hip joints. Subsequently, the second stage is devoted to segmentation, classification, and other related tasks.

The rest of this paper is organized as follows: Related work (Sect. 2); Methodology (Sect. 3); Results and discussion (Sect. 4); Conclusions (Sect. 5).

2   Related Works

In recent years, a growing body of literature has focused on object detection in medical imaging. In 2021, Liu et al. [10] introduced a deep learning-based framework for ROI detection utilizing a single-shot multi-box detector. Their study involved a dataset of 7399 anteroposterior pelvic radiographs from three diverse sources. The proposed model achieved impressive results: an average intersection over union (IoU) of 0.81 and an average precision with a threshold IoU of 0.5 (AP50) equal to 0.99. This highlights the model's ability to accurately detect and localize ROIs within the medical images. McEvoy et al. [11], also in 2021, employed a two-stage transfer learning approach for ROI detection in

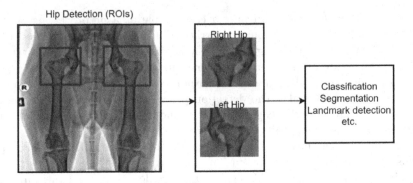

Fig. 1. Pipeline illustration of two-stage system.

the same domain. Their initial step involved training a tiny Yolov3 model to predict the bounding boxes for each hip joint within the images. This initial stage achieved an impressive IoU score of 0.85, indicating precise localization of the hip joints. Subsequently, using the cropped images obtained from the previous stage, the same model was trained for binary classification, distinguishing between dysplasia and non-dysplasia cases. The results showed a sensitivity of 0.53 and a specificity of 0.92. Gomes et al. [12] pursued a similar strategy in 2021. However, they did not focus on ROIs but considered the entire image to classify whether a dog exhibited dysplastic features. They utilized an Inception-V3-based neural network, achieving a specificity of 0.66. While the model's performance on test images may not have been outstanding, when integrated with McEvoy's research, it showcased the ability of machine learning to conduct initial classification for assessing canine coxofemoral joint morphology. However, we believe that precise hip joint detection is an indispensable step for further feature analysis.

3   Methodology

3.1   YOLO Architecture

The YOLO (You Only Look Once) framework has gained considerable recognition within the area of computer vision due to its remarkable equilibrium between speed and accuracy. This framework facilitates the rapid and reliable identification of objects in images, thereby establishing its wide acceptance and acclaim [13]. Over time, the YOLO family has undergone multiple iterations, with each version building upon its predecessors to address limitations and enhance overall performance. YOLOv8 [14], introduced in 2023, maintains some of the core concepts from YOLOv5 [15] while also being meticulously designed to integrate the strengths of multiple real-time object detectors. As a result, YOLOv8 introduces significant advancements compared to the previous iterations of the YOLO series.

One of the challenging aspects encountered in earlier YOLO models is the utilization of anchor boxes [17]. This complexity arises from introducing predefined anchors, which necessitates the specification of additional hyperparameters to define their sizes and aspect ratios. Consequently, while these predefined anchor boxes may aptly capture the distribution of the target benchmark's boxes, they may not adequately reflect the distribution prevalent within custom datasets [18]. One of the notable advancements in YOLOv8 is the adoption of anchor-free detection. This approach entails directly predicting the object center instead of estimating the offset from a predefined anchor box. As a result, the number of box predictions is reduced, leading to an acceleration of the Non-Maximum Suppression (NMS) process [13]. NMS is a post-processing step that filters the detection boxes based on the Intersection over Union (IoU) metric [19].

YOLOv8 shares a similar backbone with YOLOv5 but with a significant modification in the C3 module. In YOLOv8, the C3 module is substituted with the C2f module, which is built upon the Cross-Stage Partial (CSP) concept [20]. This architectural update in YOLOv8 incorporates valuable insights from the Efficient Layer Aggregation Network (ELAN) paradigm introduced in YOLOv7 [16]. The C2f module, which combines aspects from both C3 and ELAN, not only enhances the flow of gradient information but also provides a lightweight design [21].

Nevertheless, a notable characteristic of YOLOv8 is its extensibility. YOLOv8 is specifically engineered to be compatible with all iterations of YOLO, enabling seamless switching between versions and facilitating straightforward performance comparisons. Moreover, it exhibits versatility by being capable of running on diverse hardware platforms, including CPU and GPU, thereby offering strong flexibility [21].

3.2 Dataset and Preprocessing

For this study, 133 DICOM images were gathered from the Veterinary Teaching Hospital of the University of Trás-os-Montes and Alto Douro (UTAD). Subsequently, manual annotation was performed on each X-ray using the open-source graphical image annotation tool, LabelImg [22]. Specifically, the annotations were focused on identifying the right and left hip. Afterward, all radiographs from the two classes were converted to the .png format, and their dimensions were adjusted to 640 × 640 pixels.

Furthermore, we divide the dataset into three subsets: training, validation, and test sets, maintaining an 80–10-10 ratio, respectively. Since the available data was limited, we implemented *on-the-fly* data augmentation techniques to ensure a more robust model. These transformations, including translation, scale, and rotation, along with the addition of mosaic augmentation, were applied. Importantly, these transformations were carefully selected not to alter the essential characteristics of the images.

3.3 Training and Evaluation

The training process encompassed 200 epochs, with a batch size of 8. In cases where the model failed to demonstrate improvement within 50 epochs, the training procedure was terminated (Early Stopping). Stochastic gradient descent (SGD) was utilized as the optimization algorithm for training the model [23]. The training employed an initial learning rate of 0.1, a momentum value of 0.937, and a weight decay 0.0005. To overcome the limitations posed by the scarcity of available data, transfer learning techniques were employed by using weights pre-training on the COCO dataset [24].

The proposed approach was evaluated using an Intersection over Union (IoU) threshold of 0.5. IoU, defined in equation (1), represents the ratio between the intersection area of the ground truth (X_G) and predicted bounding box (X_P) and the union area of the ground truth and predicted bounding box.

$$IoU = \frac{X_G \cap X_P}{X_G \cup X_P} \tag{1}$$

Mean Average Precision (mAP), as explained in equation (2), is utilized to calculate the AP across various classes (n). AP is determined by interpolating the Precision (P) and Recall (R) curve at equally spaced recall levels.

$$mAP = \frac{1}{n} \sum_{n}^{i=1} AP_i \tag{2}$$

Precision and recall are computed using equations (3) and (4), respectively, where TP, FP and FN correspond to true positives, false positives, and false negatives, respectively.

$$P = \frac{TP}{TP + FP} \tag{3}$$

$$R = \frac{TP}{TP + FN} \tag{4}$$

4   Results and Discussion

In our study, we set out to determine the best-performing variations of YOLOv8: YOLOv8n (nano), YOLOv8s (small), and YOLOv8m (medium). The training performance results, showed in Fig. 2, include two types of loss: box loss and classification loss. The box loss measures the model's accuracy in locating the center of an object and accurately predicting its bounding box. On the other hand, the classification loss indicates the algorithm's ability to predict the object's class correctly. The study also compares these versions based on their mAP results at IoU threshold of 0.5 and ranging from 0.5 to 0.95.

Interestingly, the small variant of YOLOv8 exhibited superior performance compared to the other two iterations. YOLOv8s achieved a minimal box loss of 0.005, whereas the nano and medium versions recorded higher box losses of 0.006 and 0.007, respectively. Furthermore, the small version demonstrated a minimal classification loss value of 0.003, while the medium and nano versions displayed double the loss at 0.004. Regarding mAP results at different IoU thresholds, the small version achieved the highest performance, with a maximum mAP of 0.79 at IoU 0.5 to 0.95. The nano version closely followed with an mAP of 0.77, while the medium version attained a score of 0.75.

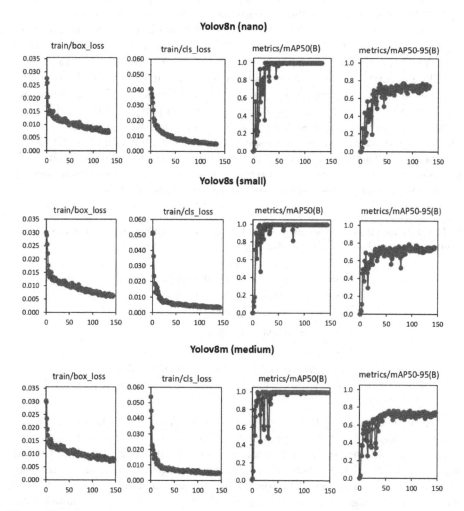

Fig. 2. Performance comparison of the scaled versions of YOLOv8 during training. The graphs illustrate the Box Regression Loss (Box Loss) and Classification Loss (Cls Loss), while the last two figures display the Mean Average Precision (mAP) for IoU thresholds greater than 0.5 and within the range of 0.5 to 0.95.

After training the model, we conducted model inference by feeding unseen pictures into the models, using a confidence threshold of 0.7. The results for mean mAP at IoU > 0.5 and 0.5 > IoU > 0.95 are presented in Table II. Upon closer examination of the table, it becomes evident that training the YOLOv8s model outperforms the other two models. Notably, the YOLOv8s model achieves an increased mAP50:95 value of 0.81. Additionally, we compared two scaled versions of YOLOv7 and found that both iterations yielded inferior results compared to YOLOv8, particularly the YOLOv7x variant. Furthermore, during training, we observed that the YOLOv8 versions exhibited significantly faster performance than YOLOv7, demonstrating a good balance between speed and accuracy.

The improved performance of YOLOv8s can be attributed to the observed correlation between the number of parameters and the network's learning capacity. Furthermore, when contrasted with a more complex network (YOLOv8n), it becomes evident that a simpler neural network has the potential to generate superior outcomes. This advantage arises from the ability to retrain complex networks, resulting in the improved performance of the simpler network. In addition, using fewer parameters can also function as a type of regularization, thereby improving the simpler network's capacity to generalize effectively [25].

Table 1. Evaluation performance of YOLOv8 and YOLOv7 models for the overall average of both classes (right and left hip).

Models	mAP50	mAP50:95	R	P
YOLOv8n	0.945	0.758	0.896	1
YOLOv8s	0.995	0.806	1	1
YOLOv8m	0.995	0.780	1	1
YOLOv7n	1	0.699	1	1
YOLOv7x	0.777	0.450	0.970	0.773

We further analyzed the detection results for hip ROI visualization on the testing dataset. In Fig. 3, we present three radiographs as examples: one displaying text outside the key hip area, another exhibiting dislocation in the left hip, and the third showcasing artifacts near our ROI. These results indicate that YOLOv8 is a robust detector for hip objects, making it applicable to a wide range of images with different qualities. It can be potentially valuable for the automated assessment of pathological signs related to CHD. However, it is crucial for future research to evaluate the model's performance on radiographs containing plates and total hip replacements.

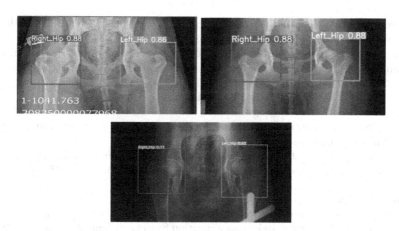

Fig. 3. The visualization of hip ROI detection results on the testing dataset is presented in this figure. In all instances, the ROIs were accurately detected for both hips. The top row displays a radiograph containing text outside the relevant hip area and another radiograph exhibiting left hip dislocation. On the bottom row, a radiograph with artifacts present near the left hip is showcased.

5   Conclusion

This study aimed to automate the detection of right and left hip joints in X-ray images using a YOLOv8-based object detector. Multiple experiments were conducted with different models to determine the most effective one yielding the highest performance. The results of these experiments confirmed that utilizing the YOLOv8s model produced superior outcomes compared to the previous version, YOLOv7, mainly working with a small dataset. The proposed approach for ROI detection demonstrates a clear methodology and holds practical significance for future applications in medical imaging. However, further investigations are necessary to evaluate the model's performance on a more diverse and heterogeneous dataset.

Acknowledgments. This work was financed by project Dys4Vet (POCI-01–0247-FEDER-046914), co-financed by the European Regional Development Fund (ERDF) through COMPETE2020 - the Operational Programme for Competitiveness and Internationalisation (OPCI). The authors are also grateful for all the conditions made available by FCT- Portuguese Foundation for Science and Technology, under the projects UIDP/00772/2020, LA/P/0059/2020, and Scientific Employment Stimulus Institutional Call-CEECINST/00127/2018 UTAD.

References

1. Kaur, M., Wasson, V.: ROI Based medical image compression for telemedicine application. Procedia Comput. Sci. (2015)

2. Alexander, J.W.: The pathogenesis of canine hip dysplasia. Vet Clin North Am Small Anim Pract. (1992). https://doi.org/10.1016/s0195-5616(92)50051-1

3. Pinna, S., Tassani, C., Antonino, A., Vezzoni, A.: Prevalence of Primary Radiographic Signs of Hip Dysplasia in Dogs. Animals (Basel). (2022). https://doi.org/10.3390/ani12202788

4. Allan, G., Davies, S.: Chapter 21 - Radiographic Signs of Joint Disease in Dogs and Cats, Textbook Vet. Diagn. Radiol. (Seventh Edition), pp. 403–433 (2018)

5. Wang, S., et al.: (2021). Review and Prospect: artificial intelligence in advanced medical imaging. Frontiers Radiol. (2021)

6. Sun, S., Zhang, R.: Region of interest extraction of medical image based on improved region growing algorithm. (2017). https://doi.org/10.2991/mseee-17.2017.87

7. Joshi, A., Charan, V., Prince, S.: A novel methodology for brain tumor detection based on two stage segmentation of MRI images, In: 2015 International Conference on Advanced Computing and Communication Systems, Coimbatore, India, (2015). https://doi.org/10.1109/ICACCS.2015.7324127

8. Xie, L., et al.: Automatic lung segmentation in dynamic thoracic MRI using two-stage deep convolutional neural networks. Proc. SPIE- Int. Soc. Opt. Eng. (2022). https://doi.org/10.1117/12.2612558

9. Pawar, P., Talbar, S.: Two-Stage hybrid approach of deep learning networks for interstitial lung disease classification. Biomed. Res. Int. (2022). https://doi.org/10.1155/2022/7340902

10. Liu, F-Y., et al.: Automatic hip detection in anteroposterior pelvic radiographs-A labelless practical framework. J. Personalized Med. (2021). https://doi.org/10.3390/jpm11060522

11. Mcevoy, F., et al.: Deep transfer learning can be used for the detection of hip joints in pelvis radiographs and the classification of their hip dysplasia status. Vet. Radiol. Ultrasound. (2021)

12. Gomes, D.A., Alves-Pimenta, M.S., Ginja, M., Filipe, V.: Predicting Canine Hip Dysplasia in X-Ray Images Using Deep Learning. In: Pereira, A.I., Fernandes, F.P., Coelho, J.P., Teixeira, J.P., Pacheco, M.F., Alves, P., Lopes, R.P. (eds.) OL2A 2021. CCIS, vol. 1488, pp. 393–400. Springer, Cham (2021). https://doi.org/10.1007/978-3-030-91885-9_29

13. Terven, J., Cordova-Esparza, D-M.: A Comprehensive Review of YOLO: From YOLOv1 to YOLOv8 and Beyond (2023)

14. Jocher, G., Chaurasia, A., Qiu, J.: YOLO by Ultralytics. https://github.com/ultralytics/ultralytics. Accessed 1 Jun 2023

15. Ultralytics YOLOv5. Ultralytics YOLOv5 - Ultralytics YOLOv8 Docs. https://docs.ultralytics.com/yolov5. Accessed 31 May 2023

16. Wang, C-Y., Bochkovskiy, A., Liao, H.: YOLOv7: Trainable bag-of-freebies sets new state-of-the-art for real-time object detectors. (2022). https://doi.org/10.48550/arXiv.2207.02696

17. Solawetz, J., Francesco.: What is YOLOv8? The Ultimate Guide. https://blog.roboflow.com/whats-new-in-yolov8. Accessed 1 Jun 2023

18. Zand, M., Etemad, A., Greenspan, M.: ObjectBox: From Centers to Boxes for Anchor-Free Object Detection (2022)

19. Wang, D., Li, C., Wen, S., Nepal, S., Xiang, Y.: Daedalus: Breaking Non-Maximum Suppression in Object Detection via Adversarial Examples (2019)

20. Li, Y., Fan, Q., Huang, H., Han, Z., Gu, Q.: A modified YOLOv8 detection network for UAV aerial image recognition (2023). https://doi.org/10.3390/drones7050304

21. Lou, H., et al.: DC-YOLOv8: Small-Size object detection algorithm based on camera sensor. Electronics (2023). https://doi.org/10.3390/electronics12102323
22. Tzutalin. LabelImg. (2015). https://github.com/tzutalin/labelImg
23. Ruder, S.: An overview of gradient descent optimization algorithms. (2016)
24. Lin, T-Y., et al.: Microsoft COCO: Common Objects in Context. (2014)
25. Horvat, M., Jelečević, L., Gledec, G.: A comparative study of YOLOv5 models performance for image localization and classification (2022)

Using LiDAR Data as Image for AI to Recognize Objects in the Mobile Robot Operational Environment

Marek Nowakowski[1](✉) [iD], Jakub Kurylo[6] [iD], João Braun[2,3,4] [iD],
Guido S. Berger[2,4,5] [iD], João Mendes[2,4] [iD], and José Lima[2,3,4] [iD]

[1] Military Institute of Armoured and Automotive Technology, Okuniewska 1, 05-070
Sulejówek, Poland
marek.nowakowski@witpis.eu

[2] Research Centre in Digitalization and Intelligent Robotics (CeDRI) - Instituto Politécnico de
Bragança, Campus de Santa Apolónia, Bragança, Portugal
{jbneto,guido.berger,jllima}@ipb.pt

[3] INESC Technology and Science, Porto, Portugal

[4] Laboratory for Sustainability and Technology in Mountain Regions (SusTEC) - Instituto
Politécnico de Bragança, Bragança, Portugal

[5] Engineering Department, School of Sciences and Technology, Universidade de
Trás-os-Montes e Alto Douro (UTAD), 5000-801 Vila Real, Portugal

[6] Bialystok University of Technology, 45A, Wiejska Street, 15-351 Bialystok, Poland

Abstract. Nowadays, there has been a growing interest in the use of mobile robots
for various applications, where the analysis of the operational environment is a crucial component to conduct our special tasks or missions. The main aim of this work
was to implement artificial intelligence (AI) for object detection and distance estimation navigating the developed unmanned platform in unknown environments.
Conventional approaches are based on vision systems analysis using neural networks for object detection, classification, and distance estimation. Unfortunately,
in the case of precise operation, the used algorithms do not provide accurate data
required by platforms operators as well as autonomy subsystems. To overcome this
limitation, the authors propose a novel approach using the spatial data from laser
scanners supplementing the acquisition of precise information about the detected
object distance in the operational environment.

In this article, we introduced the application of pretrained neural network
models, typically used for vision systems, in analysing flat distributions of LiDAR
point cloud surfaces. To achieve our goal, we have developed software that fuses
detection algorithm (based on YOLO network) to detect objects and estimate their
distances using the MiDaS depth model. Initially, the accuracy of distance estimation was evaluated through video stream testing in various scenarios. Furthermore,
we have incorporated data from a laser scanner into the software, enabling precise
distance measurements of the detected objects.

The paper provides discussion on conducted experiments, obtained results,
and implementation to improve performance of the described modular mobile
platform.

Keywords: Convolutional Neural Network · Depth Estimation · Point Clouds

A. I. Pereira et al. (Eds.): OL2A 2023, CCIS 1982, pp. 118–131, 2024.
https://doi.org/10.1007/978-3-031-53036-4_9

1   Introduction

Mobile robots have emerged as versatile tools that can be utilized for a wide range of applications, including internal logistics, security operations, reconnaissance, special-purpose field operations, visual inspections as well as demining tasks [1–3]. In conflict-affected regions like Ukraine, the presence of landmines and unexploded ordnance poses a significant threat to civilian populations and hinders post-conflict recovery efforts. The clearance of these hazardous remnants of war is a critical undertaking that requires careful planning, specialized equipment, and skilled personnel. Mobile robots equipped with advanced perception systems have emerged as valuable assets in demining operations, enhancing safety and efficiency while reducing the risk to human lives.

In addition to demining requirements in open outdoor areas, the detection of explosive materials remains a crucial challenge, especially in crowded buildings such as airports, where the persistent threat of terrorism is a concern. Ensuring public safety requires the integration of advanced technologies based on mobile platforms, equipped with innovative navigation systems, to effectively operate in complex indoor environments as well as using some additional devices [4]. Advanced perception systems, such as vision-based object recognition and depth estimation, empower mobile robots to precisely identify and locate suspicious objects.

The versatility of mobile robots in various environments underscores the imperative of their adoption in security operations. Different configurations and constructions have been developed including wheeled, tracked, or legged platforms as well as aerial and underwater unmanned vehicles [5, 6]. Each type of platform offers unique advantages for specific applications and environments. The choice of platform structure depends on factors such as terrain, mobility requirements, payload capacity, and the tasks the robot needs to perform. Researchers and engineers continue to explore and develop innovative platform designs to meet the diverse needs of mobile robotic systems. Moreover, the selection of an appropriate perception system, as well as efficient object analysis and classification algorithms, plays a significant role in enabling accurate and timely decision-making during missions. Certain tasks and missions may demand autonomous modes of operation for mobile robots, which highlights the need for the development of robust navigation algorithms. In the existing literature, numerous methods have been extensively studied and documented, focusing on the integration of vision systems and active sensors such as 3D LiDARs [7, 8]. While vision systems remain a principal component for object recognition and depth estimation, they are susceptible to adverse weather conditions commonly encountered in outdoor environments, such as dust, heavy rain, and fog [9]. These conditions can degrade the accuracy and reliability of vision-based distance estimation. LiDARs offer high-resolution scans and precise distance measurements, making them an attractive alternative.

In this article, the importance of advanced perception systems for mobile robots in special-purpose applications is highlighted. The selection of a suitable perception system, considering environmental conditions and mission objectives is described. Object analysis and classification techniques are introduced. The paper investigates the usage of vision systems for object recognition and depth estimation, discussing their advantages and limitations in different operational environments. Additionally, developed software was examined using pretrained neural network models for analysing flat distributions of LiDAR point cloud surfaces to precise measuring distance from detected object. The conducted experiments, presenting the obtained results and exploring potential implementations for scenarios requiring accurate spatial in special-purpose applications are discussed.

2 Described of Developed Mobile Robot Platform

The developed wheeled mobile robot represents a versatile solution that can be effectively deployed for a wide range of tasks in both indoor and outdoor environments as shown in Fig. 1. Its modular design allows the integration of different modules and components according to operational requirements. Developed architecture enables users to control the robot from a safe distance while also benefiting from its ability to perform tasks autonomously according to advanced defined paths.

a)   b)

Fig. 1. View of developed mobile robot platform (a) and control station (b).

The mobile platform is equipped with key modules including electric drives, batteries, and control panels, as well as electric energy distribution circuits. These modules provide the necessary power and control systems for the robot's movement and overall operation. Their robust design ensures reliable performance in challenging outdoor environments.

The remote operation system is equipped with radio communication modules allowing to transfer control data and vision stream from installed cameras. The onboard computer processes the data received from the robot's sensors, performs advanced algorithms for decision-making, and enables real-time operation (Fig. 2). The radio communication transceivers facilitate reliable and efficient command transmission between the robot and the control station.

The developed platform is suitable for optional modules that can be installed exclusively on the specific mission requirements. One of the proposed integrations (Fig. 3) is a neutron-based explosives detector module that can facilitate demining operations, allowing the robot to identify explosive materials in the environment [10]. Alternatively,

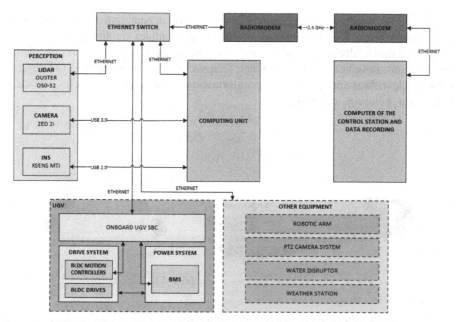

Fig. 2. The modular architecture of the developed mobile robot system.

an observation head module can be employed for reconnaissance purposes, providing enhanced visual capabilities and intelligence gathering capabilities.

Fig. 3. Integration example of the robot equipped with the neutron-based detector [10].

The control station, equipped with a user application as the interface between the operator and the mobile robot. It enables operators to monitor and control the robot's actions, access real-time data, and interact with the robot's functionalities. The user application provides a user-friendly interface that facilitates efficient command and control operations, allowing operators to make informed decisions and adjust the robot's behaviour as needed.

Critical to the robot's operational capabilities is the perception system, which plays a crucial role in environment analysis. The basic system is based on vision and incorporates distinct types of cameras such as stereo, daylight, or thermal, along with optional active sensors like LiDARs or radars. Based on captured data from sensors, the robot can detect objects, estimate distances, and create a detailed understanding of its environment. Perception system allows the robot to navigate through complex layouts, avoid obstacles, and make informed decisions, ensuring safe and efficient operation in various operational environments, both indoors and outdoors. Despite hardware it is required to integrate software algorithms and tools to gather information about objects, obstacles, vehicles, pedestrians, buildings, and more.

a)   b)

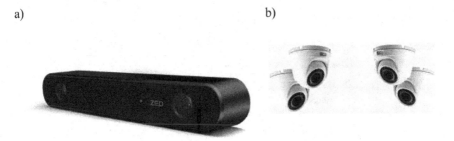

Fig. 4. View of ZED 2 stereo camera (a) and IP cameras (b).

The selection of a vision system for a mobile robot depends on its specific needs and operating conditions, with options ranging from monocular cameras for basic obstacle detection to stereo and RGB-D cameras for enhanced depth perception and environmental analysis. In our mobile platform, we commonly use the ZED 2 stereo camera (Fig. 4) from Stereolabs which has two 4K resolution sensors that capture images from different perspectives with a maximum resolution of 3840×2160 pixels for colour and 2560×720 pixels for depth [11]. In the case of advanced missions like reconnaissance, the integration of the Mobile Surveillance Head can enhance the mobile robot's capabilities. This solution incorporates high-resolution cameras, advanced video analytics, and real-time monitoring, enabling detailed imagery, intelligent object detection, and tracking for enhanced situational awareness and reconnaissance tasks.

Navigation in outdoor environment requires localization technologies that combines GNSS signal and Aided Inertial Navigation System (INS) in conjunction with fitted external wheel speed sensors to provide precise position estimation and motion tracking capabilities. The GNSS signal, received from satellite constellations such as GPS, GLONASS, or Galileo, allows the mobile platform to determine its global position with high accuracy. Processing signals from multiple satellites, the robot can calculate its coordinates and align itself with a global reference system to follow predefined paths or reach specific waypoints. In situations where GNSS signal reception may be disturbed, such as in urban canyons or dense foliage, the Aided Inertial Navigation System (INS) are used to estimate the robot's position, velocity, and orientation using data from accelerometers and gyroscopes.

Unknown environments pose significant challenges for mobile platforms navigation, requiring systems that can accurately perceive and map the surroundings. In some conditions vision-based systems have limitations due to adverse weather conditions like rain, snow, or dust significantly reducing reliable perception and obstacle detection. To overcome these limitations, it is necessary to integrate 3D sensors like LiDARs that emit pulses and utilize time-of-flight measurements [12]. Laser scanners can accurately capture detailed information about the environment, including object distances and positions.

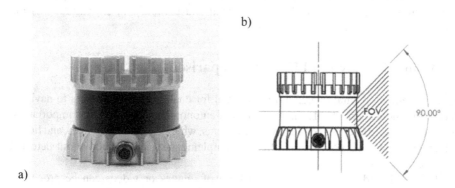

Fig. 5. View of Ouster LiDAR (a) and indicated field of view (b) [17].

The optical signal from the laser is modulated to carry information about the surrounding environment. Analysing the reflected signals, the LiDAR system can gather information not only about distance but also reflectivity and other properties of objects and surfaces in the environment. Combining the distance information from multiple laser pulses, the system can build a real-time 3D map of the environment. This map provides detailed spatial information, allowing the robot to operate effectively in various lighting conditions and weather. LiDARs are not affected by factors such as darkness or precipitation, enabling reliable object detection at a long range. This capability provides early warnings to the path-planning system, enabling the robot to adapt its trajectory accordingly.

In the architecture of developed mobile platform, different type of Ouster LiDARs (Fig. 5) are used due to long-range capabilities and high-resolution imaging resulting in a precise and dense point cloud representation of the surrounding environment. The sensor data is seamlessly integrated into the mobile platform's perception and decision-making systems in real-time through Ethernet communication, using UDP packets (Table 1).

Table 1. Main parameters of used Ouster LiDARs.

Parameter	Ouster OS0-32	Ouster OS1-128
Channels	32	128
Range accuracy	±1.5–5 cm	±0.7–5 cm
Field of view (vertical)	90°	45°
Angular resolution (vertical)	2.125°	0.35°
Points per second	655,360	2,621,440

This integration of the described perception system enables the mobile platform to operate in both indoor and outdoor environments. Remote control and optional autonomous functions can be used for a wide range of tasks, including security operations, reconnaissance, demining, and more. Its modular structure and adaptable sensor and module integration make it a powerful and flexible tool for various mission requirements and operational scenarios.

3   Vision Sensors and LiDARs Comparison

Accurate environmental perception is essential for enabling mobile robots to navigate their surroundings effectively. In the context of autonomous operation, it is important to understand the differences between vision systems, which capture 2D images, and lidars, which generate a 3D point cloud offering complementary information about detected objects.

Data collected from cameras in the form of images or videos can be processed using computer vision techniques to extract valuable information. Vision systems can provide detailed information about the appearance and characteristics of objects in the environment. The following methods are commonly employed for analysing image data [13]:

- Image Segmentation:
  Image segmentation divides an image into multiple segments, where each segment corresponds to a different object in the scene. Techniques such as thresholding, edge detection, or region growing can be used to perform image segmentation. Segments can then be classified as obstacles or other objects of interest. Authors in [18] do an extensive explanation on the subject.
- Object Detection:
  Object detection involves detecting instances of objects within an image, such as vehicles, pedestrians, or buildings. Deep learning-based object detection algorithms, such as Faster R-CNN or YOLO, are commonly used for this task. These algorithms can learn to detect objects of interest by training on large datasets. The innovation in this area is recent and long. For a better understanding, the reader is referred to [19].
- Deep Learning-Based Semantic Segmentation:
  Semantic segmentation assigns a label to each pixel in an image, such as "car," "building," or "obstacle." Deep learning-based semantic segmentation algorithms, such as U-Net or SegNet, can learn to segment an image into different classes of objects. This provides a more detailed understanding of the scene. A comprehensive review can be seen in [20].
- Stereo Vision:
  Stereo vision utilizes two cameras to estimate the depth of objects in a scene, as shown in Fig. 6. Computing disparities between the two images, the depth of each pixel can be estimated. Stereo vision can be used to detect obstacles by identifying regions in the depth image that correspond to objects in front of the camera.

LiDAR-based obstacle recognition presents a different approach, utilizing point cloud data to perceive the environment. LiDAR systems emit laser pulses and measure the time it takes for the pulses to bounce back, allowing for the creation of detailed

Fig. 6. Captured Image from the ZED2i stereo camera.

3D maps. The following methods are commonly used for analysing LiDAR data [14, 21].

- Point Cloud Segmentation:
  Point cloud segmentation involves separating LiDAR data into distinct groups of points that correspond to different objects in the environment. Clustering algorithms, such as the k-means algorithm or the Euclidean clustering algorithm, can be used to group points that are close to each other in space. The resulting clusters can be classified as obstacles or other objects of interest.
- Ground Segmentation:
  Ground segmentation aims to remove ground points from the LiDAR data and extract non-ground objects. The RANSAC (Random Sample Consensus) method is commonly employed, which fits a plane to the ground points and separates them from the rest of the data. The remaining points can then be classified as obstacles.
- Simultaneous Localization and Mapping (SLAM):
  SLAM combines LiDAR data with other sensory information, such as wheel odometry or IMU data, to build a real-time map of the environment. SLAM algorithms can detect obstacles by analysing differences between the current and previous maps and identifying changes corresponding to the presence of obstacles.

Vision systems for mobile robot navigation have limitations that can affect precision, such as sensitivity to lighting, adverse weather conditions and limited field of view. However, these limitations can be overcome by incorporating LiDAR sensors as a separate data source, complementing the capabilities of vision sensors. It should underline that vision sensors provide high-resolution imagery, but LiDAR sensors offer additional parameters such as distance to objects and signal strength (indicated in the scale at the lower right corner), which provide valuable information about the environment (Fig. 7).

A typical environment with dense vegetation poses significant challenges regarding the classification of objects against the complex background. However, the integration of LiDAR technology proves to be highly advantageous in this scenario. LiDAR's ability to capture high-resolution point clouds allows the robot to overcome these challenges and achieve more accurate data.

This information can be particularly useful in scenarios where visual data from cameras may be limited, such as low-light conditions or when objects are partially

a)

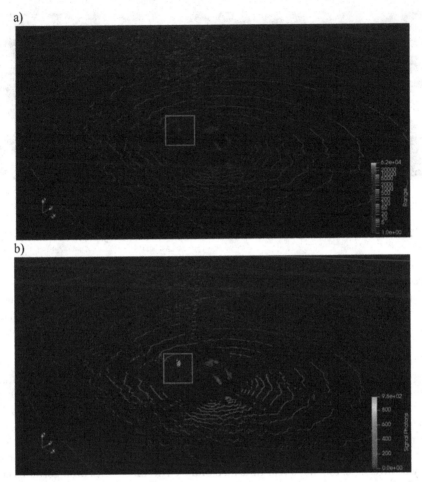

b)

Fig. 7. 3D environment representation considering the distance from the sensor (a) and reflected energy as signal photons (b).

obscured. The proposed approach in the paper uses LiDAR data as source for already trained neutral network for vision system to utilize additional parameters, enabling more accurate object detection, classification, and scene understanding for precise navigation and decision-making in various mobile robot applications.

4 Implementation of AI for Object Recognition in Operational Environment

Precisely measuring the distance to objects is not only important for mobile robot navigation but also critical in certain scenarios like operation in dangerous zones to mitigate any potential risks. This capability to perceive the spatial layout of surroundings in real-time enhances the overall safety and reliability of the unmanned platforms. Accurate distance estimation is particularly critical in operational environments where the robot may encounter complex terrains, dynamic obstacles, or narrow passageways.

Vision systems are valuable sources of object detection for mobile robots, utilizing neural network models (Fig. 8) such as AdaBins for absolute depth maps and MiDaS for inverse depth estimations [15]. These advanced models enhance distance estimation and object recognition, enabling mobile robots to navigate and interact with their environment more effectively, improving their overall capabilities.

For instance, authors in [16] proposed an overall system for monocular depth estimation, shown in Fig. 8. It consists of a front-end CNN with an encoder and decoder (blue blocks) that extracts features and generates an initial depth map from the input image. The researchers propose a Structured Attention guided CRF model (grey box) to refine the depth estimation further. This CRF model incorporates attention maps (green boxes) to highlight essential regions in the image and jointly inferred features (light blue boxes) through a message-passing algorithm. Integrating attention into the CRF framework aims to enhance depth estimation accuracy by leveraging contextual information.

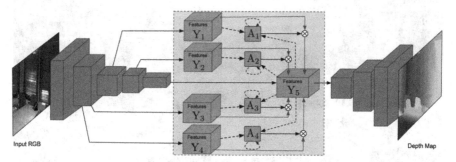

Fig. 8. Architecture for depth estimation using convolutional neural network [16].

In our study, we have evaluated precision of developed model fusing the object detection algorithm You Only Look Once (YOLO) and depth estimation using machine learning model from an arbitrary input image (MiDaS). The model employs a convolutional neural network architecture, specifically a fully convolutional neural network (FCN). The FCN architecture allows the model to take an entire image as input and produce a corresponding depth map. Typically, the depth regression represents the distance of each pixel from the camera in a grayscale, where brighter pixels indicate objects that are closer to the camera and darker pixels represent objects that are quite far.

This software was extensively assessed in operational environments to assess its performance and reliability. Tests were conducted based on typical traffic scenarios to evaluate the accuracy of our distance estimation under good weather, lighting, and environmental conditions.

The results depicted in Fig. 9 rely solely on vision-based distance estimations. Throughout the testing phase, the operational environment division into two zones. ˅ The first one is the Near Zone, encompassing distances up to 4.5 m from the mobile robot, requiring precise operation. This zone demands high accuracy and responsiveness to navigate around nearby obstacles or potential hazards. The second region is the Far

a)

b)

Fig. 9. Examples of detected objects using fused model in operational environment with assigned estimated distance.

Zone, where objects are positioned beyond the 4.5-m, allowing the mobile robot to move freely without hindrance.

Unfortunately, all measurements did not provide the expected level of precision required for effective operation in various conditions. Our investigation highlighted the crucial role of precise distance measurements for efficient operation in dynamic environments, leading us to investigate the integration of LiDAR sensors (that provide precise measured distance as a parameter in their output data).

5 Flat View Projection from LiDAR as Source for AI Models

In our work, we have proposed an innovative approach that combines data from lidars represented as flat images as source (Fig. 10) for already trained neutral network models for object detection. Integrating laser scanner data into the analysis, we achieve precise distance estimation for the detected objects utilizing data from the high-quality OS1-128 LiDAR sensor, based on an existing dataset provided by the manufacturer [17].

Fig. 10. Example of flat view from Ouster OS1–128 LiDAR point cloud surfaces.

Using the same neutral network model YOLO, like in-depth analysis of vision system, we have classified the trained objects in operational environment. After object detection it is possible to accurately determine the distance and gain additional information provided by the Ouster sensor.

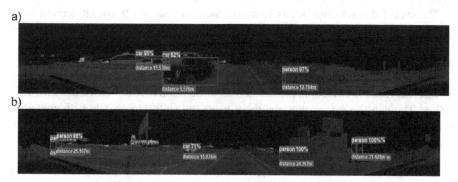

Fig. 11. Examples of detected objects using flat view with assigned precise distance.

The integration of convolutional neural network model (YOLO) for real-time object detection system with laser scanner data in our approach allows achieve precise object detection and accurate distance estimation, as shown in Fig. 11.

Each point has also encoded distance and due to high resolution dense point cloud can be treated like image form camera as source for already trained CNN. Calculating the average distance from a classified set of points (associated with the recognized object) our approach enables accurate localization and distance estimation even in complex spatial environments.

Laser scanners provide precise measurement from dense point cloud that enhance the perception system of mobile robots, enabling comprehensive environmental information. This innovative method opens new possibilities for advanced object detection, accurate length estimation, and leveraging the rich data from laser scanners to improve decision-making in diverse mobile robot applications.

6   Results Discussion

The article presents a detailed overview of a wheeled robot with a modular construction designed to conduct special missions in challenging terrains. These tasks often require precise object detection and accurate distance estimation capabilities. Considering operational capabilities dedicated software was developed that utilizes the YOLO algorithm and the MiDaS model for image analysis. We utilised data collected from unstructured and unexplored environments to validate the estimation model detailed in Sect. 4. Distance estimation was obtained through camera data captured across two distinct settings: one imitating real-world scenarios in densely vegetated surroundings and the other in a characteristic urban structure.

The limitations of vision systems concerning distance estimation are underlined. To overcome this challenge, the authors proposed a solution that uses a developed neural network model to analyse the projection of LiDAR point cloud distributions. This approach provides more accurate and reliable distance information, enhancing the robot's capabilities in terms of situation awareness and control.

The spatial dataset used in this study is based on Ouster 128 output derived from a typical urban landscape. This dataset was obtained by downloading high-resolution point cloud representation with precise distance measurements and flat-view imaging from the manufacturer's website [17].

The proposed approach combining vision systems and LiDAR technology enables the wheeled robot to overcome the limitations of traditional vision-based distance estimation. Through this integration, the robot gains the ability to operate with enhanced precision and efficiency, effectively navigating and perceiving its surroundings. The results of this approach are illustrated in Fig. 11.

Acknowledgments. This work was supported under research work no. 55.23615.PR and 55.2022489.PL at the Military Institute of Armoured and Automotive Technology.

References

1. Petrişor, S.M., Simion, M., Bârsan, G., Hancu, O.: Humanitarian demining serial-tracked robot: design and dynamic modeling. Machines **11**, 548 (2023). https://doi.org/10.3390/machines11050548
2. Rubio, F., Valero, F., Llopis-Albert, C.: A review of mobile robots: concepts, methods, theoretical framework, and applications. Int. J. Adv. Robot. Syst. **16**(2) (2019). https://doi.org/10.1177/1729881419839596
3. Jung, Y.H., et al.: Development of multi-sensor module mounted mobile robot for disaster field investigation. Gottingen Copernicus GmbH (2022). https://doi.org/10.5194/isprs-archives-XLIII-B3-2022-1103-2022
4. Janczak, D., Walendziuk, W., Sadowski, M., Zankiewicz, A., Konopko, K., Idzkowski, A.: Accuracy analysis of the indoor location system based on bluetooth low-energy RSSI measurements. Energies **15**, 8832 (2022). https://doi.org/10.3390/en15238832
5. Janos, R., Sukop, M., Semjon, J., et al.: Conceptual design of a leg-wheel chassis for rescue operations. Int. J. Adv. Robot. Syst. **14**(6) (2017). https://doi.org/10.1177/1729881417743556

6. Russo, M., Ceccarelli, M.: A survey on mechanical solutions for hybrid mobile robots. Robotics **9**, 32 (2020). https://doi.org/10.3390/robotics9020032

7. Guo, Y., Wang, H., Hu, Q., Liu, H., Liu, L., Bennamoun, M.: Deep learning for 3D point clouds: a survey. IEEE Trans. Pattern Anal. Mach. Intell. **43**(12), 4338–4364 (2021). https://doi.org/10.1109/TPAMI.2020.3005434

8. Khan, D., Cheng, Z., Uchiyama, H., Ali, S., Asshad, M., Kiyokawa, K.: Recent advances in vision-based indoor navigation: a systematic literature review. Comput. Graph. **104**, 24–45 (2022). https://doi.org/10.1016/j.cag.2022.03.005. ISSN 0097-8493

9. Zhang, Y., Carballo, A., Yang, H., Takeda, K.: Perception and sensing for autonomous vehicles under adverse weather conditions: a survey. ISPRS J. Photogram. Remote Sens. **196**, 146–177 (2023). https://doi.org/10.1016/j.isprsjprs.2022.12.021. ISSN 0924-2716

10. Silarski, M., Nowakowski, M.: Performance of the SABAT neutron-based explosives detector integrated with an unmanned ground vehicle: a simulation study. Sensors **22**, 9996 (2022). https://doi.org/10.3390/s22249996

11. https://www.stereolabs.com/zed-2/. Accessed 02 June 2023

12. Yang, T., et al.: 3D ToF LiDAR in mobile robotics: a review. arXiv preprint arXiv:2202.11025 (2022)

13. Sivaraman, S., Trivedi, M.M.: Looking at vehicles on the road: a survey of vision-based vehicle detection, tracking, and behavior analysis. IEEE Trans. Intell. Transp. Syst. **14**(4), 1773–1795 (2013)

14. Alaba, S., Gurbuz, A., Ball, J.: A Comprehensive Survey of Deep Learning Multisensor Fusion-based 3D Object Detection for Autonomous Driving: Methods, Challenges, Open Issues, and Future Directions. TechRxiv (2022)

15. Ranftl, R., Bochkovskiy, A., Koltun, V.: Vision transformers for dense prediction. In: 2021 IEEE/CVF International Conference on Computer Vision (ICCV), pp. 12159–12168 (2021). https://doi.org/10.1109/ICCV48922.2021.01196

16. Xu, D., Wang, W., Tang, H., Liu, H., Sebe, N., Ricci, E.: Structured attention guided convolutional neural fields for monocular depth estimation. In: 2018 IEEE/CVF Conference on Computer Vision and Pattern Recognition, pp. 3917–3925 (2018). https://doi.org/10.1109/CVPR.2018.00412

17. https://ouster.com/resources/lidar-sample-data/autonomous-vehicle-sample-data/. Accessed 02 June 2023

18. Wu, Q., Castleman, K.R.: Image segmentation. In: Microscope Image Processing, pp. 119–152. Academic Press (2023)

19. Zou, Z., Chen, K., Shi, Z., Guo, Y., Ye, J.: Object detection in 20 years: a survey. Proc. IEEE **111**(3), 257–276 (2023). https://doi.org/10.1109/JPROC.2023.3238524

20. Minaee, S., Boykov, Y., Porikli, F., Plaza, A., Kehtarnavaz, N., Terzopoulos, D.: Image segmentation using deep learning: a survey. IEEE Trans. Pattern Anal. Mach. Intell. **44**(7), 3523–3542 (2022). https://doi.org/10.1109/TPAMI.2021.3059968

21. Gomes, T., Matias, D., Campos, A., Cunha, L., Roriz, R.: A survey on ground segmentation methods for automotive LiDAR sensors. Sensors **23**(2), 601 (2023)

Adaptive Convolutional Neural Network for Predicting Steering Angle and Acceleration on Autonomous Driving Scenario

Ive Vasiljević[1,2] , Josip Musić[1] , João Mendes[3,4] , and José Lima[3,4(✉)]

[1] Faculty of Electrical Engineering, Mechanical Engineering and Naval Architecture,
Rudera Boskovica 32, 21000 Split, Croatia
ivasil00@fesb.hr
https://eng.fesb.unist.hr/
[2] Polytechnic Institute of Bragança, Campus de Santa Apolónia,
5300–253 Bragança, Portugal
[3] Research Centre in Digitalization and Intelligent Robotics (CeDRI),
Instituto Politécnico de Bragança,
5300–253 Bragança, Portugal
[4] Laboratório Associado para a Sustentabilidade e Tecnologia em Regiões de
Montanha (SusTEC), Instituto Politécnico de Bragança,
5300–253 Bragança, Portugal

Abstract. This paper introduces a novel approach to autonomous vehicle control using an end-to-end learning framework. While existing solutions in the field often rely on computationally expensive architectures, our proposed lightweight model achieves comparable efficiency. We leveraged the Car Learning to Act (CARLA) simulator to generate training data by recording sensor inputs and corresponding control actions during simulated driving. The Mean Squared Error (MSE) loss function served as a performance metric during model training. Our end-to-end learning architecture demonstrates promising results in predicting steering angle and throttle, offering a practical and accessible solution for autonomous driving. Results of the experiment showed that our proposed network is ≈ 5.4 times lighter than Nvidia's PilotNet and had a slightly lower testing loss. We showed that our network is offering a balance between performance and computational efficiency. By eliminating the need for handcrafted feature engineering, our approach simplifies the control process and reduces computational demands. Experimental evaluation on a testing map showcases the model's effectiveness in real-world scenarios whilst being competitive with other existing models.

Keywords: Autonomous Vehicles · End-to-end Learning · CARLA Simulator · Convolutional Neural Network · Deep Learning

1 Introduction

The autonomous driving phenomenon has significantly advanced over the years of its development. The automotive tech industry has made significant enhance-

A. I. Pereira et al. (Eds.): OL2A 2023, CCIS 1982, pp. 132–147, 2024.
https://doi.org/10.1007/978-3-031-53036-4_10

ments to the capability and reliability of sensors, cameras, and vehicle-to-everything (V2X) communication [16]. Collectively, these features generate many consumer benefits, even so, autonomous driving may also produce additional value for the auto industry [17]. To ensure that automotive companies are following a well-established standard, whilst announcing their progress on the state of their autonomous driving systems, Society of Automotive Engineers (SAE), a standards developing organization, has come up with six levels of driving automation. Each level puts less constraint on the human driver, meaning less attention to the road and actions are needed. Additionally, each level contributes with more features, like line centring and adaptive cruise control, automatic emergency break, etc.

The current state of autonomous driving industry is monopolized by the larger companies including Tesla, Ford, Mercedes, General Motors and Kia / Hyundai. Notably, these companies are considered to have the most reliable systems in place, however, they seem to differ in what SAE level they fall into. Yet, the best level most companies have to offer, including once industry leader Tesla, is only Level 2 as defined by the SAE standard [17]. The Level 2 standard includes constant supervision from a human driver, and making specific actions according to the situation to maintain safety. Features provide steering (lane centring) and brake / acceleration support to the human driver, i.e., adaptive cruise control. As of today, Mercedes has rolled out a self-certified Level 3 system. However, this standard needs very specific conditions to work, including the feature requests, where a human driver needs to take over the control of the vehicle. Namely, a Drive Pilot, where the speed won't exceed 45 mph (ca. 72 km/h), conditions of clear weather during the day, and only on road mapped by the system [17].

Thus, these autonomous driving systems are made possible using numerous sensors attached to a car. Hence, these sensors give meaningful information about the environment. Even with all the information available, research suggests that perhaps creating autonomous driving systems was more difficult than first predicted. Evidently, 80% of self-driving is relatively simple - making the car follow the line of the road, stick to a certain side, avoid collisions. The next 10% involves more difficult situations such as roundabouts and complex junctions. The last 10% has proven to be arduous, which covers the problem of "edge cases". They are rare cases that can occur on the road, such as an animal being in the middle of the road, or a child running across the street. These final 20% is why the autonomous driving industry is still not making any significant progress [18].

Whilst developing autonomous driving systems, there are numerous approaches, that include: how many sensors to use, what information to use from those sensors, for what purpose to use them and what algorithms to use alongside these sensors. Sensors like LiDAR (Light Detection and Ranging), radar and camera are among a few that are used to sense the world around them. Furthermore, with the rising popularity of end-to-end learning, Convolutional Neural Network (CNN) has proven to be an efficient tool with providing raw data, processing large amounts, and outputting some meaningful prediction.

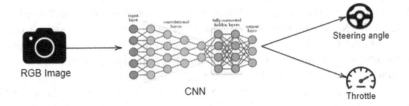

Fig. 1. End-to-end CNN

An abstract representation of an end-to-end CNN architecture is shown on Fig. 1. Firstly, the CNN is presented with a raw image data of the road that gets processed consequently as a by-product of this process, two outputs are predicted, steering angle and throttle. A more detailed explanation of each part of this configuration is presented in the methodology part of this paper, explaining image augmentation, CNN model architecture and types of resulting values. The proposed CNN architecture has proven to be more effective, accurate and with a lower complexity.

2   Related Work

CNN is a powerful tool that essentially takes the images, and transforms them into a format that is simpler to process while preserving the features that are essential for making accurate predictions. This process that is happening inside of CNN includes dealing with feature extractions, pooling layers and kernels. That is exactly what Neocognitron [1] introduced in 1980, being the first architecture of its kind, and perhaps the earliest precursor of CNNs whilst being able to perform recognition (classification). The term Convolutional Neural Network originated with the publication of LeNet [2] and it was mainly developed between 1989 and 1998 with the purpose of recognizing handwritten digits. Up until this point, many more networks have been revealed and, each respectively contributing with their own unique approach and improvements. In 2012, AlexNet [3] was the first winner of the ImageNet challenge and based on CNN. Next, in 2014, VGGNet [4] contributed with one of the major advancements. In 2015, ResNet [5] introduced the idea of "residual blocks" which went to win 1st place in all ILSVRC and COCO 2015 competitions [19]. Thus, evidentially, these networks have made a significant impact in the machine learning domain.

For the development of autonomous driving systems, a combination of different machine learning techniques is often used, including CNNs, reinforcement learning (RL), and imitation learning. In 1989, the pioneering creation of the initial self-driving vehicle, known as ALVINN [6], occurred. ALVINN employed neural networks to identify lines, segment the surroundings, steer its path, and operate autonomously. However, its progress was impeded by sluggish processing capabilities and inadequate data. In recent years, researchers have been exploring the concept of end-to-end learning and in the context of autonomous driving, end-to-end learning gained attention as a potential approach for training autonomous driving systems. Hence, there has been a plethora of research dedicated towards end-to-end learning in autonomous driving, showcasing its potential whilst also uncovering some limitations. Several pivotal works have emerged, each with their own strengths and drawbacks.

The PilotNet [7] by Nvidia introduced an end-to-end learning approach using CNNs for steering prediction. While this work demonstrated promising results, one drawback is that it relied on a vast amount of labelled data, making data collection and annotation a significant challenge.

Another important work, using Convolutional Long Short-Term Memory Recurrent Neural Network (C-LSTM) [8], pioneered the concept of directly mapping sensor inputs to steering commands. However, the limitations of this approach became apparent as it struggled to handle complex driving scenarios or generalize well to unseen situations.

Work submitted by Matthias Müller [9] combined end-to-end learning with imitation learning. While this approach showed promise in incorporating expert demonstrations, one downside is that it heavily relied on the quality and representativeness of the demonstration data, which one notes can be expensive and time-consuming to acquire.

One crucial consideration for successful end-to-end learning models in autonomous driving is the amount of data required. These models often demand vast quantities of labelled training data, which can be a significant bottleneck in terms of data collection, labelling costs, and human effort. In terms of hardware, training these models efficiently require substantial computational resources. Deep learning models used in end-to-end learning for autonomous driving, such as CNNs or RNNs, typically benefit from powerful GPUs or specialized hardware accelerators to handle the massive computational load during training. Considering this, there have been some works using a so called: "Lightweight CNNs" with a main goal of lowering the complexity of the model, so that it can be used on slower hardware with the same performance and accuracy. One such work [10] is using a smaller modified architecture with efficiency and reliability. Another similar work [15], predicts the steering angle and throttle with a lot less data needed for training to accomplish such high efficiency.

The seminal works in the field have undoubtedly laid a solid foundation for our research. Many contemporary alternatives boast lightweight characteristics, promising enhanced efficiency. However, our proposed solution not only upholds the commendable efficiency demonstrated by these modern approaches but truly shines in its small size. This compactness sets our work apart, making it an appealing and pragmatic choice for resource-constrained environments, while still delivering optimal performance. Our proposed architecture uses fewer layers altogether, fewer trainable parameters, also along the steering angle, the model predicts the throttle of the car, regulating the vehicle's speed. We used CARLA simulator [11] with custom-built town maps, with various real-world prosthetics to simulate a vehicle driving on an actual road and environment. With a solid groundwork laid by the past and our innovation addressing the challenges of the present, we proceed to the next section, where we elucidate the intricacies of our methodology.

3   Methodology

In this section of the paper, we will provide a detailed explanation of how the implementation was carried out. The primary focus will be on four key aspects: the setup of the environment, data collection, data preprocessing, and an overview of the network architecture. By explaining each of these implementation steps comprehensively, we aim to provide a clear understanding of how each of these four key aspects were executed, thereby laying the foundation for the subsequent sections of the paper.

3.1   Simulation Environment Setup

In our implementation, we harnessed the power of the CARLA simulator to construct a virtual environment where we could control a vehicle on real-life world roads. CARLA offered a wide range of sensors, including cameras, LiDARs, and radars, providing us with rich perception capabilities. However, for our specific project, we solely utilized the camera sensor to capture RGB images, which served as the only input for our vehicle control system. CARLA operates on the Unreal Engine, a robust and versatile game engine that facilitates the creation of highly realistic and immersive simulations. With its advanced physics engine, the Unreal Engine enabled CARLA to accurately model the behaviour and dynamics of vehicles, ensuring a lifelike driving experience within the simulated environment. This combination of CARLA and the Unreal Engine allowed us to achieve a realistic and adaptable platform for our research and experimentation. CARLA simulator operates using a client-server architecture, where the server generates and maintains the simulation environment, and the client interacts with the server to control vehicles, access sensor data, and receive simulation updates. Setting up CARLA simulator consists of two parts. The first part consists of downloading and installing the prerequisites, with the second part concerning building the simulator itself. The whole process is time-consuming, because of the large number of prerequisites and scripts to run.

In order to stick to the parameters of this paper, we utilized a software called RoadRunner, which is an interactive editor that aids the design of 3D scenes for simulating and testing automated driving systems [20]. Using this software, we created three maps with the typical features. As seen on Fig. 2 maps includes bus stations, roads, trees, hydrants, rubbish cans, street light poles, etc.

The first two maps were used for collecting data (C_Town01 and C_Town02), and the third map (C_Town03) was used for testing the trained network and to observe how a vehicle behaves in a new unexplored environment. Figure 3 depicts how these maps look and their set-up. Once we created the maps in RoadRunner, we exported them, and then did the finishing touches using the Unreal Editor, where we added the traffic signs. Along with some visible features, we also added invisible features, such as, spawn points at specific points on the map, waypoints for the autopilot, and speed limiters.

Houses

Crosswalks and
traffic signs

Bus stations
with trash cans

Houses
with cars

Fig. 2. Custom map's features

3.2 Data Collection

To collect data for training, first we attached a single camera sensor designed for collecting RGB images. The camera was placed at the front of the car, approximately a bit below the vehicle's hood. The vehicle we used during training and testing was a Tesla Model 3. The images were saved to a specific folder using the built-in static function, that saves an image after every frame of the simulation running. The size of the saved images was $300 \times 300 \times 3$. Along with the images, we were also keep track of steering angle and throttle values, by saving all the information inside a .csv file, where each row would represent one unique frame, that comes with an image, steering angle and throttle values. Steering values go from -1 to +1, and throttle values go from 0 to +1. Since CARLA functions at a client-server principle, the simulator was running in a synchronous mode, which means that the client and server were running at the same time. In other words, if the client is too slow, the server will wait for the client to continue executing. This proved to be helpful while collecting data, due to the fact that every frame is registered.

For the best possible quality of the data collected, we were using a built-in autopilot function. The autopilot follows a carefully positioned waypoints, and in doing so, we collected almost precise steering angle values, which will help with the feature of lane centring. Additionally, by adding invisible features, such as speed limiters, we are telling the vehicle to slow down before a cross-walk or to maintain a reasonable speed before a curve. This whole behaviour is simulating

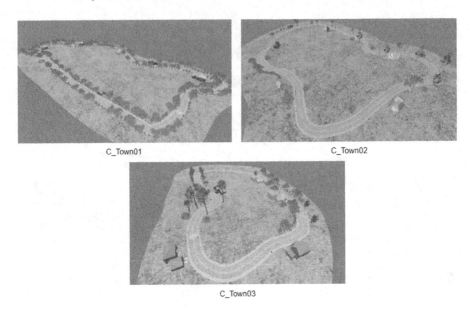

C_Town01

C_Town02

C_Town03

Fig. 3. Custom maps

a human-like driver, due to the problem of controlling a vehicle with a basic keyboard or a joystick produces a lot of noisy data that, as a result, produces an unstable model. At the end of our data collection, we ended up with 100,000 images, where each image correspond to its steering angle and throttle. From these images, two batches are created, each containing 50,000 images. The first batch containing images from the first map (C_Town01) is split into sub-batches consisting of 25,000 images. Each of these sub-batches consists of images from both directions of the road. The same process has been applied to the second batch from the second map (C_Town02).

3.3 Data Preprocessing

After collecting the images, one of the essential parts of the whole process is preprocessing the images before using them for the training. Figure 4 shows how the original images looked when they were captured during the data collection phase. Additionally, important to point out is that the images were captured with a specific attribute of field of view (FOV), with the value of 130. The first step in data preprocessing was resizing images from the dimensions of $300 \times 300 \times 3$ to $224 \times 224 \times 3$. Additionally, after resizing, images were cropped by extracting regions of interest (ROI) from images. After that, the dimensions were reduced to $114 \times 224 \times 3$. Figure 5 depicts how the images looked after cropping them. Lowering the dimensions of the images, lowers the training time significantly, and raises the model's efficiency by extracting important features from the images. The last preprocessing that was applied was image normalisation, which helps

Fig. 4. Original image

Fig. 5. Cropped image

to stabilize the gradient descent step, allowing us to use larger learning rates or help models converge faster for a given learning rate [21]. Figure 6 shows how images looked like after applying normalisation. The images are normalized by subtracting the mean (μ) of each feature and a division by the standard deviation (σ). This way, each feature has a mean of 0 and a standard deviation of 1 [22]. The normalization follows the following formula.

$$x = \frac{x - \mu}{\sigma} \qquad (1)$$

Before normalisation, we had to calculate the mean and standard deviation of our image dataset. We calculated the mean by summing the pixel values divided by the total number of pixel values. After that, we calculated the standard deviation with the following formula.

$$\sigma = \sqrt{E[X^2] - (E[X])^2} \qquad (2)$$

$E[X^2]$ represents the mean of the squared data, while $(E[X])^2$ represents the square of the mean of the data [22].

Fig. 6. Normalized cropped image

3.4 Data Splitting

When the data was collected, we used the first two maps to collect data. Furthermore, we decided to split that data into data for training and data for validation with the ratio of 80:20. We also used data loaders, which help in providing the model with images in specific number of batches. What number of batches is close to optimal is discussed in later sections of the paper. Additionally, every time we would split the data, we would choose randomly which images would be used for training and which for validation. The validation data was used to monitor the state of the model. In some cases it can happen that model overfits, and using the validation data, that can be detected.

3.5 Network Architecture

The proposed architecture draws inspiration from a well-established architecture developed by hminle [23]. The network uses a lightweight approach in the sense of how many convolutional layers were used, while at the same time maintaining high accuracy. During the implementation of the network, we experimented with some parameters, such as the dimensions of the images, batch sizes, colour model for the images and number of features for some layers. After a few experiments, we ended up with the following architecture depicted in Fig. 7. The network is split up into two parts. The first part is concerned with convolution and consists of two convolutional layers, one max-pool layer, one dropout layer and one exponential linear unit (ELU) (activation function). The first convolutional layer has 3×3 kernel size with a stride of 2, then after that come ELU activation function. The second convolutional layer has 3×3 kernel size with a stride of 2. Then comes the max-pooling layer with 4×4 kernel size and a stride of 4. At the end of the first part there is a dropout layer with the dropout rate of 25%. The second part is where we transitioned from convolution to linear neural network by flattening the pooled feature map. In other words, we transformed a two-dimensional shape of data into a one dimension so that we can do further operations on the same data. The first linear layer input's consists of 3,744 neurons and 50 output neurons, which is a direct consequence of the convolutional part of the network. Before the second linear layer, we added an ELU activation function for a better convergence. The second linear layer has 50 input neurons and 10 output neurons, while the last linear layer has 10 input neurons and ends

```
===================================================================================
Layer (type:depth-idx)                    Output Shape              Param #
===================================================================================
CNNModel                                  [64, 1]                   --
├─Sequential: 1-1                         [64, 48, 6, 13]           --
│    └─Conv2d: 2-1                        [64, 24, 56, 111]         672
│    └─ELU: 2-2                           [64, 24, 56, 111]         --
│    └─Conv2d: 2-3                        [64, 48, 27, 55]          10,416
│    └─MaxPool2d: 2-4                     [64, 48, 6, 13]           --
│    └─Dropout: 2-5                       [64, 48, 6, 13]           --
├─Sequential: 1-2                         [64, 2]                   --
│    └─Linear: 2-6                        [64, 50]                  187,250
│    └─ELU: 2-7                           [64, 50]                  --
│    └─Linear: 2-8                        [64, 10]                  510
│    └─Linear: 2-9                        [64, 2]                   22
===================================================================================
```

Fig. 7. Proposed network architecture

with 2 output neurons. Those 2 output neurons are the ones that gave a prediction for our steering angle and throttle. The idea is that after the first part of the network where we ended with convolution and started with fully connected layer, we transformed the ending dimension of $48 \times 6 \times 13$ into a single vector of 3,744 neurons. Those neurons are transferred forward to the fully connected layer. We also used the Adam algorithm with a learning rate of 0.0001.

For keeping track of the network performance during training, we used an MSE loss as a criterion between each element in the input and target, or in other words between our steering angle and throttle that we captured versus predicted steering angle and throttle. MSE criterion uses the following formula to make the difference between two values.

$$MSE = \frac{1}{n} \sum_{i=1}^{n} (y_i - \hat{y}_i)^2 \tag{3}$$

At the end, we ended up with just 198,870 trainable parameters. Where the first part contains 11,088 parameters and the second part 187,762 parameters.

4   Results and Discussion

The proposed architecture was built, trained and tested using Python programming language (v. 3.8.10) and PyTorch (v. 1.13.0+cu117), along with some additional PyTorch utilities (DataLoader, Torchvision, etc.), as well as other Python libraries, such as NumPy (v. 1.23.5) and Pandas (v. 1.5.2). Additionally, we used a machine with an NVIDIA GeForce GTX 1070 with 8 GB GDDR5 memory graphics card. The captured images took just over 16 GB of disk memory, containing 100,000 images in total.

4.1 Experimenting with Different Batch Sizes

Batch size is an important hyperparameter in neural network training that determines the number of training examples used in each iteration. During the training process, the data is divided into batches, and the model's parameters are updated based on the average gradient computed from the loss values of the examples within the batch. The batch size affects the speed, generalisation, and resource utilisation of the training process. Choosing the best batch size depends on several factors, including the nature of the dataset, model complexity, and available resources. There is no universally optimal batch size that works for all scenarios. However, there are some general guidelines, and in the past there has been work done on this matter, which proves that smaller batch sizes are believed to have a higher likelihood of escaping local minima and uncovering the global minimum [12–14]. Due to this, we trained and tested our model using different batch sizes in the range from 16 to 512. Since we noticed that using anything above 512 produced similar results, we stopped there. The results from our work are presented in Table 1. From these results we concluded that indeed, the smaller the batch size, the loss is lower. Additionally, with smaller batch size the convergence is faster, but this comes with one draw back. Generally, training time gets higher with the lower batch size. Since the model has to update its parameters more frequently and taking a smaller batch of images every iteration means the model will take a longer time to go over the whole dataset, and when the batch of images is bigger, it will consume more memory resources. In our case, we got the lowest loss values with a batch size of 16. Training times were not as expected, moreover we expected much longer times with smaller batches, but that was not the case, as the batch size 128 had the smallest training time. Of course, all that matters is the model with the best generalization and loss, so we decided to choose the batch size of 16. Figure 8 shows the training and validation losses during the training process per epoch. The benefits of choosing the batch size of 16 can also be seen on Fig. 9 which depicts how a model with a batch size of 16 converges faster than a model with a batch size of 256.

Table 1. Model results by batch size

Batch size	16	32	64	128	256	512
Training Loss	0.001980	0.002664	0.004344	0.006746	0.012418	0.014073
Validation Loss	0.002752	0.002777	0.003730	0.006049	0.011686	0.012982
Testing Loss	0.036393	0.036763	0.036604	0.038049	0.038737	0.039210
Training time	19236 s	19280 s	19075 s	18779 s	20000 s	19345 s

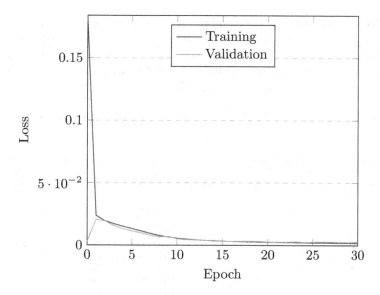

Fig. 8. Training and validation loss

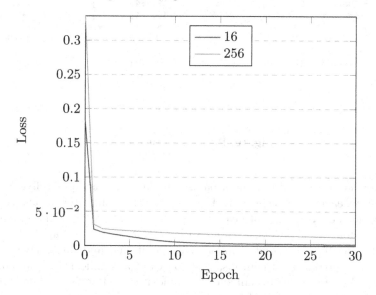

Fig. 9. Convergence difference between two batch sizes - 16 and 256

4.2 Comparison to PilotNet

As an end product, our vehicle manoeuvres around the map without crashing, maintaining the maximum speed of 40 km/h, slowing down when it encounters a cross-walk or a curve, and again speeds up when it finds it suitable to do so. While being a lightweight network and being able to recognize a correlation with an image and steering angle and throttle. Brake has not been implemented, due to the environment being free of obstacles and the regenerative braking of the vehicle is enough to stop the vehicle. Inference time was 0.02 s, and for reliability reasons we ran the simulation in 30 frames per second, to allow the model to react properly to the images. To further strengthen the significance of our model, we decided to compare it to the Nvidia's PilotNet. For a more contextual comparison, the architecture of the PilotNet is shown on Fig. 10.

```
================================================================
Layer (type:depth-idx)            Output Shape          Param #
================================================================
NvidiaModel                       [16, 1]                  --
├─Sequential: 1-1                 [16, 64, 7, 21]          --
│    └─Conv2d: 2-1                [16, 24, 55, 110]      1,824
│    └─ELU: 2-2                   [16, 24, 55, 110]        --
│    └─Conv2d: 2-3                [16, 36, 26, 53]      21,636
│    └─ELU: 2-4                   [16, 36, 26, 53]         --
│    └─Conv2d: 2-5                [16, 48, 11, 25]      43,248
│    └─ELU: 2-6                   [16, 48, 11, 25]         --
│    └─Conv2d: 2-7                [16, 64, 9, 23]       27,712
│    └─ELU: 2-8                   [16, 64, 9, 23]          --
│    └─Conv2d: 2-9                [16, 64, 7, 21]       36,928
│    └─Dropout: 2-10              [16, 64, 7, 21]          --
├─Sequential: 1-2                 [16, 2]                  --
│    └─Linear: 2-11               [16, 100]            940,900
│    └─ELU: 2-12                  [16, 100]                --
│    └─Linear: 2-13               [16, 50]               5,050
│    └─ELU: 2-14                  [16, 50]                 --
│    └─Linear: 2-15               [16, 10]                 510
│    └─Linear: 2-16               [16, 2]                   22
================================================================
```

Fig. 10. PilotNet architecture

The PilotNet consists of two main parts. The first part comprises five convolutional layers, each followed by an ELU activation function. After the last convolutional layer, there is a dropout layer with a dropout rate of 25%. The second part consists of four linear layers, with an ELU activation function applied between the first two. The increased number of convolutional and linear layers, along with more interconnected neurons, contributes to a significantly more complex structure. As a result of this enhanced complexity, the PilotNet is larger in size, leading to a higher number of trainable parameters.

To train the PilotNet we used the same data we used to train our proposed model. Additionally, with the same learning rate, Adam optimizer, and MSE loss. Table 2 shows the comparison between PilotNet and our network.

PilotNet has lower training and validation losses, but whereas our proposed network has a lower testing loss and the overall lower size of the network. Number of trainable parameters is $\approx$ 5.4 times lower. Furthermore, the network size is $\approx$ 5.3 times lower. This makes our proposed network much more suitable for lower end hardware, that is in need for the same kind of performance and

Table 2. Comparison between PilotNet and our proposed network

Network	Proposed Network	PilotNet
Training Loss	0.001980	0.000668
Validation Loss	0.002752	0.001589
Testing Loss	0.036393	0.039372
Training time	19236 s	19706 s
Network size	0.80 MB	4.31 MB
No. of parameters	198,870	1,077,830

efficiency. All in all, our proposed network shows some notable advantages when compared against PilotNet using the same data, and testing in the same context.

5 Conclusion

Our work presented a novel approach to predicting steering angle and throttle in autonomous vehicles using a simple and lightweight architecture. Our proposed model showcased impressive performance on the testing map, demonstrating its effectiveness in real-world scenarios. Furthermore, our study highlights the concept of end-to-end learning in autonomous vehicles. End-to-end learning refers to a paradigm where a single neural network is trained to directly map sensor inputs to control outputs, such as steering and throttle. This approach eliminates the need for handcrafted feature engineering and allows the system to learn representations and control policies directly from raw sensor data. It is worth noting that while our architecture achieved remarkable results, there are alternative approaches available in the field. These alternatives often employ architectures with significantly higher numbers of parameters, leading to increased computational complexity. Comparing our proposed network against PilotNet, our proposed network has a lower testing loss and is significant lighter than PilotNet. In summary, our research showcases the potential of lightweight architectures for predicting steering angle and throttle, providing a promising avenue for further advancements in autonomous driving technology. By offering a balance between performance and computational efficiency, our model open up possibilities for deploying autonomous systems in various real-world applications, while reducing the computational demands and implementation complexities associated with other architectures.

Acknowledgment. The authors are grateful to the Foundation for Science and Technology (FCT, Portugal) for financial support through national funds FCT/MCTES (PIDDAC) to CeDRI (UIDB/05757/2020 and UIDP/05757/2020) and SusTEC (LA /P/0007/2021).

References

1. Fukushima, K.: Neocognitron: a self-organizing neural network model for a mechanism of pattern recognition unaffected by shift in position. Biol. Cybern. **36**, 193–202 (1980)
2. Lecun, Y., Bottou, L., Bengio, Y., Haffner, P.: Gradient-based learning applied to document recognition. Proc. IEEE **86**(11), 2278–2324 (1998). https://doi.org/10.1109/5.726791
3. Krizhevsky, A., Sutskever, I., Hinton, G.: ImageNet classification with deep convolutional neural networks. Neural Inf. Proc. Syst. **25**,(2012). https://doi.org/10.1145/3065386
4. Simonyan, K., Zisserman, A.: Very deep convolutional networks for Large-Scale image recognition. Preprint at. https://arxiv.org/abs/1409.1556
5. Kaiming, H., Xiangyu, Z., Shaoqing, R., Jian, S.: Deep residual learning for image recognition. Preprint at. https://arxiv.org/abs/1512.03385
6. Pomerleau, D.A.: ALVINN: an autonomous land vehicle in a neural network. In: Proceedings of the 1st International Conference on Neural Information Processing Systems (NIPS'88). MIT Press, Cambridge, MA, USA, pp. 305–313
7. Bojarski, M., Del Testa, D., Dworakowski, D., Firner, B. Flepp, B., Goyal, P., et al.: End to End Learning for Self-Driving Cars. Preprint at. https://arxiv.org/abs/1604.07316
8. Navarro P.J., Miller L., Rosique F., Fernández-Isla C., Gila-Navarro A.: End-to-End deep neural network architectures for speed and steering wheel angle prediction in autonomous driving. Preprint at. https://arxiv.org/abs/1710.03804
9. Codevilla, F., Muller, M., Lopez, A., Koltun, V., Dosovitskiy, A.: End-to-end driving via conditional imitation learning. Preprint at. https://arxiv.org/abs/1710.02410
10. Imtiaz Ul, H., Huma, Z., H.Sundus, F., Syed Adnan, Y., Muhammad, K., Noé López P.: A lightweight convolutional neural network to predict steering angle for autonomous driving using CARLA Simulator. Model. Simul. Eng. 2022 (2022). https://doi.org/10.1155/2022/5716820
11. Dosovitskiy, A., Ros, G., Codevilla, F., Lopez, A., Koltun, V.: CARLA: an open urban driving simulator. Preprint at. https://arxiv.org/abs/1711.03938
12. Keskar Shirish, N., Mudigere, D., Nocedal, J., Smelyanskiy, M., Tang, P. T. P.: On large-batch training for deep learning: generalization gap and sharp minima. Preprint at. https://arxiv.org/abs/1609.04836
13. Dinh, L., Pascanu, R., Bengio, S., Bengio, Y.: Sharp minima can generalize for deep nets. Preprint at. https://arxiv.org/abs/1703.04933
14. Kandel, I., Castelli, M.: The effect of batch size on the generalizability of the convolutional neural networks on a histopathology dataset. ICT Express **6**(4), 312–315 (2020)
15. Zhang, J., Huang, H., Zhang, Y.: A convolutional neural network method for self-driving cars. In: Australian and New Zealand Control Conference (ANZCC). Gold Coast, QLD, Australia **2020**, pp. 184–187 (2020). https://doi.org/10.1109/ANZCC50923.2020.9318398
16. The State of Level 3 Autonomous Driving in 2023: Ready for the Mass Market?. https://autocrypt.io/the-state-of-level-3-autonomous-driving-in-2023/. Accessed 4 Jun 2023
17. The State of Self-Driving Cars: Autonomous Advances. https://www.techspot.com/article/2644-the-state-of-self-driving-cars/. Accessed 4 Jun 2023

18. How self-driving cars got stuck in the slow lane. https://www.theguardian.com/technology/2022/mar/27/how-self-driving-cars-got-stuck-in-the-slow-lane. Accessed 4 Jun 2023
19. Convolutional Neural Networks: A Brief History of their Evolution. https://medium.com/appyhigh-technology-blog/convolutional-neural-networks-a-brief-history-of-their-evolution-ee3405568597. Accessed 6 Jun 2023
20. RoadRunner. https://www.mathworks.com/products/roadrunner.html. Accessed 6 Jun 2023
21. Using Normalization Layers to Improve Deep Learning Models. https://machinelearningmastery.com/using-normalization-layers-to-improve-deep-learning-models. Accessed 6 Jun 2023
22. How To Calculate the Mean and Standard Deviation - Normalizing Datasets in PyTorch. https://towardsdatascience.com/how-to-calculate-the-mean-and-standard-deviation-normalizing-datasets-in-pytorch-704bd7d05f4c. Accessed 8 Jun 2023
23. Car Behavioral Cloning using PyTorch. https://github.com/hminle/car-behavioral-cloning-with-pytorch/. Accessed 11 Jun 2023

Deep Learning-Based Classification and Quantification of Emulsion Droplets: A YOLOv7 Approach

João Mendes[1,3(✉)] , Adriano S. Silva[1,2,3] , Fernanda F. Roman[2,3] ,
Jose L. Diaz de Tuesta[4] , José Lima[1,3] , Helder T. Gomes[2,3] ,
and Ana I. Pereira[1,3]

[1] Research Centre in Digitalization and Intelligent Robotics (CeDRI), Instituto
Politécnico de Bragança, 5300-253 Bragança, Portugal
{adriano.santossilva,jllima,apereira}@ipb.pt
[2] Centro de Investigação de Montanha (CIMO), Instituto Politécnico de Bragança,
5300-253 Bragança, Portugal
{roman,htgomes}@ipb.pt
[3] Laboratório Associado para a Sustentabilidade e Tecnologia em Regiões de
Montanha (SusTEC), Instituto Politécnico de Bragança, 5300-253 Bragança, Portugal
joaocmendes@ipb.pt
[4] Chemical and Environmental Engineering Group, ESCET, Rey Juan Carlos
University, Madrid, Spain
joseluis.diaz@urjc.es

Abstract. This study focuses on the analysis of emulsion pictures to understand important parameters. While droplet size is a key parameter in emulsion science, manual procedures have been the traditional approach for its determination. Here we introduced the application of YOLOv7, a recently launched deep-learning model, for classifying emulsion droplets. A comparison was made between the two methods for calculating droplet size distribution. One of the methods, combined with YOLOv7, achieved 97.26% accuracy. These results highlight the potential of sophisticated image-processing techniques, particularly deep learning, in chemistry-related topics. The study anticipates further exploration of deep learning tools in other chemistry-related fields, emphasizing their potential for achieving satisfactory performance.

Keywords: YOLOv7 · Image processing · Learning method

1 Introduction

Emulsions are systems comprised of two immiscible liquids in which one liquid is dispersed in the other. There are many applications of emulsions in cosmetics, personal care products, pharmaceutical, and food industries [23]. Due to the high surface energy between the two immiscible liquids, the system is thermodynamically unstable and tends to separate. Conventional emulsions are stabilized by amphiphilic polymers or surfactants that reduce the lipophilic-hydrophilic

A. I. Pereira et al. (Eds.): OL2A 2023, CCIS 1982, pp. 148–163, 2024.
https://doi.org/10.1007/978-3-031-53036-4_11

interfacial tension and form a molecular film around the liquid droplet [11]. The conventional methods explored to stabilize emulsified systems have drawbacks associated with foaming, biological interactions, and air entrapment. For this reason, one alternative explored in the literature is the stabilization of emulsions using solid particles [3]. Emulsions formed exploring this particular strategy are known as Pickering emulsions. The scientists Ramsden [17] and Pickering [15] were the first scholars to study the stabilization of colloidal suspensions using solid particles at the beginning of the 20th century.

The stabilization mechanism of Pickering emulsions is related to the partial adsorption of solid particles by both oil and water phases (*i.e.*, dual wettability). The driving force stabilising the emulsion is decreasing the surface energy between the immiscible liquids. Several factors need to be considered to understand the energy-related mechanisms behind emulsion formation, such as the interaction between particles and both interfaces [1]. Pickering emulsions can be categorized as oil-in-water (O/W) emulsions (stabilized by hydrophilic particles) and water-in-oil (W/O) emulsions (stabilized by hydrophobic particles) [27]. In the last few years, scholars have also demonstrated that using amphiphilic particles (interacts with both oil and water phase) can lead to higher stability of the emulsions [14].

No matter the application one is exploring for the Pickering emulsions, one of the most important parameters affecting the performance of the emulsion is the droplet size. The quantitative methods applied to determine this important property have several issues to be solved. For instance, the main challenge in this task is the lack of proper techniques to process many images and avoid misleading calculations. For instance, there are software able to process images of regular emulsions and perform a reasonable identification and determination of droplet sizes, such as the open-source ImageJ (see https://imagej.nih.gov/ij/index.html). However, the higher complexity of Pickering emulsion images does not allow the software to identify and quantify the droplet. In this scenario, the alternative used by scholars is the manual counting of the images, a process that demands exhaustive time and may lead to the misclassification of images due to biased analysis and human error. The complete task can be divided into steps, starting with the droplet selection, area measurement, conversion to real scale based on resolution and amplification, and finally the droplet size distribution analysis. The most challenging aspect of the task is the droplet identification and area measurement.

In this scenario, the utilization of advanced image processing technologies could be used to improve the process of Pickering emulsion analysis. Object detection algorithms in deep learning are one example of an information and communication tool that could be used to analyze the entire microstructure characteristics of large amounts of sample images. These algorithms have been largely applied in self-driving cars [12], facial recognition [9], disease detection [25], and the agricultural sector [21]. By using various images and extracting feature vectors in object detection, the algorithm can recognize specific targets in the images and classify them according to the desired characteristic. Despite the considerable number of applications of deep learning algorithms for a wide variety of object detection, few studies are devoted to the analysis of emulsion images to classify and quantify droplet size.

Therefore, in this work, Pickering emulsions were prepared using carbon nanotubes and 50/50% oil/water mixture. The emulsion images were recorded with an electronic microscope, and YOLOv7 (You Only Look Once) was used to process the images and classify the droplets. The parameters of interest (*i.e.*, average droplet size and droplet size distribution) were further determined based on 2 methods. The first method was based on the droplet's dimension, and the second used a more sophisticated technique to determine the average diameter of the droplet. The results obtained with the algorithms applied were compared to the human classification of the images to validate the methodology and study both methods' performance. The rest of the paper is organized to present the most relevant literature in Sect. 2, the methodology used in Sect. 3, the results and discussion in Sect. 4, and the conclusion in Sect. 5.

2   Related Literature

The research to explore the utilization of image processing techniques applied to Pickering emulsions is very scarce, which makes it difficult to find relevant literature on this topic. For this reason, to amplify the search and find more related studies, the keywords "droplet size" and "image processing" were used to gather the most relevant literature in Scopus and Web of Science databases. The results were processed in the Scientopy application to remove the duplicates, and Fig. 1 brings an overview of the most relevant keywords among the published studies.

The literature analysis result revealed a few works dedicated to exploring the utilization of ICT tools applied in droplet size distribution calculation. Nonetheless, the works reported in the literature are devoted to applying the algorithms in other contexts of droplet size analysis rather than Pickering emulsions. The overall advance published will be briefly reviewed in the next sections.

2.1   General Strategies

The chemistry field is enriched with applications demanding particle size distributions, from emulsion sizes to aerosol particle sizes. No matter the application, the need to explore new strategies to determine particle or droplet size is constant. For this purpose, some authors have reported methods and algorithms based on different strategies, such as digital image processing, laser image processing, and learning techniques. Some of the methods depend on further modifications in the sample studied or even the use of specific equipment to capture the images. The utilization of dynamic light scattering analysis has been accepted in the field as a more reliable and accurate technique. However, the operation of the equipment has several drawbacks, such as the effect of the photomultiplier coupled in the equipment on the particle size distribution due to interaction with

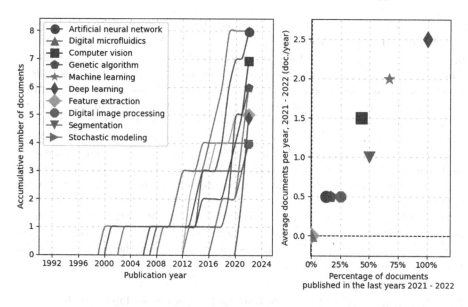

Fig. 1. Evolution of most relevant keywords amongst the published studies.

the sample. Additionally, the technique relies on the low value of droplet/particle for better results, which limits the utilization of the equipment for a wide variety of samples.

For instance, Schuster *et al.* have studied the statistical image processing of Confocal Laser Scanning Microscopy (CLSM) to determine the droplet size distribution of water-in-oil-in-water emulsions (double emulsion) [22]. The CLSM technique is widely used to study single emulsions, but the equipment is not used to classify and quantify double emulsions due to problems recording the images. In light of this limitation, the authors presented one methodology to analyze double emulsions by coupling experimental procedures with statistical image processing. For this purpose, the authors have explored the effects of slicing and limited image field of view on accurately determining droplet size distribution, comparing the results obtained with other measuring techniques. The main contribution of this paper is to present algorithms for error correction and estimation of a statistically relevant number of objects. The strategy was validated using one specific type of double emulsions that were measured by another technique already accepted by the scientific community. Despite the interesting approach shown in this study, the counting process previous to the algorithm applied to enable the utilization of this equipment to study the specific emulsion was performed in ImageJ software. Furthermore, the strategy was validated for only one emulsified system type, making it difficult to predict if the strategy can be used for other similar emulsions.

Jin *et al.* have studied the utilization of advanced image processing techniques to determine droplet size distribution in the dispersed flow film boiling regime during the reflood state [8]. In these systems, the size of the liquid droplets in the gas stream is important because they determine the thermal-hydraulic behavior of the two-phase mixture, which can significantly affect the reactor operation. The system used by the authors is based on utilising a system known as Oxford Lasers Firefly Imaging system, which can be used for droplet data measurement and analysis. The system comprises various components, including an infrared laser, a high-resolution camera, control equipment, and the software VisiSize. The software is mainly responsible for image processing and operates based on stages. First, the software will distinguish particle shadows from illuminated backgrounds. Next, the software will exclude blurred particles hindering further image processing steps. After analyzing the degree of droplet sphericity, border contact condition, and focus criterion, the software returns the size distribution of up to 1000 particles per frame captured. The application of the advanced image processing system proposed by the authors in this application is well described in the paper. Still, the overall discussion is based on utilising the proposed system, which represents a drawback.

2.2   Learning Algorithms Applied to Droplet Size Distribution

Learning algorithms were also studied for measuring particle or droplet size distribution in different chemistry fields. Farzi *et al.*, for example, have published a study showing the utilization of convolutional neural networks (CNN) algorithm for in-situ measurement of spherical and non-spherical droplets in the emulsion [5]. The results were compared to measurement using a laser diffraction analyzer to validate the algorithm's performance. The authors presented the detailed procedure using a new algorithm based on both CNN and Linear Matrix Inequality (LMI) to analyze images in a semi-simultaneous system that allows real-time monitoring of droplet size, which greatly impacts the reaction studied. The main challenge approached by the authors is related to edge detection in a dynamic and non-disturbed system, allowing one to obtain information close to the real reaction conditions. For this purpose, the authors used a training template for noise reduction and edge detection of CNN, which they named LMI. The CNN used is a 2D model based on the connection of the processing units with neighbors, so only near cells can affect each other during the algorithm runs. Despite the interesting study presented in this paper, the authors did not mention the ability of their algorithm to analyze static images of emulsions, which could be interesting to increase the versatility of their approach.

Zhang *et al.* have presented one alternative for measuring microdroplet size distribution using deep learning technique in their study [28]. The proposed method can segment microdroplets with deep learning, fitting the boundaries to obtain precise size distribution curves. Their results demonstrated that even small-sized satellites and overlapped droplets are accounted for, which other studies in this strand did not achieve. The authors have shown that their method improves by around 1000 times the measurement performed manually, achieving errors as low as 0.75 μm. The method proposed is based on instant segmentation of the images to distinguish between shapes and fit according to the shape to determine accurately the size distribution. The main feature of this work is the segmentation method, which is divided into feature extraction, region proposal, and result interference steps. This detailed image analysis of the figures allows for improving the precision of identifying single droplets, improving the overall measurement and classification of the droplets as a consequence.

Another study published by Patil *et al.* presented one alternative for measuring droplet size in fluid-fluid dispersions using the Faster R-CNN method [13]. The strategy explored by the authors represents an improvement to be implemented in the traditional microscopic probes inserted in chemical reactors to collect images to characterize dispersion behaviors. Usually, the technique used to characterize the system is known as the multi-stage filtered Hough method. In their work, the authors compared the droplet detection performance of their algorithm with the traditional method, yet compared both strategies with manual detection. The system considered to perform the experiments was a stirred tank with Exxsol D80 oil emulsion. The results demonstrated that the Faster R-CNN method overcame the performance of the traditional advanced filtered Hough. The Faster R-CNN used by the authors comprises two modules: the first is responsible for identifying candidate regions for potential objects, and the second is responsible for performing the measurements and confirming the droplet presence in the potential region.

The development of image-processing techniques to analyze Pickering emulsions is scarce in the literature. For instance, one paper published by Huang *et al.* discusses using deep learning techniques to classify and quantify Pickering emulsions [6]. Their paper presented a new technique for evaluating Pickering emulsions through classification and quantification using an object detection algorithm. The trained neural network used by the authors can distinguish between different individual emulsion droplets and morphological mechanisms from the studied system. The capabilities of their algorithm include the classification of the emulsion morphology, the microstructure abundance, the statistical analysis of individual droplets, properties correlation, and the quantification of emulsion droplets. The breakthrough methodology adopted by the authors represents one step forward to understanding the correlation between the emulsions properties and the images loaded with lots of data that were not being properly used. Despite the interesting development presented in this study, the quantification mechanism explored could be improved to allow quantification during the image recordings, for example. Furthermore, the lack of studies in this particular application represents one opportunity to seek for alternative solutions to classify and quantify Pickering emulsion droplets.

3   Methodology

This section will discuss the applied methodology to prepare the materials used to stabilize the Pickering emulsions, the preparation of the emulsions, and the techniques used to classify and quantify the droplets. The methodology for preparing materials and emulsions will be discussed briefly since the study's main goal is related to the image-processing technique presented for the classification and determination of droplet size distribution of the emulsions. Figure 2 brings a graphical representation of the study performed.

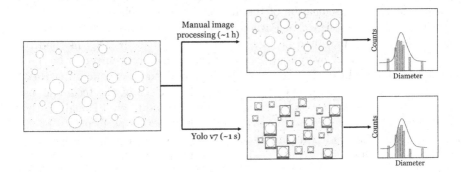

Fig. 2. Graphical illustration of the study performed.

3.1 Carbon Nanotubes Synthesis, Emulsion Preparation and Recording

The Carbon Nanotubes (CNTs) used in this study were prepared by Chemical Vapor Deposition using pure polyolefin as the carbon source and a metal substrate in a one-chamber reactor equipped with three heating zones, as described in other study [4]. In brief, the metal substrate was synthesized by adapting a sol-gel procedure for the obtention of nickel ferrite supported on alumina. This material was further loaded in the lower zone of the CNTs reactor, and a 5 g of a mixture of polypropylene (40%), low-density polyethylene (35%), and high-density polyethylene (25%) was loaded in the upper zone. The material recovered from the reactor was washed with sulfuric acid 50% (v/v) solution to remove metal impurities (140 °C for 3 h).

The Pickering emulsions were prepared following the procedure described in a previous study [19]. In brief, a mixture of 2, 2, 4-trimethylpentane and water (pH 3.0) at an oil-water ratio (O/W) of 50:50 was mixed with the material (2.5 g L^{-1}). The emulsion was formed by sonication (Ultrasounds-H, JP-Selecta) for at least 10 min. The emulsified layer was observed in a Nikon Eclipse 50i coupled to a Nikon digital sight DS-SM camera. The images captured are a static representation of the emulsion state.

The emulsion is formed between thin-layered lamels, ensuring droplet formation occurs in a 2D shape. For this reason, the images acquired following this methodology will have no droplet overlapping problems.

3.2 Image Processing

Choosing the best method for classifying images is one of the most important processes to determine droplet size distribution, this will be responsible for identifying and counting all of the droplets, even though the area detection process is a separate process from this as shown in the Fig. 3 will have all its structure linked to the first stage the identification [10]. In this way, considering the number of algorithms available for this purpose, two were selected, and several tests were carried out by comparison. The choice of methods relied mainly on their speed and ease of application, opting for one-stage identification methods, namely two versions of the YOLO model were chosen, the V4 version and the V7 version. The first serves as a ground truth based on the principle that it is a stable model with several proven results in the most diverse areas, from autonomous driving [2] to the agronomic [20], and the second takes advantage of the author's announced improvements like the speed and accuracy [26].

Similar processes were performed for both algorithms, the first step was the creation of a dataset duly annotated and adapted to the problem in question. To this end, considering the problem's difficulty, which can exceed 500 objects in just one image, a small but representative dataset (32 images) was used. The images, all in RGB format with different sizes, of Pickering emulsions were properly annotated by a qualified technician, varying his annotations between 3 objects and 191. This dataset used 26 images (80%) to train the algorithms and the remaining 6 to validate (20%).

The second step is the pre-processing of the images, here, normalization and resize techniques are applied taking into account the input of the algorithm in question. In this step, divergences between the algorithms emerge, with the YOLOv4 version trained with 416×416 images and the YOLOv7 version 640×640. The remaining parameters of the algorithms were kept in their original default, with only the necessary parameters being changed to adapt the training to the machine used. In the YOLOv4 training, the Darknet [18] framework was used, and the pre-trained weights of AlexeysAB's Darknet[1] (yolov4.con.137). These were trained during 5000 iterations, using an NVIDIA RTX3060 graphics card with 6GB RAM, with the best weights being kept based on Precision, Recall, Mean Average Precision (mAP), and Intersection over Union (IoU). The YOLOv7 training process was similar to its competitor, however, the darknet framework was not used, and the GPU used was an Nvidia TITAN V with 12GB RAM. The number of training batches was also changed to 8 instead of the 64 used in YOLOV4. The training process was also 5000 iterations with the best results appearing approximately 300 iterations earlier in YOLOv7. In both cases, the versions of the libraries were similar, using version 4.7.0.72 of OpenCV [7] and version 0.2.7 of CVlib [16] in the case of YOLOv4, as programming language version 3.6.13 of Python was used, combined with version 11.7 of CUDA on both devices.

Its performance was measured according to a test group of 21 images never seen before by any of the algorithms. In this process, the algorithms detected objects for each image, and this number was compared with the detection of the qualified technician. Here the results demonstrate an advantage of YOLOv7, essentially in images with a greater number of objects, showing the ability to detect smaller objects in the image. Also, the metrics used reveal a better behav-

---

[1] https://github.com/AlexeyAB/darknetaccessedinMay20,2023.

ior of YOLOv7, thus choosing the classification algorithm to be used. Once the best classification algorithm for the problem in question was chosen, the area of each of the droplets was counted. For this, two different algorithms were developed.

The first method resorts only to the clipping performed by the classification algorithm. The bounding boxes presented by the classification algorithm are considered. The smallest side value of the bounding box is used, and from this, the area of the circle is calculated assuming that the smallest side is the diameter.

The second algorithm (Fig. 3) is more complex, using some segmentation techniques. It starts with transforming the clipping provided by the classification algorithm and changing it from its RGB format to the Gray format. From this, the area of the bounding box in question is calculated, and the pixels of the four edges are measured (assuming that these are external to the droplet), obtaining their average. In continuity, the values corresponding to the height and width of the bounding box are read, from which the area of the droplet will be estimated, taking into account that if any of the sides is greater than twice the opposite side, we are working with only half of a droplet, forcing to redo the area calculations. A radius tolerance is also calculated in parallel with this process, equivalent to $radius*0.2$, and the center of the droplet is measured. With these data an average of the pixels (circular) with the center in the center of the droplet and with a radius of the radius tolerance is figured, assuming that these pixels constitute the coloration inside. Next, the averages of the outer pixels are compared with those of the inner ones to segment the image using threshold techniques. In this case, an inverted binary threshold was used (all values above the threshold are replaced by zero and the rest by 255) if the internal mean exceeds the external mean. In the inverse case, the opposite function is used (all values above the threshold value are replaced by 255 and the remaining 0). Finally, using the segmented image, for both cases, the OpenCV library's contour identification function is used to contour the pixels in the form present in Fig. 3. The largest identified contour is selected from this list of identified contours, and an area value is taken from it. This value is also used to carry out another condition that if the identified area is less than 65% and greater than 85% of the bounding box, it must be ignored and must be considered as the final value of the droplet area 0.75% of the bounding box area if on the other hand, it is between these values, the calculated value must be assumed as the final value of the area.

4   Results and Discussion

This section will present the results obtained for image classification considering different conditions. All the images used to evaluate the performance of the methods and YOLOv7 were different from the training dataset (independent validation). The tool's capacity to classify the images was evaluated based on the number of droplets identified with the tool and manually. The best training condition was further used to classify and quantify the images according to the 2 methods described in more detail in Sect. 3.

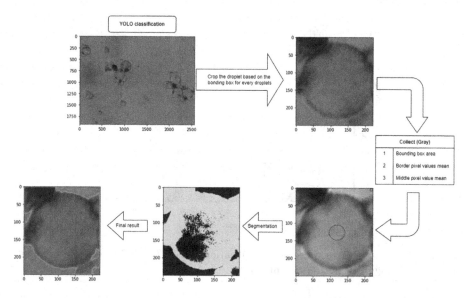

Fig. 3. Second method structure.

4.1   Classification

The number of droplets identified with YOLOv7 was compared to those identified with a manual procedure using ImageJ software. For this purpose, 10 images from the test dataset (not used for training) were randomly chosen, and the result obtained is shown in Fig. 4.

On average, images with many droplets can take as long as 2 h to be analyzed. Using YOLOv7, the results can be obtained within a couple of seconds, which is a significant improvement compared to manual counting. The result obtained here demonstrates that YOLOv7 found the droplets with errors in the range of 4.3%–18% (average 12.2% error) when compared with the ground truth of the technician's identification. The error in the classification of Pickering emulsion is mainly related to the presence of particles in the pictures, which increases the difficulty for the algorithm to find the droplets based on the training. Nonetheless, the error found in this work is acceptable, considering the tool's efficiency assessed here. It is important to highlight that identifying the number of droplets is only one step of this study, and the real efficiency of the complete strategy should be assessed considering the average droplet size and droplet size distribution, which is the main goal here.

4.2   Quantification

In most cases, the determination of average droplet size is not representative enough to illustrate the nature of an emulsion. For this reason, most studies report the droplet size distribution of the studied samples. Here, the average

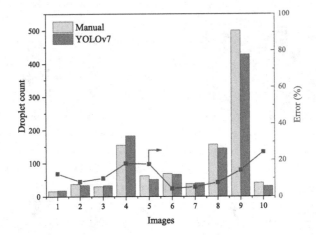

Fig. 4. Comparison between droplet classification using YOLOv7 (green) and manual procedure (orange). (Color figure online)

size was determined based on manually counting the validation dataset and the 2 methods. The results obtained were then compared graphically using a scatterplot (Fig. 5) that compares the set of YOLOv7 results with reference data (parity plot) to evaluate the performance of both methods.

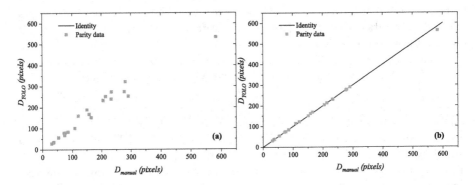

Fig. 5. Parity plot obtained using the (a) first method, and the (b) second method.

The results demonstrate that both methods have a considerable performance to determine the average droplet size compared to manual handling of the images. On average, a human can take as long as 2 h to perform the task, and the most common practice is cropping the image in the most representative region to perform the counting task. However, this can lead to biased image analysis since the analyst might consider the region that will return the most interesting result. On the other hand, YOLOv7 can process the complete image and return a most representative droplet counting, which can help further discussions that depend on the droplet size. Despite the good performance of both methods considering the processing time to return the response, the second method has an increased performance compared to the first. For instance, the average error obtained for the second method is 2.74%, whereas the first method had an average error of 22.5% in average droplet size determination.

The increased performance of the second method compared to the first one is related to the technique considered for each method. The first method has a simpler assumption to determine the droplet diameter, which is not considering the different droplet shapes to determine the most representative diameter. In contrast, the second method is based on an algorithm that can accurately determine the droplet frontiers based on the combination of pixels found in this region. The most accurate determination of the droplet region leads to increased precision in determining the droplet diameter.

As mentioned, the average droplet size is often presented along with droplet size distribution, which is the most useful data representation technique to study emulsion dispersibility. In other words, the average alone cannot illustrate how dispersed the droplets are in a sample. A comparison between the best and worst average droplet size results obtained with the training images is represented in Fig. 6.

The best (image 9) and worst (image 2) results obtained for average droplet size revealed significant visual differences with the droplet size distribution. For instance, comparing Fig. 6(a) with Fig. 6(c) and Fig. 6(e) shows a visual difference in the histogram, which reflects in the higher errors observed using both methodologies. In contrast, comparing the droplet size distribution in Fig. 6(b) with Fig. 6(d) and Fig. 6(f) shows higher similarity in the histogram. The comparison can be extended to the average values and standard deviations found for each image, with errors of 18.7% and 10% for the first method in images 9 and 2; and 5.3% and 0.03% errors using the second method in images 2 and 9.

The comparison of deep learning methods applied to Pickering emulsion classification is rather complicated due to the lack of studies dealing with this approach. Regarding the utilization of learning models to classify and quantify other emulsion types, Unnikrishnan et al. [24] have reported poor performance of the Vanilla Neural Network (VNN) and Convolutional Neural Network (CNN) with pharmaceutical emulsions. Their VNN achieved 89% and 85.3% in cross-validation and independent datasets, while the CNN was not able to cross-validate due to low performance (<50% accuracy in cross-validation dataset). The authors justified the low accuracy of the deep learning models due to the limited data size used in the training stage. Another study reported in the literature by Patil et al. [13] considered the utilization of a CNN algorithm (Faster R-CNN) and Hough filter to classify and quantify Exxsol D80 oil-water emulsions. The algorithm revealed errors in the range 0.2%–11.6% (average 6.7%), which performed significantly better than the Hough filter method (average 25% error). Nonetheless, the combined strategy used here for droplet detection using YOLOv7 and the second method to quantify the droplet size achieved an accu-

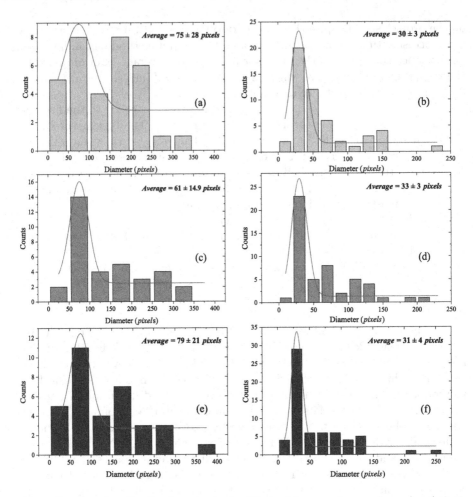

Fig. 6. Droplet size distribution obtained with (a, b) manual procedure, (c, d) first method, and (e, f) second method. (a, c, e) belongs to image 9 from the dataset, and (b, d, f) belongs to image 2.

racy of 97.26%, which is significantly better than what is currently reported in the literature.

For instance, the error in classification shown in the previous Sect. (4) is not significantly affecting the capacity of the coupled solution to determine the average droplet size and the droplet size distribution. This can be described due to the non-representative character of the droplets that are escaping the algorithm's classification since the overall error in the quantification step is lower compared to the classification one.

5   Conclusion and Future Work

In this study, we showed one approach for classifying and quantifying Pickering emulsions using advanced image processing techniques. YOLOv7 was used to classify the droplets in the microphotographs, and two different methods were considered for droplet size determination for comparison purposes. To the best of our knowledge, no other study is devoted to exploring deep learning techniques to quantify droplet size distribution in Pickering emulsions. The most challenging aspect of these emulsions is related to the presence of solid particles in the images, which are used to stabilize the emulsions. Images of Pickering emulsions are often loaded with "dots" which complicates object detection algorithms' operation. Nonetheless, the result reported here was able to overcome the accuracy of other deep-learning models used to classify and quantify regular emulsions.

The approach presented in this study for static images previously recorded in the laboratory could be extended to dynamic utilization of YOLOv7 coupled with the second method to classify and quantify the produced emulsions instantly. For future studies, the strategy presented here will be tested for other Pickering emulsion systems and also for other emulsion types to evaluate other utilization possibilities. In addition, the dynamic application of YOLOv7 trained with static images will be evaluated using a piece of hardware still to be explored.

Acknowledgements. This work has been supported by FCT - Fundação para a Ciência e Tecnologia within the R&D Units Project Scope: UIDB/05757/2020, UIDP/05757/2020, UIDB/00690/2020, UIDB/50020/2020, and UIDB/00319/ 2020. Adriano Silva was supported by Doctoral Grant SFRH/BD/151346/2021 financed by the Portuguese Foundation for Science and Technology (FCT), and with funds from NORTE 2020, under MIT Portugal Program. Fernanda F. Roman was supported by FCT and FSE with the PhD research grant SFRH/BD/143 224/2019.

References

1. Berton-Carabin, C.C., Schroën, K.: Pickering emulsions for food applications: background, trends, and challenges. Ann. Rev. Food Sci. Technol. **6**, 263–297 (2015). https://doi.org/10.1146/annurev-food-081114-110822
2. Cai, Y., et al.: Yolov4-5d: an effective and efficient object detector for autonomous driving. IEEE Trans. Instrument. Meas. **70** (2021). https://doi.org/10.1109/TIM.2021.3065438
3. Chevalier, Y., Bolzinger, M.A.: Emulsions stabilized with solid nanoparticles: pickering emulsions. Colloids Surf. A **439**, 23–34 (2013). https://doi.org/10.1016/j.colsurfa.2013.02.054
4. de Tuesta, J.L.D., et al.: Polyolefin-derived carbon nanotubes as magnetic catalysts for wet peroxide oxidation of paracetamol in aqueous solutions. Catal. Today **419**, 114162 (2023). https://doi.org/10.1016/j.cattod.2023.114162
5. Farzi, G.A., Nejad, A.P.: An image-based technique for measuring droplet size distribution: the use of CNN algorithm. J. Dispersion Sci. Technol. **37**(10), 1444–1452 (2016). https://doi.org/10.1080/01932691.2015.1090321

6. Huang, Z., Ni, Y., Yu, Q., Li, J., Fan, L., Eskin, N.M.: Deep learning in food science: an insight in evaluating pickering emulsion properties by droplets classification and quantification via object detection algorithm. Adv. Coll. Interface. Sci. **304**, 102663 (2022). https://doi.org/10.1016/j.cis.2022.102663

7. Itseez: Open source computer vision library (2015). https://github.com/itseez/opencv

8. Jin, Y., et al.: Uncertainty analysis on droplet size measurement in dispersed flow film boiling regime during reflood using image processing technique. Nucl. Eng. Des. **326**, 202–219 (2018). https://doi.org/10.1016/j.nucengdes.2017.11.013

9. Ma, T., Tian, W., Xie, Y.: Multi-level knowledge distillation for low-resolution object detection and facial expression recognition. Knowl.-Based Syst. **240**, 108136 (2022). https://doi.org/10.1016/j.knosys.2022.108136

10. Maiti, N., Desai, U., Ray, A.: Application of mathematical morphology in measurement of droplet size distribution in dropwise condensation. Thin Solid Films **376**(1), 16–25 (2000). https://doi.org/10.1016/S0040-6090(00)01396-1

11. McClements, D.J., Jafari, S.M.: Improving emulsion formation, stability and performance using mixed emulsifiers: a review. Adv. Coll. Interface. Sci. **251**, 55–79 (2018). https://doi.org/10.1016/j.cis.2017.12.001

12. Mobahi, M., Sadati, S.H.: An improved deep learning solution for object detection in self-driving cars. In: 2020 28th Iranian Conference on Electrical Engineering (ICEE), pp. 1–5. IEEE (2020). https://doi.org/10.1109/ICEE50131.2020.9260870

13. Patil, A., Sægrov, B., Panjwani, B.: Advanced deep learning for dynamic emulsion stability measurement. Comput. Chem. Eng. **157**, 107614 (2022). https://doi.org/10.1016/j.compchemeng.2021.107614

14. Pera-Titus, M., Leclercq, L., Clacens, J.M., De Campo, F., Nardello-Rataj, V.: Pickering interfacial catalysis for biphasic systems: from emulsion design to green reactions. Angew. Chem. Int. Ed. **54**(7), 2006–2021 (2015). https://doi.org/10.1002/anie.201402069

15. Pickering, S.U.: Cxcvi.-emulsions. J. Chem. Soc. Trans. **91**, 2001–2021 (1907)

16. Ponnusamy, A.: cvlib - high level computer vision library for python (2018). https://github.com/arunponnusamy/cvlib

17. Ramsden, W.: Separation of solids in the surface-layers of solutions and 'suspensions' (observations on surface-membranes, bubbles, emulsions, and mechanical coagulation).-preliminary account. Proc. Roy. Soc. Lond. **72**(477–486), 156–164 (1904)

18. Redmon, J.: Darknet: open source neural networks in c (2013–2016). http://pjreddie.com/darknet/

19. Roman, F.F., de Tuesta, J.L.D., Sanches, F.K., Silva, A.S., and P.M.: Selective denitrification of simulated oily wastewater by oxidation using janus-structured carbon nanotubes. Catal. Today 114001 (2023). https://doi.org/10.1016/j.cattod.2023.01.008

20. Roy, A.M., Bhaduri, J.: Real-time growth stage detection model for high degree of occultation using densenet-fused yolov4. Comput. Electron. Agric. **193** (2022). https://doi.org/10.1016/j.compag.2022.106694

21. Roy, A.M., Bose, R., Bhaduri, J.: A fast accurate fine-grain object detection model based on yolov4 deep neural network. Neural Comput. Appl. 1–27 (2022). https://doi.org/10.1007/s00521-021-06651-x

22. Schuster, S., et al.: Analysis of w1/o/w2 double emulsions with CLSM: statistical image processing for droplet size distribution. Chem. Eng. Sci. **81**, 84–90 (2012). https://doi.org/10.1016/j.ces.2012.06.059

23. Shewan, H.M., Stokes, J.R.: Review of techniques to manufacture micro-hydrogel particles for the food industry and their applications. J. Food Eng. **119**(4), 781–792 (2013). https://doi.org/10.1016/j.jfoodeng.2013.06.046

24. Unnikrishnan, S., Donovan, J., Macpherson, R., Tormey, D.: In-process analysis of pharmaceutical emulsions using computer vision and artificial intelligence. Chem. Eng. Res. Des. **166**, 281–294 (2021). https://doi.org/10.1016/j.cherd.2020.12.010

25. Walia, R., Sharma, S., Shrivastava, S.: A methodology for early detection of plant diseases using real time object detection algorithm. In: Boumerdassi, S., Ghogho, M., Renault, É. (eds.) SSA 2021. CCIS, vol. 1470, pp. 122–139. Springer, Cham (2021). https://doi.org/10.1007/978-3-030-88259-4_9

26. Wang, C.Y., Bochkovskiy, A., Liao, H.Y.M.: Yolov7: trainable bag-of-freebies sets new state-of-the-art for real-time object detectors (2022)

27. Yang, Y., et al.: An overview of pickering emulsions: solid-particle materials, classification, morphology, and applications. Front. Pharmacol. **8**, 287 (2017). https://doi.org/10.3389/fphar.2017.00287

28. Zhang, S., Liang, X., Huang, X., Wang, K., Qiu, T.: Precise and fast microdroplet size distribution measurement using deep learning. Chem. Eng. Sci. **247**, 116926 (2022). https://doi.org/10.1016/j.ces.2021.116926

Identification of Late Blight in Potato Leaves Using Image Processing and Machine Learning

Renan Lemes Leepkaln[1] , Angelita Maria de Ré[1] ,
and Kelly Lais Wiggers[2]([⊠])

[1] Midwestern Parana State University, Guarapuava, Paraná, Brazil
r138265@gmail.com, angelita@unicentro.br
[2] Federal Technological University of Paraná, Pato Branco, Paraná, Brazil
kwiggers@utfpr.edu.br

Abstract. Potato is a widely consumed food worldwide, and its productivity has increased due to new varieties and the use of technologies related to irrigation, nutrition, and soil preparation, among others. However, diseases such as late blight disease can often affect the crop, impacting many farmers around the world. As a way to help production, technology in agriculture is increasing. Among the various computational techniques that can be applied, those based on digital image processing associated with machine learning algorithms stand out, producing excellent results. This work aimed to develop a methodology for recognizing late blight disease in potato leaves using digital image processing techniques and machine learning algorithms. It was possible to obtain promising results. The experiments were carried out in a set of images from a public database containing images of healthy and unhealthy leaves (with late blight). We compare the performance of machine learning algorithms using feature vectors obtained with SIFT algorithm and RGB descriptors. The best performance was using the Decision Tree algorithm and SIFT vectors, with 99.24% of accuracy.

Keywords: Automatic disease recognition · Digital Image · Machine Learning · Computer Vision

1 Introduction

Potatoes are one of the most consumed foods on the planet, second only to dairy products, wheat, and rice. The tuber is planted in more than 130 countries, covering about 20 million hectares and producing more than 400 million tons of potatoes annually. In Brazil, it is estimated that there are 100,000 hectares of the crop spread across different states of Brazil, generating a production of 3.8 million tons, according to the Brazilian Institute of Geography and Statistics [1].

Productivity has been increasing due to more productive varieties and new technologies related to irrigation, nutrition, soil preparation, and the use of quality seed potatoes. Most of this production is sold fresh, with around 25–30%

A. I. Pereira et al. (Eds.): OL2A 2023, CCIS 1982, pp. 164–177, 2024.
https://doi.org/10.1007/978-3-031-53036-4_12

destined for industrial processing, in the form of frozen pre-fried (500,000 tons), chips, and straw potatoes (250,000 tons) [22].

However, diseases can affect the plantation, and these are usually caused by microorganisms, such as bacteria, fungi, nematodes, and viruses, but a lack or excess of essential factors for plant growth, such as nutrients, water, and light can also cause them.

The growing maturation and development of agricultural technology, in general, is remarkable, with the emergence of new applications and software to facilitate the day-to-day life of agricultural producers. Among these, techniques based on digital image processing are widely used. Image processing performs operations on an image to obtain an improved image or extract some useful information from it. It is a type of signal processing where the input is an image, and the output can be an image or features associated with that image. Several techniques can be explored, mainly in agriculture, due to the variety of plants that can present diseases.

Furthermore, along with these processing techniques, machine learning algorithms can help detect diseases, pests, or even production estimates, such as the work of Kadir et al. [14] and Trindade and Basso [25]. Specifically in disease identification, Arnaud et al. [2] aimed to develop an application that identifies disease diagnoses using deep learning techniques. Pallathadka et al. [19] detected grape diseases. Lawrence et al. [18] to recognize leaf diseases using individual lesions. Carmo et al. [6] identified the best time and sensor to detect the disease caused by Pectobacterium carotovorum in lettuce, using images obtained by multispectral sensors in Unmanned Aerial Vehicle (UAV).

Therefore, this paper aims to develop a methodology for recognizing late blight disease in potato leaves by exploring digital image processing techniques and machine learning algorithms. This way, image samples of healthy potato leaves and leaves with late blight disease were selected to form a database. We performed experiments using image processing techniques to obtain the best representation from this base. Finally, relevant algorithms from the literature were trained and evaluated, allowing the definition of a promising approach to identifying the disease. The main contribution was finding a feature extraction strategy and a traditional machine learning algorithm, which bring promising results, avoiding more complex structures, such as deep learning approaches.

The rest of the paper is organized as follows: Sect. 2 describes the previous works of disease detection of different plants and Sect. 3 explains the dataset and the proposed approach. The experimental results are illustrated in Sect. 4. Finally, Sect. 5 concludes the work, including the future plans.

2   Related Work

Machine learning algorithms involving classification tasks are increasingly important and popular. The main goal of algorithms is to learn a general rule that maps inputs to outputs correctly. Several techniques have been used to detect and categorize plant diseases. These various techniques could be observed in the relevant and recent literature articles that we found, in which the authors performed disease classification on images of agricultural data.

Hughes [16] created a database with 50,000 expertly curated images of agricultural leaves available on the PlantVillage online platform. The goal was to develop an application that identifies disease diagnoses using machine learning techniques. This database allows several researchers to use it in different experiments. For example, Pallathadka et al. [19] used Support Vector Machine (SVM), Naïve Bayes, and Convolution Neural Network (CNN) to detect diseases of rice leaves. The SVM was the algorithm with the better performance, with 96.2% accuracy.

Ngugi et al. [18] recognize leaf diseases using individual lesions. A segmentation algorithm was trained using only 90 hand-labeled critical illness images. However, manually labeling or cutting lesions that do not have clearly defined borders but gradually merge with healthy leaf tissue makes it difficult to be consistent when labeling lesions manually. The proposed automatic lesion segmentation techniques work in experimental settings.

Carmo et al. [6] identified the best time and the best sensor to detect the disease caused by Pectobacterium carotovorum in lettuce, using images obtained by multispectral sensors in an Unmanned Aerial Vehicle (UAV). For this, an experiment was installed in a greenhouse at the Federal University of Uberlândia, Mount Carmel Campus. The authors used Support Vector Machine (SVM) and Naive Bayes (NB) classifiers to evaluate groups of data composed of spectral bands, vegetation indices, and the combination of bands and indices obtained from a conventional visible camera and a Mapir Survey 3W multispectral camera, as well as agronomic parameters.

Trindade et al. [25] investigate three computational methods to detect soybean leaves. Thus, they carried out a systematic literature review to map the methods applicable to the problem, characterizing techniques for detecting plant diseases and generating important information. They selected three methods for training Neural Networks Convolutional (RNCs), and each one was tested and compared, generating very motivating results that prove the efficiency of using image data augmentation techniques as an essential pre-processing step.

In the case of potatoes, Biondo et al. [4] present a system developed to classify the types of potato disease, such as late blight and early blight, based on leaf conditions, using Deep Learning as a model of conventional neural network architecture, through the proposed model had an accuracy of 92.57% in identifying diseases. Islam et al. [13] implemented AVM to classify healthy leaves and those affected by late and early blight diseases using 300 potato images. The system's cross-validated accuracy was 95%.

Sanjeev et al. [24] implemented a classifier based on a neural network to predict and classify potato image samples. The Feed Forward Neural Network (FFNN) Model was used to predict and classify unknown leaves. The accuracy of the model is achieved at 96.5%.

Pires et al. [21] used Convolutional Neural Networks (CNN) to classify tree species by leaf images. The work compared Darknet-19 and GoogLeNet

(Inception-v3). The Darknet and GoogLeNet models achieved recognition rates of 86.2% and 90.3%, respectively.

Generally, many researchers use ANN and Deep Learning as algorithms for training the classifier. However, this may require more computational resources and relies on a large volume of data for training. Thus, we decide to explore some traditional feature extraction techniques and machine learning algorithms to classify late blight disease and compare the results of our approaches.

3 Methodology

Machine learning is one of the areas of artificial intelligence that uses algorithms and mathematics, specifically statistics, to accomplish learning tasks. Currently, various databases are available where experiments can be performed integrating techniques for automatic recognition. Thus, the need arose to process and obtain useful information from these databases. Consequently, the machine learning area gained prominence since it is impracticable to process and analyze data currently available manually, and tasks can be automated, simulating human behavior [8]. However, it is necessary to carry out studies and define stages of data preparation, as well as the algorithms and parameters to be implemented.

Therefore, for the development of this work, four main stages were defined: 1. Image search and selection; 2. Preprocessing; 3. Feature extraction and machine learning algorithm training, and 4. analysis of results.

The developed method includes exploratory experiments with digital image processing techniques to allow the formation of feature vectors for each image in the database. With these vectors, experiments were carried out with supervised machine learning algorithms to allow the automatic identification of leaves that have late blight disease. Figure 1 shows the schematic of the order in which the development steps are carried out, and the descriptions are presented below.

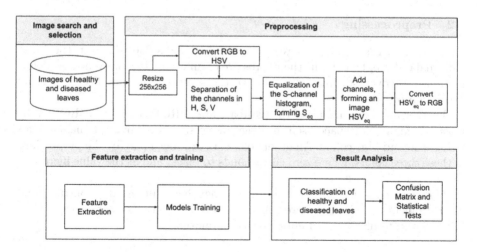

Fig. 1. Development Stages

The technologies used for the development of this project were: Python programming language; Libraries: Numpy; Pandas; csv; Tqdm; Sklearn; Skimage; OpenCV; Matplotlib; posthoc.

3.1 Image Search and Selection

The database used in the experiments is formed by selecting public images from the Plant Village website[1]. This database is a collection of plant and leaf images and corresponding metadata, which are used to train machine learning models in plant disease recognition and diagnosis tasks. In this way, there are 4864 images in the selected dataset. The first class is formed by 2432 images of healthy leaves. The second class is formed by 1216 slightly diseased and 1216 extremely diseased. Figure 2 shows healthy and late blight leaf examples, respectively.

(a) Healthy leaf   (b) Late blight leaf

Fig. 2. Example of selected leaf images from PlantVillage database

3.2 Preprocessing

At this stage, firstly, all images were resized to 256×256, since, in the Plant Village database, by default, the photos are of different sizes or even show deformation. Moreover, all images must have the same size for an effective feature extraction process.

Furthermore, the images of the database are in RGB color space. RGB is the most common color space used in image processing, with one channel each for red, green, and blue colors. All other colors are produced only by the proportions of these three colors, where zero corresponds to black, and as the value increases, the intensity increases.

However, considering that the images may have luminosity, contrast, and color problems, the images were transformed from the RGB color space to HSV (Hue, Saturation, Value) to improve the luminosity.

---

[1] https://plantvillage.psu.edu/.

In color space HSV, the image consists of three channels: Hue, Saturation, and Value. A color component represents the H; the S suggests the percentage of the color; usually, this value is between 0 and 1, and the V represents the intensity of the chosen color and varies from 0 to 100 [10]. Thus, we equalized the S channel histogram after transforming the image to HSV. Subsequently, the images were converted back to RGB.

The histogram equalization aims to balance the distribution of pixel frequency values, reducing accentuated differences and highlighting previously unnoticed details. The algorithm normalizes the brightness and increases the contrast of the image. Figure 3 presents an example of equalizing the histogram of an RGB image. Thus, given an image *src*, the equalization is given by steps 1 to 4, according [10] and OpenCV implementation[2].

1. Calculate the histogram H for *src*.
2. Normalize the histogram so that the sum of histogram bins is 255.
3. Compute the integral of histogram using:

$$H_i' = \sum_{0 \leq i \leq L} H(i) \tag{1}$$

4. Transform the image using H' as a look-up table:

$$img_{eq}(x, y) = H'(src(x, y)) \tag{2}$$

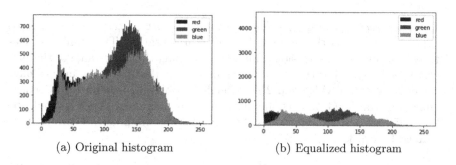

(a) Original histogram   (b) Equalized histogram

Fig. 3. Example of histogram equalization. Source: the authors.

3.3 Feature Extraction

The feature extraction stage aimed to extract the information of interest (sheet), generating the feature vectors of the images. For this work, we evaluated two types of characteristics:

---

[2] https://docs.opencv.org/2.4/modules/imgproc/doc/histograms.html?highlight=equalizehist.

– *Automatic vectors extracted by the Scale-Invariant Feature Transform (SIFT) algorithm:* It starts by identifying the patterns, called descriptors, that is, characteristic points, looking for the edges of each object. Edges in the image are discovered by calculating the magnitude of the x- and y-axis frequencies using a kind of "high-pass" filter to enhance the edges of the image.

Once this task is completed, the method tests and evaluates the possibility of image standard deviation creating different highlights in the image [15]. However, this algorithm requires the formation of a vocabulary to generate the feature vectors using the K-means algorithm. Figure 4 shows an example of identifying SIFT descriptors in a leaf image.

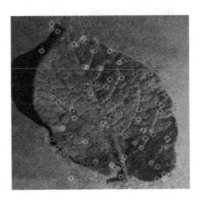

Fig. 4. Example of points of interest found by the SIFT extractor. Source: the authors.

– *Extracted vectors based on color information: feature vector from the RGB color space:* This is the simplest form of representation. The number of features will be a one-dimensional matrix containing the color value of the pixels of the images. For this scenario, as previously described, the images have dimensions 256 in width and 256 in height, formed by 3-channel gray scales, which are the R, G, and B channels. The total number of pixels would be $256 \times 256 \times 3$, the average values of the images for each pixel i of each channel defined by Eq. 3.

$$RGB_{vector} = \sum_{n=0}^{i} \frac{R_i + G_i + B_i}{3}; \; with \; 0 < i \leq L \qquad (3)$$

R is the red channel, G is the green channel, B is the blue channel, and L is the limit edge of the 256-pixel image, then transformed into a single 1-dimensional channel with the same width and height.

3.4   Machine Learning

Machine learning models were selected to carry out the experiments in this step. Therefore, the objective is to identify patterns based on the features provided by the images in the database.

As an experimental protocol, we split the database into 70% for training and validation, and 30% for tests. Also, in the training set, we performed ten runs to analyze the results [7], and cross-validation (k-folds) with different values of K. This technique consists of randomly dividing the database into K subsets (K is previously defined), with approximately the same amount of samples in each of them. At each iteration, training, and validation, a set formed by K-1 subsets is used for training, and the remaining subset will be used for validation, generating a metric result for evaluation. For the experiments, the values of K = 5 were defined, with sets formed in a stratified manner. These experiments were performed to avoid overfitting or underfitting. Overfitting means that the model has a high accuracy score on the training data but a low score on the test data, i.e. the model is not generalized. On the other hand, underfitting occurs when the algorithm used to build the prediction model has low performance already on the training data [5].

After some experiments and state-of-the-art studies, we define the machine learning models: Random Forest (RF) [20], Decision Tree (DT) [17], K-Nearest Neighbors (KNN) [3], Support Vector Machine (SVM), LinearSVM [12] and Stochastic Gradient Descent (SGD) [23].

3.5   Metrics for Evaluating Results

The experiments were evaluated using statistical analysis through Accuracy (Eq. 4), Precision (Eq. 5), Recall (Eq. 6), and Confusion Matrix, because they are essential tools for evaluating the performance of a classification algorithm. [9,11].

$$accuracy = \frac{TP + TN}{TP + TN + FP + FN} \tag{4}$$

where TP: true positive, TN: true negative, FP: false positive, and FN: false negative

$$precision = \frac{TP}{TP + FP} \tag{5}$$

$$recall = \frac{TP}{TP + FN} \tag{6}$$

The Kruskal-Wallis statistical test, with a significance of 0.5, was applied to the results. The Kruskal-Wallis tests the null hypothesis that the population median of all algorithms being compared is equal. The test works on two or more independent samples with different sizes. If the value (p) is less than or equal to 0.05, the hypothesis that all samples have equal medians is rejected with 95% confidence, i.e., there are at least one pair of algorithms that is significantly different between them. Otherwise, the hypothesis is accepted, the performance of all algorithms is statistically equivalent. Rejecting the null hypothesis does not indicate which of the algorithms is different. Thus, post hoc comparisons between algorithms are needed to determine which algorithms differ. This work used Conover [7] as a post hoc test.

4   Experimental Results

Firstly, the images were read using the OpenCV library and stored as a tuple containing the image name and the image itself. Then, experiments were carried out using pre-processing and image feature extraction techniques. Table 1 shows the database's pre-processing results applied to healthy and late blight leaves. Thus, it is possible to observe that regions of the leaf that present late blight disease were more intensified in the pre-processed image. In addition, green color pigments and sparkles also had increased contrast, mainly in disease leaves.

Table 1. Examples of preprocessing results applied in dataset imagens

Class	Original image	HSV image	Equalized	Preprocessed
healthy leaf				
late blight leaf				

Next, we describe the results using feature extraction techniques and machine learning algorithms. The first technique used was the SIFT algorithm to detect the points of interest in each image and extract the corresponding descriptors, totaling 2214 descriptors. The descriptors were stored in a list. Subsequently, we used the K-Means clustering algorithm with 50 clusters to group the descriptors into similar clusters, creating a vocabulary to describe the features of the images.

Once the descriptors were grouped into clusters, a histogram was created for each image using the results of running K-Means. Each descriptor is assigned to the closest cluster, and the histogram is created by counting the occurrence in the image. Finally, we saved the histograms in a text file for later use in the classification task. Therefore, 4864 training samples were created, each with 50 feature descriptors. Afterward, the base was separated for training, validation, and test set. Thus, 3404 samples were used for training/validation, k-folds with $k = 5$, and 1460 images for testing. All analyzes are based on ten runs independent of the algorithms and calculated the mean values for accuracy, precision, and recall. The results of the experiments on the test samples are in Table 2.

It is possible to observe in Table 2 that the algorithms SGDClassifier and LinearSVM presented lower performance. The best results use Decision Tree and Knn algorithms, with 99.24% accuracy. In general, the results obtained were

Table 2. Results of experiments using SIFT vectors (in %)

Model	Accuracy	Precision	Recall
Decision Tree	**99.24**	98.45	100
KNN	**99.24**	98.45	100
Randon Forest	99.16	98.27	100
SVM	99.17	98.31	100
LinearSVM	95.50	93.38	97.90
SGD	92.80	88.87	98.43

satisfactory, as using the SIFT algorithm allowed the creation of robust image descriptors. Applying the K-Means clustering algorithm allowed the identification of similar features between the images, mainly observing the proportion between precision and recall. In this way, it is possible to conclude that using SIFT descriptors is a promising alternative for identifying late blight through images of the leaves.

The Decision Tree model was selected to analyze the confusion matrix (Table 3). Thus, 1460 images were selected for test samples. There was low confusion in differentiating healthy leaves from diseased ones; only 11 leaves were classified incorrectly.

Table 3. Confusion matrix using SIFT descriptors and Decision Tree algorithm

		Detected	
		Healthy leaves	Diseased leaves
Real	Healthy leaves	752	11
	Diseased leaves	0	697

The second set of experiments used RGB descriptors as feature vectors. Table 4 shows that the best performance was obtained using the SGD algorithm, with approximately 79% accuracy, followed by the LinearSVM with only 0.05% difference. Analyzing the SGD confusion matrix (Table 5), 759 healthy leaves and 392 diseased leaves were classified correctly. However, the major confusion was in 305 samples that were classified incorrectly as healthy leaves. In addition, the results obtained using vectors with the average of RGB colors presented better precision, however, low recall. This shows that color features may not be able to correctly distinguish diseased parts of potato leaves. Thus more experiments must be performed in further works, preparing the feature vectors.

Table 4. Results of experiments using RGB descriptors (in %)

Model	Accuracy	Precision	Recall
Decision Tree	78.00	97.79	55.17
KNN	66.23	100.00	29.26
Randon Forest	76.21	99.43	50.47
SVM	76.30	98.88	50.93
LinearSVM	78.79	99.74	55.72
SGD	**78.84**	98.42	56.67

Table 5. Confusion matrix using RGB descriptors and SGD algorithm algorithm

		Detected	
		Healthy leaves	Diseased leaves
Real	Healthy leaves	759	4
	Diseased leaves	305	392

Figures 5a and 5b show the statistical analysis, and when $p < 0.05$ (p-value) means that there is a statistical difference in favor of the method that has highest mean accuracy. In these figures, the p values represented by the green colors (the greater the color intensity, the greater the difference between the algorithms) indicate statistical differences between the pair of algorithms in row x column. The pink color represents statistical equivalence. For both sets of descriptors, the statistical tests show that there is a statistical difference between some pairs of compared versions. Except for the SIFT-KNN and SIFT-DT, RGB-LinearSVM and RGB-SGD, and RGB-RF and RGB-SVM.

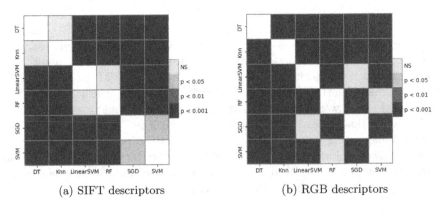

(a) SIFT descriptors   (b) RGB descriptors

Fig. 5. Pair-by-pair analysis of post-hoc testing of machine learning algorithms on the data set

Many papers with similar problems do not provide the bases used in their experiments. However, with the samples selected for the experiments, promising results were obtained in identifying late blight on potato leaves. For comparison, the most recent papers that classify potato diseases were in Table 6. Though methods like artificial neural networks and deep neural networks, applied by [4] and [24], show good accuracies, they come with high computational costs. In addition, [4] used a deep learning approach, however, with few samples of healthy and diseased leaves. This implies performing data augmentation, with we did not perform in our work. Thus, we can observe that our proposed method, using Decision Tree and SIFT vectors, outperformed the results.

Table 6. Comparison of the state of the art

Reference	Technique	Accuracy
This work	RGB features + SGD	78.84%
This work	SIFT descriptors + DT	99.24%
Islam et al. [13]	Color and texture + SVM	95.00%
Biodo [4]	Deep Features + CNN	92.57%
Sanjeev [24]	Color, shape and texture + ANN	96.7%

5 Conclusion

The present study aimed to develop a methodology for recognizing late blight disease in potato leaves using digital image processing techniques and machine learning algorithms. Firstly, we collected images from a public database. Through a bibliographic survey, available images were found, as well as the main image processing techniques used.

We used two feature extraction techniques to perform comparative experiments. We observe that using vectors of the RGB color space with the use of the SGD algorithm presented promising results. However, the SIFT points presented robust feature vectors, which increased the results, mainly using DT and KNN model. In addition, we evaluated the significant difference between machine learning models and concluded some significant differences between the algorithms evaluated.

In future work, we intend to conduct experiments on a specific database, created from the collection of images of greenhouse potato leaves located in the Cedeteg campus of Unicentro, Paraná. In addition, further research is needed to identify other models of automatic feature extraction and machine learning algorithms, allowing to increase in the amount of the image database, with greater data variability.

References

1. Abba: Situação atual da produção de batata no Brasil. Batata Show **20**(58) (2020)
2. Arnaud, S.E., Rehema, N., Aoki, S., Kananu, M.L.: Comparison of deep learning architectures for late blight and early blight disease detection on potatoes. Open J. Appl. Sci. **12**(5), 723–743 (2022)
3. AWS: Amazon sagemaker documentation (2023). https://docs.aws.amazon.com/sagemaker/index.html
4. Biodo, D.R.: Classificação de doenças em batata baseado em imagens das folhas de batata utilizando Deep Learning. Masters, UFSCar (2021)
5. Bonaccorso, G.: Machine Learning Algorithms. Packt Publishing, Birmingham (2017)
6. Carmo, G., Castoldi, R., Martins, G., Castoldi, R., Zilvani, A.: Detecção de podridão mole em alface por Pectobacterium carotovorum subsp. carotovorum por algoritmos de aprendizado de máquina a partir de imagens multiespectrais. Master in agriculture and geospatial information, Universidade Federal de Uberlândia (2021)
7. Conover, W.J.: Practical Nonparametric Statistics, 3rd edn. Wiley, Hoboken (1999)
8. Escovedo, T.: Machine learning; conceitos e modelos - parte i: Aprendizado supervisionado (2020). https://tatianaesc.medium.com/machine-learning-conceitos-e-modelos-f0373bf4f445
9. Ferri, C., Hernández-Orallo, J., Modroiu, R.: An experimental comparison of performance measures for classification. Pattern Recogn. Lett. **30**(1), 27–38 (2009)
10. Gonzalez, R., Woods, R.: Processamento digital de imagens, vol. 3. Pearson Prentice Hall, Upper Saddle River (2010)
11. Hossin, M., Sulaiman, M.N.: A review on evaluation metrics for data classification evaluations. Int. J. Data Mining Knowl. Manag. Process **5**(2), 1 (2015)
12. Iniyan, S., Jebakumar, R., Mangalraj, P., Mohit, M., Nanda, A.: Plant disease identification and detection using support vector machines and artificial neural networks. In: Dash, S.S., Lakshmi, C., Das, S., Panigrahi, B.K. (eds.) Artificial Intelligence and Evolutionary Computations in Engineering Systems. AISC, vol. 1056, pp. 15–27. Springer, Singapore (2020). https://doi.org/10.1007/978-981-15-0199-9_2
13. Islam, M., Dinh, A., Wahid, K., Bhowmik, P.: Detection of potato diseases using image segmentation and multiclass support vector machine, pp. 1–4 (2017). https://doi.org/10.1109/CCECE.2017.7946594
14. Kadir, A., Nugroho, L., Susanto, A.: Performance improvement of leaf identification system using principal component analysis. J. Theor. Appl. Inf. Technol. **44**, 113–124 (2021)
15. Lowe, D.G.: Distinctive image features from scale-invariant keypoints. Int. J. Comput. Vision **60**, 91–110 (2004). https://doi.org/10.1023/B:VISI.0000029664.99615.94
16. Hughes, D., Salathe, M.: An open access repository of images on plant health to enable the development of mobile disease diagnostics (2015). https://arxiv.org/abs/1511.08060
17. Mada, M.S.: Decision trees algorithms (2017). https://medium.com/deep-math-machine-learning-ai/chapter-4-decision-trees-algorithms-b93975f7a1f1
18. Ngugi, L.C., Abdelwahab, M., Abo-Zahhad, M.: A new approach to learning and recognizing leaf diseases from individual lesions using convolutional neural networks. Inf. Process. Agric. **10**(1), 11–27 (2023)

19. Pallathadka, H., Ravipat, P., Phashinam, G.S.K., Kassanuk, T., Sanchez, T.: Application of machine learning techniques in rice leaf disease detection. Mater. Today Proc. **51**, 2277–2280 (2022)

20. Paul, A., Mukherjee, D.P., Das, P., Gangopadhyay, A., Chintha, A.R., Kundu, S.: Improved random forest for classification. IEEE Trans. Image Process. **27**(8), 4012–4024 (2018). https://doi.org/10.1109/TIP.2018.2834830

21. Pires, W.O., Fernandes, R.C., de Paula Filho, P.L., Candido Junior, A., Teixeira, J.P.: Leaf-based species recognition using convolutional neural networks. In: Pereira, A.I., et al. (eds.) OL2A 2021. CCIS, vol. 1488, pp. 367–380. Springer, Cham (2021). https://doi.org/10.1007/978-3-030-91885-9_27

22. Rampazo, A.: Cenário atual da cultura da batata e os principais desafios (2020). https://www.agrolink.com.br

23. Russel, S., Norvig, P.: Artificial Intelligence - A Modern Approach, 4th edn. Pearson, Boston (2022)

24. Sanjeev, K., Gupta, N.K., Jeberson, W., Paswan, S.: Early prediction of potato leaf diseases using ANN classifier. Orient. J. Comput. Sci. Technol. **13**(2), 129–134 (2021)

25. Trindade, L., Basso, F.: Investigando técnicas de processamento de imagens com IA na detecção de ferrugem em folhas de soja. Professional master's in software engineering, Universidade Federal do Pampa (2021)

Machine Learning and AI in Robotics

Deep Learning-Based Localization Approach for Autonomous Robots in the RobotAtFactory 4.0 Competition

Luan C. Klein[1,2(✉)], João Mendes[2,3], João Braun[2,3,4,5], Felipe N. Martins[6], Andre Schneider de Oliveira[1], Paulo Costa[4,5], Heinrich Wörtche[6,7], and José Lima[2,3,5]

[1] Universidade Tecnológica Federal do Paraná, Campus Curitiba, UTFPR/PR, Curitiba, Brazil
luanklein@alunos.utfpr.edu.br, andreoliveira@utfpr.edu.br
[2] Research Centre in Digitalization and Intelligent Robotics (CeDRI), Instituto Politécnico de Bragança, Bragança, Portugal
{joao.cmendes,jbneto,jllima}@ipb.pt
[3] Laboratory for Sustainability and Technology in Mountain Regions (SusTEC), Instituto Politécnico de Bragança, Bragança, Portugal
[4] Faculty of Engineering of the University of Porto, Porto, Portugal
paco@fe.up.pt
[5] INESC Technology and Science, Porto, Portugal
[6] Sensors and Smart Systems Group, Institute of Engineering, Hanze University of Applied Sciences, Groningen, The Netherlands
{fe.nascimento.martins,h.j.wortche}@pl.hanze.nl
[7] Department of Electrical Engineering, Eindhoven University of Technology, Eindhoven, The Netherlands

Abstract. Accurate localization in autonomous robots enables effective decision-making within their operating environment. Various methods have been developed to address this challenge, encompassing traditional techniques, fiducial marker utilization, and machine learning approaches. This work proposes a deep-learning solution employing Convolutional Neural Networks (CNN) to tackle the localization problem, specifically in the context of the RobotAtFactory 4.0 competition. The proposed approach leverages transfer learning from the pre-trained VGG16 model to capitalize on its existing knowledge. To validate the effectiveness of the approach, a simulated scenario was employed. The experimental results demonstrated an error within the millimeter scale and rapid response times in milliseconds. Notably, the presented approach offers several advantages, including a consistent model size regardless of the number of training images utilized and the elimination of the need to know the absolute positions of the fiducial markers.

Keywords: Indoor Localization · CNN · Robotic Competition

1 Introduction

A necessary skill for agents in numerous circumstances, notably in robotics with Autonomous Mobile Robots (AMR), is the ability to localize themselves in an

A. I. Pereira et al. (Eds.): OL2A 2023, CCIS 1982, pp. 181–194, 2024.
https://doi.org/10.1007/978-3-031-53036-4_13

environment. Solving the localization problem means determining the pose—a combination of position and orientation—concerning some reference frames, often the global reference frame. Several strategies have been created employing sensor data and different techniques. Artificial intelligence approaches are also increasingly being used to solve this issue.

Many countries have created robotic competitions to encourage research and inspire students. In this study, the Portuguese Competition RobotAtFactory 4.0 was chosen to carry out the methods and validate the concepts proposed here. In this competition, an AMR must move boxes through a model warehouse in the shortest possible time.

One of the current approaches used in this competition to solve the robot localization issue is presented in [1], in which previous knowledge of the location of fiducial markers (ArUcos markers) in the environment is used. The robot's pose is estimated using the relative pose of the robot's camera concerning the ArUcos, through geometry. A limitation of this approach is that the pose of all ArUcos in the field must be precisely known. This is acceptable in a known scenario (like the competition) but can be challenging in situations in which the position of the markers is not precisely known, such as in potentially hazardous circumstances. To overcome this issue, we investigated some Machine Learning (ML) approaches in previous works [2] and [3]. However, the dependency on the tag's identification remains since the approaches presented are based on the relative ArUco's pose.

Within this context, the present work aims to explore and validate the application of Convolutional Neural Networks (CNN) to the robot localization problem. In the proposed approach, there is no need to know the pose of the ArUco markers, neither in the global reference frame nor relative to the robot's camera. As in our previous works, we use the RobotAtFactory 4.0 competition as a scenario for the reported experiments and results.

The rest of the text is divided into four sections: Sect. 2 presents related works; Sect. 3 presents theoretical concepts and explains how the work was developed, namely the data collecting, pre-processing of data and the models used; Sect. 4 presents the results and the discussions; Finally, Sect. 5 presents the conclusion and future works.

2   Related Work

The study of localization is crucial in various contexts, especially in the AMR. Given its importance, research in this area has generated considerable interest. There are two categories of localization: Outdoor and Indoor. The widespread Global Positioning System (GPS) is a frequent method for outside settings, but due to physical restrictions, it is ineffective indoors [4]. So, multiple alternatives have been explored and developed. Base future decisions on wrong pose estimations might have terrible consequences [5]. Therefore recognizing the associated uncertainty in pose estimation is crucial.

Many strategies have been developed, and one of the most well-known is the Kalman Filter, first introduced in [6]. It is a mathematical method that uses (noisy) measurements over time to produce estimates that approximate the real values. The Kalman filter was designed for linear systems, but a similar approach can be used in nonlinear situations, such as the Extended Kalman Filter (EKF) [7]. Another interesting approach is Markov Localization, a probabilistic algorithm that maintains a probability distribution throughout all hypotheses instead of just one [8]. An alternative method is the Monte Carlo Localization, which uses numerous samples (particles) with different weights, which represent hypotheses of the interest variable [9] [10].

More techniques for localization include map-matching algorithms such as Perfect Match [11], Iterative Closest Point (ICP) [12], and Normal Distributions Transform (NDT) [13]. A comparative analysis of these approaches was performed in [14]. Further approaches were developed using landmarks in the environment, such as the use of fiducial markers [15]. Using them in a SLAM (Simultaneous Localization and Mapping) problem with other localization techniques was also explored [16].

Recent years have seen a substantial increase in the use of machine learning techniques due to improvements in computing capacity. Various methods for feature extraction, selection, and regression in the localization context were examined in a survey in 2020 [17]. This survey highlights that this field is still in its early stages, and several problems require further exploration.

Additionally, by employing pictures from the robot's camera and other sensors, Convolutional Neural Networks (CNN) have been used to support robot localization [18] [19]. An interesting study on this topic is in [20], where the authors employed images for localization in a 6-DoF (Degrees of Freedom) scenario. They applied transfer learning from GoogLeNet [21] and achieved promising outcomes in outdoor and indoor environments.

Focusing on the RobotAtFactory 4.0 competition, one of the current methods utilized to address the localization issue is considering the stored data of the ArUcos pose and its relative position to the camera reference frame [1]. Based on these two pieces of information, analytical geometry estimates the robot's pose concerning the global reference frame. Stochastic filters like the EKF and Mahalanobis filters are also used to aggregate the guesses and improve their accuracy.

The analytical approach's disadvantage is that it necessitates accurate information about each ArUco's pose, which might be difficult to get in hostile conditions. In [2], a machine learning (ML) solution is proposed to overcome this restriction, where prior knowledge about the ArUcos' pose is not required. However, the demand for the ArUcos to be recognized in the images remains.

3   Background and Methodology

This section is divided into three parts: Sect. 3.1 is focused on the theoretical explanation of the CNNs, exploring the transfer-learning concept and the VGG16 model. Section 3.2 aims to explain the competition scenario, explaining the robot, the scenario, and the simulator. Finally, Sect. 3.3 describes how the work was done, the data collection, the model training, and the metrics considered to evaluate the models.

3.1 Theoretical Background

Artificial Neural Networks (ANN) were developed to replicate how the human brain works. This method was founded on the premise that brain cells, or neurons, and the connections between them, or synapses, are the root of mental activity. The earliest neuron model was created in 1943 [22] and involves multiple inputs, each with an associated weight. These inputs are multiplied by the corresponding weights before being added along with a bias term. The neuron output is obtained by passing the resultant sum through an activation function. An ANN is, in essence, a collection of neurons arranged in layers. Feeding data into a neural network in which each neuron's output serves as an input for the layer above it is known as feedforward. Backpropagation is the process of determining optimal weights and biases. It uses the learning rate as a critical variable to control how rapidly the network may modify its weights and biases [23].

Convolutional Neural Networks (CNN) are a particular type of ANN frequently employed in deep learning for processing data with a known grid-like architecture, such as images [24]. The use of the convolution operation in at least one layer, as described in [25], is the distinguishing feature of CNN. In summary, the two basic components of CNN are feature extraction and classification/regression. The first one consists of filters, using convolutional layers and layer-pooling techniques that reduce the size of the representation, speed up computation, and improve feature resilience. Fully connected layers handle the classification or regression operation.

Most AI approaches have been trained to perform a specific task. Coming later to the conclusion that the learning acquired for a specific function can be reused, a new field called transfer learning emerged. Several pre-trained models are accessible, particularly in CNN[1]. To carry out this work, the pre-trained network VGG16[2] was chosen [26], due to its ease of interpretation and possible modification of hyperparameters. This, despite its age and not guaranteeing the best results today, continues to be a good choice considering several parameters, such as the simplicity of its structure, the reduced number of parameters if used as a transfer-learning model, and the low computational capacity required by it.

The VGG16 model's architecture was initially proposed with a fixed input ConvNet (224×224 RGB image), and only necessitating normalization of the image pixel values during pre-processing [26]. Compared to other presented models, VGG16 demonstrated a deeper structure with 16 weight layers (13 convolutional layers and three fully-connected layers) using 3×3 filtering to extract

---

[1] Some examples are available at https://keras.io/api/applications/.

[2] The ranking of the approaches considering the ImageNet dataset are available at https://paperswithcode.com/sota/image-classification-on-imagenet.

features from the input image effectively. To reduce information volume, a 2×2 max-pooling layer was applied at the end of the filter stack. In the ImageNet-trained[3] model version, the final max-pooling layer is connected to a fully connected layer containing 4096 neurons. This layer's output is then fed into a softmax layer for 1000 classifications. A graphical representation of the VGG16 architecture is presented in Fig. 1.

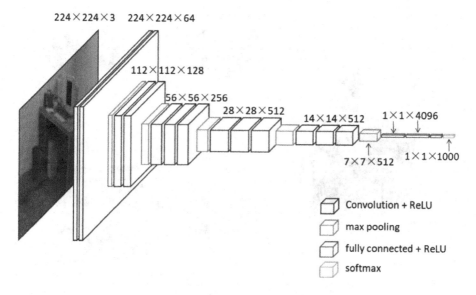

Fig. 1. VGG16 architecture. Adapted from [27].

3.2   Scenario Context

This study investigates if the localization problem in the RobotAtFactory 4.0 Competition[4] can be resolved using CNN. In this competition, an AMR must move as many boxes as possible in the shortest time around the warehouse. This challenge aims to replicate a condition in automated factories, such as warehouses, where several procedures to meet the requirements are necessary. Since the warehouse is part of an automated system, robots may replace human workers, increasing efficiency and safety.

The robot must comply with some rules to participate in this competition, including fitting in a cube of $30 \times 30 \times 30$ cm and being entirely autonomous-any connection with an external system the organization does not provide is forbidden.

---

[3] Details in https://www.image-net.org/.
[4] More details at https://www.festivalnacionalrobotica.pt/2023/robotfactory-4-0/.

The principal parts of the robot are depicted in Fig. 2: While the Arduino Uno handles the low-level control of the robot, such as motors and encoders, the Raspberry Pi handles the high-level control of the robot, managing, for instance, the RGB camera, localization, navigation, and decision-making [28].

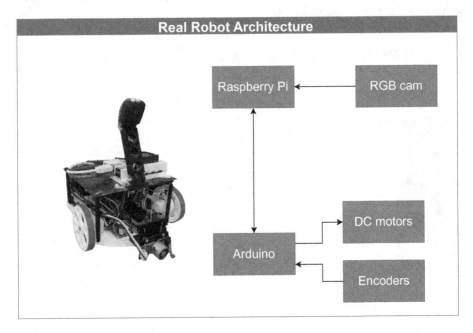

Fig. 2. A representation of robot architecture. Two boards compose the system: the Raspberry Pi, which manages decision-making and regulates the RGB camera, and the Arduino, which is in charge of interfacing with low-level hardware such as the motors and encoders. Source: [2].

Additionally, the competition organization created a simulation setting of the competition[5]. This simulator works with rigid-body dynamics interactions and constraints [29]. The user can interact with a variety of features on the simulator. For instance, an editor for XML files allows the user to modify definitions for the robot and the surroundings. A code editor in the Pascal language is another feature that makes it possible to develop the robot's programming, for example, by creating an algorithm to define the robot's route [28]. More details about the simulator can be found in [29]. The simulator depicted in Fig. 3 presents a virtual version of the RaF competition field. Additionally, Fig. 4 displays an image taken by the robot's camera in the simulator.

---

[5] Available at: https://github.com/P33a/SimTwo.

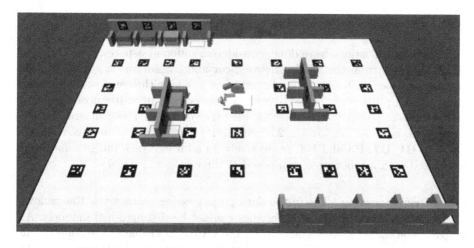

Fig. 3. Simulation scene that displays the robot and the competition's simulated environment.

Fig. 4. Example of an image taken by the robot's camera in simulation.

3.3   Methodology

Data Collection. Only data from a simulated scenario was used in this study to facilitate implementing and evaluating the proposed solutions. The field was discretized into a grid to gather the data, and the robot was placed in each open spot - that is, a spot without obstacles - to collect data. The robot rotates

360° while taking about 60 photos in each location to build a database for ML training.

Five data collections were done, considering different aspects. The **Dataset A** have images from the whole environment and considering a grid resolution equals 1 cm, i.e., each square in the grid has a side with a size equal to 1 cm. Only a small portion of the field—a square measuring 10×10 cm in the field's center—was considered while creating the other datasets. The grid's resolutions considered were 10 mm, 5 mm, 2.5 mm, and 1 mm, creating, in this way, the datasets **B1**, **B2**, **B3** and **B4**, respectively. In addition, each image collected is associated with a robot pose, composed of three values: $\{x, y, \theta\}$.

Data Preprocessing. The initial data preprocessing necessary is the removal of "ambiguous images", i.e., images that can not be distinguished uniquely. An image is considered "ambiguous" when no ArUco[6] is visible in the frame. This restriction was done to avoid images that do not improve the training and the validation of the models. Furthermore, this limitation will be treated in future works, for example, by using filters and odometry. After this, the preprocessing in each image is done using the pre-defined function specific to the VGG16 model[7].

Aiming to improve the quality of the estimations, two different CNNs were built, with the same structure: one model to estimate the robot position (x and y); and the other to estimate its orientation (θ). Each model is based on transfer-learning from the VGG16 model, as explained in Sect. 3.1. The model's adaptation was based on removing the last layers (dense and softmax) and adding three dropouts (with factor 0.2), three dense layers, 2 with 4096 neurons, and 1 with 1072. Finally, the output layer has a linear activation function and 1 or 2 outputs (with one output for the model to estimate θ and with two outputs to estimate x and y). It is essential to highlight that only the new layers were trained, and all the original weights of VGG16 were maintained, i.e., no fine-tuning was done. Figure 5 presents the adapted model.

To evaluate the quality of the models, four metrics were used: Mean Absolute Error (MAE), Root Mean Squared Error (RMSE), Normalized Root Mean Squared Error (NRMSE), and R^2 [30]. The following equations give these metrics:

$$MAE = \frac{1}{n} \sum_{i=1}^{n} |y_i - \hat{y}_i|, \tag{1}$$

$$RMSE = \sqrt{\frac{1}{n} \sum_{i=1}^{n} (y_i - \hat{y}_i)^2}, \tag{2}$$

$$NRMSE = \frac{RMSE}{y_{max} - y_{min}}, \tag{3}$$

---

[6] To identify the ArUcos, the OpenCV library was used: https://docs.opencv.org/4. x/d5/dae/tutorial_aruco_detection.html.

[7] More detail at https://www.tensorflow.org/api_docs/python/tf/keras/applications/ vgg16/preprocess_input.

$$R^2 = 1 - \frac{\sum\limits_{i=1}^{n}(y_i - \hat{y}_i)^2}{\sum\limits_{i=1}^{n}(y_i - \overline{y}_i)^2}, \tag{4}$$

where y_i represents the true value and the $\hat{y}_i$, represents the predicted value, for instance, i, y_{max} and y_{min} represents the max and min value, respectively, of the observations, while $\overline{y}$ represents the mean. The best value possible for MAE and RMSE is 0, and the worst value is $+\infty$, while for R^2, the range is $(-\infty, 1]$, where $-\infty$ is the worst possible value, and one is the best.

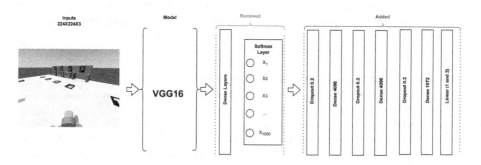

Fig. 5. Architecture of the proposed model.

The datasets were divided into three parts: 80% to training, 10% to validation, and 10% to testing. Since the goal of this study is to propose a possible solution and not a final localization system, the traditional split of the datasets was done aiming to keep it the most as simple as possible. In this way, these data were applied to the CNN models. The cross-validation technique was applied, aiming to avoid overfitting. This way, the data was divided again (independent of the previous division), and a new model was trained and tested with the latest data. This process was done three times, and the final results were based on the average of metrics calculated for the three executions.

Furthermore, as part of the training process, the x and y values were scaled by a factor of 1000 due to their small initial magnitude to facilitate significant improvements. Subsequently, after the estimation phase, the values were rescaled by dividing them by 1000 to restore their original scale.

In addition to the scaling operation, various settings were configured for the Convolutional Neural Network (CNN) model. Specifically, the training was executed over 200 epochs, utilizing an adaptive learning rate strategy[8] with an initial value of 0.0005. The MAE metric was employed for monitoring purposes, with a reduction factor of 0.8, the patience of three epochs, and a minimum

---

[8] https://pytorch.org/docs/stable/generated/torch.optim.lr_scheduler.
ReduceLROnPlateau.html.

value constraint set at 0.00000001. Furthermore, an early stopping criterion was defined, terminating the training process after ten epochs.

All the tests were performed using a GPU NVIDIA A100, with 16GB. The operating system used was Ubuntu 22.04.2 LTS (Jammy Jellyfish), the Python version used was 3.10.6, and the libraries used were: Pandas 2.0.0 and Tensorflow 2.12.0. The CUDA version used was 11.8, with CUDNN 8.9.1.

4   Results and Discussions

The first result to be shown is considering the entire field, using the grid's resolution equal a 1 cm. These results are presented in Table 1, where each column shows a metric for each one of the three components of the pose. Each value is the average of the three executions, and the respective standard deviation is presented.

Table 1. Results obtained considering the whole field.

	MAE			RMSE			NRMSE			R2		
	x[m]	y[m]	$\theta[°]$	x[m]	y[m]	$\theta[°]$	x	y	θ	x	y	θ
Avg.	0.0100	0.0070	6.05	0.0211	0.0142	11.79	0.015	0.019	0.033	0.997	0.996	0.985
Std. Dev.	0.0029	0.0017	2.72	0.0091	0.0028	5.05	0.007	0.004	0.014	0.002	0.002	0.012

The average training time required to train the model for the position (x, y) was 10,047.15 s, with a standard deviation of 3,412.12 s. On the other hand, the model for the orientation (θ) required 5078.67 s with a standard deviation of 1334.86 s. Regarding the inference, the necessary time to estimate the pose of a preprocessed image was 1.9 ms to x and y, and 1.9 ms to θ, with standard deviations of 0.7 ms and 0.5 ms, respectively. In this way, the total time to estimate the complete pose was around 3.8 ms, not considering the necessary time to preprocess the image.

The second result is considering the limited part of the field but varying the grid's resolution. Table 2 presents the results, where the columns represent the resolutions and the lines the metrics for each pose component. All the values (except for the training time) are averages of the three executions.

Comparing the result in the whole field, presented in Table 1 with the results presented in [2], it is possible to see a similarity between the random forest (RF) and CNN. To emphasize, the RF was the approach that presented the best results in that previous study, with errors equal 7 mm in x, 6 mm in y, and 3.05° in θ. Comparing with the results in the current study, a millimeter difference was obtained in x and y (3 mm and 1 mm, respectively), while the difference in θ was 3.0°. In addition, the RMSE and NRMSE presented by the CNNs were similar to that presented by the RF. Furthermore, all the results presented a small standard deviation for the three executions (considering the cross-validation process), indicating that the results of the models were satisfactory and trusty.

Table 2. Results obtained considering the limited part of the field, using different grid's resolution, with *Avg.* columns indicating the average and *Std. Dev.* indicating the standard deviation.

Grid's Resolution		10 mm		5 mm		2.5 mm		1 mm	
Quantity of images		8306		33,291		113,596		655,130	
		Avg.	Std. Dev.	Avg.	Std. Dev.	Avg.	Std. Dev.	Avg.	Std. Dev.
MAE	x[m]	0.0026	0.0001	0.0026	0.0004	0.0023	0.0002	0.0023	0.0006
	y[m]	0.0026	0.0000	0.0027	0.0004	0.0023	0.0004	0.0023	0.0007
	θ[°]	2.97	0.29	2.76	0.14	1.58	0.10	4.51	3.82
RMSE	x[m]	0.0034	0.0002	0.0033	0.0005	0.0029	0.0002	0.0029	0.0006
	y[m]	0.0038	0.0006	0.0042	0.0002	0.0032	0.0003	0.0030	0.0007
	θ	6.03	1.50	7.09	0.76	4.06	0.71	6.99	3.80
NRMSE	x	0.0307	0.0015	0.0302	0.0043	0.0293	0.0026	0.0262	0.0059
	y	0.0345	0.0053	0.0368	0.0021	0.0292	0.0031	0.0279	0.0062
	θ[°]	0.02	0.00	0.02	0.00	0.01	0.00	0.02	0.01
R2	x	0.990	0.001	0.990	0.003	0.990	0.002	0.989	0.005
	y	0.985	0.005	0.984	0.002	0.990	0.002	0.990	0.004
	θ	0.996	0.002	0.995	0.001	0.998	0.001	0.994	0.006
Training time (Position) [s]		678.63	80.85	898.40	153.75	4505.48	647.51	8281.08	233.89
Training time (Orientation) [s]		592.89	80.17	1437.00	401.92	17369.99	3399.39	18509.41	8368.63
Inference time (Position) [ms]		2.95	0.74	2.02	0.07	2.44	0.35	2.06	0.15
Inference time (Orientation) [ms]		2.46	0.12	2.04	0.05	2.22	0.19	1.96	0.40

Another exciting result of this work is the constant size of the models regardless of the number of images used. Each model has a size equal to 512 MB, totaling, in this way, 1024 MB for the complete pose estimation. This size is fixed due to the structure of the CNN, where only the values of parameters are updating, and not the architecture of the CNN. This is interesting because some ML approaches, such as Random Forest, can increase the size considerably since the structure of the model can vary, i.e., the trees can be deeper, according to the problem [3].

Analyzing the results presented in Table 2, it is possible to notice the errors were practically constant for all resolutions. This behavior differs from that found for the same test done in [2], where the prediction quality improved with the grid's resolution. So, it indicates that for the proposed model, the trade-off found in [2] is not applied here. Nevertheless, for the resolutions 10 mm, 5 mm, and 2.5 mm, the results using CNN were better or equal to that presented by random forest, and only for 1 mm the CNN results were worst than RF. Again, all the presented results show a small standard deviation, indicating that the results for all three executions in the cross-validation were close to each other.

5   Conclusions

The results confirm the main hypothesis and show that using CNN to address the localization issue in RobotAtFactory 4.0 is an effective strategy. Therefore, the main goal of this study was achieved. Comparing the results presented with the ones in [2], a significant improvement is seen, showing better results when the whole field is considered. When different grid resolutions are considered (10 mm, 5 mm, and 2.5 mm), the performance of the proposed CNN is similar to the ML techniques shown in [2]. Furthermore, the uniformity of the predictions, i.e., through the RMSE, evidence that the CNN presents more stable results than the other ML approaches.

In addition, another advantage to the ML approaches, especially Random Forest, was the stable size of the models. While the Random Forest can drastically vary the size of the trained models, such as presented in [3], the CNN models were constantly the same size, due to a pre-defined structure, before the training. This is an exciting advantage because it is important to understand the necessary resources if these models are executed in an embedded system.

Another exciting advantage to the ML approaches presented in [2] is that CNN does not necessarily the identification of ArUco's markers. While the input of the ML models is the relative pose of each ArUco, in the CNN, this identification is irrelevant since the input is just the image. However, it is essential to emphasize that the presented approaches are not the final system to pose estimation but a part of that. A complete localization system, which can include filters such as the Extended Kalman Filter, can solve problems with ambiguous images and improve the quality of the estimations.

Finally, in future work, we aim to embed the complete localization system and implement it in a real environment, making necessary adjustments, such as retraining the models with images from the real scenario. In addition, it is planned to explore various conditions and scenarios and assess their respective impacts on localization accuracy. Another interesting work is exploring other transfer-learning models and performing fine-tuning in the models, aiming to improve their quality.

Acknowledgments. The project that gave rise to these results received the support of a fellowship from "la Caixa" Foundation (ID 100010434). The fellowship code is LCF/BQ/DI20/11780028. João Braun is a PhD Student at the Faculty of Engineering, University of Porto (FEUP).

References

1. Braun, J., et al.: A robot localization proposal for the RobotAtFactory 4.0: a novel robotics competition within the Industry 4.0 concept. Front. Rob. AI **9** (2022). https://doi.org/10.3389/frobt.2022.1023590
2. Klein, L. C., et al.: A machine learning approach to robot localization using fiducial markers in RobotAtFactory 4.0 competition. Sensors **23**(6), 3128 (2023). https://doi.org/10.3390/s23063128
3. Klein, L.C., et al.: Using machine learning approaches to localization in an embedded system on RobotAtFactory 4.0 competition: a case study. In: 2023 IEEE International Conference on Autonomous Robot Systems and Competitions (ICARSC), pp. 69–74. IEEE (2023)
4. Grewal, M.S., Weill, L.R., Andrews, A.P.: Global Positioning Systems, Inertial Navigation, and Integration. John Wiley & Sons, Hoboken (2007)

5. Huang, S., Dissanayake, G.: Robot localization: an introduction. In: Wiley Encyclopedia of Electrical and Electronics Engineering, pp. 1–10 (1999)
6. Kalman, R.E.: A new approach to linear filtering and prediction problems. J. Basic Eng. **82**(1), 35–45 (1960). https://doi.org/10.1115/1.3662552
7. Welch, G., Bishop, G.A.: An introduction to the kalman filter. New York EBooks **1**(4), 1–16 (1995). https://academic.csuohio.edu/simond/reduce/ijar.pdf
8. Fox, D., Burgard, W., Thrun, S.: Markov localization for mobile robots in dynamic environments. J. Artif. Intell. Res. **11**, 391–427 (1999)
9. Gordon, N.J., Salmond, D.J., Smith, A.F.: Novel approach to nonlinear/non-Gaussian Bayesian state estimation. In IEE Proceedings F (Radar and Signal Processing), vol. 140, no. 2, pp. 107–113. IET Digital Library (1993)
10. Arulampalam, M.S., Maskell, S., Gordon, N., Clapp, T.: A tutorial on particle filters for online nonlinear/non-Gaussian Bayesian tracking. IEEE Trans. Signal Process. **50**(2), 174–188 (2002)
11. Lauer, M., Lange, S., Riedmiller, M.: Calculating the perfect match: an efficient and accurate approach for robot self-localization. In: Bredenfeld, A., Jacoff, A., Noda, I., Takahashi, Y. (eds.) RoboCup 2005. LNCS (LNAI), vol. 4020, pp. 142–153. Springer, Heidelberg (2006). https://doi.org/10.1007/11780519_13
12. Besl, P.J., McKay, N.D.: Method for registration of 3-D shapes. In: Sensor Fusion IV: Control Paradigms and Data Structures, vol. 1611, pp. 586–606. Spie (1992)
13. Biber, P., Straßer, W.: The normal distributions transform: A new approach to laser scan matching. In: Proceedings 2003 IEEE/RSJ International Conference on Intelligent Robots and Systems (IROS 2003) (Cat. No. 03CH37453), vol. 3, pp. 2743–2748. IEEE (2003)
14. Sobreira, H., et al.: Map-matching algorithms for robot self-localization: a comparison between perfect match, iterative closest point and normal distributions transform. J. Intell. Rob. Syst. **93**, 533–546 (2019)
15. Michail, K., Cain, B., Carroll, S., Anand, A., Camden, W., Nikolaos, V.: Fiducial markers for pose estimation. J. Intell. Rob. Syst. **101**(4) (2021)
16. de Oliveira Júnior, A., Piardi, L., Bertogna, E. G., & Leitão, P.: Improving the mobile robots indoor localization system by combining slam with fiducial markers. In 2021 Latin American Robotics Symposium (LARS), 2021 Brazilian Symposium on Robotics (SBR), and 2021 Workshop on Robotics in Education (WRE), pp. 234–239. IEEE (2021)
17. Nessa, A., Adhikari, B., Hussain, F., Fernando, X.N.: A survey of machine learning for indoor positioning. IEEE Access **8**, 214945–214965 (2020)
18. Sadeghi Esfahlani, S., Sanaei, A., Ghorabian, M., Shirvani, H.: The deep convolutional neural network role in the autonomous navigation of mobile robots (SROBO). Remote Sens. **14**(14), 3324 (2022)
19. Atanasyan, A., Roßmann, J.: Improving self-localization using CNN-based monocular landmark detection and distance estimation in virtual testbeds. In: Tagungsband des 4. Kongresses Montage Handhabung Industrieroboter, pp. 249–258. Springer, Heidelberg (2019). https://doi.org/10.1007/978-3-662-59317-2_25
20. Kendall, A., Grimes, M., Cipolla, R.: Posenet: a convolutional network for real-time 6-dof camera relocalization. In: Proceedings of the IEEE International Conference on Computer Vision, pp. 2938–2946 (2015)
21. Szegedy, C., et al.: Going deeper with convolutions. In: Proceedings of the IEEE Conference on Computer Vision and Pattern Recognition, pp. 1–9 (2015)
22. McCulloch, W.S., Pitts, W.: A logical calculus of the ideas immanent in nervous activity. Bull. Math. Biophys. **5**, 115–133 (1943)

23. Rumelhart, D.E., Hinton, G.E., Williams, R.J.: Learning representations by back-propagating errors. Nature **323**(6088), 533–536 (1986)

24. Goodfellow, I., Bengio, Y., Courville, A.: Deep Learning. MIT press, Cambridge (2016)

25. LeCun, Y., Bengio, Y., Hinton, G.: Deep learning. Nature **521**(7553), 436–444 (2015)

26. Simonyan, K., Zisserman, A.: Very deep convolutional networks for large-scale image recognition. arXiv preprint arXiv:1409.1556 (2014)

27. Chen, Y., Chen, R., Liu, M., Xiao, A., Wu, D., Zhao, S.: Indoor visual positioning aided by CNN-based image retrieval: training-free, 3D modeling-free. Sensors **18**(8), 2692 (2018)

28. Braun, J., Júnior, A.O., Berger, G.S., Lima, J., Pereira, A.I., Costa, P.: RobotAtFactory 4.0: a ROS framework for the SimTwo simulator. In: 2022 IEEE International Conference on Autonomous Robot Systems and Competitions (ICARSC), pp. 205–210. IEEE (2022)

29. Costa, P., Gonçalves, J., Lima, J., Malheiros, P.: Simtwo realistic simulator: a tool for the development and validation of robot software. Theory Appl. Math. Comput. Sci. **1**(1), 17–33 (2011)

30. Sammut, C., Webb, G.I. (eds.): Encyclopedia of Machine Learning. Springer, Heidelberg (2011). https://doi.org/10.1007/978-0-387-30164-8

Deep Learning and Machine Learning Techniques Applied to Speaker Identification on Small Datasets

Enrico Manfron[1,2,3]($\boxtimes$) ⓘ, João Paulo Teixeira[1,2] ⓘ, and Rodrigo Minetto[3] ⓘ

[1] Research Centre in Digitalization and Intelligent Robotics (CeDRI), Instituto Politécnico de Bragança, Campus de Santa Apolónia, 5300-253 Bragança, Portugal
enricomanfron@alunos.utfpr.edu.br, joaopt@ipb.pt
[2] Associate Laboratory for Sustainability and Technology (SusTEC), Instituto Politécnico de Bragança, Campus de Santa Apolónia, 5300-253 Bragança, Portugal
[3] Federal University of Technology - Paraná, Curitiba 80230-901, Brazil
rminetto@utfpr.edu.br
https://cedri.ipb.pt

Abstract. In this study, we explore the capabilities of speaker recognition technology for biometric authentication developing speaker recognition-based access control systems and serving as a resource for future research and improvements in secure and efficient speaker identification solutions. We focused on developing and evaluating machine learning and deep learning models for speaker identification. The models were trained and tested on private datasets with 32 speakers and public datasets with 1251 to 6112 speakers. The Gaussian Mixture Model performed well with our private datasets, with 93,10%, and 95% accuracy in correctly identifying the speakers. The Multilayer Perceptron achieved a peak accuracy of 93.33% on the Framed Trim private dataset. The VGG-M model, after initial training on larger datasets, achieved an accuracy of 90.34% and 98.33% on our private datasets. At last, the model ResNet50 slightly outperformed the other models on two versions of our private dataset, achieving accuracies of 97.93% and 100%.

Keywords: Speaker Identification · Convolutional Neural Network · Deep Learning

1 Introduction

The speaker recognition technology can be used for biometric authentication in secure environments, particularly in access control systems. In recent times, there has been significant advancement in speaker recognition technology, including the creation of complex algorithms and machine learning models. This technology can accurately identify individuals by analyzing their unique vocal traits, thus allowing access to restricted areas.

A. I. Pereira et al. (Eds.): OL2A 2023, CCIS 1982, pp. 195–210, 2024.
https://doi.org/10.1007/978-3-031-53036-4_14

In this work, we discuss the strategies for developing and testing four models for recognizing speakers: Gaussian Mixture Model (GMM), Multilayer Perceptron (MLP), Visual Geometry Group Medium (VGG-M) model used in the VoxCeleb1 [1], and ResNet50 model discussed in the VoxCeleb2 [2]. The main objective of this paper is to investigate speaker recognition-based access control systems to grant access to CeDRI's laboratory. Future work will involve deploying the most effective model on a device such as a Raspberry Pi or a computer. We explored the application of different models and compared the results specifically for the speaker identification task for a small audio dataset of Portuguese speakers (European, Brazilian, African, and foreign speakers).

The paper begins with a review of the existing literature on speaker recognition in Sect. 2. In Sect. 3, we provide a detailed description of the methodologies employed to develop the models, including the GMM, MLP, VGG-M, and ResNet-50, and the datasets used for training, validation, and testing. Section 4 presents a comparative performance analysis of these models across different datasets. The paper concludes in Sect. 5 with an analysis and evaluation of the experimental results obtained from evaluating the models.

2   Related Work

Speaker recognition (SR) experienced significant progress in recent years, thanks to the development of new techniques and the increased availability of large datasets. Consequently, many academic papers have been published, delving into many SR aspects, from fundamental concepts and methodologies to the most recent cutting-edge models.

In 1995, Reynolds and Rose [3] introduced the Gaussian Mixture Model. This model served as the basis for speaker recognition for over a decade [4]. GMM models are applied in many applications in computer vision, speech recognition, and speaker recognition due to their ability to approximate complex distributions using a combination of simple Gaussian distributions. However, in recent years, deep learning has presented exceeding results for the speaker recognition task [5,6].

The study by Hanifa et al. [7] provides an extensive overview of SR models, focusing on crucial aspects such as background noise, lack of data, and model attacks. It presents a timeline of the field's evolution, highlighting the developed technologies and advancements. Researchers have explored various preprocessing methods, standard features used in the field, potential model types and classifiers, and application areas.

A study conducted in 2010 [8] utilized three Discrete Wavelet Transform (DWT) with different coefficients, employing an MLP and a GMM as classifiers. Both models achieved high accuracy (ACC) (98% and 99%), but the MLP could be trained with audio samples half the duration of those used in the GMM model. In the subsequent years, research focused on neural networks, such as the Fuzzy Min-Max Neural Network (FMMNN) [9], variations of the GMM model [10], and comparisons with the Hidden Markov Model (HMM), all using Mel Frequency Cepstral Coefficients (MFCC) vectors as input [11].

Different attempts have been made to improve upon the MFCC features, including exploring variations such as Normalized Dynamic Spectral Features (NDSFs) and Linear Prediction Cepstral Coefficients (LPCCs) to determine if they provide better feature representation than MFCCs [12]. The field has now moved towards using x-vectors due to their robustness to noise [13]. Recent surveys have shown that a combination of features, such as MFCCs + Power Normalized Cepstral Coefficients (PNCC) [14] and Linear Discriminant Analysis (LDA) + MFCCs [15], have also been used to improve these features.

In 2018, Chung et al. [2] built a dataset with over 6,000 speakers and compared CNN models and training strategies that can effectively recognize identities from voice under diverse conditions. These models exceeded the performance of previous works.

3 Methodology

For this study, we implemented early SR approaches such as the GMM and the MLP model. Then we moved on to more recent models that use CNN and ResNet networks. By comparing and contrasting these various approaches, we comprehensively understood the underlying concepts and challenges associated with SR.

3.1 Audio Features

This section explains the specific audio features used in this study. As indicated by Fernandes et al. [16] and J. P. Teixeira et al. [17], these features have demonstrated good performance and are frequently utilized in the field with better results, also presented in the literature review in Sect. 2.

- **Mel Frequency Cepstral Coefficients (MFCCs):** Are the cepstral formant coefficients extracted from the Discrete Cosine Transform calculation from a Mel-scaled Log Power Spectrum from an audio signal. In other words, this coefficient describes how the frequency components of a sound signal are built.
- Δ **MFCCs** are derivatives of the MFCCs that provide the rate of change of the MFCCs, adding temporal information to the features.
- Δ^2 **MFCCs** are second-order derivatives of the MFCCs that provide the rate of change of the Delta MFCCs, adding another level of temporal information.
- **Chroma STFT** represents the audio where the spectrum's magnitude is divided into bins representing different pitches or chroma.
- **Root Mean Square (RMS)** measures the audio signal's power. It is calculated by squaring the amplitude values, averaging them, and then taking the square root.
- **Spectral Centroid (SC)** measures that indicate where the "center of mass" of the spectrum is located. It is used in digital signal processing to measure a sound's brightness.

- **Spectral Bandwidth (SBW)** measures how wide the power distribution is across different frequencies.
- **Spectral Rolloff (SRO)** measures the shape of the signal's power spectrum. It represents the frequency below which a specified percentage of the total spectral energy lies.
- **Zero Crossing Rate (ZCR)** is the rate at which the signal changes from positive to negative or back.
- **Short-Time Fourier Transform (STFT)** is a Fourier transform that is applied to short intervals in order to analyze a signal. By examining local sections of the signal over time, it can determine each section's sinusoidal frequency and phase content and provide information about its frequency.
- **Spectrogram** is a visual representation of the different frequencies in a sound or signal over time. The time axis is represented horizontally, the frequency axis is represented vertically, and the plot's color or intensity represents each frequency's power at a specific time.

3.2 Datasets

This work aims to create a speaker recognition system to grant access to CeDRI's laboratory. To accomplish this, we utilized a unique dataset from CeDRI members' speeches. This dataset comprises 169 distinct utterances, with durations varying from 2.7 s to as long as 21.5 s. These utterances were collected by text-reading from 32 individuals, all of whom are Portuguese-speaking. The gender distribution of the speakers is approximately 69% male and 31% female. The dataset contains contemplates various accents and dialects from different Portuguese-speaking regions such as Portugal (37.5%), Angola (18.60%), São Tome (15.6%), Cabo Verde (12.5%), Mozambique (6.3%), Brazil (6.3%), and Spain (3.1%). The age distribution of our speakers is in the primarily early twenties. The data distributions of our dataset are illustrated in Fig. 1.

In addition to our dataset, we also utilized the VoxCeleb1 [1] and VoxCeleb2 [2] datasets for training our convolutional models. The VoxCeleb1 is a large-scale dataset of over 100,000 utterances from 1,251 unique speakers. The VoxCeleb2 dataset is significantly larger, containing over a million utterances from over 6,000 speakers. Both datasets are collected from open-source media and include various ethnicities, accents, professions, and ages. The datasets contain audio segments affected by real-world noise, such as background chatter, overlapping speech, laughter, and different room acoustics providing a rich source of variability and complexity.

3.3 Models

In this section, we provided a detailed explanation of the models used in this study and details about their characteristics and implementations.

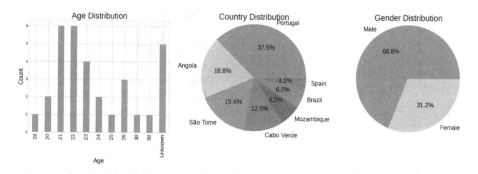

Fig. 1. Distribution Analysis showcasing age, country, and gender distributions within the dataset.

GMM. The GMM [3] is a statistical model that can identify subpopulations within a dataset without requiring explicit labels. When a new utterance is introduced, acoustic features X are extracted. Assuming we have S candidate speakers, with the GMM parameters λ_S, the model computes the likelihood of the utterance for each speaker's GMM. Then, to find the closest speaker among all candidates, we identify the speaker s that maximizes the likelihood as the best match using the Eq. 1.

$$s = \arg \max_{1 \leq s \leq S} \ln p(X|\lambda_S) \tag{1}$$

We used our dataset with 32 speakers, each represented by a GMM model. Each model consisted of 23 Gaussian components and utilized a diagonal covariance matrix. The input to these models were features extracted from audio files. We experimented many combinations of features such as MFCCs, along with their first and second derivatives, Chroma STFT, RMS, SC, SBW, SRO, and ZCR. The model takes the extracted features from the audio input and generates an embedding that matches against stored speaker profiles to generate dissimilarity scores. These scores are then thresholded to produce the final identification results.

MLP. Based on the work done by Kral et al. [8], we implemented an MLP model for speaker recognition. We began with a simple MLP model that classified 32 speakers during the initial testing phase. The model used 33 to 77 input features, similar to the features used in GMM model, including MFCC(20), Δ MFCC(20), Δ^2 MFCC(20), Chroma STFT(12), RMS, SC, SBW, SRO, and ZCR in the experiments. The MLP architecture consisted of an input layer, fc1, with variable input and 256 neurons; two hidden layers, fc2 and fc3, with 128 and 64 neurons, respectively; and an output layer fc4, with 32 neurons representing the number of classes of the dataset. Table 1 shows the architecture of the MLP model used in the study.

Table 1. MLP Architecture. N represents a variable number of inputs.

Layer (type)	Input Shape	Output Shape
fc1	N	256
fc2	256	128
fc3	128	64
fc4	64	32

VGG-M. The VGG-M model is a CNN characterized by high efficiency and good audio classification performance. In [2], the VGG-M was modified by replacing the fully connected fc6 layer with two layers: a fully connected layer of 9×1 and an average pool layer with support $1 \times n$, where n relates to the input speech segment length. With this modification, the network can rely on temporal aspects rather than frequency while also maintaining the output dimensions of the original fully connected layer and reducing the number of network parameters.

We used the VGG-M model in this work due to its proven effectiveness in the VoxCeleb1 [1]. The model's invariance to temporal position and sensitivity to frequency aligns well with the nature of speech data. Inspired by Guedes et al. [18], we also employed the pre-trained VGG-M model to conduct transfer learning on our dataset to identify our 32 speakers. This involved re-creating the classifier after training on the VoxCeleb dataset, specifically to classify our 32 speakers, changing the model's output, and training now for our database. The architecture of VGG-M is shown in Table 2.

Table 2. VGG-M Architecture.

Layer (type)	Support	Input Dim	Output Dim	Stride
conv1	7×7	1	96	2×2
mpool1	3×3	-	-	2×2
conv2	5×5	96	256	2×2
mpool2	3×3	-	-	2×2
conv3	3×3	256	384	1×1
conv4	3×3	384	256	1×1
conv5	3×3	256	256	1×1
mpool5	5×3	-	-	3×2
fc6	9×1	256	4096	1×1
apool6	$1 \times n$	-	-	1×1
fc7	1×1	4096	1024	1×1
fc8	1×1	1024	1251	1×1

ResNet50. The ResNet architecture adapts a standard CNN with skip connections, which allows the layers to add residuals to an identity mapping on the channel outputs. The VoxCeleb2 [2] explores ResNet-34 and ResNet-50, adapting their layers to accommodate the spectrogram input. In our study, we adopted the ResNet-50 architecture and trained it on the VoxCeleb2 data. Following the same idea as the VGG-M model, we performed transfer learning by modifying the output layer and retraining the model on our specific dataset. The architecture of the ResNet-50 model is in Table 3.

Table 3. Modified Res-50 architecture. Each row specifies the number of convolutional filters and their sizes as $size \times size$, # filters.

Layer (type)	ResNet-50
conv1	7×7, 64, stride 2
pool1	3×3 max pool, stride 2
conv2_x	$\begin{bmatrix} 1 \times 1 & 64 \\ 3 \times 3 & 64 \\ 1 \times 1 & 256 \end{bmatrix} \times 3$
conv3_x	$\begin{bmatrix} 1 \times 1 & 128 \\ 3 \times 3 & 128 \\ 1 \times 1 & 512 \end{bmatrix} \times 4$
conv4_x	$\begin{bmatrix} 1 \times 1 & 256 \\ 3 \times 3 & 256 \\ 1 \times 1 & 1024 \end{bmatrix} \times 6$
conv5_x	$\begin{bmatrix} 1 \times 1 & 512 \\ 3 \times 3 & 512 \\ 1 \times 1 & 2048 \end{bmatrix} \times 3$
fc1	9×1 2048 stride 1
pool_time	$1 \times N$ $avgpool$ stride 1
fc2	1×1 5994

3.4 Data Preparation

We exclusively used CEDRI's laboratory dataset to train the GMM. This dataset contains audio files of varying lengths, ranging from 2.7 to 21.5 s, as shown in Fig. 2. To standardize our dataset, we initially applied two filters. The first was a silence removal filter, eliminating audio sections below a 30db threshold. The second was a trim filter, which removed silence from the beginning and end of the audio, also at a 30db threshold. Based on this process, we created two versions of the original dataset: one with silence removed and the other with silence trimmed from the start and end of the audio.

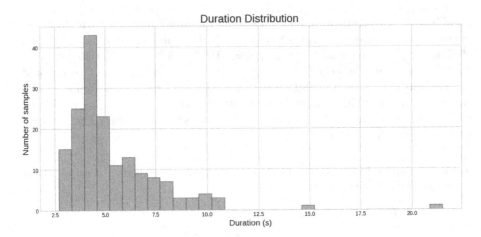

Fig. 2. Histogram showcasing the duration distribution of audios.

The silence removal dataset had a range of 1.824 s to 10.35825 s, and the trim dataset had a range of 1.888 s to 12.608 s. These datasets were then processed to segment the audio files so that all had the same duration. For instance, the audio files in the silence removal dataset were divided to all have a length of 1.824 s, while those in the trim dataset were adjusted to 0.944 s. Subsequently, 70% of the audio files from the silence and trim datasets were designated as training data, 10% to validation, and the remaining 20% as test data, as shown in Table 4. However, for the GMM model, the validation splits were considered training data.

From Framed Trim and Framed Silence Removed datasets, we extracted features such as Chroma STFT, RMS, SC, SBW, SRO, ZCR, and MFCCs to feed into the models GMM and MLP. For the VGG-M and ResNet50 models, we utilized the VoxCeleb1 and VoxCeleb2 datasets. We extracted the STFT from the audio and used this as input to the VGG-M. For the ResNet50 model, we extracted the spectrogram and performed normalization before feeding it into the ResNet50. Initially, we randomly selected 40 speakers from the VoxCeleb1 dataset and used their audio files for testing both the VGG-M and ResNet50 models.

In the case of the VGG-M model, to maximize the use of the audio length in the VoxCeleb1 dataset, we created a framed version of the dataset. In this version, each audio file was divided into multiple 3-second segments, effectively increasing the number of audio files available for training.

When we moved on to the VoxCeleb2 dataset, which is significantly larger, we had to use the training approach proposed in the original VoxCeleb2 [2] due to the large volume of data. We randomly selected a 3-second frame from each audio file and computed the STFT or Spectograms of the audio. The VoxCeleb1 and VoxCeleb2 datasets were split into training, validation, and testing subsets, as shown in Table 4.

We also extracted the STFT and Spectrograms for the VGG-M and ResNet50 models during the transfer learning stage from our Framed Silence Removed and Framed Trim datasets. Given that the duration of these audios is less than 3 s, we performed padding to match the model's input requirements.

Table 4. Separation of data in Framing Trim, Framing Silence Removed, VoxCeleb 1, and VoxCeleb 2 datasets

Dataset	Total	Train	Test	Validation
Framed Trim	724	523 (72.24%)	145 (20.03%)	56 (7.73%)
Framed Silence Removed	289	197 (68.16%)	60 (20.76%)	32 (11.07%)
VoxCeleb 1	148, 642	104, 590 (70.36%)	29, 738 (20.01%)	14, 314 (9.63%)
Framed VoxCeleb 1	332, 918	233, 587 (70.16%)	66, 589 (20.00%)	32, 742 (9.83%)
VoxCeleb 2	1, 092, 009	766, 917 (70.23%)	218, 373 (20.00%)	106, 719 (9.77%)

4   Experimental Results and Discussion

In this section, we present the development and experimentation process of the four models used in this study: the GMM, the MLP, the VGG-M, and the ResNet-50. We will discuss the characteristics of each model, the modifications made to adapt them to our task, and the results obtained from our experiments.

4.1   GMM Experiments

For the first GMM implementation step, we focused on the task of Speaker Identification and used the Framed Silence Removal and Trim datasets. The development of the GMM model required the creation of a unique GMM model to represent each speaker. Each model has 23 Gaussian components and also a diagonal covariance matrix. Once trained, when a new audio sample is introduced, the features from this audio are extracted and passed through all the models. The model that generates the highest score is selected as the speaker identified. To calculate the score, we used a function that calculates the average log-likelihood per sample of the provided data.

To evaluate the model's performance, we passed each test audio through the models and asked them to classify the speaker. Then, we counted the correct classifications and calculated the accuracy with which the model identified the speakers. Considering this evaluation, we conducted several experiments by varying the input data to compare the best set of input features for the GMM model. The results of these experiments are summarized in Table 5.

The Framed Silence Removed dataset and the Framed Trim dataset were the primary data sources for these experiments. We can notice that the Silence dataset demonstrated higher accuracy across various feature combinations. This observation could happen for two reasons, and the first one is because the Silence

Removed dataset has lesser data to classify, and the second one is that the Silence Removed data is cleaner than the trim dataset. We could also notice that the model's accuracy decreased as we increased the input parameters for both datasets. This suggests a potential trade-off between the complexity of the model and its performance.

In summary, the performance of the GMM model in Speaker Identification depends on data quality and input parameters. Clean data works best, as shown by higher accuracy with Silence Removed. Adding more parameters can decrease accuracy, indicating sensitivity to complexity.

Table 5. Accuracy of the GMM model with different feature combinations

Dataset	Input Features	Accuracy (%)
Silence Removed	MFCC(13)	95.00
	MFCC(13), ΔMFCC(13), Δ^2MFCC(13)	93.00
	MFCC(13), Chroma STFT, RMS, SC, SBW, SRO, ZCR	91.66
	MFCC(20)	93.00
	MFCC(20), ΔMFCC(20), Δ^2MFCC(20)	90.00
	MFCC(20), Chroma STFT, RMS, SC, SBW, SRO, ZCR	93.33
	MFCC(20), ΔMFCC(20), Δ^2MFCC(20), Chroma STFT, RMS, SC, SBW, SRO, ZCR	91.66
Trim	MFCC(13)	90.34
	MFCC(13), ΔMFCC(13), Δ^2MFCC(13)	86.89
	MFCC(13), Chroma STFT, RMS, SC, SBW, SRO, ZCR	86.20
	MFCC(20)	93.10
	MFCC(20), ΔMFCC(20), Δ^2MFCC(20)	86.20
	MFCC(20), Chroma STFT, RMS, SC, SBW, SRO, ZCR	90.34
	MFCC(20), ΔMFCC(20), Δ^2MFCC(20), Chroma STFT, RMS, SC, SBW, SRO, ZCR	88.27

4.2   Multilayer Perceptron Experiments

Inspired by Kral et al. [8] study, we implemented an MLP model to initially test Artificial Neural Networks in the field of Speaker Identification and then gain more experience in DL development. In order to do that, just the Framed Trim dataset served as the input data for these experiments. We developed a basic MLP model to classify 32 speakers, using the first 13 MFCCs, Δ MFCCs, and Δ^2 MFCCs as input features, resulting in a descriptor size of 39 features. The MLP model, containing three hidden layers with 256, 128, and 64 neurons, respectively, was trained for 50 epochs using CrossEntropy as the loss function. This initial setup yielded an accuracy of 74%.

In the second experiment, we adjusted the data allocation for training, validation (early stopping), and testing to 70%, 10%, and 20%, respectively. We initially set the early stopping criteria based on the loss function but later shifted to accuracy as we observed that accuracy could still improve despite an increase in loss. This model achieved an accuracy of 91.12% on the test data. The increase in loss with improved accuracy could be attributed to class imbalance arising from varying audio lengths among speakers, leading to different numbers of MFCC vectors extracted per speaker.

In the third experiment, we expanded the model's feature set to include chroma STFT, RMS, SC, SBW, SRO, ZCR, and additional MFCCs (20 columns), resulting in a total descriptor size of 77 features. The model, trained over 500 epochs, achieved a validation accuracy of 93.48% and a test accuracy of 92.19%. The training process became more stable with the increased number of features, although the loss continued to increase.

In the final experiment, we reduced the learning rate from 0.001 to 0.0001, which led to more stable training and a further improvement in accuracy. The model achieved a validation accuracy of 93.40% and a test accuracy of 93.33%.

Table 6 provides a comparison of the MLP network's results.

Table 6. Performance of MLP Model Across Attempts

Experiments	Input Features	Validation ACC (%)	Test ACC (%)
Experiment 1	MFCC(13), ΔMFCC(13), Δ^2MFCC(13)	–	74.00
Experiment 2	MFCC(13), ΔMFCC(13), Δ^2MFCC(13)	91.76	91.12
Experiment 3	MFCC(20), ΔMFCC(20), Δ^2MFCC(20), chroma SFTF(12), RMS(1), SC(1), SBW(1), SRO(1), ZCR(1)	93.48	92.19
Experiment 4	MFCC(20), ΔMFCC(20), Δ^2MFCC(20), chroma SFTF(12), RMS(1), SC(1), SBW(1), SRO(1), ZCR(1)	93.40	93.33

4.3 VGG-M and ResNet50 Experiments

For conducting experiments using the convolutional neural networks ResNet and VGG-M, initially, we downloaded the VoxCeleb1 dataset, which contains 1,251 speakers. We implemented the model proposed in the VoxCeleb1 [1], a modified VGG-M model designed to accept STFT data instead of an image. To extract the STFT data, we process audio data segmented into 3 s, sampled at 16kHz, using a window of 25ms and a step of 10ms. The data was then normalized and passed to the VGG-M model for classification.

We processed the data as described in the VoxCeleb [2] and built the model architecture to classify into 40 classes. For this training, we reduced the number of speakers to 40 chosen randomly, which still resulted in more than 1GB of data. This reduction was made because this dataset has a large amount of data, so we could perform tests more quickly. The best accuracy achieved during training was 92.20% for validation data and 90.25% for test data.

We also implemented the model proposed in the VoxCeleb2 [2], which recommends using a ResNet50 model. The input for this model is similar to the VGG-M, but instead of the STFT, the input is a Spectrogram derived from the

STFT. The dimensions and sampling rate are the same. We also modified the first convolutional layer to accept one-dimensional spectrograms, as the original network accepts three-dimensional RGB images. We also removed the final layers described in the VoxCeleb2 [2] and added the classifier described in the paper.

After training the model, we achieved an accuracy of 88.60% for validation data and 86.40% for test data for this reduced data set with 40 speakers. The accuracy of the ResNet50 model was lower than that of the VGG-M model because the dataset used was undersized. The VoxCeleb2 [2] used a larger dataset with about 6,000 speakers. The more significant amount of data used in training the ResNet50 resulted in better generalization results.

After this initial test, we chose the best model to train with the complete Framed VoxCeleb 1 dataset, created from The VoxCeleb1 dataset was then processed to separate the audio into 3 s frames and separated into 70% for training, 20% for testing, and 10% for validation. This dataset was used to train the VGG-M, with a learning rate of 0.0001 and a Cross Entropy Loss function. The model achieved an accuracy of 85.66% on validation data and 86.20% on test data, which is higher than the first VoxCeleb1 [1] results.

Next, we conducted additional experiments using the VoxCeleb2 dataset. This dataset is considerably larger than VoxCeleb1, with 1,092,009 speeches from 5,994 speakers. Previously, the VoxCeleb1 data was separated into 3 s frames and then used in training the models. However, with over 1 million audio, adopting another strategy described in the VoxCeleb2 [2] was necessary. In this strategy, a 3 s audio segment is randomly selected for each audio and then used for training. This way, different parts of a recording can be used at different times during training.

Then, we trained the VGG-M network for the VoxCeleb2 data, now with 5,994 output classes. This model improved when the data increased. With the VoxCeleb1 data, we obtained an accuracy of 85.66% for validation data and 86.20% for test data. However, with the VoxCeleb2 data, the accuracy increased to 89.34% for validation data and 89.19% for test data. We trained the model for 100 epochs using a learning rate of 1e-05 to achieve this.

For the ResNet50 model, with the VoxCeleb2 data, we achieved an accuracy of 95.22% for validation data and 95.09% for test data after 100 training epochs

Table 7. Summary of the accuracy results for the VGG-M and ResNet50 models on the VoxCeleb1 and VoxCeleb2 datasets.

Model	Dataset	Validation ACC (%)	Test ACC (%)
VGG-M	VoxCeleb1 (40 speakers)	92.20	90.25
ResNet50	VoxCeleb1 (40 speakers)	88.60	86.40
VGG-M	VoxCeleb1	85.66	86.20
VGG-M	VoxCeleb2	89.34	89.19
ResNet50	VoxCeleb2	95.22	95.09

with a learning rate of 1e-05. This one performed the best of all the models we trained with the VoxCeleb datasets (Table 7).

After training the VGG-M and ResNet50 models with the VoxCeleb1 and VoxCeleb2 datasets, we selected the models with the highest accuracies to proceed with the transfer learning stage. The best-performing models were the VGG-M trained with the VoxCeleb2 dataset and the ResNet50 also trained with the VoxCeleb2 dataset.

For the VGG-M model, the transfer learning process began by importing the weights from the best-performing VGG-M model. We then reset the **f7** layer and adjusted the output of the **f8** layer to classify 32 classes, corresponding to the number of speakers in our dataset. The process for the ResNet50 model was similar. We imported the weights from the best-performing ResNet50 model, reset the **fc1** layer, and adjusted the output of the **fc2** layer to classify 32 classes. Following these adjustments, all layers were kept trainable, and then we trained these adjusted models.

The ResNet50 and the VGG-M model were retrained in this stage for 20 and 60 epochs, respectively. We trained each model on our two personal datasets, the Framed Trim and Framed Silence Removed. Given that the audio samples in these datasets are shorter than 3 s, we performed padding to study the models' responses. We padded the audio samples adding zeros at the end until they reached a length of 3 s, and in other testing sessions, we conducted the training without padding. The results of all these training sessions are in Table 8.

Table 8. Summary of Transfer Learning Results for ResNet50 and VGG-M Models

Model	Dataset	Padding	Accuracy (%)
ResNet50	Framed Trim	N	97.93
		Y	93.10
	Framed Silence Removed	N	100.00
		Y	100.00
VGG-M	Framed Trim	N	88.97
		Y	90.34
	Framed Silence Removed	N	88.33
		Y	98.33

Analyzing the results, it is observable that for the ResNet50 model, the accuracy decreased when adding padding to the Framed Trim dataset. On the other hand, for the VGG-M model, adding padding to the Framed Trim dataset did not seem to make a significant difference, but there was a slight improvement in the Framed Silence Removed dataset. Since the Framed Silence Removed dataset is smaller than the Trim dataset and its audio files are longer, the accuracy is expected to be slightly higher when testing on Framed Silence Removed dataset. The 100 percent accuracy means the system identified correctly all the speakers in the test set.

4.4 Discussion

The GMM model demonstrated sensitivity to the input features' complexity and the data quality. As we increased the number of input parameters, the model's accuracy decreased, indicating a potential trade-off between the model's complexity and performance. The GMM model achieved the highest accuracy with the Framed Silence Removed dataset, which is cleaner and has fewer data to classify than the Trim dataset.

The MLP model was tested with different feature sets and data allocations. The model's accuracy improved as we expanded the feature set and adjusted the data allocation for training, validation, and testing. The highest accuracy achieved with the MLP model was 93.33% on the Framed Trim dataset.

The VGG-M and ResNet-50 models were initially trained on the larger Vox-Celeb1 and VoxCeleb2 datasets for transfer learning. We processed the audio data into 3-second segments for both models and computed the STFT or spectrogram of the audio for input. During the training of the VGG-M in the VoxCeleb1 dataset, the model achieved an accuracy of 86.20% which outperformed the best accuracy in the first VoxCebeb 1 paper. Then the VGG-M model achieved the best accuracy of 89.19%, classifying 5994 people over the VoxCeleb2 data. At the same time, the best ResNet-50 model in this step reached an accuracy of 95.09% for test data within the VoxCeleb2 data.

In the transfer learning stage, the VGG-M and ResNet50 models were fine-tuned using our datasets, Framed Trim and Framed Silence Removed. The VGG-M model achieved the best accuracy of 90.38% on the Framed Trim dataset and 98.33% on the Framed Silence Removed dataset. The ResNet50 model, on the other hand, achieved the best accuracy of 97.93% on the Framed Trim dataset and 100% on the Framed Silence Removed dataset.

Both models adapted well to the new data. However, the ResNet50 model slightly outperformed the VGG-M model on all datasets, training in fewer epochs than VGG-M, suggesting that it might be more robust to variations in the data making it the best-performing model in our study.

It's also important to mention that the Framed Silence Removed dataset is smaller, provides audio with a more extensive duration, and is cleaner than the Framed Trim dataset. These characteristics contribute to all models achieving higher accuracy in this dataset in comparison Framed Trim dataset, not meaning that this dataset is better, just easier to classify. The comparison of all best models over the Framed Trim and Framed Silence Removed datasets are summarized in Table 9.

Table 9. Summarized results from comparing the best models.

Dataset	Best Models	Acurracy (%)
Framed Trim Dataset	GMM	93.10
	MLP	93.33
	VGG-M	90.34
	ResNet50	**97.93**
Silence Removed Dataset	GMM	95.00
	VGG-M	98.33
	ResNet50	**100.00**

5 Conclusion

This study explored different machine learning and deep learning models for speaker recognition technology, which can be used to build a biometric authentication system in the future. We tested models such as GMM, MLP, VGG-M, and ResNet50 on various datasets. These models were trained on different datasets, including Framed Trim and Framed Silence Removed.

The GMM accurately identified speakers with 93.10% in Framed Trim dataset and 95% in accuracy Framed Silence Removed dataset. The Multilayer Perceptron performed on the Framed Trim dataset with an accuracy of 93.33%. The VGG-M model, after initial training on larger datasets, achieved 90.34% in Framed Trim dataset and 98.33% in Framed Silence Removed dataset. Finally, the ResNet-50 model outperformed the others, achieving the highest accuracy of 100% on the Framed Silence Removed dataset and 97.93% on Framed Trim dataset, suggesting that it might be more robust to variations in the data. However, it's important to note that the Framed Silence Removed dataset, which is smaller and cleaner than the Framed Trim dataset, contributed to all models achieving higher accuracy.

In summary, the performance of each model in speaker identification depends on various factors, including the quality and complexity of the input data, the choice of features, and the model architecture. Our research provides insights into developing speaker recognition-based access control systems. It serves as a resource for future research and improvements in secure and efficient Speaker Identification solutions.

Acknowledgment. The authors are grateful to the Foundation for Science and Technology (FCT, Portugal) for financial support through national funds FCT/MCTES to CeDRI (UIDB/05757/2020 and UIDP/05757/2020) and SusTEC (LA/P/0007/2021).

References

1. Nagrani, A., Chung, J.S., Zisserman, A.: VoxCeleb: a large-scale speaker identification dataset. In: Interspeech 2017. ISCA (2017)
2. Chung, J.S., Nagrani, A., Zisserman, A.: VoxCeleb2: deep speaker recognition. In: Interspeech 2018. ISCA (2018)
3. Reynolds, D.A., Rose, R.C.: Robust text-independent speaker identification using gaussian mixture speaker models. IEEE Trans. Speech Audio Process. 3(1), 72–83 (1995)
4. Bai, Z., Zhang, X.-L.: Speaker recognition based on deep learning: an overview. Neural Netw. 140, 65–99 (2021)
5. Snyder, D., Garcia-Romero, D., Sell, G., Povey, D., Khudanpur, S.: X-vectors: robust DNN embeddings for speaker recognition. In: 2018 IEEE International Conference on Acoustics, Speech and Signal Processing (ICASSP), pp. 5329–5333 (2018)
6. Lei, Y., Scheffer, N., Ferrer, L., McLaren, M.: A novel scheme for speaker recognition using a phonetically-aware deep neural network. In: 2014 IEEE International Conference on Acoustics, Speech and Signal Processing (ICASSP), pp. 1695–1699 (2014)
7. Hanifa, R.M., Isa, K., Mohamad, S.: A review on speaker recognition: technology and challenges. Comput. Electr. Eng. 90, 107005 (2021)
8. Kral, P.: Discrete wavelet transform for automatic speaker recognition. In: 2010 3rd International Congress on Image and Signal Processing. IEEE (2010)
9. Jawarkar, N.P., Holambe, R.S., Basu, T.K.: Use of fuzzy min-max neural network for speaker identification. In: 2011 International Conference on Recent Trends in Information Technology (ICRTIT). IEEE (2011)
10. Krishnamoorthy, P., Jayanna, H.S., Prasanna, S.R.M.: Speaker recognition under limited data condition by noise addition. Expert Syst. Appl. 38(10), 13487–13490 (2011)
11. Tolba, H.: A high-performance text-independent speaker identification of Arabic speakers using a CHMM-based approach. Alex. Eng. J. 50(1), 43–47 (2011)
12. Chougule, S.V., Chavan, M.S.: Robust spectral features for automatic speaker recognition in mismatch condition. Procedia Comput. Sci. 58, 272–279 (2015)
13. Villalba, J., et al.: State-of-the-art speaker recognition for telephone and video speech: the JHU-MIT submission for NIST SRE18. In: Interspeech 2019. ISCA (2019)
14. Bharath, K.P., Rajesh, K.M.: ELM speaker identification for limited dataset using multitaper based MFCC and PNCC features with fusion score. Multimed. Tools Appl. 79(39–40), 28859–28883 (2020)
15. Zergat, K.Y., Selouani, S.A., Amrouche, A.: Feature selection applied to g.729 synthesized speech for automatic speaker recognition. In: 2018 IEEE 5th International Congress on Information Science and Technology (CiSt). IEEE (2018)
16. Fernandes, J.F.T., Freitas, D., Junior, A.C., Teixeira, J.P.: Determination of harmonic parameters in pathological voices—efficient algorithm. Appl. Sci. 13(4), 2333 (2023)
17. Teixeira, J.P., Freitas, D.S.: Segmental durations predicted with a neural network. In: Proceedings of Eurospeech 2003 - International Conference on Spoken Language Processing, pp. 169–172 (2003)
18. Victor, G., et al.: Transfer learning with audioset to voice pathologies identification in continuous speech. Procedia Comput. Sci. 164, 662–669 (2019)

Impact of EMG Signal Filters on Machine Learning Model Training: A Comparison with Clustering on Raw Signal

Ana Barbosa[1,2,3(✉)] , Edilson Ferreira[1,2,3] , Vinicius Grilo[1,2,3] ,
Laercio Mattos[2], and José Lima[1,3]

[1] Research Centre in DIgitalization and Intelligent Robotics (CeDRI), Instituto
Politécnico de Bragança, 5300-253 Bragança, Portugal
edilsonsfc@live.com, {viniciusgrilo,jllima}@ipb.pt
[2] Centro Federal de Educação Tecnológica de Minas Gerais (CEFET-MG), Minas
Gerais, Brazil
cb_ana@outlook.com, laercio.mattos@gmail.com
[3] Laboratório Associado para a Sustentabilidade e Tecnologia em Regiões Montanha
(SusTEC), Instituto politécnico de Bragança, 5300-253 Bragança, Portugal

Abstract. Our current society faces challenges in integrating individuals with disabilities, making this process difficult and painful. People with disabilities (PwD) are often mistakenly considered incapable due to the difficulties they face in daily tasks due to the lack of adapted means and tools. In this context, assistive technologies play a crucial role in improving the quality of life for these individuals. However, assistive technologies still have various limitations, making research in this area essential to enhance existing solutions and develop new approaches that meet individual needs, aiming to promote inclusion and equal opportunities. This paper presents a research project that focuses on the study of electromyography (EMG) signal processing generated by individuals who have undergone amputations. These signals are essential in assistive technologies, such as myoelectric prostheses. The study focuses on the impact of different filters and machine learning training methods on this processing. The results of this study have the potential to provide relevant findings for the development of more efficient assistive technologies. By understanding the processing of EMG signals and applying machine learning techniques, it is possible to improve the accuracy and response speed of prosthetics, increasing the functionality and naturalness of movements performed by users, as well as paving the way for the emergence of new technologies.

Keywords: Assistive technologies · Electromyography (EMG) signal processing · Machine learning

1 Introduction

In our society, certain body features are associated with beauty, health, and perfection, while others are seen as flaws. Different bodies are often viewed as disadvantages, complicating the integration of individuals carrying these features, leading to a challenging and painful process. In this context, people with disabilities (PWD) are frequently considered imperfect and incapable. This perception is further exacerbated by the lack of adapted means and tools, resulting in numerous difficulties in performing everyday tasks. Consequently, these individuals are further alienated from what society deems a "normal" life.

Amputees, for example, face significant physical and psychological challenges, and the possibility of using assistive technologies such as prosthetics, which represent the most comprehensive solution to this issue, plays a crucial role in rehabilitation and improving the quality of life. However, even with advancements in assistive technology, these technologies still have limitations in replicating all movements of the biological limb and are generally expensive.

In light of this reality, this article explores the use of EMG signals, which represent the electrical activity associated with muscle contraction, along with machine learning algorithms aiming to enhance existing technologies and develop new solutions, focusing on the impacts of different filters on the training methods. Despite the evident applicability of EMG signals and machine learning techniques for the development of advanced assistive technologies, there is still a gap in recent studies evaluating the impact of different types of filters on the performance of machine learning algorithms in classifying multi-channel EMG signals. Previous research has mainly focused on signal classification applications and specific machine learning methods, without conducting a systematic comparison of filters in conjunction with these different classification algorithms.

Therefore, this article employs an approach that applies four filters (bandpass, Kalman, moving average, and Nocth) to EMG signals. These filtered signals are used to train three supervised machine learning methods: Decision Tree, Random Forest, and SVM, as well as an unsupervised clustering method. The goal is to identify the most efficient combinations for the classification and interpretation of EMG signals

2   Theoretical Background and Related Work

In this section, an overview of the relevant theoretical foundations related to the study topic will be presented. Fundamental concepts and theories will be addressed, establishing a solid foundation for understanding and developing the research at hand.

2.1   EMG Signal

The main focus of this study is centered on the analysis and treatment of a specific type of signal that originates from muscle movement.

Muscles play a crucial role in generating force and movement in the human body. Muscle force is the result of muscles' ability to convert chemical energy into mechanical energy. There are three types of muscle tissue in the human body: smooth, cardiac, and skeletal. In this context, our focus is on skeletal muscles, which are directly involved in body movement.

To understand muscle contraction and stretching, it is necessary to explore the macroscopic and microscopic anatomy of muscles. Muscles are composed of muscle fibers, which in turn contain myofibrils. These myofibrils consist of myosin and actin filaments, responsible for muscle contraction. The sarcoplasm, the fluid filling the spaces between myofibrils, contains various substances and protein enzymes. The sarcoplasmic reticulum stores calcium ions (Ca++) and releases them during muscle contraction.

Voluntary control of skeletal muscles is achieved through somatic motor neurons. Action potentials, which are electrical signals generated in response to stimuli, originate at the neuromuscular junction where the somatic motor neuron connects with the muscle fiber. Communication between these cells occurs through the release of a neurotransmitter called acetylcholine (ACh). When ACh binds to receptors on the muscle fiber, ion channels open, allowing the flow of sodium ions (Na++) and triggering a muscle action potential. This action potential propagates along the muscle fiber, causing the sarcoplasmic reticulum to release stored calcium ions, resulting in muscle contraction. [10]

This brings us to electromyography (EMG), a technique used to record and monitor the electrical activity of muscles. It captures the summation of action potentials generated in muscle fibers during contraction. EMG signals provide valuable information about muscle function and are widely used in studies of muscular diseases, assessment of muscle performance during physical exercises, and the development of assistive technologies. Understanding myoelectric signals and the use of EMG are essential for advancing in the field of rehabilitation, myoelectric prosthetics, and other applications related to the interface between muscles and technology [18].

2.2   Signal Filters: Definition and Types

In the present context, the effects of filters on signal processing will be explored, as they play a role in modifying the spectral content of these signals. The various types of filters employed in this research will be discussed, with the purpose of describing their characteristics and specific applications. The main objective is to provide an in-depth understanding of these filters, thus establishing a solid foundation for comprehending the present study.

– **Bandpass Filter** A bandpass filter allows a specific range of frequencies to pass while attenuating or rejecting frequencies outside that range. It can be created by combining a highpass and a lowpass filter [21,22].
  The gain of a bandpass filter is ideally maximum within the passband and minimum outside of it, and the attenuation rate is determined by the design requirements [19,21,22].
  Designing a bandpass filter involves determining the center frequency, the width of the passband, and the attenuation rate for frequencies outside the passband. There are different configurations of bandpass filters, such as Butterworth and Chebyshev, each with its own frequency response and implementation characteristics [19,21,22].

- **Kalman Filter** The Kalman Filter is a mathematical estimator used to solve the linear-quadratic problem by estimating the state of a linear dynamic system affected by random noise. It provides optimal statistical estimation of the state based on measurements that are linearly related to the state but corrupted by white noise [9].

  From a practical perspective, the Kalman Filter has found wide applications in controlling complex dynamic systems such as manufacturing processes, aircraft, ships, and spacecraft. It allows for inferring missing information from indirect and noisy measurements, enabling a better understanding of system behavior. Furthermore, the Kalman Filter is useful for predicting future behavior in uncontrollable dynamic systems like river flows, celestial body trajectories, or commodity prices [9].

- **Moving Average Filter** Moving Average Filters (MAFs) are cost-effective and easy to implement linear-phase FIR filters. They operate by continuously calculating the average value of input signals within a sliding time window T_W. This helps reduce undesired harmonics and distortion. MAFs exhibit a low-pass filtering behavior, providing unity gain at zero frequency and attenuating frequencies at regular intervals determined by the window size. They are commonly used as ideal low-pass filters under specific conditions [15,27]. Due its characteristics, the MAF suffers a response delay on T_W. Typically, a smaller T_W means a shorter MAF response delay; however, the filtering performance is also dependent on T_W [27].

- **Notch Filter** A notch filter is a linear filter that selectively eliminates a specific frequency component, known as the notch frequency, while maintaining unit gain at other frequencies. These filters are widely used in various applications where targeted frequency components need to be removed [22].

  However, FIR notch filters often have a wide bandwidth, resulting in significant attenuation of nearby frequencies. To address this, poles can be introduced into the filter to create resonance and reduce the notch bandwidth. However, this may introduce a slight ripple in the passband, which can be minimized by adding more poles and/or zeros. Nevertheless, this approach is considered ad hoc and relies on trial-and-error, presenting a notable challenge [22].

2.3   Machine Learning: Concepts and Applications

Machine Learning is a field of artificial intelligence research in prominence and in constant evolution today that focuses on the development of algorithms and models capable of making predictions or decisions from data collection without the need for explicit programming, as in classical programming. These algorithms cover a wide range of concepts and techniques that allow the extraction of patterns and decision-making from data sets, with applications in several areas, such as signal processing, computer vision, data analysis, among others [25].

For Machine Learning concepts to be applied, a few core elements are required. First of all, is needed to have a relevant amount of data. This data is used to train the model and needs to be representative and contain meaningful information for the problem. The preparation and processing of data are also extremely important steps in building a good machine learning model.

The learning techniques of a machine learning model can be divided into three types:

- **Supervised:** Supervised learning involves the presence of an external instructor who imparts knowledge about the environment through sets of examples in the format of input-output pairs. The machine learning algorithm leverages these examples to extract a representation of the acquired knowledge. The primary goal is to generate a representation that can accurately produce desired outputs for novel inputs that have not been encountered before [11].
- **Unsupervised:** Unsupervised learning operates without the presence of a teacher, meaning there are no labeled examples provided. This algorithm, employed in such scenarios, strives to acquire a representation or grouping of the given inputs based on a quality measure. These techniques are predominantly utilized when the goal is to uncover patterns or trends that facilitate comprehension of the data [23].
- **Reinforcement:** Reinforcement Learning (RL) is a dynamic method to learn optimal actions through trial and error in an interactive environment. Unlike other approaches that rely on pre-existing labeled data, RL operates in an environment where the agent learns by taking actions and observing the resulting feedback or rewards. This feedback serves as a signal for the algorithm to adjust its decision-making process and maximize its long-term objective, known as the reward function [3].

2.4   Training Methods

Some examples of training methods are:

- **Decision tree** emerged as versatile tools for prediction and classification, and were one of the pioneering statistical algorithms to be implemented in electronic form during the widespread adoption of digital circuits for computational purposes in the last decades of the 20th century. Over time, they have evolved into highly adaptive and computationally intensive methods that find applications in a variety of disciplines. Decision trees now serve as general-purpose mechanisms for prediction and classification, as well as indispensable components in artificial intelligence, machine learning, knowledge discovery, and inductive rule construction. Their use extends to a diverse range of tasks in data mining, knowledge discovery, machine learning, and artificial intelligence [8].
  A key feature of decision trees lies in their recursive subset approach, employed to analyze a target data field based on the values of associated input fields or predictors. This methodology facilitates the creation of partitions within the data set, resulting in descending subsets of data called leaves or nodes. Notably, these leaves or nodes contain progressively similar intra-leaf (or intra-node) target values, while exhibiting progressively different inter-leaf (or inter-node) values at each level of the tree. This hierarchical organization allows decision trees to effectively discern patterns and

relationships within the data, enabling robust predictive and classification capabilities. This unique feature, combined with the computational intensity and interdisciplinary applicability of decision trees, contributes to their broad utility in a variety of research and practice domains [8].

- **Random forest** The method called random forest is an extension of decision tree models and consists of creating multiple individual decision trees through a process called "ensemble learning". Each tree in a random forest is built and trained using variables or a set of random information in the dataset, allowing each tree to learn different characteristics of the data set decision trees [26].

  When a prediction is required, after the model is trained, each tree performs its individual prediction and then a final decision is made by the model. This collective process reduces overfitting and consequently improves the generalizability of the model.

  One of the main advantages of Random Forests is their ability to handle large data sets while maintaining robustness, since in a sense the problem is divided into several decision trees. Furthermore, they are less sensitive to outliers and noise when compared to individual decision trees [4].

- **Support Vector Machine or SVM** is a widely used machine learning algorithm for classification and regression. Its main goal is to find the optimal hyperplane that separates the input data into distinct classes, seeking the largest margin between the closest training samples. Such samples are called support vectors and play a crucial role in the definition of the hyperplane [17]. For non-linearly separable data sets we use mapping tricks to a higher dimensional space, where linear separation through a hyperplane is possible [17].

  This machine learning technique has good generalization capabilities, since the optimization process is based on margin maximization, which tends to avoid unwanted overfittings. The possibility of application to non-linearly separable problems makes SVMs extremely flexible and able to handle a wide variety of classification and regression problems [17].

  However, the training process of an SVM can become computationally demanding for large data sets, so it is necessary to evaluate the size of the data set when using the SVM as a learning algorithm [16].

- **Clustering** is a technique used to group similar objects or data points based on their intrinsic characteristics, aiming to discover patterns, structures, or relationships within a dataset without prior knowledge of the specific groups or classes [7].

  The challenge lies in dividing the data into groups in a way that maximizes their similarity. Clustering has been extensively studied due to its diverse applications in data mining and machine learning, including summarization, segmentation, and targeted marketing [2].

  There is a wide variety of problems that can be solved with clustering algorithms, such as Collaborative Filtering, Data Summarization, Biological Data Analysis, and Social Network Analysis [2].

2.5 Related Work

The study of electromyographic (EMG) signals has advanced significantly, with applications in medicine, biomedical engineering, biomechanics, and neuro-science [18]. Improvements in the acquisition, processing, and interpretation of EMG signals have been achieved, allowing for a greater understanding of muscle function and the diagnosis of neuromuscular disorders, in addition to the control of assistive devices [14]. Techniques such as decomposition into individual motor units, machine learning, and brain-machine interfaces have been explored [24].

However, EMG signals can be compromised due to noise and artifacts. Studies have sought ways to remove these noises and recover the actual muscle signal. [6] analyzed four filtering procedures, finding that the wavelet method stood out for preserving all information and having greater accuracy.

Recent studies have also explored the application of machine learning in EMG signal analysis. One study developed a control system for a robotic hand using an Artificial Neural Network (ANN), achieving an accuracy of 84.78% in the identification of hand movements [20]. Another study used the Q-Tuned Wavelet Transform (TQWT) for feature extraction and applied various machine learning classifiers, achieving the highest success rate with Random Forest (RF), 98.64% in the classification of neuromuscular disorders [1].

There are also works exploring the use of EMG features in early detection of medical conditions, such as hand osteoarthritis [12]. In assistive technology, EMG signal processing and machine learning techniques are used to enhance prosthesis functionality, increasing accuracy and response speed [13]. Studies like [5] also demonstrate significant advancements in motion estimation and EMG signal classification to enhance prosthesis functionality.

In sum, the field of EMG signal processing and the use of machine learning is very promising. Advancements in this field have the potential to improve the quality of life for many individuals.

3 Methodology

This section describes the methods and procedures used in this study to collect and analyze the data. It provides a clear overview of how the research was conducted.

3.1 Data Acquisition

For data acquisition, the Myo Gesture Armband, developed by THALMCLABS, was used, which is capable of capturing electromyographic (EMG) signals from the forearm muscles. In addition to EMG signals, the armband also provides additional information such as accelerometers and gyroscopes. Although this device was not originally designed for this specific purpose, it can be used as a non-invasive tool to capture the electrical signals generated by the muscles during contraction. With its 8 channels, it is possible to obtain signals from distinct muscles during movement, allowing comprehensive data acquisition.

The main objective of this step was to create a suitable database for training the machine learning methods presented earlier. For this purpose, data were collected from 12 volunteers, including 5 women and 7 men, all between the ages of 20 and 30, in good health and without amputations. The armband was placed on the right forearm of each volunteer, and 60 files were recorded for each of them. Of these, 30 files correspond to the execution of the hand closing and opening movement, varying in duration and the force applied in each capture. The other 30 files correspond to the absence of movement, meaning the volunteer did not perform any specific movement. Each capture had a duration of 3 s. The stored files vary in the number of samples, ranging from 600 to 800 samples, depending on the file.

Subsequently, the collected data was saved in CSV files, where each column represents an EMG channel, facilitating data processing. In Fig. 1, It is possible to observe at the top in black the 8 channels during the execution of the movement, while at the bottom of the figure we have in blue the same 8 channels during the absence of movement.. These collected and organized data files provide the foundation for the subsequent steps of analysis and training of the machine learning algorithms.

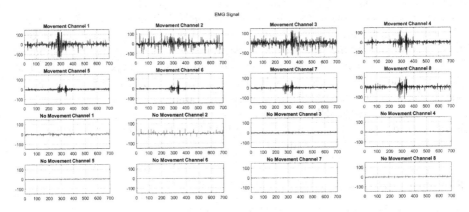

Fig. 1. Comparison of 8-channel EMG signals during movement execution (Black) and absence of movement (Blue). (Color figure online)

Upon observing Fig. 1, it is evident that the movement is characterized by signals with higher amplitudes. Specifically, when the volunteer performs the movement, the EMG signals exhibit larger amplitudes, whereas in the absence of movement, only small amplitudes are observed. Furthermore, it can be noted that, for the hand-closing movement, the signal is not uniformly reproduced across all channels, indicating varied muscular activation intensities based on their respective contributions to the execution of the movement.

3.2   Data Filtering

After properly storing the data, we proceeded to process it. In order to gain a better understanding of the filters that operate in the frequency domain, we performed the Fourier transform to visualize the frequencies present in the signal, as well as their magnitude. Figure 2 displays the applied transform for each channel, represented in black for the movement data and in blue for the non-movement data.

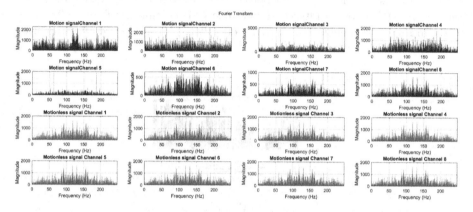

Fig. 2. Fourier Transform of Raw Signal during movement execution (Black) and absence of movement (Blue). (Color figure online)

The first filter applied was the bandpass filter, with a passband ranging from 5 Hz to 500 Hz. This range was chosen based on the frequency range typically present in healthy skeletal muscle action potentials.

Next, with the cutoff frequencies defined, the bandpass filter was applied to all files in the database. The filter was applied to each column of the files, using the Fourier transform to perform the filtering. The result of this filtering can

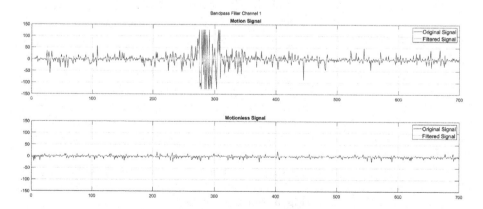

Fig. 3. Bandpass Filtering

be observed in Fig. 3, where the original signal is represented in black and the filtered signal is represented in red. For better visualization, only channel one is being presented.

It is evident that the filter performed well in attenuating the signal, even with the removal of a relatively narrow frequency range. It is important to note that although the filter was designed to eliminate all frequencies below 5 Hz and above 500 Hz, only frequencies below 5 Hz were effectively eliminated. This is because in the original signal, the maximum frequency present is around 250 Hz, so there were no frequencies above 500 Hz to be removed. The application of the Fourier transform to the filtered signal allows visualizing the filter's effect. As shown in Fig. 4, frequencies below 5 Hz were efficiently suppressed after the filter application.

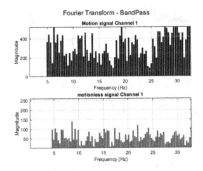

Fig. 4. Fourier Transform of Bandpass Filtering

Another filter used for frequency elimination is the notch filter, which aims to remove a specific frequency. In this case, the filtering process was performed to eliminate the 50 Hz frequency, which represents the interference caused by the

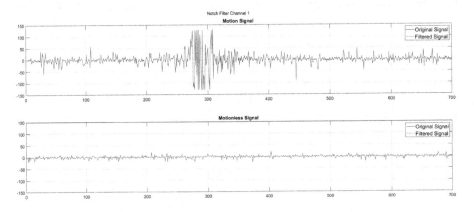

Fig. 5. Notch Filtering

power grid in Portugal, where the data was captured. Similar to the passband filter, the notch filter is also applied to each column of the files. The effectiveness of the filtering can be observed in Fig. 5, where the original signal is represented in black and the filtered signal is represented in red. It is important to note that only channel one is presented for better visualization of the results.

By performing the Fourier transform of the filtered signal, as illustrated in Fig. 6, we can observe that the filter was effective in attenuating the frequencies near 50 Hz. However, it is notable that the elimination of this single frequency did not have a significant impact on the signal, as the filtered signal overlaps almost completely with the original signal. This indicates that the 50 Hz interference caused by the power grid was not a dominant source of distortion in the captured signal.

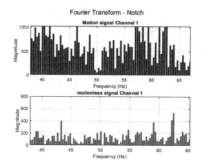

Fig. 6. Fourier Transform of Notch Filtering

The next step involved applying the moving average filter, testing different window sizes, including 3, 5, 10, 50, and 100 samples. The result of this filtering can be observed in Fig. 7, where the left side shows the filtering of the signal with

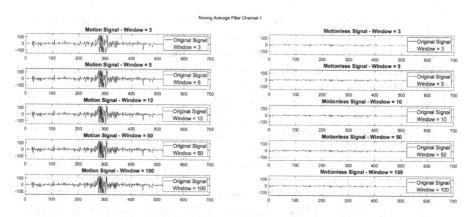

Fig. 7. Moving Average Filtering

movement, and the right side shows the filtering of the signal without movement. It is noticeable that as the window size increases, the signal is more attenuated, meaning there is a greater smoothing of the signal.

Finally, the last filter applied was the Kalman filter, which is implemented in the prediction and update steps. In the prediction step, the filter estimates the next state of the system based on the previous state, while in the update step, the filter corrects the estimated state based on the actual measurement. The result of this filtering can be observed in Fig. 8, where a significant attenuation of the signal is evident.

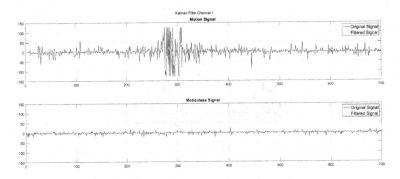

Fig. 8. Kalman Filtering

3.3   Training of Machine Learning Methods

After the proper data prepossessing, it's time to start training the models. We have selected three supervised models and one unsupervised model, which will be explained below. Training and evaluating these models will allow valuable insights into the relationship between filtered EMG signals and the accuracy of the tested models.

– **Supervised models** In this supervised training process, the general operating structure remains consistent, differing only in the applied training model, which includes Decision Trees, Random Forests, and Support Vector Machines (SVM). Each of these models has its peculiarities, but the overall workflow to apply them remains the same.

  The first step of this process involves reading data from CSV files. These files contain data classified as 'movement' and 'non-movement,' which form the two classes that the models will try to predict. The data is read and combined into a single DataFrame, one for each class, to facilitate subsequent processing. This step is crucial as it allows all information to be gathered into a single coherent data structure.

  After data consolidation, the next step is to split the data into training, validation, and test sets. These sets represent 70%, 20%, and 10% of the data, respectively. Splitting the data this way is a common practice in machine learning. The training set is used to train the model, the validation set is used to adjust hyperparameters and assess the model's performance during training, and the test set is used to evaluate the model's performance on unseen data. One point to consider is that many machine learning models cannot handle null values. To address this, in this process, any missing values in the data are filled with the mean of existing values.

After data preparation, the selected model is trained. The model learns patterns from the training data that enable it to predict whether a given example belongs to the 'movement' or 'non-movement' class. Then the model is evaluated by running the validation and test sets and comparing the model's predictions with the actual labels. This provides a measure of the model's performance, usually expressed as a percentage of correct predictions, known as accuracy. Finally, the trained model is saved to a file, allowing it to be reused later without the need for retraining.

- **Unsupervised model** In this context, the process of unsupervised training maintains a similar operational structure to supervised cases, albeit with some specific nuances. The learning model used here is k-means, a clustering algorithm. The first step involves reading data from CSV files and combining this information into a single DataFrame. Similar to the supervised case, this data is then partitioned into training, validation, and test sets, following the proportions of 80%, 10%, and 10%, respectively. Like many models, k-means also does not handle missing values well, so these values are filled with the mean of existing ones.

The data preparation phase continues with the selection of specific columns from the DataFrame that represent Electromyography (EMG) signals. These signals are then normalized to ensure that all signals are on the same scale, facilitating the clustering process. Next, the k-means algorithm is applied to the training data, learning the centroids of the clusters. Once trained, the model is used to make predictions on the validation and test sets, and the predicted labels are stored for further evaluation.

The model's performance is evaluated by comparing the predicted labels with the true ones, generating an accuracy measure. Finally, just as in supervised cases, the trained model is saved in a file to be reused later, eliminating the need for retraining.

The four machine learning models, including K-means, Decision Tree, Random Forest, and SVM, consistently utilize "train_test_split", "test_size", "random_state", and "SimpleImputer". Specific parameters include "n_clusters" for K-means, and the default values of "gini" and "min_samples_split" for Decision Tree and Random Forest, as well as C and gamma for SVM. Although adjustable, these parameters remained unchanged to prevent the introduction of an additional variable to the analysis, which could lead to overfitting of the data. The focus of the study is the impact of the filter on the data, maintaining the model parameters at their default values to establish a consistent reference.

4 Results

The results of the accuracy calculations for each of the training methods are presented in Table 1, showing the accuracies of the supervised training methods for each of the filters applied to the dataset.

Table 1. Accuracy of Trained Models

	BandPass	Moving Average					Kalman	Notch
		3	5	10	50	100		
Decision Tree								
Accuracy Test	0,811	0,775	0,762	0,769	0,825	0,866	0,771	0,805
Accuracy Validation	0,809	0,775	0,759	0,772	0,823	0,865	0,770	0,802
Random Forest								
Accuracy Test	0,876	0,850	0,838	0,845	0,882	0,901	0,843	0,871
Accuracy Validation	0,874	0,850	0,836	0,844	0,881	0,900	0,843	0,869
SVM								
Accuracy Test	0,819	0,812	0,805	0,807	0,799	0,788	0,806	0,812
Accuracy Validation	0,820	0,810	0,803	0,806	0,798	0,788	0,806	0,811

Based on the obtained results, it can be observed that the Random Forest model consistently demonstrated the highest accuracies for all applied filters. In particular, the Moving Average filter with a window size of 100 exhibited exceptional performance, achieving an accuracy of 0.90. The SVM and Decision Tree models showed significant variations in performance depending on the applied filter. Except for the Moving Average filter with a window size of 100, which yielded satisfactory results of 0.866 in the test set and 0.865 in the validation set for the Decision Tree method, no other combination surpassed the performance of the Random Forest. These results suggest that the Random Forest was the most effective method for the analyzed dataset.

When evaluating the different filters, it was consistently observed that the Moving Average filter with a window size of 100 displayed the best performance in the Decision Tree and Random Forest models. Additionally, the Moving Average filter with a window size of 50 yielded satisfactory results, while the BandPass filter also achieved good results. The Notch filter and Moving Average filters with window sizes of 3 and 10 produced intermediate results. The Kalman filter and Moving Average filter with a window size of 5 exhibited inferior performance compared to the other filters in both machine learning models considered.

Regarding the SVM method, it was found that the BandPass filter obtained the best performance, followed by the Notch filter. The Moving Average filters with window sizes of 3, 5, and 10, as well as the Kalman filter, showed intermediate results, while the Moving Average filters with window sizes of 50 and 100 had the lowest accuracy compared to the other filters applied to this method.

Analyzing the validation results, it was observed that the BandPass filter performed well in all methods, being particularly effective in SVM. The Notch filter also stood out by consistently yielding accuracies above 0.800 across all methods. On the other hand, the Moving Average filter with a window size of 5 displayed lower results in all methods, suggesting a limited impact on improving accuracy compared to the other filters.

The results indicate that the SVM method exhibited less variation in performance with respect to the different filters, suggesting that this method may be less sensitive to the considered filter types and may not benefit as much from the applied variations. The analysis of moving average filters reveals significant differences in the performance of different machine learning models depending on the window size used. The choice of window size for the moving average filter should consider the nature of the machine learning model to be used, as well as the trade-off between noise reduction and data reactivity preservation.

For instance, window sizes of 100 and 50 demonstrated the best performance in Decision Tree and Random Forest models. This can be attributed to the larger window's ability to more effectively smooth out data noise, allowing the model to focus on general trends rather than short-term fluctuations. However, larger window sizes may introduce more significant delays, which could be a disadvantage in real-time applications.

On the other hand, the same window sizes of 100 and 50 showed inferior performance in the SVM method, which seeks to find the optimal hyperplane that maximizes the margin between classes. Excessive data smoothing, which can occur with a large moving average filter window, may make the features of support vectors less distinct, and these features are crucial for constructing the SVM's decision boundary. In contrast, smaller window filters may not smooth out data noise sufficiently for Decision Tree and Random Forest models, resulting in a model that could be overly influenced by short-term variations. However, these smaller window filters may be useful for SVM, preserving some important details for constructing the decision boundary.

These assumptions are based on the observations of the results and may vary depending on the nature and quality of the data under consideration. Therefore, the choice of window size should be made carefully, considering the machine learning model to be used and the specific characteristics of the data.

The analysis of the unsupervised model showed considerably lower training accuracies (0.535 for test data and 0.534 for validation data) compared to the supervised methods discussed earlier. These results suggest that the clustering method may be less effective in classifying the dataset used in this article compared to supervised methods. However, it is worth noting that further tests, including the use of filtered data or a different dataset size, can provide a more reliable evaluation of the clustering method's performance in comparison to the supervised methods

The goal of testing this method was to explore the possibility of classifying motion without the need for filtering, which could be of interest in the future for classifying multiple motions. The idea behind the used clustering was to group the data based on similar characteristics. Eliminating the need for filtering would reduce the processing time required for real-time motion classification, contributing to reducing the response time of related technologies. However, the results obtained were not satisfactory for the dataset used in this project.

5   Conclusion

This study focuses on analyzing electromyographic (EMG) signals from individuals with amputations and utilizing machine learning techniques for training. It explores the effects of different filters (bandpass, Kalman, moving average, and notch) and training methods (decision tree, random forest, and support vector machines) to optimize the classification and interpretation of EMG signals.

This research contributes to the field of assistive technology by demonstrating the potential of using EMG signals and machine learning to enhance the functionality and efficiency of assistive technologies. By investigating various filter and training method combinations, it aims to advance assistive technologies, promote inclusivity, social integration, and equal opportunities for individuals with disabilities.

In summary, this study investigated the effectiveness of specific filters in signal analysis, creating possibilities for future research. To further advance this field, future studies will include different types of filters and explore various combinations. Comprehensive analyses of the results, including testing multiple movements, are crucial. Additionally, upcoming tests will analyze EMG signals from individuals with amputations. These future efforts will improve our understanding of filter applications and their impact on outcomes, leading to the development of more accurate and efficient techniques in signal analysis.

Acknowledgment. The authors are grateful to CeDRI (UIDB/05757/2020, UIDP/05757/2020), SusTEC (LA/P/0007/2021) and SmartHealth (NORTE-01-0145-FEDER-000045).

References

1. Abdel-Maboud, N.F., Parusheva, S.S., Alfonse, M., Salem, A.B.M.: Comparative study of machine learning techniques based on TQWT for EMG signal classification. In: 2022 5th International Conference on Computing and Informatics (ICCI), pp. 374–377 (2022). https://doi.org/10.1109/ICCI54321.2022.9756080
2. Aggarwal, C.C., Reddy, C.K. (eds.): Data Clustering. Chapman & Hall/CRC Data Mining and Knowledge Discovery Series. CRC Press, Boca Raton, FL (2013)
3. Alharin, A., Doan, T.N., Sartipi, M.: Reinforcement learning interpretation methods: a survey. IEEE Access **8**, 171058–171077 (2020)
4. Ao, Y., Li, H., Zhu, L., Ali, S., Yang, Z.: The linear random forest algorithm and its advantages in machine learning assisted logging regression modeling. J. Petrol. Sci. Eng. **174**, 776–789 (2019)

5. Briouza, S.: EMG signal classification for human hand rehabilitation via two machine learning techniques: KNN and SVM. In: 2022 5th International Conference on Advanced Systems and Emergent Technologies (IC_ASET), pp. 412–417 (2022). https://doi.org/10.1109/IC_ASET53395.2022.9765856

6. Conforto, S., D'Alessio, T., Pignatelli, S.: Optimal rejection of movement artefacts from myoelectric signals by means of a wavelet filtering procedure. J. Electromyogr. Kinesiol. **9**(1), 47–57 (1999). https://doi.org/10.1016/S1050-6411(98)00023-6, https://www.sciencedirect.com/science/article/pii/S1050641198000236

7. Coradine, L.C., Lopes, R.V.V., Maciel, A.F.: Mineração de dados: Uma introdução. J. Braz. Neural Netw. Soc. **9**, 168–184 (2011). https://doi.org/10.21528/LNLM-vol9-no3-art3

8. De Ville, B.: Decision trees. Wiley Interdisc. Rev. Comput. Stat. **5**(6), 448–455 (2013)

9. Grewal, M.S., Andrews, A.P.: Kalman Filtering: Theory and Practice with MATLAB. Wiley, Hoboken (2014)

10. Hall, J.E.: Tratado de Fisiologia Médica. Elsevier Health Sciences (2021)

11. Haykin, S.S.: Neural Networks: A Comprehensive Foundation. Prentice Hall, Hoboken (1999)

12. Jarque-Bou, N.: Toward early and objective hand osteoarthritis detection by using EMG during grasps. Sensors **23**, 5 (2023). https://doi.org/10.3390/s23052413

13. Kristoffersen, M.: User training for machine learning controlled upper limb prostheses: a serious game approach. J. NeuroEngineering Rehabil. **18**, 1–5 (2021). https://doi.org/10.1186/s12984-021-00831-5

14. Lennon, O., et al.: A systematic review establishing the current state-of-the-art, the limitations, and the desired checklist in studies of direct neural interfacing with robotic gait devices in stroke rehabilitation. Front. Neurosci. **14**, 578 (2020)

15. Liu, C., Jiang, J., Jiang, J., Zhou, Z.: Enhanced grid-connected phase-locked loop based on a moving average filter. IEEE Access **8**, 5308–5315 (2020). https://doi.org/10.1109/ACCESS.2019.2963362

16. Liu, T.Y., Yang, Y., Wan, H., Zeng, H.J., Chen, Z., Ma, W.Y.: Support vector machines classification with a very large-scale taxonomy. ACM SIGKDD Explor. Newsl. **7**(1), 36–43 (2005)

17. Lorena, A.C., De Carvalho, A.C.: Uma introdução às support vector machines. Revista de Informática Teórica e Aplicada **14**(2), 43–67 (2007)

18. Merletti, R., Parker, P.J.: Electromyography: Physiology, Engineering, and Noninvasive Applications, vol. 11. Wiley, Hoboken (2004)

19. Mitra, S.K.: Digital Signal Processing: A Computer Based Approach. McGraw-Hill Companies, New York (2006)

20. Núñez-Montoya, B., Valarezo Añazco, M., Saravia-Avila, A., Loayza, F.R., Valarezo Añazco, E., Teran, E.: Supervised machine learning applied to noninvasive EMG signal classification for an anthropomorphic robotic hand. In: 2022 IEEE ANDESCON, pp. 1–6 (2022). https://doi.org/10.1109/ANDESCON56260.2022.9989874

21. Oppenheim, A.V., Schafer, R.W., Yoder, M.A., Padgett, W.T.: Discrete-time Signal Processing, 3rd edn. Pearson, Upper Saddle River, NJ (2009)

22. Proakis, J.G., Manolakis, D.G.: Digital Signal Processing: Principles, Algorithms, and Applications. Prentice Hall, Hoboken (1996)

23. Souto, M.C.P., Lorena, A.C., Delbem, A.C.B., Carvalho, A.C.P.D.L.F.: Técnicas de aprendizado de máquina para problemas de biologia molecular (2003)

24. Stashuk, D.: EMG signal decomposition: how can it be accomplished and used? J. Electromyogr. Kinesiol. **11**(3), 151–173 (2001)

25. Suvrit, S., Sebastian, N., Stephen J.W.: Optimization for Machine Learning. In: Neural Information Processing Series, The MIT Press, Cambridge (2012). https:// mitpress.mit.edu/9780262537766/optimization-for-machine-learning

26. Xu, G., Liu, M., Jiang, Z., Söffker, D., Shen, W.: Bearing fault diagnosis method based on deep convolutional neural network and random forest ensemble learning. Sensors **19**(5), 1088 (2019)

27. Xue, H., Ruan, M., Cheng, Y.: A fixed length adaptive moving average filter-based synchrophasor measurement algorithm for P class PMUs. Energies **12**(21), 4168 (2019). https://doi.org/10.3390/en12214168

Fault Classification of Wind Turbine: A Comparison of Hyperparameter Optimization Methods

Danielle Pinna[1], Rodrigo Toso[2], Gustavo Semaan[3], Fernando de Sá[3], Ana I. Pereira[4(✉)], Ângela Ferreira[4], Jorge Soares[1], and Diego Brandão[1]

[1] Centro Federal de Educação Tecnológica Celso Suckow da Fonseca, Rio de Janeiro, Brazil
danielle.pinna@eic.cefet-rj.br, {jorge.soares,diego.brandao}@cefet-rj.br
[2] Microsoft, Redmond, USA
rfran@microsoft.com
[3] Universidade Federal Fluminense, Rio de Janeiro, Brazil
{gustavosemaan,fernandosa}@id.uff.br
[4] Research Center in Digitalization and Intelligent Robotics, Instituto Politécnico de Bragança, Bragança, Portugal
{apereira,apf}@ipb.pt

Abstract. The last few years have been marked by the insertion of renewable technologies in the global energy matrix, such as wind and solar energy, which are considered clean energies with low environmental impact. Wind turbines, responsible for the energy conversion process, are complex equipment that are expensive and susceptible to numerous failures. Monitoring turbine components can help detect failures before they occur, reducing equipment maintenance costs. This work compares the training time of different techniques for tuning hyperparameters in supervised machine-learning models for fault detection in wind turbines. Results show the importance of data optimization during model training.

Keywords: Wind turbine · Machine learning · Fault classification

1 Introduction

Wind energy is an important clean and renewable energy resource available in nature that has been increasingly used. The main benefits of wind energy are related to environmental aspects since it does not emit any harmful greenhouse gases into the atmosphere in the energy conversion process. In addition, and considering the technological development of these systems, the levelized energy cost of onshore wind turbines is nowadays competitive which adds these systems an economic interest [1].

In 2022, 77 GW of new wind power installations were added to power grids worldwide, bringing total installed wind capacity to 906 GW, a 9% growth compared to 2021. Although new onshore installations were down 5% compared to

A. I. Pereira et al. (Eds.): OL2A 2023, CCIS 1982, pp. 229–243, 2024.
https://doi.org/10.1007/978-3-031-53036-4_16

the previous year, 2022 was still the third-highest year in history for additions. In terms of cumulative installs, the top five markets at the end of 2022 were unchanged. China, USA, Germany, India and Spain together accounted for 72% of the world's total wind energy installed capacity [2].

The wind turbine is the technical structure responsible for the conversion of wind energy into electrical energy. With this global growth in power generation, there are also challenges related to reducing the operation and maintenance (O&M) costs of turbines, which are sophisticated, complex, and expensive systems. According to [3], O&M of turbines are responsible for around 25% to 35% of generation costs. The turbine system is composed of several external and internal components, such as the tower, rotor, generator and blades.

Currently, wind turbines are hosted with a data collection and storage system known as the Supervisory Control and Data Acquisition - SCADA, which monitors and stores data on the entire functioning of the turbines through sensors installed in their components. These variables can be, for example, oil temperature and pitch angle, and also meteorological variables, such as temperature, atmospheric pressure, and wind speed. The advantage of dealing with real-time data measurement is that they represent the real state of health of the turbine, which is directly related to the possibility of reducing maintenance costs. Furthermore, SCADA has proven to be an excellent system for preventive maintenance based on data [4].

Most studies on fault detection in wind turbines use operational and event data sets, such as those provided by SCADA [5]. Such data can be used for the development of fault detection models in wind turbines, like machine learning models. A machine learning model uses training data to learn the relationship between input and output data, and can be used to classify new input data. One of the most important parts of machine learning is selecting the optimal hyperparameters to ensure an accurate and efficient model.

This paper aims to compare different hyperparameter tuning techniques in machine learning models, considering a data-centric approach, to help detect faults in wind turbine components extracted from real SCADA data. The novelty of the manuscript is an application of machine learning hyperparameter optimization methods in a real problem.

The work is organized as follows: Sect. 2 introduces several related works; Sect. 3 discusses the main algorithms to implement machine learning based on the type of problem to be solved, discusses the hyperparameter optimization as a crucial step in the machine learning pipeline and the predictive model performance evaluation; Sects. 4 and 5 introduce the dataset and the methodology, respectively, being the results and discussion presented in Sect. 6. Finally, the paper rounds up with the main conclusions and future work.

2   Related Works

In recent years, with the growing volume of data generated and the greater complexity of the problems to be computationally treated, more sophisticated and autonomous computational tools have become necessary. One example is machine learning (ML) algorithms that can model data and solve complex problems.

An extensive literature review on ML models used in wind turbine monitoring, including the fault detection task, can be seen at [5]. The authors analyzed the following ML stages: data source, attribute selection, model choice and validation, and decision-making. They concluded that most works use SCADA data with classification models.

A discussion of the need for most articles in the literature to be based on models and not on data pre-processing is presented in [6]. The authors emphasize that more efforts should be put into the quality of the dataset in order to improve the performance of the classification measures. Furthermore, they propose a data-centric methodology, where data-driven steps are performed iteratively in detecting faults in wind turbine components.

A review of SCADA data's state of the art for monitoring wind turbines is provided in [4]. The authors point out that feature selection can increase model accuracy and reduce computational time, as SCADA data contains many redundant variables.

A comprehensive review of recent approaches on fault diagnosis and lifetime prognosis methods for condition monitoring of wind turbines is provided in [7]. The study summarizes the last 20 years of research in wind turbine condition monitoring, highlighting the state-of-art methods developed for treating faults in their components.

A statistical approach based on structural break detection in SCADA data for condition monitoring and fault diagnosis of wind turbines is developed in [8]. The five-step Chow's test-based computation procedure is used to test a multiple linear regression model based on gearbox and generator temperature data as the independent variables and generator speed data as the dependent variable. The proposed test evaluates the coefficient instability, which means a structural change in the regression model, whose behavior can be interpreted as the occurrence of a fault in the wind turbine.

As can be seen, the works in the literature presented do not address the determination of the hyperparameters of the developed models. Thus, this work introduces this subject, comparing three techniques for determining hyperparameters in the context of identifying faults in wind turbines.

3   Machine Learning

Mitchell [9] defines machine learning as improving performance in executing a task through experience. For Marsland [10] machine learning consists of making computers modify or adapt their actions to become more accurate.

Machine learning algorithms have several subdivisions based on the type of problem that needs to be solved [11,12], as described hereinafter.

Supervised machine learning algorithms exploits labeled data. The algorithm learns from example data and associated target responses, which may consist of numerical values or string labels, such as classes, to predict the correct answer later when presented with new examples. The types of problems can be regression when predicting some numerical value or classification when trying to predict some class [11].

On the other hand, for Unsupervised machine learning algorithms, data is not labeled. The algorithm learns from simple examples with no associated response, leaving it to the algorithm to determine patterns in the data independently [11].

Semi-Supervised machine learning algorithms use labeled and unlabeled data for model training. A mixture of supervised and unsupervised methods is generally used [11]. Another subdivision is the Reinforcement machine learning algorithms, where the algorithms learn from the environment. If it performs well, it gets a reward, and the goal is to maximize the reward [11].

3.1   Hyperparameter Optimization

In machine learning, hyperparameter optimization, or tuning, is the process of finding the right combination of hyperparameter values to get maximum data performance in a reasonable amount of time. A prerequisite to training machine learning models in general, is to come up with a particular combination of values of hyperparameters. Only after a specific set of hyperparameters has been chosen can the training process tune the parameters of the model [13]. This can be particularly important when comparing the performance of different machine learning models on a dataset.

Hyperparameters are parameter values used to control the learning process and significantly affect the performance of models. According to [14], machine learning models are composed of two different types of parameters: Hyperparameters i.e., parameters that the user can define arbitrarily before starting the training, and Model Parameters, the ones learned during model training.

Most of these machine-learning algorithms come with default values for their hyperparameters. But default values don't always work well in different types of machine learning projects. That's why you need to optimize them to get the right combination to give you the best performance. Some common examples of hyperparameters include learning rate, dropout, and activation function for neural networks, maximum tree depth for random forests, and regularization rate for regularized linear regression, among others.

Professionals often tune these hyperparameters using standard brute-force methods, such as systematically searching a grid of hyperparameters (grid search) or randomly sampling hyperparameters (random search). Among the existing methods to speed up hyperparameter optimization, successive halving has emerged as a popular and state-of-the-art early stopping algorithm [15].

Grid Search uses a brute-force approach to test all combinations of a predefined list of hyperparameter values and find the model with the best set of parameters that provide maximum accuracy. This method is the safest way to find the best set of hyperparameters since all combinations are evaluated, but it also has its drawbacks. One of the main disadvantages of grid search is that when it comes to dimensionality. It suffers when the number of hyperparameters grows exponentially, requiring more time to run.

Random search is a less time and resource-consuming method than grid search. It randomly picks hyperparameters from random combinations of a range of values, creates a set, and trains the model on it. This method may not find the best set of hyperparameters but can provide a model that comes close to the ideal in terms of performance, saving a lot of computational time.

Finally, Successive Halving Search implements a tournament strategy in succession. It is an early-stopping hyperparameter optimization algorithm. This means it starts with a few training cases to identify and select unpromising candidate models quickly. Models that survive to the next round are evaluated using a larger proportion of the available data. This process repeats until only a few candidate models are trained and evaluated using all available data [16].

Figure 1 shows a hyperparameter tuning problem with a 2D search space, whereas each point represents a specific hyperparameter configuration, and warmer colors correspond to better performance. It is noteworthy that adaptive selection methods for hyperparameter tuning, such as successive halving, proceed sequentially and concentrate on promising regions of the search space [15].

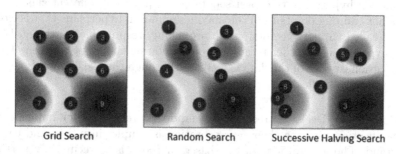

Grid Search   Random Search   Successive Halving Search

Fig. 1. Hyperparameter tuning problem with a 2D search space. Source: Adapted from https://blog.ml.cmu.edu/2018/12/12/massively-parallel-hyperparameter-opt imization/

3.2 Classification Algorithms

In this study, the interest is in the supervised machine learning problem, more specifically in the binary classification problem, to recognize the faults and the flawless operations of a wind turbine. The binary classification algorithm only deals with two classes, 0 or 1. Class 0 indicates a fault-free (healthy) observation, and class 1 indicates fault (defective) observations.

Naive Bayes: It is based on applying Bayes' theorem with the "naive" assumption of conditional independence between each pair of features, given the value of the class variable. The classifier is a simple and effective classification algorithm due to its robustness [11,12].

Logistic Regression: It is a type of generalized linear model (GLM) used for binary classification. It aims to estimate discrete values (binary values such as 0/1, yes/no, and true/false) based on a given set of explanatory variables. Commonly, logistic regression uses a function "Sigmoid" (logistic function), which has an "S" curve, used for the binary classification that converts values to the interval [0,1], which can be interpreted as the probability that a given instance belongs or does not belong to a given class [11,12].

k-Nearest Neighbors (kNN): It is a method based on the concept of distance, that is, on the proximity between the data, which uses information from the data of k-neighbors made by a classifier based on memory. According to [17], the base hypothesis is that similar data tend to be concentrated in the same region in the input space and, in the same way, data that are not similar will be distant from each other. The k parameter is user-defined, and in classification problems, it is common to use odd values to avoid ties [11,12].

Support Vector Machine (SVM): The algorithm seeks to find the maximum margin hyperplane that best separates the points of different classes. The equidistant training points from the maximum margin hyperplane that is closest to it are called support vectors, which are mainly responsible for the authority of this hyperplane. In order to accommodate non-linear limits between classes, the dimensional space of the data is increased through the use of *kernels*, making the algorithm more flexible [18].

Decision Tree: Decision trees are an important technique for implementing the classification task, as their representation is simple, intuitive, and easy to understand. The general idea of tree-based methods is to recursively partition space into rectangles (subregions), in which a simple model is learned. These models use the divide and conquer strategy: a complex problem is decomposed into simpler sub-problems, and recursively this technique is applied to each sub-problem [11,12].

Random Forest The Random Forest method is a supervised learning algorithm that consists of a set of decision trees generated within the same object. Each object (set of trees) goes through a voting mechanism (bagging) that elects the most voted classification and regression. Such a method is a combination of tree predictors, such that each tree depends on the values of a random vector sampled independently and with the same distribution for all trees in the forest [19].

3.3 Predictive Model Performance Evaluation

To measure the performance of classification algorithms and verify the model's ability to generalize to unseen data examples, several metrics can be used in the context of binary classification, such as the confusion matrix, and the resulting performance measures, such as accuracy, precision, sensitivity, and F1-Score [20].

The confusion matrix is displayed in Fig. 2, which gives the predicted and observed quantities in each class of the response variable.

		Predicted Class	
		Faulty	Not Fault
Actual	Faulty	True Positive (TP)	False Negative (FN)
Class	Not Fault	False Positive (FP)	True Negative (TN)

Fig. 2. Binary classification problem confusion matrix.

True Positives (TP): number examples of the positive class that were correctly classified. In this case, it represents the correct detection of failures; True Negatives (TN): number examples of the negative class that were correctly classified, that is, the examples that had no failures; False Positives (FP): number examples of the negative class that were incorrectly classified by the model, including false alarms; and False Negatives (FN): number examples of the positive class that were incorrectly classified, that is, failures not detected.

The performance measures shown in the confusion matrix are described below:

- **Accuracy** (Acc) - The accuracy is the ratio of true cases to all cases, as follows:

$$Acc = \frac{TP + TN}{TP + TN + FP + FN} \tag{1}$$

- **Precision** ($Prec$) - The ratio of correct positive predictions to the total predicted positives, i.e.,

$$Prec = \frac{TP}{TP + FP} \tag{2}$$

- **Sensitivity or Recall** - Is the probability of obtaining correctly classified for TP, given by

$$Recall = \frac{TP}{TP + FN} \tag{3}$$

- **F1-Score** - Is the harmonic mean of precision and recall, given by

$$F_1-score = 2 \times \frac{Prec \times Recall}{Prec + Recall} \tag{4}$$

– **Matthew's Correlation Coefficient (MCC)** - The MCC takes values between -1 and 1. A score of 1 indicates perfect agreement between the predicted and actual values, and is defined by

$$MCC = \frac{TP \times TN - FP \times FN}{\sqrt{(TP + FP)(TP + FN)(TN + FP)(TN + FN)}} \tag{5}$$

– **Area Under the Curve (AUC) ROC** - Receiver Operating Characteristic (ROC) Curve is a probability curve and AUC represents the degree or measure of separability. It tells how much the model is capable of distinguishing between classes. The higher AUC, the better is the model.

4   Data Description

The database used is provided by the company Energias de Portugal (EDP) [21]. This is one of the most complete free datasets available for wind resource analysis and wind turbine performance research [22].

The availability of this data was based on a challenge proposed by the company in which the objective was to detect failures in wind turbines. The records were extracted from a SCADA system of 5 wind turbines measured in 2016 and 2017.

The information provided by EDP is as follows [21]:

– *Signals*: Dataset of SCADA system sensor variables for each turbine's most important components and production values, read every 10 min. It has 81 variables related to wind speed and direction, generator, transformer, etc.
– *Metmast*: Dataset of weather mast variables, measured every 10 min. Data is pulled from a single tower. It has 40 variables related to wind speed and direction (2 anemometric sensors), temperature, atmospheric pressure, humidity, and precipitation.
– *Failures*: Dataset with the record of occurrences of failures of the five components of the wind turbine, measured in the time of each occurrence. The faulty components are Transformer, Generator Bearing, Hydraulic Group, Generator, and Gearbox.

Table 1 presents each dataset's total number of observations and variables, more details about the data can be found in [6, 22–24].

Table 1. Description of datasets.

Dataset	Number of observations	Number of variables
Signals	498,338	83
Metmast	87,528	41
Failures	28	4

The *Failures* set provides the history of failures that occurred in the years 2016 and 2017. Figure 3 presents the failures for each component of the turbines, and, as can be seen, the Hydraulics was the component that failed the most in this period, containing eight failures in total, followed by the Generator with seven failures.

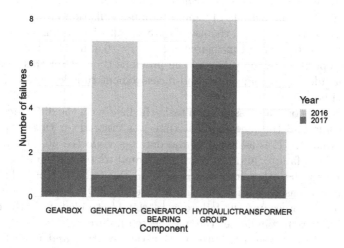

Fig. 3. Frequency of Failures in Wind Turbine Components.

5   Methodology

The pipeline adopted for each component failure of the wind turbine is illustrated in Fig. 4 and consists of steps: 1) Data Preprocessing; 2) Feature selection; and 3) Training of supervised ML algorithms with hyperparameter tuning and model performance evaluation.

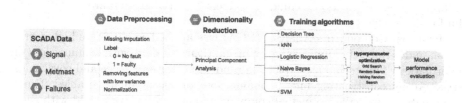

Fig. 4. Pipeline of the adopted methodology.

5.1 Data Preprocessing

The application of data preparation techniques is important to improve data quality and to help machine learning algorithms to build models more faithful to the real distribution of data [17].

An initial preprocessing step involves the inclusion of meteorological data (*Metmast*) in the sensor database (*Signals*) by the measurement time variable (*Timestamp*). In some instants of time, the non-acquisition of data by the sensors, for some reason, required the use of data imputation techniques so that the series was complete with all measurements every 10 min. This imputation was due by the repetition of the values of the previous time. After this step, failure data was included by turbine code, and measurement time less than or equal to the failure time.

As the focus is on the classification task, the field with the difference between the failure time and the measurement time was created for this purpose. The class label equal to '1' is assigned to the data set collected 60 days before the occurrence of the failure, and the class label equal to '0' is assigned to the data sets collected in the other intervals related to the failure record. The 60-day limit was defined based on an evaluation released by EDP, which determined the period of 60 days preceding the failure as reasonable to identify in the captured data the behavior that indicates the unexpected failure.

In pre-processing, the attributes with little variation and named as offset were still necessary to be removed from the data set. Many of the variables contained information with minimum, maximum, mean, and variance values for the measurement time every 10 min, having a high correlation between them. Thus, in order to remove redundant attributes, only the average values of each variable in the data set were selected, totaling 60 features. Numerical data normalization was performed to eliminate the discrepancy of measurement units between variables.

5.2 Dimensionality Reduction

Often real data sets contain many attributes; however, not all of them are informative for the process they are supposed to describe. In this way, it is necessary to apply resource selection techniques to identify variables that are actually useful for the analysis problem.

Principal Components Analysis (PCA) was applied to eliminate high correlation and reduce the dimensionality of multivariate data with minimal loss of information. This technique explains a random vector's variance and covariance structure by constructing linear combinations of the original variables. These combinations are called principal components and are not correlated with each other.

The information in the original p variables is replaced by the information in the uncorrelated principal components k ($k < p$). The selection of the number of principal components was defined, keeping 98% of the data variance.

5.3 Training Algorithms

The classifiers used were Naive Bayes (NB), Logistic Regression (LR), k-Nearest Neighbors (KNN), Decision Tree (DT), Random Forest (RF), and Support Vector Machine (SVM). In the search for the best combination of hyperparameters, three optimization techniques will be evaluated to measure the computational training time of the models. Grid Search tests all possible combinations of hyperparameters, and Random Search tests random combinations of a range of hyperparameters. At the same time, Halving Random Search uses a random search strategy that starts with a few resources and iteratively selects the best candidates, using more and more resources.

A widely used method to analyze the results produced by the classifiers is the confusion matrix and the performance measures that result from it, such as Accuracy, Recall, Precision, F_1 score, AUC, and Matthew's correlation coefficient. All these measures are used to measure the quality of ratings.

6 Results and Discussions

The experiments were performed using computational routines implemented in Python version 3.10.6, on an Intel(R) Xeon(R) Gold 5120 CPU 2.20GHz, with 28 cores and 192 GB of RAM. The libraries used were *pandas*[1] version 1.5.3, *numpy*[2] version 1.24.2 and *scikit-learn*[3] version 1.2.2.

The database was divided into 80% for model training and 20% for testing, maintaining the order of the data set. To arrive at the most optimized model, the hyperparameter optimization techniques with cross-validation with five folds were used to define the hyperparameters with the best result by the metric F_1 Score. The wind turbine Transformer component will be used to evaluate the optimization methods.

Tables 2-7 present the performance metrics of the models in the test base: F_1-score, AUC, Accuracy, Precision, Recall, and Matthews Coefficient for each of the classifiers with the respective optimization method of hyperparameters, in addition to the training time in seconds and the combination of values of the hyperparameters of each model that resulted in the highest F_1-Score. More details about the parameters of the ML models can be found in [25].

In all models, the halving method obtained a low computational cost and F_1-Score similar to Grid and Random Search. That is, it did not lose in the model's predictive performance. The SVM model with halving search was the one that had the most savings in processing, with a difference of 9 h concerning the grid and random search. On the other hand, Naive Bayes is not a valid method to improve the fit of hyperparameters, as there are no hyperparameters to tune in the same sense as different ML classifiers (Table 3).

---

[1] https://pandas.pydata.org/.

[2] https://numpy.org/.

[3] https://scikit-learn.org/stable/.

Table 2. Result of the Decision Tree model for each optimizer referring to the Wind Turbine Transformer component in the test base. The results are presented in %.

Tunnig	F1-Score	AUC	Acc	Prec	Recall	MCC	Time (s)	Best Model
Grid Search	5.1	50.8	70.5	51.5	2.7	6.0	24.15	criterion = 'entropy', max_depth = 5
Random Search	6.2	51.1	70.6	55.8	3.3	7.6	21.78	criterion = 'log_loss', max_depth = 10, max_features = 'log2'
Halving Random Search	4.9	51.0	70.7	62.6	2.6	8.0	5.55	criterion = 'log_loss', max_depth = 100

Table 3. Result of the kNN models for each optimizer referring to the Wind Turbine Transformer component in the test base. The results are presented in %.

Tunnig	F1-Score	AUC	Acc	Prec	Recall	MCC	Time (s)	Best Model
Grid Search	2.6	50.3	70.3	41.8	1.3	2.6	39.37	n_neighbors = 9, weights = 'distance'
Random Search	2.6	50.3	70.3	41.8	1.3	2.6	63.29	n_neighbors = 9, weights = 'distance'
Halving Random Search	2.6	50.3	70.3	41.8	1.3	2.6	0.59	n_neighbors = 9, weights = 'distance'

In [6], the F1-Score for the Transformer component was not elevated too, they obtained F1-Score the 8.08%, the difference is that they used a decision tree model with a high correlation filter in the feature selection. A possible explanation for the values of the metrics obtained are not high is that as the failure data in wind turbines resemble rare events, it may be necessary to apply special techniques to balance the classes and thus improve the metrics. Another point is that as the SCADA data is a multidimensional time series, a future strategy is to consider the previous time dependence in dimensionality reduction (Tables 4, 5, 6 and 7).

Table 4. Result of the Logistic Regression models for each optimizer referring to the Wind Turbine Transformer component in the test base. The results are presented in %.

Tunnig	F1-Score	AUC	Acc	Prec	Recall	MCC	Time (s)	Best Model
Grid Search	23.9	56.5	73.9	85.5	13.9	27.6	165.87	penalty = None, solver = 'newton-cg'
Random Search	23.9	56.5	73.9	85.5	13.9	27.6	496.40	penalty = None
Halving Random Search	23.9	56.5	73.9	85.6	13.9	27.6	35.58	solver = 'sag'

Table 5. Result of the Naive Bayes models for each optimizer referring to the Wind Turbine Transformer component in the test base. The results are presented in %.

Tunnig	F1-Score	AUC	Acc	Prec	Recall	MCC	Time (s)	Best Model
Grid Search	46.3	64.1	76.0	68.5	34.9	36.0	0.11	
Random Search	46.3	64.1	76.0	68.5	34.9	36.0	0.14	
Halving Random Search	46.3	64.1	76.0	68.5	34.9	36.0	0.11	

Table 6. Result of the Random Forest models for each optimizer referring to the Wind Turbine Transformer component in the test base. The results are presented in %.

Tunnig	F1-Score	AUC	Acc	Prec	Recall	MCC	Time (s)	Best Model
Grid Search	0.7	50.1	70.5	63.3	0.4	3.0	1,950.96	criterion = 'log_loss', max_depth = 10
Random Search	0.7	50.1	70.5	57.4	0.4	2.6	703.59	max_depth = 10
Halving Random Search	0.8	50.2	70.5	73.3	0.4	3.8	106.89	criterion = 'entropy', max_depth = 50, max_features = 'log2'

Table 7. Result of the SVM models for each optimizer referring to the Wind Turbine Transformer component in the test base. The results are presented in %.

Tunnig	F1-Score	AUC	Acc	Prec	Recall	MCC	Time (s)	Best Model
Grid Search	1.1	50.3	70.6	98.0	0.6	6.1	36,167.51	C = 0.1
Random Search	1.1	50.3	70.6	98.0	0.6	6.1	33,406.22	C = 0.1
Halving Random Search	0.9	50.2	70.5	68.5	0.4	3.7	781.48	C = 100

7 Conclusions and Future Works

Wind turbines are complex systems that require maintenance, and as data acquisition increases, so does the possibility of applying machine learning algorithms combining data-centric training approaches with model training optimization in order to have a better quality of the data entering the models and savings in computational time.

Fault detection was performed on a wind turbine component from a real SCADA system dataset. Dimensionality reduction was applied, creating a new set of variables with minimal loss of information and without correlated variables. The initially proposed methodology was able to compare hyperparameter optimization methods and identify the best algorithm that has the shortest computational time, that is, the most economical. As the next steps, the objective is to test other types of algorithms, such as those of the ensemble class and neural networks, oversampling methods for balancing between classes, and other dimensionality reduction techniques that consider the temporal dependence of the data.

References

1. Kost, C, et al.: Levelized Cost of electricity- Renewable Energy Technologies. Fraunhofer Institute for Solar Energy Systems (ISE), June 2021. https://www.ise.fraunhofer.de/en/publications/studies/cost-of-electricity.html
2. GWEC "Global Wind Energy Council - Global Wind Report 2023". https://gwec.net/globalwindreport2023/. Accessed 15 May 2023
3. Blanco, M.A., et al.: Impact of target variable distribution type over the regression analysis in wind turbine data. In: International Conference and Workshop on Bioinspired Intelligence (IWOBI), pp. 1–7 (2017)
4. Pandit, R., Astolfi, D., Hong, J., Infield, D., Santos, M.: SCADA data for wind turbine data-driven condition/performance monitoring: a review on state-of-art, challenges, and future trends. Wind Eng. 47(2), 422–441 (2023)
5. Stetco, A., et al.: Machine learning methods for wind turbine condition monitoring: a review. Renew. Energy 133, 620–635 (2019)
6. Garan, M., Tidriri, K., Kovalenko, I.: A data-centric machine learning methodology: application on predictive maintenance of wind turbines. Energies 15(3), 826 (2022)
7. Badihi, H., Zhang, Y., Jiang, B., Pillay, P., Rakheja, S.: A comprehensive review on signal-based and model-based condition monitoring of wind turbines: fault diagnosis and lifetime prognosis. Proc. IEEE 110(6), 754–806 (2022)
8. Dao, P.B.: Condition monitoring and fault diagnosis of wind turbines based on structural break detection in SCADA data. Renew. Energy 185, 641–654 (2022)
9. Mitchell, T.M.: Machine Learning, vol. 1. McGraw-hill, New York (2007)
10. Marsland, S.: Machine Learning: An Algorithmic Perspective. CRC Press, Boca Raton (2015)
11. Bishop, C.M., and Nasrabadi, N.M.: Pattern Recognition and Machine Learning, vol. 4. No. 4. Springer, New York (2006)
12. Russell, S.J.: Artificial Intelligence A Modern Approach. Pearson Education Inc., London (2010)
13. Japa, L., Serqueira, M., Mendonça, I., Aritsugi, M., Bezerra, E., González, P.H.: A Population-based Hybrid Approach for Hyperparameter Optimization of Neural Networks. IEEE Access (2023)
14. Agrawal, T.: Hyperparameter Optimization in Machine Learning: Make your Machine Learning and Deep Learning Models More Efficient. Apress, New York (2021)
15. Li, L., Jamieson, K., Rostamizadeh, et al.: A system for massively parallel hyperparameter tuning. Proc. Mach. Learn. Syst. 2, 230–246 (2020)
16. Soper, D.S.: Hyperparameter optimization using successive halving with greedy cross-validation. Algorithms 16(1), 17 (2022)
17. Norvig, P., Russell, S.: Artificial Intelligence: A Modern Approach, Pearson Education, London (2021)
18. Gareth, J., Daniela, W., Trevor, H., Robert, T.: An Introduction to Statistical Learning: with Applications in R. Springer, New York (2013). https://doi.org/10.1007/978-1-4614-7138-7
19. Breiman, L.: Random forests. Mach. Learn. 45, 5–32 (2001)
20. Kohavi, R., Provost, F.: "Glossary of terms," Glossary of Terms Journal of Machine Learning. https://ai.stanford.edu/ronnyk/glossary.html. Accessed 08 Jul 2022
21. EDP Open Data. https://opendata.edp.com/pages/homepage/. Accessed 15 Aug 2021

22. Menezes, D., Mendes, M., Almeida, J.A., Farinha, T.: Wind farm and resource datasets: a comprehensive survey and overview. Energies **13**(18), 4702 (2020)

23. de Sá, F. P., et al.: Wind turbine fault detection: a semi-supervised learning approach with automatic evolutionary feature selection. In: 2020 International Conference on Systems, Signals and Image Processing (IWSSIP), pp. 323–328. IEEE (2020)

24. Pinna, D., et al.: Fault identification in wind turbines: a data-centric machine learning approach. In: International Conference on Computational Science and Computational Intelligence (CSCI) (2022)

25. Géron, A.: Hands-on machine learning with Scikit-Learn, Keras, and TensorFlow. "O'Reilly Media, Inc".. (2022)

Realistic Model Parameter Optimization: Shadow Robot Dexterous Hand Use-Case

Tiago Correia$^{(\boxtimes)}$ (ID), Francisco M. Ribeiro (ID), and Vítor H. Pinto (ID)

SYSTEC (DIGI2), ARISE and ECE Department, Fac. de Engenharia, Universidade do Porto, Rua Dr. Roberto Frias, 4200-465 Porto, Portugal
{tpcorreia,fmribeiro,vitorpinto}@fe.up.pt

Abstract. The notable expansion of technologies related to automated processes has been observed in recent years, largely driven by the significant advantages they provide across diverse industries. Concurrently, there has been a rise in simulation technologies aimed at replicating these complex systems. Nevertheless, in order to fully leverage the potential of these technologies, it is crucial to ensure the highest possible resemblance of simulations to real-world scenarios. In brief, this work consists of the development of a data acquisition and processing pipeline allowing a posterior search for the optimal physical parameters in MuJoCo simulator to obtain a more accurate simulation of a dexterous robotic hand. In the end, a Random Search optimization algorithm was used to validate this same pipeline.

Keywords: Optimization · realistic simulation · model · pipeline

1 Introduction

Industry 4.0 is changing and adjusting the current manufacturing standards, adapting the traditional manufacturing system to a more intelligent and autonomous one. In parallel with this change, new technologies emerged and became a crucial factor in the industry.

Simulation technologies have emerged as indispensable factors in various industries, facilitating the virtual representation of real systems. This capability offers the opportunity to safely conduct tests, validate, and monitor the system's actual state. In the context of highly intricate systems like a dexterous robotic hand, simulations play a pivotal role. They provide a safe testing environment, minimizing the risk of damaging costly components and enabling the implementation of diverse control techniques, including Machine Learning (ML) approaches such as Reinforcement Learning (RL). It is evident that performing thousands of movements using a real dexterous hand would be time-consuming, costly, and pose a significant risk of component damage. Conversely, simulations allow for the execution of these movements within a controlled environment and even permit the utilization of multiple simulated hands, thereby drastically expediting the process.

A. I. Pereira et al. (Eds.): OL2A 2023, CCIS 1982, pp. 244–255, 2024.
https://doi.org/10.1007/978-3-031-53036-4_17

Numerous physics engines allow a virtual representation of a real robot. Still, a particular one called MuJoCo [1] has gained some attention from the community, mainly due to the release of its source code online. The library provides a C API for interaction with the virtual environment, and the acquisition of data from sensors in the simulation depends on this same API. When compared to other physic engines, in the case of Bullet PhysX, Havok and Open Dynamics Engin (ODE), MuJoCo outperforms them in key factors such as speed and accuracy [2]. Also, Ribeiro *et al.* [3], compared several physics engines. The aim of the study was to assess the usability of these simulators in realistically simulating a dexterous robotic hand and manipulator system for highly detailed tasks and concluded that MuJoCo demonstrates more promising results compared to several physics engines present in Gazebo.

After understanding the importance and the bases of those technologies, there is a necessity to grant the viability and the similarity between both real and virtual systems. This resemblance can be achieved by adjusting the physical parameters of the simulation so that the environment in the simulation reacts as similarly as possible to the real environment. These parameters establish how objects interact with each other in their environment and are defined as constants and represent *inertia, friction loss, stiffness, damping, range* and numerous more.

In order to obtain the best possible parameters so that the simulated hand movement resembles the real hand movement, it is necessary to optimize those parameters.

However, to implement an algorithm with the goal of optimizing those physical parameters, it is necessary to develop a pipeline capable of extracting the data from the real and from the simulated hand, process and analyse that same data and compare it. Subsequently, this comparison allows the attainment of an objective function so that it can be used for the optimization algorithm.

2   Robotic Hand

Physical Component. As mentioned before, the robotic system used in this project is the Shadow Dexterous Hand [4]. It is a humanoid robotic hand with a high degree of precision, with 24 joints, 20°C of freedom and four under-actuated movements and can be seen in Fig. 1a.

To obtain data from the real hand, all sensor values have a specific sampling rate, depending on the type. In the case of positional sensors used to sense the rotation of each joint, the typical rate is 1000 Hz.

It is used a Hall effect sensor with a resolution of 0.2o. The emphHand Sensor node is responsible for providing all the information from the sensors to the communication bus. On this hand, EtherCAT bus (Ethernet for Control Automation Technology) is used for communication between the robotic system and the NUC (Next Unit of Computing). This last is responsible for the control loop of the real hand.

Simulation Component. As said before, the physics engine in use on the simulator is MuJoCo. MuJoCo models are defined in an XML derivation file with MuJoCo Modeling XML File (MJCF) format. This file describes the dynamics, kinetics, and properties of rigid bodies in the simulator. In this file, we can find physical parameters that, when adjusted, can approximate the simulation model to the real hand, allowing a more realistic reproduction of the system. The hand model in the MuJoCo Simulator can be observed in Fig. 1b).

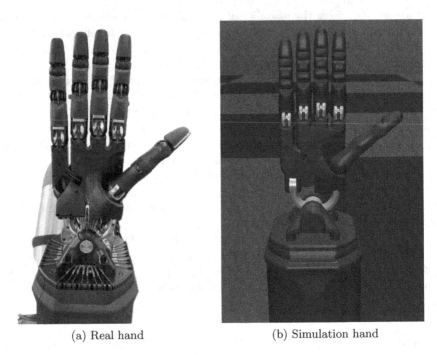

(a) Real hand   (b) Simulation hand

Fig. 1. (a) Represents the real hand. (b) Represents the Simulation model in MuJoCo Simulator.

3   Methodology

The chart that can be observed in Fig. 2 covers the fundamental steps to find the best parameters present in the hand model in MuJoCo so that the simulation resembles reality the most.

In the graph, we may visualise that in order to find the optimal parameters in the MuJoCo model, is inevitable the development of a pipeline capable of obtaining the data from the physical hand and from the simulator. Furthermore, considering the comparison between the trajectories of the physical hand and the simulator, it is imperative to process the data to extract crucial information. This

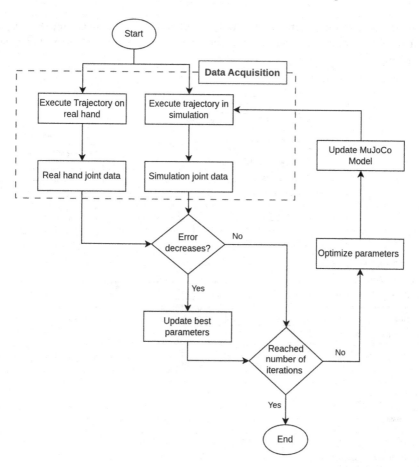

Fig. 2. Algorithm used to obtain the best parameters for simulation similarity with the real world.

data processing step is essential for optimizing the algorithm to its maximum potential.

However, it is important to enhance that the main focus of this article is the pipeline that enables the attainment of data from both the real and simulated hand, allowing posterior integration of an optimization algorithm.

3.1 Data Processing Pipeline

In Fig. 3, a class diagram offering a detailed illustration of the data acquisition and processing algorithm along with its connection to the main optimization algorithm can be found. It clarifies the connections and interdependencies between the different classes interacting with the system. The class diagram provides a formal representation that enables a clearer understanding of the data flow and integration points between the data gathering, processing, and optimization components by illustrating the structure and interactions inside the algorithm.

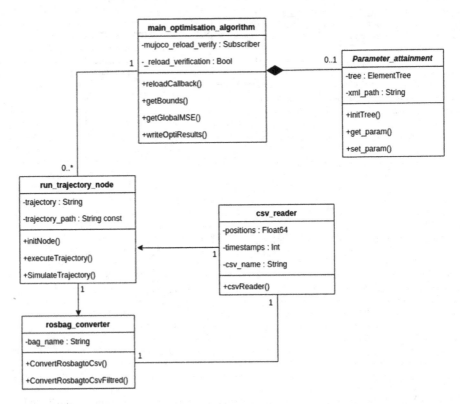

Fig. 3. Detailed Class Diagram Illustrating Data Acquisition and Processing algorithm.

Rosbag Converter Module (rosbag_converter): To compare both the angles from the real and the simulated robotic hand, it is mandatory to have the data from the real hand and the simulated one.

Starting with the real, while executing the predefined trajectory of the hand, a topic called *joint_states* was recorded in a rosbag. This topic contains information about the joint names, the angle of each joint (position) in radians, and the velocity of that joint and the effort. This last effort can be intended as a force applied in each joint. Beyond this information, we can also acquire information about the timestamp, which will be crucial later.

The same must be done in every simulation execution during the optimization. However, the rosbag does not always start at the same exact moment nor

stop because of different system loads and delays at the beginning of each trajectory. Moreover, to facilitate a comparison between each trajectory generated
in the simulation and the actual hand movement, it is essential to synchronize
their starting points. To address this challenge, a dedicated module needs to be
developed. This module will effectively filter the data obtained from the rosbag
and convert it into a CSV format (Comma-Separated Values). The CSV file can
then be accessed and utilized for a comprehensive comparison with the real hand
trajectory.

In this module, it was first implemented a simple program, using pandas
Python module [5], that converts the rosbag to a CSV with only the necessary
information, such as the position of each joint to be later used on the main algorithm, the velocity, so that it could be known when the trajectory has started,
and the timestamp of every reading. This allows us to have a global view of
the trajectory and confirm that during the execution of different trajectories, a
different number of readings were recorded.

After that, based on the previous one, a program was implemented that, in
addition to converting the rosbag to a CSV, also filters the data. It starts by
checking where the movement has begun based on the velocity of the joints,
defines the hand movement pre-defining the number of iterations, and ends up
removing all unnecessary data since the beginning of rosbag's record and the
start of the hand trajectory, along with the end of the trajectory and the shutdown of the rosbag's record.

CSV Interpreter Module (csv_reader): Having all the necessary data organized and filtered in a CSV file, a module was created to interpret this file and
return only the absolutely essential information. In brief, this program takes into
input the filtered CSV file and returns the angle of each joint and the instant
that occurred each reading. It is relevant to note that this process must be executed in every simulation and, for that reason, must be computationally light so
as not to unnecessarily extend the execution time of each iteration in the main
optimization program.

Parameter Attainment Module (Parameter_attainment): Considering
the preceding points, determining optimal parameters requires the capacity to
access and modify the parameters specified in the MuJoCo model file. To fulfil
this requirement, the xml.etree.ElementTree library [6] in Python was employed.
This library offers a user-friendly and efficient API for generating and interpret-
ing XML data.

However, it is crucial to remember that some parameters, such as the *range*,
have multiple values in the same attribute of a specific element, which hinders
the use of this module. To overcome this problem, two separate functions were
created to read and process the attribute values depending on the number of
floats in that same attribute. Despite that, it was also developed a way to read
and update the attributes of a particular defined element or all the elements

simultaneously from the XML file and save them on an array, depending on the pretended result and input.

Control Trajectory Node Module (run_trajectory_node): In this module, we can find the node responsible for the execution of the defined trajectory in the simulator and also in the real robotic hand. It is liable for the initialization of that same node, the trajectory selection and the rosbag's recording during the simulation of that same trajectory. On another note, the trajectories are all defined in a YAML format file, where a name characterises each trajectory and contains the goal of each joint and the time duration until the objective is reached.

In addition to what has been mentioned, to execute a specific trajectory, a method that takes the pretended trajectory's name and previously initialised node as input was developed. This program, in brief, sends the order to execute a particular trajectory to the node mentioned before.

In parallel with this previous method, another program focuses on starting the record of the *joint_states* topic before the start of the trajectory's execution. It also ensures that the record is ceased after the end of that trajectory.

This module establishes direct interaction with the Rosbag Converter module. The output derived from the aforementioned method, consisting of a Rosbag containing positional information and timestamps, serves as the raw data input for subsequent processing within the Rosbag Converter module.

Similarly, the CSV Interpreter module interfaces directly with the Rosbag Converter module, creating an additional dependency on the present module. This is due to the fact that each filtered CSV file returned by the Rosbag Converter module is utilized as input for the CSV Interpreter module. As a result, the main optimization program gains access to the joint angle values, enabling comprehensive analysis and subsequent optimization.

Main Algorithm (main_optimisation_algorithm): Lastly, this module encompasses the main optimization algorithm, leveraging the functionalities provided by all the previously mentioned programs. The objective is to find the set of parameters that best match the real-world hand movement data.

Due to the high complexity of the system, it would be very computationally heavy to try to find the best possible fit for the hand model. However, by significantly augmenting the publication rates of the *joint_states* topic in the simulation, more data points will be generated, thereby reducing the errors associated with comparing unsynchronised points in time. In essence, the augmented publication rate in the simulation ensures a higher density of points along the trajectory, creating a more accurate representation when compared to the relatively lower publication rate of real-world data.

For that reason, it was developed several helper functions used for the optimisation process. One of these functions includes finding the closest points in an array so that comparing the real movement and the simulated one can produce the best possible results.

Furthermore, it incorporates functionalities for computing the MSE of individual joints, individual fingers, or the overall median MSE across all hand joints. This will subsequently serve as the cost function within the optimisation algorithm. It is important to note that the value of the MSE may have a slight variation between simulations with the exact same parameters. This is due to the error that is generated from the discrepancy between the sample rate in the simulated and real trajectory, which was previously explained. The difference in the sample rates of each component causes a maximum error equal to half of the period of the component with a higher sample rate, in this case, the simulated trajectory. In this specific case, the sample rate of the trajectory angles is 250 Hz, provoking a maximum discrepancy of 0.002 seconds. This variance, however, is very small and does not affect the overall outcome of this algorithm.

Additionally, this implementation includes methods to establish predetermined bounds within a specified percentage and to generate random parameters within those previously established limits.

To ensure the preservation and subsequent analysis of all algorithmic data, a method was implemented to write the results of each iteration from the optimization algorithm onto a file. This file provides a comprehensive overview of the evolution of the error throughout the optimization process, offering a global perspective.

The main program starts by initializing variables and setting up some components of ROS (Robot Operating System). It reads real hand movement data from a CSV file and prepares it for comparison with simulated data. Bounds for the parameters are defined based on the provided numeric parameters. The main optimization loop proceeds by iteratively comparing the positions of the simulated hand with those of the real hand. The MSE is computed within each iteration to measure the disparity between these positions. If it has been verified that the error has diminished, the best parameters and the minimum error are globally updated.

In addition, once all the parameters have been updated in the MuJoCo model during each iteration, it becomes essential to reload this same model. A ROS publisher and a subscriber were implemented in both this module and the main ROS program responsible for the MuJoCo model to enable this operation. These components establish communication through a new topic named *mujoco_reload_verify*, which indicates whether reloading is feasible and confirms whether the reloading process has occurred.

It is worth highlighting that this algorithm was not specifically developed for a particular type of optimization. Consequently, its general implementation enables its utilization in a vast range of black-box, simulation-based optimization scenarios.

3.2 Optimization

With the aim of verifying the pipeline previously developed, there is a necessity to develop and implement an optimization method. This method must allow the implementation of black-box optimization, which in turn is the type of optimization required for this specific scenario.

Considering the general form of an optimization expression:

$$\min_{\mathbf{x} \in \Omega} f(\mathbf{x}), \tag{1}$$

where Ω is the feasible region and $f(\mathbf{x})$ is the objective function.

A black-box optimization may be interpreted as the analysis of the function $f(\mathbf{x})$ where the constraints defining Ω are unknown or non-existent [7].

In this specific scenario, the evaluation of the objective function requires the execution of simulations due to the involvement of an unknown function representing the model of the hand.

In this project, a Random Search optimization algorithm was utilised. This method may be used for optimizing gradient-free objective functions and can be adapted to address black-box optimization problems effectively.

In this particular case, the algorithm implemented involves random changes to the parameters and saves the best solution encountered up to the current iteration.

However, despite not being the most efficient and even the best overall algorithm for this situation, this method presents some advantages compared to other gradient-free methods, being those mainly:

- *Simplicity.* When compared to other optimization methods, it is considerably easy to implement and does not depend on hyperparameters, as opposed to other gradient-free methods.
- *Parallelization.* Keeping in mind that each iteration is independent of others enables the execution of multiple instances simultaneously, exploring, in parallel, different parts of the search space. As a result, the overall process can be accelerated.

A profound explanation of this method can be encountered in [8].

3.3   Approach

The main approach for optimization does not consider the *range* parameter. After analyzing the motion of the real hand, it was observed that the limits of joint movement slightly deviated from the default value of 1.57 rad. However, the magnitude of this deviation is not very significant.

In this strategy, a trajectory was created that, starting from an open hand position, closes the middle, first, ring and little finger and then stretch them again.

In addition, finding appropriate initial values for all the parameters is essential. Since these parameters are sensitive, it is crucial that their initial values hold physical significance. This ensures that the search space of the optimization aligns with the intended behaviour and characteristics of the system. It is important to refer that in the simulation, by default, both the middle, first, ring and little finger are considered to be identical, with only a slight position displacement. This can be observed in Fig. 1. This basically means that both of these fingers have the same model and, as a consequence, the same parameters. This indicates that all the joints within a specific category share the same default parameters.

In the end, the search space was also limited so that the algorithm would not consider values totally meaningless, causing a more inefficient execution of the algorithm. The limits were defined as a 40% deviation from the default values.

4   Results

After optimisation, the initial Mean Squared Error (MSE) of all the joints present in the hand was 0.056864, which is significant for tasks requiring high precision.

Applying the optimisation algorithm, we may see a rapid reduction of the MSE in the first 100 iterations, as can be seen, in Fig. 4.

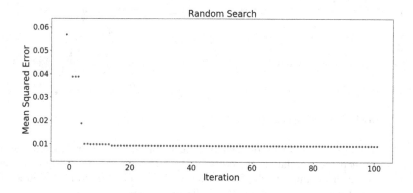

Fig. 4. MSE evolution in the first 100 iterations.

However, after reaching 100 iterations, the error begins to converge, decreasing by smaller decimal places. This can be seen in Fig. 5.

The final MSE was 0.0084706, which corresponds to a considerable decrease compared to the initial error. Approximately, is an 85% reduction in the error.

In Fig. 6 can be observed an overview of each joint angle position during the trajectory execution. In Fig. 6a, the red line represents the real hand trajectory, and the green line the trajectory of the hand in the simulation environment before optimisation in the FJ1 joint. Putting into context, the FJ1 joint corresponds to the articulation between the distal phalanx and the middle phalanx. In Fig. 6b, the red line also represents the real hand trajectory, and the green line the trajectory of the hand in the simulation environment after optimisation in the FJ1 joint.

However, it is important to highlight that this algorithm has a very limited search space and was mainly used to prove the correct implementation of the previous pipeline.

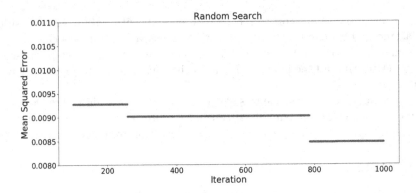

Fig. 5. MSE evolution after 100 iterations

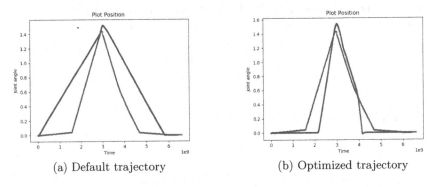

(a) Default trajectory   (b) Optimized trajectory

Fig. 6. (a) Represents the angle of each reading before optimization, in red the real hand and in green the simulated trajectory of the FJ1 joint (b) Represents the angle (in radians) of each reading after optimization, in red the real hand and in green the simulated trajectory of the FJ1 joint. (Color figure online)

5   Conclusion and Future Work

This research proposes a pipeline designed to access and process data from sensors and simulations, with the ultimate objective of enhancing the realism of the simulator. Specifically, the focus lies in optimizing the physical parameters of the hand model defined in the MuJoCo model file. The proposed solution not only addresses these parameters but also encompasses methods for acquiring and updating the values associated with the hand MuJoCo model. Finally, a simple Random Search Optimization algorithm was implemented to validate the proper implementation of the pipeline. In future works, a more advanced and efficient algorithm may be explored and implemented, which, in turn, can significantly minimize the error. Additionally, expanding the number of parameters utilized in the optimization process may contribute to further error reduction.

Acknowledgments. The authors acknowledge the support of R&D Unit SYSTEC Base (UIDB/00147/2020) and Programmatic (UIDP/00147/2020) and the ARISE Associated Laboratory (LA/P/0112/2020), as well as the support of GreenAuto Agenda: Green Innovation for the Automotive Industry, no. C644867037-00000013, investment project no. 54, from the Incentive System to Mobilising Agendas for Business Innovation, funded by the Recovery and Resilience Plan and by European Funds NextGeneration EU.

References

1. Todorov, E., Erez, T., Tassa, Y.: MuJoCo: a physics engine for model-based control. In: 2012 IEEE/RSJ International Conference on Intelligent Robots and Systems (2012). https://doi.org/10.1109/IROS.2012.6386109
2. Erez, T., Tassa, Y., Todorov, E.: Simulation tools for model-based robotics: comparison of bullet, Havok, Mujoco, ode and Physx, Proceedings - IEEE International Conference on Robotics and Automation 2015, vol. 2015-June, pp. 4397–4404 (2015). https://doi.org/10.1109/ICRA.2015.7139807
3. Ribeiro, F.M., Correia, T., Lima, J., Gonçalves, G., Pinto, V.H.: Modeling and realistic simulation of a dexterous robotic hand: SVH hand use-case. In: 2023 IEEE International Conference on Autonomous Robot Systems and Competitions (ICARSC), Tomar, Portugal, pp. 132–138 (2023). https://doi.org/10.1109/ICARSC58346.2023.10129643
4. Shadow robot. https://www.shadowrobot.com/dexterous-hand-series/. Accessed 12 Apr 2023
5. McKinney, W.: Data structures for statistical computing in Python. In: Proceedings of the 9th Python in Science Conference, pp. 51–56 (2010)
6. Python Software Foundation xml.etree.ElementTree. https://docs.python.org/X/library/xml.etree.elementtree.html. Accessed 24 May 2023
7. Alarie, S., Audet, C., Gheribi, A.E., Kokkolaras, M., Le Digabel, S.: Two decades of blackbox optimization applications. EURO J. Comput. Optim. **9**, 100011 (2021). https://doi.org/10.1016/j.ejco.2021.100011
8. Andradóttir, S.: An overview of simulation optimization via random search. In: Handbooks in Operations Research and Management Science, vol. 13, pp. 617–631. Elsevier (2006). https://doi.org/10.1016/S0927-0507(06)13020-0

Performance of Heuristics for Classifying Leftovers from Cutting Stock Problem

Glaucia Maria Bressan[1]([✉])(iD), Esdras Battosti da Silva[2](iD),
Matheus Henrique Pimenta-Zanon[3](iD), Elisângela Aparecida da Silva Lizzi[1](iD),
and Fabio Sakuray[4](iD)

[1] Mathematics Department, Universidade Tecnológica Federal do Paraná (UTFPR),
Alberto Carazzai, 1640, Cornélio Procópio, PR 86300-000, Brazil
{glauciabressan,elisangelalizzi}@utfpr.edu.br
[2] Electrical Engineering Department, Universidade Tecnológica Federal do Paraná
(UTFPR), Alberto Carazzai, 1640, Cornélio Procópio, PR 86300-000, Brazil
esdras.2019@alunos.utfpr.edu.br
[3] Computer Science Department, Universidade Tecnológica Federal do Paraná
(UTFPR), Alberto Carazzai, 1640, Cornélio Procópio, PR 86300-000, Brazil
[4] Computer Science Department, State University of Londrina (UEL), Rodovia Celso
Garcia Cid, Pr 445 Km 380 C.P. 10.011, Londrina, PR 86057-970, Brazil
sakuray@uel.br

Abstract. The one-dimensional cutting stock problem is defined in the
literature as a branch of the classic cutting stock optimization problem,
involving one dimension in the cutting process, like cutting bars. The bar
cutting optimization problem can generate leftovers - reusable- or losses
- disposable. The objective of this paper is to compare the performance
of OptimizationDistBSP and OptimizationTREE heuristics (proposed
in [2]) for classifying leftovers or losses, from the cutting stock problem
(specifically from cutting one-dimensional bars), using the dataset proposed in [3], since this dataset allows the application of Machine Learning
methods, which are: Logistic Regression, Naive Bayes, Decision Tree and
Random Forest, to classify the output data as leftover or loss. Results
show that the OptimizationDistBSP and OptimizationTREE heuristics
provide better performance in the classification task than the Greedy
heuristic used in [2]. Thus, we can conclude that the heuristics can be
applied in a more realistic problem, using bars of different sizes, and
the dataset can be validated, providing good results for the classification
using heuristics other than Greedy.

Keywords: One-dimensional cutting stock problem · Leftover
classification · Machine learning · Comparison of heuristics

1 Introduction

The cutting stock problem is a classic optimization problem, first addressed by
Gilmore and Gomory [13].

This problem involves cutting a set of objects (larger-sized) available in stock to produce the required items (smaller-sized) with specific quantities and dimensions, with the aim of optimizing (maximize or minimize) a known objective function [17], such as production costs or cutting-related losses. In [14], higher dimensional cutting stock problems are modeled as linear programming problems.

When the cutting process involves only one dimension, we can define the one-dimensional cutting stock problem, as cutting steel bars, paper rolls and tubes [7,8]. The cutting process can generate leftovers - which can be reused in a new demand - or losses, which are discarded. In this context, the called *usable leftover cutting stock problems* [7] is a branch of the cutting stock problem and it purposes to determine the cutting patterns and to analyze the leftovers generated by the cutting process. This problem is of the one-dimensional cutting stock problem type, wherein the non-used material from the cutting process can be stored for future utilization, provided it meets the required size, that is, if large enough [6]. In order to optimize this type of problem, different heuristic methods have been developed [4,5,10].

In the paper [2], two heuristic methods, called OptimizationDistBSP and OptimizationTREE, have been proposed to minimize the quantity of bars required for cutting known item demands in the one-dimensional cutting process with no stock. The problem considers an unlimited quantity of just one type of bar. The numerical values used in simulations are based on [5].

Normally, in the literature, some numerical data generators can be found [11,12], which are used to test algorithms and heuristics for the cutting stock problem optimization. In the existing literature, it is challenging to find and access numerical data sets that consist of a substantial number of instances suitable for training algorithms and dealing with optimization problem variables like demands, objects, and items to be cut. These datasets are relatively scarce and not readily available [3]. For this reason, in [3], a methodology for generating a numerical data set, considering items demand data and cut objects, for the problem of classifying leftovers or losses from the cutting stock process, is presented. For that, the FFD (*First Fit Decreasing* heuristic [5]), which consists of a Greedy heuristic, was applied in order to use input variables and to determine whether the output corresponding to that set of items is loss or leftover, in the face of a given object. This large dataset can be used in supervised training algorithms for classification tasks.

In this context, considering the dataset proposed by [3] and the heuristics from [2], the objective of this paper is to compare the performance of heuristics OptimizationDistBSP and OptimizationTREE for classifying leftovers or losses, from the cutting stock problem (specifically from cutting one-dimensional bars), using the dataset proposed in [3]. In this way, the heuristics proposed in [2] are applied in a more real problem, using bars of different sizes, and the dataset can be validated, since the classic Greedy heuristic is replaced by two new heuristics for the classification task.

The remainder of the paper is organized as follows. Section 2 presents the methodology used in this paper to apply the heuristics, obtain the classification results and evaluate the performance of the heuristics. The algorithm shows the procedure to obtain the results. Section 3 presents the numerical results and discussion. Lastly, Sect. 4 presents the conclusion and discuss potential directions for further exploration in subsequent works.

2   Methods

Considering the proposal to compare the performance of heuristic methods OptimizationDistBSP and OptimizationTREE [2] for classifying leftovers or losses, this study uses the dataset generated in [3]. The Python programming language is used, including parameters from [12] and [19], statistical methods and the Greedy heuristic FFD capable of determining the labels of the output. This dataset presents 350 lines and 19 columns, which allows the application of Machine Learning methods to make predictions, since it is a satisfactorily large dataset. The number of lines of the dataset corresponds to the number of objects and the user can define it.

For comparison purposes with the FFD heuristic results, the following supervised methods were used for the classification task: Decision Trees, Random Forests, Naive Bayes and Logistic Regression. The theoretical description of these classification methods can be seen in [1]. These supervised methods will determine the output class as leftover or loss, considering a set of items, demands and object.

Algorithm 1 describes the procedure proposed in this paper in order to evaluate the performances of the OptimizationDistBSP and OptimizationTREE heuristics [2] for classifying leftovers from cutting stock problem. The inputs of the algorithm are the minimum and maximum sizes of items (l_{min}, l_{max}), the minimum and maximum sizes of objects (L_{min}, L_{max}), the minimum and maximum sizes of demand for items (d_{min}, d_{max}), so that it contains l_{types}, L_{types} or d_{types} subintervals, respectively. The number of items (n_{items}) and the number of objects (n_{obj}) are also defined, according to [3].

The concepts associated with the algorithms OptimizationDistBSP and OptimizationTREE can be briefly described. The OptimizationTREE algorithm is based on a tree structure and it has two phases: item selection and loss reduction. First, the demanded items are arranged in descending order of size. Then, for each selected item, one unit is subtracted from the number of items to be cut. The objective is to utilize larger elements first and then fill the remaining space with smaller elements on the cutting bar. In the OptimizationDistBSP algorithm, once the demanded items are sorted in descending order of size, the subsequent step involves replacing one selected item with two smaller ones. This replacement is done by selecting smaller items that result in a smaller leftover bar after the cutting process [2].

Algorithm 1: Performance Evaluation of Dataset with OptimizationDistBSP and OptimizationTREE

---

1 **Function** HeuristicsPerformance(l_{min}, l_{max}, l_{types}, L_{min}, L_{max}, L_{types}
   d_{min}, d_{max}, d_{types}, n_{items}, n_{obj})**:**

2     $items$, $demands$, $objs$ = Dataset(l_{min}, l_{max}, l_{types}, L_{min}, L_{max}, L_{types}
   d_{min}, d_{max}, d_{types}, n_{items}, n_{obj})

3     $leftover_{BSP}$, $loss_{BSP}$ = OptimizationDistBSP($items$, $demands$, $objs$)

4   **if** $loss_{BSP} > leftover_{BSP}$ **then**

5 | $label_{BSP} = loss$

6   **end**

7   **else**

8 | $label_{BSP} = leftover$

9   **end**

10   **PerformanceEvaluation** ($items$, $demands$, $objs$, $label_{BSP}$)

11    $leftover_{TREE}$, $loss_{TREE}$ = OptimizationTREE($items$, $demands$, $objs$)

12   **if** $loss_{TREE} > leftover_{TREE}$ **then**

13 | $label_{TREE} = loss$

14   **end**

15   **else**

16 | $label_{TREE} = leftover$

17   **end**

18   **PerformanceEvaluation**($items$, $demands$, $objs$, $label_{TREE}$)

19 **end**

In order to evaluate the performance of the classifiers and to compare the results generated from heuristics procedures, the Cross-Validation and the Confusion Matrix concepts [1] are employed as efficient measures for evaluating the analysis results. Specifically, the *stratified k-fold cross validation* is applied, since data might be unbalanced. This technique divides the data into k distinct subsets of comparable sizes, ensuring that each subset retains a similar proportion of instances belonging to each class C_i, making them stratified subsets [1,20]. The $k = 10$ was opted as it is a widely used value in the literature and aligns well with the complexity of the problem under investigation.

Important statistical measures are also considered to compare the results. The *Matthews Correlational Coefficient* (MCC) [18] is a consistent evaluation for unbalanced datasets, avoiding bias, as a complement to accuracy [9]. The coefficient varies between $[-1, 1]$ assesses the extent to which the performance of the utilized classifier surpasses that of a completely random classification. It provides a measure of how much better the classifier performs in making predictions than random methods. In addition, the evaluation metrics *F1-score* and the *Area Under the Curve (AUC) of the Receiver Operator Characteristic (ROC)* curve are also presented.

The F1-score consists of a valuable classification error metric for assessing the performance of classification algorithms. It is particularly useful for evaluating binary classification predictions. To calculate the F1-score, precision and recall are employed. On the other hand, the AUC-ROC (Area Under the Receiver Operating Characteristic curve) provides how well the performance of binary classifiers is in Machine Learning. A higher AUC-ROC value indicates that the classifiers are performing better at distinguishing between the two output classes (e.g., leftover and loss).

In summary, when both the F1-score and AUC-ROC values are closer to 1, it indicates that the classifiers have superior performance in accurately distinguishing between the two output classes in binary classification tasks.

3 Results

Considering the characteristics of the classifiers and their algorithms, the cross-validation process was conducted using a stratified k-folds approach, where k was set to 10. This technique ensures that the data is divided into 10 distinct subsets of similar sizes, maintaining a balanced representation of instances belonging to each class in the original dataset. Table 1 presents the results from the classification methods, using the OptimizationTREE heuristic. In the sequence, Table 2 presents the results from the classification methods, using the OptimizationDistBSP heuristic. The numerical values of these tables are obtained by calculating the average of the 10 rounds of the stratified 10-folds.

Table 1. Results from stratified 10-folds for each classifier, using the Optimization-TREE heuristic

Classifiers	Precision	Recall	F1-Score	Accuracy	AUC ROC	MCC
Logistic Regression	0.8934	0.7438	0.8035	0.8955	0.9381	0.9373
Naive-Bayes	0.7285	0.8224	0.7679	0.8538	0.9372	0.9342
Decision Tree	0.8360	0.7859	0.8021	0.8880	0.9123	0.9373
Random Forest	0.8513	0.8112	0.8232	0.8989	0.9396	0.9373

Table 2. Results from stratified 10-folds for each classifier, using the OptimizationDistBSP heuristic

Classifiers	Precision	Recall	F1-Score	Accuracy	AUC ROC	MCC
Logistic Regression	0.9100	0.7378	0.8068	0.8968	0.9353	0.9342
Naive-Bayes	0.8621	0.7323	0.7818	0.8803	0.9300	0.9303
Decision Tree	0.8512	0.7451	0.7855	0.8805	0.8877	0.7980
Random Forest	0.8457	0.7775	0.8046	0.8880	0.9335	0.9342

Observing Table 1, we can conclude that Logistic Regression and Random Forest classification methods provide the best performances, according to their statistical measures, using the OptimizationTREE heuristic. The levels of accuracy, for example, for the Logistic Regression is 0.8955 and for the Random Forest is 0.8989. However, Naive Bayes and Decision Tree classification methods also present good performances, with accuracies 0.8538 and 0.8880, respectively. Due to the fact that they have algorithms with less computational complexity [15, 16], they can also be considered for the classification task based on the OptimizationTREE heuristic. Since the values of F1-score and AUC-ROC are close to 1, then the classifiers are distinguishing the two output classes well: leftover and loss.

Due to the closely comparable statistical measures between the Random Forest and Decision Tree methods, the decision trees are deemed more practical and suitable for use. The decision tree method demonstrated outstanding results, particularly in specificity (recall), signifying its exceptional ability to distinguish between different classes effectively. Hence, the decision tree approach is considered highly effective and preferred for the given context.

After that, observing Table 2, we can notice that the performance of the classifiers are very close, using the the OptimizationDistBSP heuristic. A small advantage of the Logistic Regression and Random Forest methods can be seen, for example, the accuracy of these classifiers are, respectively, 0.8968 and 0.8880. The values of F1-score and AUC-ROC are also close to 1, then all the classifiers used are distinguishing the two output classes well and can be considered for the classification task based on the OptimizationDistBSP heuristic.

The coefficient MCC is especially applied in unbalanced datasets, complementing to accuracy, since it is a more reliable statistical rate [9]. If the prediction obtained good results, the coefficient MCC produces a high score. As the MCC value of the classifiers is close to 1 for both heuristics, then a good performance of the classifiers is highlighted, avoiding bias, as a complement to accuracy [9]. The coefficient ranges from -1 to 1 and measures the improvement in performance of the utilized classifier compared to a random classification. It provides a quantitative evaluation of how much better the classifier performs in making predictions compared to a random classifier.

In addition, the Confusion Matrices are obtained and presented for each classifier in Table 3, using the OptimizationTREE heuristic and in Table 4, using the OptimizationDistBSP heuristic. The matrices come from a random division of the dataset into 80% for training and 20% for testing, in order to show the good performance in classification.

The Confusion Matrices indicates the quality of the analysis results. Since the largest values are on the main diagonals of the matrices, the classifiers, using both heuristics, are labeled as loss the instances that really are loss and labeled as leftover the instances that really are leftover.

Figures 1, 2, 3 and 4 illustrate the AUC ROC curves graphics for each classifier, where part (a) refers to the OptimizationTREE heuristic and part (b) refers to OptimizationDistBSP heuristic. The stratified k-fold cross validation was used and the figures show that the adopted methods provide a good discrimination between the output classes (loss or leftover).

Table 3. Confusion matrices for methods (a) Logistic Regression, (b) Naive-Bayes, (c) Decision Tree and (d) Random Forest using the OptimizationTREE heuristic

(a) Logistic Regression	Loss	Leftover	(b) Naive-Bayes	Loss	Leftover
Loss	45	4	Loss	41	8
Leftover	5	16	Leftover	3	18
(c) Decision Tree	Loss	Leftover	(d) Random Forest	Loss	Leftover
Loss	44	5	Loss	47	2
Leftover	5	16	Leftover	4	17

Table 4. Confusion matrices for methods (a) Logistic Regression, (b) Naive-Bayes, (c) Decision Tree and (d) Random Forest using the OptimizationDistBSP heuristic

(a) Logistic Regression	Loss	Leftover	(b) Naive-Bayes	Loss	Leftover
Loss	48	1	Loss	47	2
Leftover	2	19	Leftover	8	13
(c) Decision Tree	Loss	Leftover	(d) Random Forest	Loss	Leftover
Loss	47	2	Loss	44	5
Leftover	4	17	Leftover	6	15

The ROC Curve linked to the proposed supervised models works as a metric for evaluating their prediction capability and aids in visualizing and classifying the model's discrimination based on its predictive performance. This graphical representation of the ROC curve illustrates the trade-off between the true positive rate and the false positive rate predicted by the model. Thus, when examining the graph, a model that is positioned closer to the upper-left corner indicates better classification performance.

The AUC ROC show the performance in classifying the outputs as loss or excess, associated with to the cutting problem. The figures show that all supervised methods obtained good metrics, since the curves are concentrated in the upper left corner. Thus, there was no method that mischaracterized the classification task. Emphasis on Logistic Regression and Random Forest methods, which presented the highest values of area under the curve.

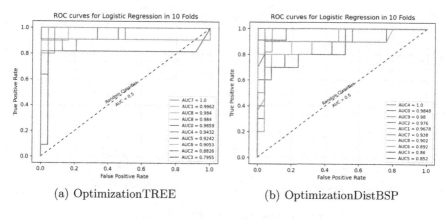

Fig. 1. AUC ROC for Logistic Regression

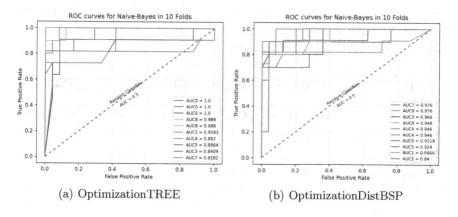

Fig. 2. AUC ROC for Naive-Bayes

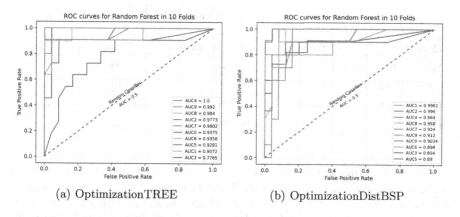

Fig. 3. AUC ROC for Random Forest

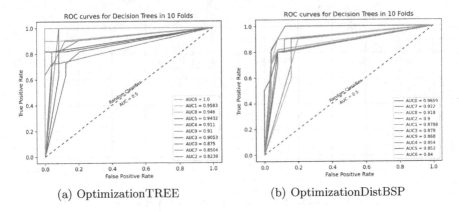

(a) OptimizationTREE   (b) OptimizationDistBSP

Fig. 4. AUC ROC for Decision Tree

For comparison purposes, Table 5 shows the mean AUC ROC and Table 6 shows the mean accuracy, considering 10 rounds of the stratified k-fold cross validation, for each one of the classifiers.

Table 5. Mean AUC ROC considering 10 rounds of k-fold cross validation

Heuristics	FFD (Greedy)	OptimizationTREE	OptimizationDistBSP
Logistic Regression	0.8862	0.9381	0.9353
Naive Bayes	0.8847	0.9372	0.9300
Decision Tree	0.8512	0.9123	0.8877
Random Forest	0.9448	0.9396	0.9335

Table 6. Mean accuracy considering 10 rounds of k-fold cross validation

Heuristics	FFD (Greedy)	OptimizationTREE	OptimizationDistBSP
Logistic Regression	0.7617	0.8955	0.8968
Naive Bayes	0.6600	0.8538	0.8803
Decision Tree	0.8606	0.8880	0.8805
Random Forest	0.8606	0.8989	0.8880

In order to facilitate the comparison and visualization of data in the Tables 5 and 6, bar graphs can be seen in Figs. 5 and 6, respectively, for the mean AUC ROC values (corresponding to Table 5) and for the mean accuracy values (corresponding to Table 6) considering the Greedy, OptimizationTREE and OptimizationDistBSP heuristics.

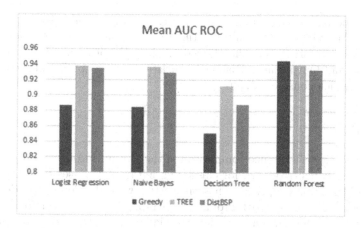

Fig. 5. Mean AUC ROC for the Greedy, OptimizationTREE and OptimizationDistBSP heuristics

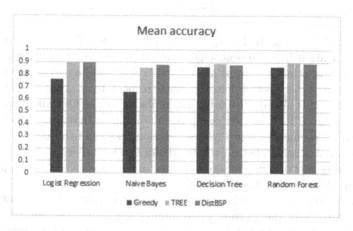

Fig. 6. Mean accuracy for the Greedy, OptimizationTREE and OptimizationDistBSP heuristics

Figure 5 shows that the Greedy heuristic presents the lowest mean AUC ROC value across all 10 rounds of the stratified 10-fold method, except for Random Forest, in which there is practically no difference between the 3 heuristics. Therefore, OptimizationTREE and OptimizationDistBSP heuristics provided better performance of the Logistic Regression, Decision Tree and Naive Bayes classifiers at distinguishing between the two output classes (leftover and loss). Using Random Forest, the 3 heuristics present the same performance.

Considering accuracy, Fig. 6 shows that the Greedy heuristic presents the lowest mean accuracy value across all 10 rounds of the stratified 10-fold method. Therefore, OptimizationTREE and OptimizationDistBSP heuristics provided a higher rate of correct answers in the classification of outputs in relation to the Greedy heuristic.

From the presented results, some questions can be answered; for example: the dataset provides good results for the classification of outputs in leftovers or losses, using heuristics other than Greedy and, on the other hand, the OptimizationTREE and OptimizationDistBSP heuristics can be applied in a case closer to reality, which considers different bar sizes.

4 Conclusion

In this paper, a performance comparison of the OptimizationDistBSP and OptimizationTREE heuristics [2], for classifying leftovers or losses from the cutting stock problem, was proposed. These heuristics were developed to address the one-dimensional cutting stock problem, which provides reusable leftovers or disposable losses. The dataset used for the classification task is proposed in [3], which is large enough to allow the application of Machine Learning methods to classify the output data as leftover or loss. The classifiers used in this paper are: Logistic Regression, Naive Bayes, Decision Tree and Random Forest, for comparison purposes.

In [3], the FFD heuristic is employed, which involves a Greedy approach. This heuristic is utilized to make decisions regarding the usage of input variables and to determine whether the resulting output, corresponding to a particular set of items, constitutes loss or leftover, with respect to a given object. In this current paper, this Greedy heuristic was replaced by the OptimizationDistBSP and OptimizationTREE heuristics [2]. Results indicate that these two heuristics provide better performance in the classification task than the Greedy heuristic. Therefore, we can conclude that the heuristics can be applied in a more realistic problem, using bars of different sizes, and the dataset can be validated, providing good results for the classification task.

In conclusion, the methods proposed in this study were implemented using open-source tools in the Python programming language. The source codes for these implementations have been made openly accessible and are readily available in the GitHub package repository. Researchers and practitioners can freely access and utilize these codes for their own purposes in the links below, as well as the dataset used in this study.

https://github.com/omatheuspimenta/heuristictree and
https://github.com/omatheuspimenta/heuristiciohbsp.

As prospects for continuing this research, we can indicate the use or generation of other datasets to be applied in the heuristics for the classification task and the consideration of other types of optimization problems, which allow a classification process, and comparing the performance of other different learning and training algorithms from the data.

References

1. Aggarwal, C.C. (ed.): Data Classification: Algorithms and Applications. No. 35 in Chapman & Hall/CRC Data Mining and Knowledge Discovery Series. CRC Press/Chapman & Hall, Boca Raton (2014)
2. Bressan, G.M., Pimenta-Zanon, M., Sakuray, F.: Heuristic methods for minimizing cut bars and using leftovers from the one-dimensional cutting process. Adv. Math. Sci. Appl. **31**(2), 407–433 (2022)
3. Bressan, G.M., da Silva, E.B., Pimenta-Zanon, M.H., da Silva Lizzi, E.A.: Classification of leftovers from the stock cutting process. In: Optimization, Learning Algorithms and Applications: Second International Conference, OL2A 2022, Póvoa de Varzim, Portugal, 24–25 October 2022, Proceedings, pp. 327–341. Springer, Heidelberg (2023). https://doi.org/10.1007/978-3-031-23236-7_23
4. Campello, B., Ghidini, C., Ayres, A., Oliveira, W.: A residual recombination heuristic for one-dimensional cutting stock problems. TOP **30**(1), 194–220 (2022)
5. Cerqueira, G.R.L., Aguiar, S.S., Marques, M.: Modified Greedy Heuristic for the one-dimensional cutting stock problem. J. Comb. Optim. **42**(3), 657–674 (2021)
6. Cherri, A.C., Arenales, M.N., Yanasse, H.H.: The one-dimensional cutting stock problem with usable leftover-a heuristic approach. Eur. J. Oper. Res. **196**(3), 897–908 (2009)
7. Cherri, A.C., Arenales, M.N., Yanasse, H.H.: The usable leftover one-dimensional cutting stock problem: a priority-in-use heuristic. Int. Trans. Oper. Res. **20**(2), 189–199 (2013)
8. Cherri, A.C., Arenales, M.N., Yanasse, H.H., Poldi, K.C., Vianna, A.C.G.: The one-dimensional cutting stock problem with usable leftovers-a survey. Eur. J. Oper. Res. **236**(2), 395–402 (2014)
9. Chicco, D., Jurman, G.: The advantages of the Matthews correlation coefficient (MCC) over F1 score and accuracy in binary classification evaluation. BMC Genom. **21**(1), 1–13 (2020)
10. Cui, Y., Yang, Y.: A heuristic for the one-dimensional cutting stock problem with usable leftover. Eur. J. Oper. Res. **204**(2), 245–250 (2010)
11. Foerster, H., Wascher, G.: Pattern reduction in one-dimensional cutting stock problems. Int. J. Prod. Res. **38**(7), 1657–1676 (2000)
12. Gau, T., Wäscher, G.: Cutgen1: a problem generator for the standard one-dimensional cutting stock problem. Eur. J. Oper. Res. **84**(3), 572–579 (1995)
13. Gilmore, P.C., Gomory, R.E.: A linear programming approach to the cutting-stock problem. Oper. Res. **9**(6), 849–859 (1961)
14. Gilmore, P.C., Gomory, R.E.: Multistage cutting stock problems of two and more dimensions. Oper. Res. **13**(1), 94–120 (1965)
15. Han, J., Kamber, M., Pei, J.: Classification: basic concepts. In: Data Mining, pp. 327–391. Morgan Kaufmann, Boston (2012)
16. Lantz, B.: Machine Learning with R: Learn How to Use R to Apply Powerful Machine Learning Methods and Gain an Insight into Real-World Applications. Packt Publishing Ltd., Birmingham (2013)
17. Luenberger, D.G., Ye, Y.: Linear and Nonlinear Programming. ISORMS, vol. 228. Springer, Cham (2021). https://doi.org/10.1007/978-3-030-85450-8
18. Matthews, B.: Comparison of the predicted and observed secondary structure of T4 phage lysozyme. Biochimica et Biophysica Acta (BBA) - Protein Struct. **405**(2), 442–451 (1975)

19. do Prado Marques, F., Arenales, M.N.: The constrained compartmentalised knapsack problem. Comput. Oper. Res. **34**(7), 2109–2129 (2007)
20. Purushotham, S., Tripathy, B.K.: Evaluation of classifier models using stratified tenfold cross validation techniques. In: Krishna, P.V., Babu, M.R., Ariwa, E. (eds.) ObCom 2011. CCIS, vol. 270, pp. 680–690. Springer, Heidelberg (2012). https://doi.org/10.1007/978-3-642-29216-3_74

Optimization in Control Systems Design

On Strong Anti-learning of Parity

Alexei Lisitsa[1]($\boxtimes$)(iD) and Alexei Vernitski[2](iD)

[1] Department of Computer Science, University of Liverpool, Liverpool, UK
a.lisitsa@liverpool.ac.uk
[2] Department of Mathematical Sciences, University of Essex, Essex, UK
asvern@essex.ac.uk

Abstract. On some data, machine learning displays anti-learning; that is, while the classifier demonstrates excellent performance on the training set, it performs much worse than the random classifier on the test set. In this paper we study what we call *strong anti-learning*, that is, the most surprising scenario, in which the more examples you place in the training set, the worse the accuracy becomes, until it becomes 0% on the test set. We produce a framework in which strong anti-learning can be reproduced and studied theoretically. We deduce a formula estimating anti-learning when decision trees (one of the most important tools of machine learning) solve the parity bit problem (one of the most famously tricky problems of machine learning). Our estimation formula (deduced under certain mathematical assumptions) agrees very well with experimental results (produced on random data without these assumptions).

1 Introduction

Let f be a function. For the purposes of this study, one can assume that the domain $\mathrm{dom} f$ is finite, and the image $\mathrm{im} f = \{0,1\}$. Split $\mathrm{dom} f$ into two sets, $\mathrm{dom} f = R \cup S$, $R \cap S = \emptyset$. *Machine learning* can be described as the art of using algorithms to predict the values of f on S when the values of f on R are given. In this context, R is called the *training set*, and S is called the *test set*. The percentage of the correct predictions of the values of f on S is called *accuracy*. A random predictor has accuracy 50%. The basic assumption of machine learning is that after inspecting the values of f on R, one can achieve a more than 50% accuracy on test set. It has turned out though that this basic assumption is violated in some cases for both natural and synthetic datasets and common models of machine learning. In some examples, researchers observed *anti-learning* [KC05, Kow07, RAQ+12, RRA18], that is, after learning on the values of f on R, accuracy becomes systematically less than 50%, that is worse than the performance of random binary classifier, on the test set. In [KC05] the phenomenon of anti-learning has been studied theoretically for a class of kernel-based ML methods.

It can be useful to say that anti-learning should not be confused with *overfitting*, which is an important but different phenomenon in machine learning. Overfitting can be briefly described as accuracy decreasing towards 50%, whereas anti-learning means that accuracy paradoxically decreases below 50%.

© The Author(s), under exclusive license to Springer Nature Switzerland AG 2024
A. I. Pereira et al. (Eds.): OL2A 2023, CCIS 1982, pp. 271–279, 2024.
https://doi.org/10.1007/978-3-031-53036-4_19

As we started exploring applications of machine learning in mathematics one anti-learning phenomenon that attracted our attention was that in some scenarios, as we vary the size $|R|$ from slightly more than 0 to slightly less than $|\mathrm{dom}f|$, accuracy monotically decreases from 50% to 0%. For example, Fig. 1 shows how accuracy (shown on the vertical axis) changes when we use random forests to predict the parity of a permutation (that is, to predict if a given permutation is odd or even) and vary the size $|R|$ (shown on the horizontal axis as the percentage of the size $|\mathrm{dom}f|$) of randomly chosen subset R. The effect was very robust and persisted for all reasonable values of parameters of random forest and decision tree ML models.

We propose to call such phenomenon *strong anti-learning* and notice that in previous approaches it was not explicitly addressed.

This paper is our attempt to explain the monotonically decreasing shape of the curve.

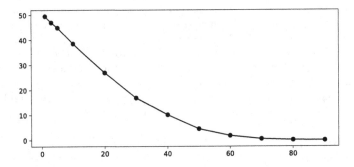

Fig. 1. Accuracy when random forests predict permutation parity. Dataset contains all permutations of size 8. WEKA Workbench [WFHP16] implementation of Random Forests with default settings is used.

To study anti-learning using mathematics, we concentrate on a combination of the parity bit problem and decision trees. Denote the two-element field GF(2) by F, and fix a positive integer n. The *parity bit* of a vector $(x_1, \ldots, x_n) \in F^n$ is the sum $x_1 + \cdots + x_n$, with the addition performed in F. The parity bit is used in many applications; in the context of machine learning, it is an example of a famously hard problem, see Examples 1, 2 below. Exploring what it takes to successfully solve the parity bit problem always leads to fruitful research discussions in machine learning; examples stretch from the 1960s discussion of what perceptrons can calculate the parity bit [MP69] to the very recent discovery that bees seem to be able to learn parity [HGAW+22].

Example 1. Let $n = 2$, and let $R = \{(0,0)(1,1)\}$ and $S = \{(0,1)(0,1)\}$. The parity bit of every vector in the training set R is 0, therefore, one predicts that the parity bit of every vector is 0. If we test this prediction on the test set S, it is wrong on all vectors of S; indeed, the parity bit of every vector in S is 1. Thus, accuracy is 0%.

Example 2. Let $n = 2$, and let $R = \{(0,0)(0,1)\}$ and $S = \{(1,0)(1,1)\}$. The parity bit of every vector (x_1, x_2) in the training set R coincides with x_2, therefore, one predicts that the parity bit of every vector is x_2. If we test this prediction on the test set S, it is wrong on all vectors of S; indeed, the parity bit of every vector in S is not x_2. Thus, accuracy is 0%.

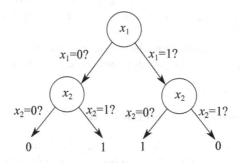

Fig. 2. A decision tree calculating the parity bit of (x_1, x_2)

Constructions used in Examples 1, 2 are rudimentary examples of a model called a *decision tree*. Figure 2 shows a decision tree calculating the parity bit of (x_1, x_2). The nodes in the tree which are not leaves instruct us to inspect the value of one position in the vector, and the leaves contain a prediction. Note that this tree is intentionally constructed to calculate the parity bit correctly for every vector (x_1, x_2); unlike Examples 1, 2 this tree is not produced by training on a subset $R \subset F^2$. This tree is *balanced*, that is, all paths from the root to a leaf have the same length. By a *leaf set* we will mean the set of vectors defined by the conditions written along one path from the root to a leaf; for example, the rightmost path in the tree defines a leaf set described by equalities $x_1 = 1$, $x_2 = 1$; in this example, the leaf set consists of one vector $\{(1,1)\}$. By the *support* of a leaf set we mean the positions in the vector which feature in the equalities defining the leaf set; for example, in this tree all leaf sets have the same support x_1, x_2. The *size* of a tree is defined as the number of its nodes; for example, the trees in Fig. 2, Example 1 and Example 2 have sizes $7, 1, 3$.

As the *main contribution* of this paper we build a theoretical model of anti-learning when a decision tree solves the parity bit problem and compare it with experimental data.

The paper [BDS10] also studies performance of decision trees at solving the parity bit problem. Theorem 1 in [BDS10] can be re-formulated as stating that accuracy is in the interval between 0% and 50%. Our approach is much more nuanced; our work culminates in producing a formula which estimates an expected value of accuracy as a function of two variables, $|S|$ and the size of the tree.

It should be noted that although the parity bit problem and decision trees are important in themselves in the study of machine learning, our research interests spread far beyond them. As we have said, we first observed anti-learning resulting in monotonically decreasing accuracy (as shown in Fig. 1) when we used random forests to predict the parity of a permutation. We also applied feedforward neural networks to predict the parity of a permutation; we observed some anti-learning, but results were so noisy and unpredictable that we could not form any conclusions or conjectures. Studying how neural networks cope with predicting the parity of permutations and with similar problems is a subject of our current research. But as to decision trees and random forests, anti-learning reliably shows itself in the shape of monotonically decreasing accuracy, as in Figs. 1 and 3. We are certain that the model presented in this paper will help us and other researchers to better understand anti-learning when it occurs in various scenarios.

2   Linear-Algebraic Constructions

By definition, every leaf set is a hyperplane in F^n. Denote by P_0 (or P_1) the set of all vectors in F^n whose parity bit is 0 (or 1). Both P_0 and P_1 are hyperplanes in F^n. These observations suggest that we can use linear algebra to estimate performance of decision trees at solving the parity bit problem. To proceed, we make two assumptions: (A1) we assume that the test set S is a hyperplane, and (A2) we assume that the tree is balanced, therefore, each leaf set has the same dimension. The assumptions (A1) and (A2) are chosen as a delicate compromise which, on the one hand, ensures that our mathematical model covers a wide range of examples and, on the other hand, makes it feasible to use linear algebra and probability theory to estimate accuracy. As we will see in Fig. 3, a mathematical model built under these assumptions predicts well accuracy in experiments produced without these assumptions.

From now on, we write vectors as columns. Let the test set S be a hyperplane of F^n defined by a matrix equation $A\mathbf{v} = \mathbf{b}$. The training set is $R = F^n \setminus S$. When we consider an individual leaf set, we denote it by L; let L be a hyperplane defined by a matrix equation $C\mathbf{v} = \mathbf{d}$. Let us denote the number of rows in A (in C) by a (by c); we will assume that the rows of A are linearly independent, and the rows of C are linearly independent. Thus, c is the size of the support of L, the dimension of S is $n - a$, and the dimension of L is $n - c$.

Recall that in machine learning, training is performed to maximise the rate of correct predictions on the training set R; therefore, for each leaf of the tree, the prediction made by the leaf is chosen to maximise the rate of correct predictions on $R \cap L$, where L is this leaf's leaf set.

Denote by $\mathbf{1}$ a vector in F^n consisting of 1s. Obviously, P_0 (or P_1) is the set of all vectors $\mathbf{v}$ such that $\mathbf{1}^{\mathrm{T}}\mathbf{v} = 0$ (such that $\mathbf{1}^{\mathrm{T}}\mathbf{v} = 1$).

Proposition 1. *The vector $\mathbf{1}^{\mathrm{T}}$ is a linear combination of rows of A and C if and only if $S \cap L$ is a subset of P_0 or P_1.*

Proof. In the notation introduced above, $S \cap L$ is a hyperplane defined by a matrix equation $\begin{bmatrix} A \\ C \end{bmatrix} \mathbf{v} = \begin{bmatrix} \mathbf{b} \\ \mathbf{d} \end{bmatrix}$. Suppose $\mathbf{1}^{\mathrm{T}}$ is a linear combination of rows of

A and C, that is, for some vector $\mathbf{t} \in F^{a+c}$ we have $\mathbf{t}^{\mathrm{T}} \begin{bmatrix} A \\ C \end{bmatrix} = \mathbf{1}^{\mathrm{T}}$. Hence, for every $\mathbf{v} \in S \cap L$ we have $\mathbf{t}^{\mathrm{T}} \begin{bmatrix} A \\ C \end{bmatrix} \mathbf{v} = \mathbf{t}^{\mathrm{T}} \begin{bmatrix} b \\ d \end{bmatrix}$. As to $\mathbf{t}^{\mathrm{T}} \begin{bmatrix} b \\ d \end{bmatrix}$, it is a scalar, that is, either 0 or 1, and it does not depend on $\mathbf{v}$. Thus, we have either $\mathbf{1}^{\mathrm{T}}\mathbf{v} = 0$ for every $\mathbf{v} \in S \cap L$ or $\mathbf{1}^{\mathrm{T}}\mathbf{v} = 1$ for every $\mathbf{v} \in S \cap L$. Hence, either every $\mathbf{v} \in S \cap L$ is in P_0 or every $\mathbf{v} \in S \cap L$ is in P_1.

Conversely, suppose that $S \cap L$ is a subset of P_0 or P_1. Then $\mathbf{1}^{\mathrm{T}}$ is contained in the orthogonal complement of the hyperplane $S \cap L$. The rows of A and C form a spanning set of the orthogonal complement of $S \cap L$. Therefore, $\mathbf{1}^{\mathrm{T}}$ is a linear combination of rows of A and C.

Proposition 2. *If $c < n$ then L contains vectors with both values of the parity bit.*

Proof. Consider an arbitrarily chosen vector $\mathbf{v} \in L$. Since $c < n$, there is a position i in $\mathbf{v}$ which is not in the support of L. Construct a vector $\mathbf{w}$ which coincides with $\mathbf{v}$ at all positions except i, and whose entry at position i is 0 (or 1) if the entry at position i is 1 (or 0) in the vector $\mathbf{v}$. Since i is not in the support of L and $\mathbf{v} \in L$ and $\mathbf{w}$ coincides with $\mathbf{v}$ at all positions except i, we conclude that $\mathbf{w} \in L$. At the same time, since $\mathbf{w}$ and $\mathbf{v}$ differ at exactly one position, we have $\mathbf{1}^{\mathrm{T}}\mathbf{v} \neq \mathbf{1}^{\mathrm{T}}\mathbf{w}$; in other words, one of the two vectors $\mathbf{w}$ and $\mathbf{v}$ is in P_0 and the other is in P_1.

Proposition 2 shows that it is realistic to assume, as we will in Theorem 3, that a leaf set contains vectors with both values of the parity bit. The only exception is $c = n$, when the leaf set contains exactly one vector. This is achieved only if the tree size is unrealistically large, so we assume that $c < n$. (For comparison, in Theorem 1 in [BDS10] large unbalanced trees are used, and leaf sets with the support of size n are explicitly considered.)

Theorem 3. *Suppose a leaf set L has a non-empty intersection with both the training set R and the test set S, and suppose L contains vectors with both values of the parity bit. Then accuracy on $S \cap L$ is either 0% or 50%. Namely, it is 0% (it is 50%) if $\mathbf{1}^{\mathrm{T}}$ is (is not) a linear combination of rows of A and C.*

Proof. Each of the subsets $L \cap P_0$ and $L \cap P_1$ is non-empty, and each of them is an $(n-c-1)$-dimensional hyperplane in F^n, therefore, $|L \cap P_0| = |L \cap P_1|$. Suppose $\mathbf{1}^{\mathrm{T}}$ is a linear combination of rows of A and C. By Proposition 1, $(S \cap L) \subseteq P_i$, where i is 0 or 1. Hence, $R \cap L$ is a union of two non-overlapping subsets, $L \cap P_{1-i}$ and $(L \cap P_i) \setminus (S \cap L)$. The former subset contains more elements than the latter, therefore, the prediction chosen on this leaf is that every vector in L is in P_{1-i}. This prediction is wrong on every vector in $S \cap L$, since $(S \cap L) \subseteq P_i$. Therefore, accuracy on $S \cap L$ is 0%.

Now suppose $\mathbf{1}^{\mathrm{T}}$ is not a linear combination of rows of A and C. By Proposition 1, $S \cap L$ has a non-empty intersection with both P_0 and P_1. Thus, $S \cap L \cap P_0$ and $S \cap L \cap P_1$ are hyperplanes in F^n having the same dimension, therefore,

$|S \cap L \cap P_0| = |S \cap L \cap P_1|$. Recall that $R = F^n \setminus S$ and $|L \cap P_0| = |L \cap P_1|$; hence, $|S \cap R \cap P_0| = |S \cap R \cap P_1|$. Thus, the same number of elements of $S \cap R$ has parity 0 and parity 1; therefore, the prediction on this leaf will be chosen 0 or 1 at random. Whichever it is, since $|S \cap L \cap P_0| = |S \cap L \cap P_1|$, this prediction will be correct on exactly a half of the vectors in $S \cap L$ and wrong on the other half of the vectors in $S \cap L$. Therefore, accuracy on $S \cap L$ is 50%.

Theorem 3 enables us to start discussing informally what accuracy we are likely to expect if the test set is small or large. If a, the number of rows in A, is small then it is 'less likely' that $\mathbf{1}^T$ is a linear combination of rows of A and C, but if a is large then it is 'more likely'. Recall that the test set S is an $(n-a)$-dimensional hyperplane of F^n, and the training set R is $F^n \setminus S$. Thus, if the training set is small and the test set is large, accuracy is 'likely' to be about 50%, whereas if the training set is large and the test set is small, accuracy is 'likely' to be about 0%. The next section refines this discussion by producing specific numerical values.

3   Estimating Accuracy

The following construction will be useful. Let X be a set of size x, and let Y, Z be two randomly chosen subsets of X having sizes y, z, respectively. Denote the probability of Y and Z having an empty intersection by $\xi(x, y, z)$. From probability theory, $\xi(x, y, z) = \frac{(x-y)!(x-z)!}{x!(x-y-z)!}$, and this value can be easily computed with the help of Stirling's approximation.

To produce an estimation of accuracy, we introduce one more assumption. Let $\langle A \rangle$ and $\langle C \rangle$ denote the spaces (of row vectors) spanned by rows of A and C, respectively, where A and C are as defined in the previous section. In other words, $\langle A \rangle$ and $\langle C \rangle$ are the orthogonal complements of S and L, respectively. Since we are working with row vectors, for convenience, we shall treat F^n as consisting of row vectors; thus, both $\langle A \rangle$ and $\langle C \rangle$ are subspaces of F^n. Our new assumption (A3) is that $\langle A \rangle$ and $\langle C \rangle$ are randomly chosen subsets of F^n. This assumption can be described as a scenario in which an algorithm building the decision tree chooses conditions at the nodes of the tree at random. When one considers other classification problems, this assumption would not be justified because the algorithm tries to optimize the tree's performance. However, the parity bit problem, by its construction, is hopelessly hard for a decision tree, therefore, we feel that it is justifiable to assume that the decision tree behaves as if it was chosen at random.

Proposition 4. *Under the assumptions of Theorem 3 and (A3), expected accuracy on $S \cap L$ can be estimated as $\frac{1}{2}\xi(2^n, 2^a, 2^c)$.*

Proof. Let p be the probability that $\mathbf{1}^T$ is not a linear combination of rows of A and C. According to Theorem 3, expected accuracy can be expressed as $0 \cdot (1 - p) + \frac{1}{2}p$. In the remaining part of the proof we will show that p can be estimated as $\xi(2^n, 2^a, 2^c)$, hence the result follows.

Recall that we assume that that $\langle A \rangle$ and $\langle C \rangle$ are random subsets of F^n. Hence, $\langle C \rangle + 1$ also is a random subset of F^n. We can express the fact that $\mathbf{1}$ is not a linear combination of rows of A and C as saying that $\langle A \rangle$ and $\langle C \rangle + 1$ do not intersect. Since $\langle A \rangle$ and $\langle C \rangle + 1$ are two randomly chosen sets of sizes $y = 2^a$ and $z = 2^c$ in F^n, whose size is $x = 2^n$, the probability of these sets not intersecting is $\xi(2^n, 2^a, 2^c)$.

Theorem 5. *Expected accuracy can be estimated as*

$$\frac{1}{2}\xi(2^n, 2^n - 2^{n-a}, 2^{n-c}) + \frac{1}{2}\left(1 - \xi(2^n, 2^n - 2^{n-a}, 2^{n-c})\right) \cdot \xi(2^n, 2^a, 2^c).$$

Proof. Consider a randomly chosen element $\mathbf{v}$ of S. Since the whole space F^n is split into leaf sets, $\mathbf{v}$ lies in a certain leaf set L. We have either $R \cap L = \emptyset$ or $R \cap L \neq \emptyset$. In the former case, due to the absence of any elements of R to base the prediction on, we assume that the prediction for the leaf corresponding to L is made at random, as either 0 or 1. Hence, expected accuracy on $S \cap L$ is 50%. In the latter case, we are in the conditions of Theorem 3, and expected accuracy is as expressed in Proposition 4.

Now estimate the probability that $R \cap L = \emptyset$. For the purposes of this estimation, we treat R as a random subset of F^n of size $x = 2^n - 2^{n-a}$, and L as a random subset of F^n of size $x = 2^{n-c}$. Hence, the probability is estimated as $\xi(2^n, 2^n - 2^{n-a}, 2^{n-c})$. By putting these fragments together, we obtain the formula in the statement of the theorem. $\square$

To perform comparison with the results of experiments produced on random data, without the linearity assumptions A1, A2 introduced in Sect. 2, we rewrite the formula in Theorem 5 as shown below, so it does not refer to dimensions of S and leaf sets, but only refers to the size of S and the size of the tree.

Corollary 6. *Expected accuracy can be estimated as*

$$\frac{1}{2}\xi(2^n, 2^n - |S|, \frac{2^{n+1}}{t+1}) + \frac{1}{2}\left(1 - \xi(2^n, 2^n - |S|, \frac{2^{n+1}}{t+1})\right) \cdot \xi(2^n, \frac{2^n}{|S|}, \frac{t+1}{2}),$$

where t is the number of nodes in the tree.

Proof. The formula is produced from the formula in Theorem 5 by substituting $c = \log(t+1) - 1$ and $a = n - \log|S|$, where log is the binary logarithm. $\square$

Using the formula in Corollary 6, we compare the estimation of Theorem 5 with the experimental results produced using WEKA machine learning software [WF05]. In Fig. 3, the horizontal axis is the size of a training set R, shown as percentage of the size of F^n, $n = 12$. The vertical axis is accuracy. In each experiment, the size $|R|$ is fixed and then R is chosen as a random subset of F^n of this size. Then WEKA is used to produce a decision tree learning on R to predict the parity bit, and then accuracy on $S = F^n \setminus R$ is measured. Note that the tree size is not constant but is, in each experiment, chosen by WEKA's algorithm and varies; we do not show the tree size on this diagram, but you can view all data in the online repository of the data of this paper[1]. Each circle in the line with circles shows accuracy produced in an experiment, and the corresponding diamond in the line with diamonds shows the estimation of accuracy produced by the formula in Corollary 6 based on the same test set size and tree size as in the experiment. What both graphs in Fig. 3 suggest is that accuracy monotonically decreases from 50% to 0% as the size of the training set increases. The overall shape of the two graphs is almost the same, so our estimation in Corollary 6 is surprisingly good, taking into account how simple our model is.

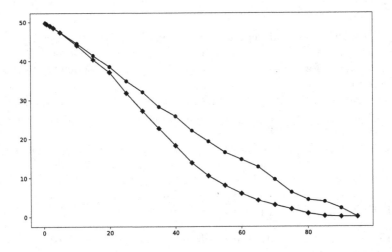

Fig. 3. Comparison of accuracy

In our experiments when we use random forests instead of decision trees, we also observe anti-learning, with approximately the same shape of a graph as in Fig. 3 (cf. Fig. 1, showing anti-learning when a random forest solves a slightly different parity problem). Of course, a mathematical model attempting to describe anti-learning of an ensemble of decision trees would have to be considerably more complicated than of one decision tree; this is why in this paper we have concentrated on modeling anti-learning of one decision tree.

4   Conclusion

While the phenomenon of *anti-learning* has been known and studied for a while, in this paper we have initiated the study of its strong variant. The proposed theoretical model is simple but describes well the experimental data obtained by applications of machine learning to mathematical structures and simple properties, such as parity. Future research directions include (1) extension of the analysis to the case of weaker assumptions, i.e. by dropping assumptions A1 and

---

[1] https://zenodo.org/record/8192737.

A2 and considering random training sets; (2) extension of the analysis to the case of Random Forest machine learning model; (3) finding manifestations and practical applications of *strong* anti-learning outside of pure mathematics, e.g. in biomedical domain, where anti-learning has already been addressed e.g. in [Kow07, RAQ+12]

Acknowledgement. This work was supported by the Leverhulme Trust Research Project Grant RPG-2019-313.

References

[BDS10] Bengio, Y., Delalleau, O., Simard, C.: Decision trees do not generalize to new variations. Comput. Intell. **26**(4), 449–467 (2010)

[HGAW+22] Howard, S.R., Greentree, J., Avarguès-Weber, A., Garcia, J.E., Greentree, A.D., Dyer, A.G.: Numerosity categorization by parity in an insect and simple neural network. Front. Ecol. Evol. **10**, 805385 (2022)

[KC05] Kowalczyk, A., Chapelle, O.: An analysis of the anti-learning phenomenon for the class symmetric polyhedron. In: Jain, S., Simon, H.U., Tomita, E. (eds.) ALT 2005. LNCS (LNAI), vol. 3734, pp. 78–91. Springer, Heidelberg (2005). https://doi.org/10.1007/11564089_8

[Kow07] Kowalczyk, A.: Classification of anti-learnable biological and synthetic data. In: Kok, J.N., Koronacki, J., Lopez de Mantaras, R., Matwin, S., Mladenič, D., Skowron, A. (eds.) PKDD 2007. LNCS (LNAI), vol. 4702, pp. 176–187. Springer, Heidelberg (2007). https://doi.org/10.1007/978-3-540-74976-9_19

[MP69] Minsky, M., Papert, S.: Perceptrons. MIT Press, Cambridge (1969)

[RAQ+12] Roadknight, C., Aickelin, U., Qiu, G., Scholefield, J., Durrant, L.: Supervised learning and anti-learning of colorectal cancer classes and survival rates from cellular biology parameters. In: 2012 IEEE International Conference on Systems, Man, and Cybernetics (SMC), pp. 797–802 (2012)

[RRA18] Roadknight, C., Rattadilok, P., Aickelin, U.: Teaching key machine learning principles using anti-learning datasets. In: 2018 IEEE International Conference on Teaching, Assessment, and Learning for Engineering (TALE), pp. 960–964. IEEE (2018)

[WF05] Witten, I.H., Frank, E.: Data Mining: Practical Machine Learning Tools and Techniques, 2nd edn. Morgan Kaufmann, San Francisco (2005)

[WFHP16] Witten, I.H., Frank, E., Hall, M.A., Pal, C.J.: The WEKA workbench. In: Online Appendix for Data Mining: Practical Machine Learning Tools and Techniques, 4th edn. Morgan Kaufmann Publishers Inc., San Francisco (2016)

Sub-system Integration and Health Dashboard for Autonomous Mobile Robots

André França[1,2]([✉]), Eduardo Loures[2][iD], Luísa Jorge[1][iD], and André Mendes[1][iD]

[1] Instituto Politécnico de Bragança, IPB, Bragança, Portugal
a54187@alunos.ipb.pt, {ljorge,a.chaves}@ipb.pt
[2] Universidade Tecnológica Federal do Paraná, UTFPR, Curitiba, Brazil
loures@utfpr.edu.br

Abstract. Data visualization has become increasingly important to improve equipment monitoring, reduce operational costs and increase process efficiency with the ever-increasing amount of data being generated and collected in various fields. This paper proposes the development of a health monitoring system for an Autonomous Mobile Robot (AMR) that allows data acquisition and analysis for decision-making. The implementation of the proposed system showed favourable results in data acquisition, analysis, and visualization for decision-making. Through the use of a hybrid control architecture, the data acquisition and processing demonstrated efficiency without significant impact on battery consumption or resource usage of the AMR embedded microcomputer. The developed dashboard proved to be efficient in navigating and visualizing the data, providing important tools for the platform manager's decision-making. This work contributes to the health monitoring of devices based on Robot Operating System (ROS), which may be of interest to professionals and researchers in fields related to robotics and automation. Furthermore, the system presented will be open source, making it accessible and adaptable for use in different contexts and applications.

Keywords: Human Machine Interface · Data visualization · Autonomous Mobile Robot · Robot Operating System · Open Source Software

1 Introduction

With the development of industry, autonomous vehicles such as Autonomous Mobile Robot (AMR), Automated Guided Vehicle (AGV) and other types of mobile robotic platforms have become increasingly popular types of equipment for companies' internal logistics, responsible for optimizing logistics processes [1,18]. Both have been identified as key enablers of smart manufacturing, underpinning the success of Factory of the Future (FoF) projects in factories worldwide.

AMRs are often considered material handling vehicles that can autonomously navigate from place to perform specific tasks, navigating autonomously using only on-board intelligence. AGVs, on the other hand, are most commonly used

A. I. Pereira et al. (Eds.): OL2A 2023, CCIS 1982, pp. 280–293, 2024.
https://doi.org/10.1007/978-3-031-53036-4_20

in industrial applications to move materials around a manufacturing floor or warehouse, often navigating with the aid of supporting infrastructure. Thus, AMRs are generally an advanced form of AGVs and can be integrated into a factory environment without supporting infrastructure such as cables, optical markers, magnets, etc.

Current autonomous vehicle schemes are familiar and widespread across manufacturing, medical and logistics, which tend to be *centralized*. The existing trend in these systems, driven by future demands for flexibility, ruggedness and scalability, is towards *distributed* systems, where the total intelligence of a system is distributed among its components [5,13].

For the proper operation of these types of vehicles, it requires effective vehicle management that addresses resource management monitoring, which has a significant impact on the performance of these systems and generates a huge amount of data to monitor [5,18].

In this context, Big Data visualization has come to the forefront of industrial decision-making, enabling the transformation of complex data into attractive and visually understandable information [4,8,14]. The use of data visualization would provide some functionality to monitor the statuses of battery, faults, and maintenance to highlight some possibilities that will limit the ability to perform tasks and need to be considered at the task assignment level.

To help collect, analyse and optimally present data, and also to act as a control point for emergencies, in centralized or distributed architectures, this paper presents an approach to monitor the "health" (*i.e*, the condition of the vehicle, its peripherals and systems) of an autonomous vehicle. The tool collects data that will contribute to the maintenance of the equipment without affecting its autonomous capabilities or having a significant impact on the use of onboard resources, such as batteries and computer usage. In addition to collecting, processing and storing the collected data, the system provides an interactive and customizable Human Machine Interface (HMI) to support strategic decisions related to the operation and check the "health" of the vehicle.

The contribution of this work may be the key to monitoring and management platforms based on Robot Operating System (ROS). Developing an open-source system, that is easily adaptable to different platforms, allows researchers and developers to get a starting point for their applications on this.

The rest of this paper is structured as follows: Sect. 2 describes the implemented system, presenting the processes and expected outputs for each hierarchical level of the system. Section 3 presents the impact of the implemented system on the resources of the robotic platform. Finally, in Sect. 4, some general conclusions are drawn about the implemented system.

2   System Description and Implementation

This section provides a brief overview of the mobile robotic platform used to develop the proposal and its primary features. It then describes the steps involved in the Remote Unit and Administrator. Following the presentation of the interface with the system manager, and the proposed method of communication between hierarchical levels.

2.1   The Robotic Platform and the Proposed System

The Magni Silver robotic platform is a mobile robot base produced by Ubiquity Robotics, acting as a target for the development of this proposal. Its characteristics and functionalities make it a useful choice for dealing with the wide range of aspects involved in HMI development, allowing multiple uses as it could model different types of mobile robotic platforms [21].

Magni has its systems embedded in the Raspberry Pi 4 microcomputer with Ubuntu 20.04 operating system, using the ROS Noetic for the execution of the required processes for the operation of the platform [20–22]. The platform can move autonomously through the space designated as through the odometry systems, LiDAR and camera for reading fiducial marks, implemented in previous work developed on the robotic platform [9].

To manage the Magni without affecting its autonomous capabilities is proposed a hybrid control architecture comprising three independent hierarchical levels: AMR, Remote Unit, and Administrator. Through the communication between these levels, it is possible to acquire, process and store the data generated by the AMR, besides providing an interactive application that enables the Administrator to analyse the data and take appropriate actions. It also allows the Remote Unit and the robotic platform to create tasks based on the available data.

2.2   Processes Internal to the AMR

The AMR is the lowest hierarchical level of the proposed architecture. It is endowed with autonomy and does not require interaction with the other hierarchical levels for its normal operation. However, it can receive instructions and tasks from the higher levels to improve its operation.

The processes belonging to the AMR and the expected information flow are visualized through Fig. 1. The processes of this flow are not developed on the ROS, and the flow starts with the initialisation of the equipment and is kept in a loop until the platform's shutdown.

The AMR performs data sampling, processing, storage, and management of the acquired data, which must be sent to the external database in the Remote Unit. Additionally, the AMR can make decisions based on the available data and create tasks that will be sent to the appropriate process for execution.

Data Acquisition and Processing in AMR. The acquisition and processing processes are executed in sequence and have a periodic behaviour, where the acquisition frequency is determined by the system manager.

This process is composed of the execution of Algorithm 1, which obtains the information of the topic and performs a callback function to process this data if required. At the end of the callback function execution, the data is packaged in a Binary JSON (BSON)[1] document and the necessary information for the final data storage is added.

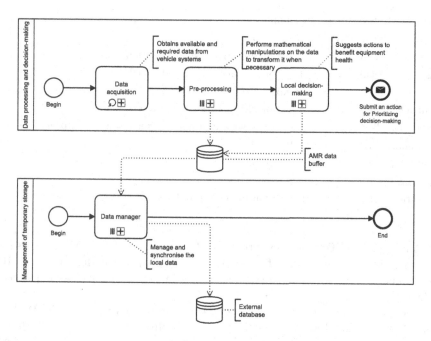

Fig. 1. AMR information flux

Algorithm 1. Get topic information

Require: *Path* as *dictionary*
Require: *Topic* as string
Require: *MessageType* as ROS message type
1: **while** *ROS.core* **is** *running* **do**
2:     *raw* ← TopicMessage(*Topic*, *MessageType*)
3:     *data* ← GetInformationRequired(*raw*)
4:     *data* ← ProcessesInformation(*data*)
5:     *dataBSON* ← EncodeBSON(*data*)
6:     createFile(*Path*, *dataBSON*)
7: **end while**

---

[1] The BSON document format is the one used by the MongoDB NoSQL Database Management System (DBMS). MongoDB is the DBMS implemented in the Remote Unit, it was selected for this project due to its ability to manage the diversity and temporal behaviour of the collected data [3,12].

Algorithm 1 is executed for all items stored in a list of dictionaries, where the information contained in these items should be following the Table 1. In this way, the acquisition, processing and buffering of the data acquired is performed.

Table 1. Dictionary structure for Data Acquisition and Pre-processing algorithms

Dictionary structure of the sample list		
Key	Data type	Description
node	string	Topic name to request information
msg	ROS message	Type of message that is published
rate	float	Sample rate for this message
callback	function	Function that executes data alterations
dataPath	dictionary	Dictionary with information concerning the storage of data
Dictionary structure of dataPath		
Key	Data type	Description
dataBase	string	Database name
collection	string	Collection name in the database

Management of Temporary Storage. The storage management process has the objective of sending the files that are stored in the buffer of the AMR. Additionally, it controls the storage size of the buffer so that it does not exceed a delimited value.

The process of sending files occurs through the PyMongo [17] Application Programming Interface (API) which establishes a connection with the database provided by the Remote Unit, allowing the sending of documents. These are stored with the instructions informed through the dictionary presented in Table 1.

The storage space control process aims to minimize the impact of information losses. Deleting documents randomly from the buffer allows the storage of new information, thus avoiding the formation of large continuous gaps in the data set. It is not expected that the process of management of the buffer space erases files during normal operating conditions, occurring only in situations of long periods without connection to the external database. This process is based on that exposed by Li, Wang, Fang, *et al.* [10], Wei and Tang [26] and Li, Wu, Li, *et al.* [11], which identifies the size of continuous gaps as an impacting factor for time series filling algorithms.

Local Decision-Making and Prioritization of Decision-Making. The decision-making process has the objective of finding anomalies in the acquired data, which in turn suggest platform hazards. It is assumed that in this decision-making process, the algorithms for anomaly detection be computationally light, not affecting the operation of the equipment. In this way, local decision-making acts as the first layer of protection and health of the equipment.

The decisions made through the decision-making process in the hierarchical levels of the AMR, Remote Unit and Administrator, are forwarded to the prioritization process of decision-making. The goal of the prioritization process is to order and classify the decisions made by the hierarchical levels, and to manage only the decisions made by the system proposed in this work. It is expected that at the end of this process, the AMR performs the most beneficial actions for the health of the platform.

2.3   Processes Internal to the Remote Unit

The Remote Unit, in the context of this work, is a cloud server made available to the project. This server is based on Ubuntu 20.04, in the same way as AMR, and through it the following services are provided: data storage, through a MongoDB Community server [16]; interactive dashboard application for the platform managers, based on React, through a Node.js server [19,25]; and data processing, through a Django server [25].

At this hierarchical level, some processes must be performed for correct information delivery. The flux is presented through Fig. 2, where it is proposed that the Remote Unit has the capability of creating and making available the dashboard for the Administrator, as well as possess the functionality to process the data and send decisions to the AMR.

Data Processing and Decision-Making. Data processing, in the Remote Unit, aims to perform data manipulation to facilitate the analysis by the other processes. It is expected, the execution of transformations of computational cost is higher than those executed at the level of the AMR, taking advantage of the server capacity available.

The decision-making process has the same objective as its equivalent process that is executed in the AMR. The difference between the processes is the analysis capacity available at the hierarchical level of the Remote Unit since the analysis algorithms performed at this level have access to a wider range of information besides possessing a greater capacity to process this data. This extra capacity allows the execution of analysis algorithms more complex than those that can be embedded in the platform.

Interface with the Administrator. The system's dashboard is a Graphical User Interface (GUI) made available in a web application format, where the system manager has access to graphical tools and stored data to assist in decision-making. Its development is based on tools for use, copy, and modification without limitations [6,23,24], for not compromising or limiting the use and availability of the application for other developments.

By comparing the established needs of this interface with the study developed by Bach, Freeman, Abdul-Rahman, et al. [2], the most appropriate dashboard

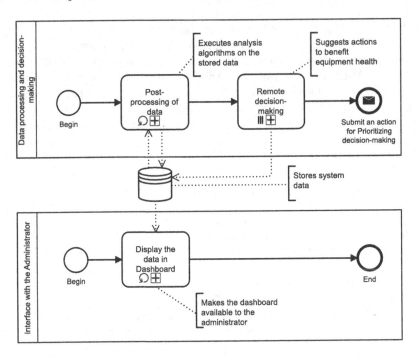

Fig. 2. Remote Unit information flux

genre is the analytic dashboard. In this way, the dashboard composition resources are established as being: an open layout and open paging structure; screen filling with information, without presenting overflow; presentation of interaction resources such as visualization, exploration, and navigation.

Figures 3a and 3b show the use of content and composition dashboard design patterns characteristics defined for this dashboard genre [2]. Various data visualization techniques such as line and area charts [14]; progress bar [2,14]; pictograms [2]; map [14]; graph [7]; and sunburst [27] can also be used by the system.

Through this application, it is also possible to send actions to the AMR, through the mechanisms described in Sect. 2.5, and through the process described in Sect. 2.2 this request is treated for its execution.

2.4   Activities of the Administrator

The Administrator is the highest hierarchical level in the proposed architecture, being the only level with the ability to impose actions on others, a capability that is intended to be used only in exceptional circumstances. The tasks assigned to the Administrator in this proposal are illustrated in Fig. 4.

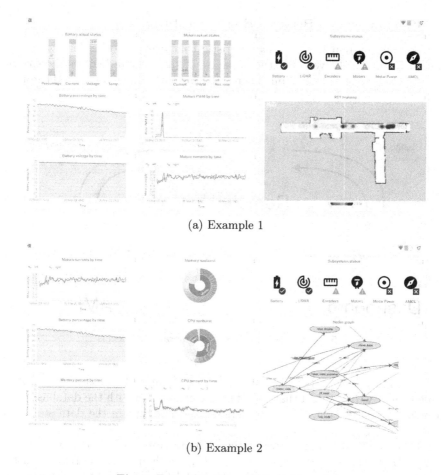

(a) Example 1

(b) Example 2

Fig. 3. Example of the AMR dashboard

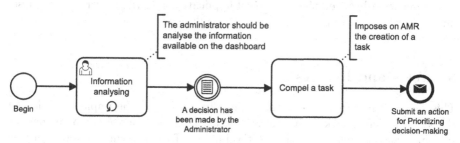

Fig. 4. Administrator information flux

The Administrator is responsible for the proper functioning of the platform, analysing the data generated and displayed through the dashboard application. Through this analysis, if necessary, the Administrator should impose an action to AMR, to preserve the health of the equipment.

2.5   Communication Between Hierarchical Levels

The proposed system has the characteristic that every information exchange, between hierarchical levels, has the database of the Remote Unit as the source or destination of this information. Therefore, this path can be illustrated through Fig. 5.

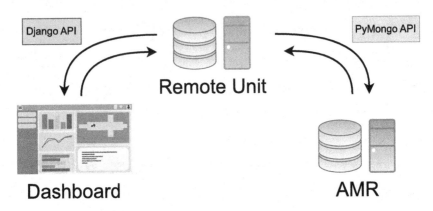

Fig. 5. Communication between hierarchical levels

The communication between the AMR and Remote Unit, is intermediated through the PyMongo API that establishes a connection with the database, and through this connection can insert, remove and manipulate the data stored in the database [17].

Information exchange between the Administrator (dashboard) and the Remote Unit is managed by a Django API, which uses HyperText Transfer Protocol (HTTP) methods such as GET and POST. This API supports the communication between the dashboard application and the server [25], requesting the server to manipulate the data through aggregation or insertion queries [15].

3   Tests and Results

This section aims to compare the result obtained with the implementation of the system, benchmarking it against the actual needs for vehicle management systems. It also aims to investigate the impact of the system developed in this paper on the battery consumption, use of CPU, volatile memory of the micro-computer, and any effect on the equipment's operation. The system's impact will be tested to ensure that it does not cause any significant issues to the equipment.

To this end, six nodes are used to obtain information about the battery, motors, location, odometry, diagnostics, and platform status. Each sampling generates approximately 3 kB of data, managed by the processes presented in Sect. 2.2.

3.1 Comparison with the Actual Challenges for Vehicle Management

The work developed in this project approached the opportunities identified by De Ryck, Versteyhe, and Debrouwere [5] and Oyekanlu, Smith, Thomas, et al. [18] in the area of Vehicle Management. These reviews highlighted points of relevance in the actual context of AGV/AMR equipment class, resource management and real-time sensor monitoring to reduce the time of analysis and decision-making being a main concern of the industry. Resource management is indicated by the authors as a bottleneck for the optimal use of this equipment, with an emphasis on battery management.

Monitoring the equipment is not a single process in this study, but the overall development outcome. The collection, processing and sharing of data between the system components and their processes provide the necessary information for autonomous or non-autonomous analysis and decision-making. The system presented an average latency of approximately 32 ms between data acquisition in the AMR and the correct storage in the Remote Unit when the system is fully connected, within the 50 ms proposed by [18] for non-critical processes.

The management of the equipment resources is a topic handled by the decision-making processes performed in all hierarchical levels of the implemented system. Through information analysis algorithms, it is possible to request that the equipment returns to the charging base autonomously when its charge is triggered or even in periods of idleness.

Finally, it can be said that this work, allowing for moving task control and monitoring to the AGV/AMR and a Remote Unit, facilitates the migration away from central control, therefore addressing the "need for a gradual transition which can migrate from a central towards a more hybrid, and eventually to a distributed architecture" [5].

3.2 Use of the Microcomputer's Resources

Two types of tests are conducted to analyse the use of the onboard microcomputer. The first test aims to verify the impact caused by the message sampling rate established by the system administrator, as presented in Sect. 2.2. The second type of test compares the equipment's operation with and without the implementation of the system to determine its impact.

Impacts of Sample Rate. Data acquisition, treatment, and management processes are executed at the AMR level. This section presents the results achieved by varying the sample rate. The purpose is to verify the impacts of the sample rate on equipment operation and the processes detailed in Sect. 2.

Through Fig. 6, it is possible to observe that the sample rate causes significant impacts on the use of the CPUs of the microcomputer. For rates higher than 5 Hz the data indicates an average usage higher than 50% of the processing cores, a value three times higher than the control test that indicated an average usage of 15%.

Moreover, Fig. 6 shows that the use of volatile memory remains relatively constant throughout the tests, indicating no significant impacts on its usage.

It is observed during these tests that sample rates between 1 Hz and 3 Hz do not affect the vehicle's motion. However, sample rates between 3 Hz and 6 Hz cause delays in the platform's environment perception, resulting in the AMR getting closer to obstacles as the sample rate increases. For sample rates higher than 7 Hz, the AMR presented a behaviour that is potentially harmful to its health, not responding in time to obstacles.

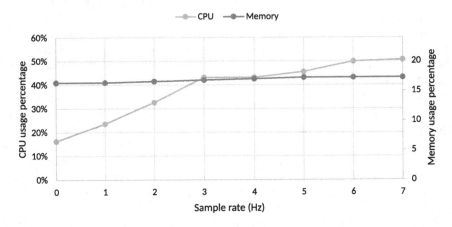

Fig. 6. Sample rate impact test on the use of the microcomputer

Impacts on Onboard Resources. This test aims to observe how the system impacts the consumption of equipment resources. The tests are longer than those described in Sect. 3.2, and the analyses are performed over time. The data is collected every five minutes while the AMR performs a route in a loop for one hour. In the test with the developed system, the data acquisition occurred with a 1 Hz of sample rate.

As shown in Fig. 7a, there were no significant impacts on battery consumption at the time. However, it is possible to detect anomalous behaviour in the discharge curve of the battery pack, which may indicate damage in the battery cells [28].

Additionally, Fig. 7b show that the system's implementation results in an increase in the consumption of the CPU and volatile memory. However, in both cases, the values are maintained at approximately 20% of utilization, not representing a significant impact on the use of total resources.

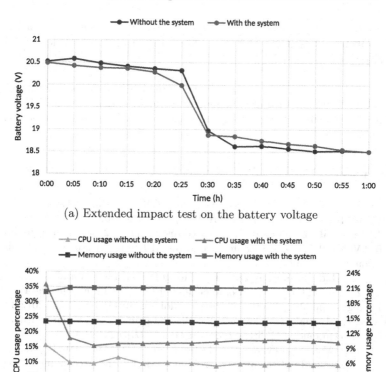

(a) Extended impact test on the battery voltage

(b) Extended impact test on the use of the microcomputer

Fig. 7. Extended impact test on the use of onboard resources

4   Conclusion

In this paper, a solution for managing robotic platforms based on ROS is proposed. The solution provides an application that allows for data analysis through customizable data visualization mechanisms that can be tailored to different situations that the equipment managers wish to investigate.

The proposed architecture produces satisfactory results for the normal operation of the equipment, enabling the acquisition of data and transmission of commands to the AMR. In this study, it was not observed the need for sample rates above 1 Hz for the platform health system. It is recommended to analyse the computational cost of the system implementation for each case, to avoid operational failures, as described in Sect. 3.

The proposed structure allows the modification and expansion of the system to accommodate new or different equipment based on ROS. The solution presents a reliable and scalable approach for managing robotic platforms with ROS. It is suggested for future work the validation of the developed system in other robotic platforms based on ROS, as well as the study and implementation of data security mechanisms.

Acknowledgment. The authors are grateful to the Foundation for Science and Technology (FCT, Portugal) for financial support through national funds FCT/MCTES (PIDDAC) to CeDRI (UIDB/05757/2020 and UIDP/05757/2020) and SusTEC (LA/P/0007/2021).

References

1. Agarwal, D., Bharti, P.S.: A case study on AGV's alternatives selection problem **14**(2), 1011–1023. https://doi.org/10.1007/s41870-018-0223-z
2. Bach, B., et al.: Dashboard design patterns **29**(1), 342–352. https://doi.org/10.1109/TVCG.2022.3209448, conference Name: IEEE Transactions on Visualization and Computer Graphics
3. Boicea, A., Radulescu, F., Agapin, L.I.: MongoDB vs oracle - database comparison. In: 2012 Third International Conference on Emerging Intelligent Data and Web Technologies, pp. 330–335 (2012). https://doi.org/10.1109/EIDWT.2012.32
4. Chawla, G., Bamal, S., Khatana, R.: Big data analytics for data visualization: review of techniques 182. https://doi.org/10.5120/ijca2018917977
5. De Ryck, M., Versteyhe, M., Debrouwere, F.: Automated guided vehicle systems, state-of-the-art control algorithms and techniques **54**, 152–173. https://doi.org/10.1016/j.jmsy.2019.12.002, https://www.sciencedirect.com/science/article/pii/S0278612519301177
6. Design, A.: Ant design. https://github.com/ant-design/ant-design/blob/822dec20a44d099e599747899d113ba6c0680c4b/LICENSE, original-date: 2015-04-24T15:37:24Z
7. Gross, J.L., Yellen, J.: Graph Theory and Its Applications, Second Edition. CRC Press
8. Ishika, Mittal, N.: Big data analysis for data visualization a review. In: 2021 9th International Conference on Reliability, Infocom Technologies and Optimization (Trends and Future Directions) (ICRITO), pp. 1–6 (2021). https://doi.org/10.1109/ICRITO51393.2021.9596423
9. Júnior, A.D.O.: Combining particle filter and fiducial markers in a SLAM-based approach to indoor localization of mobile robots
10. Li, H.M., Wang, P., Fang, L.Y., Liu, J.W.: An algorithm based on time series similarity measurement for missing data filling. In: 2012 24th Chinese Control and Decision Conference (CCDC), pp. 3933–3935 (2021). https://doi.org/10.1109/CCDC.2012.6244628, ISSN: 1948-9447
11. Li, Z.X., Wu, S.H., Li, C., Zhang, Y.: Research on methods of filling missing data for multivariate time series. In: 2017 IEEE 2nd International Conference on Big Data Analysis (ICBDA), pp. 382–385. https://doi.org/10.1109/ICBDA.2017.8078845
12. Mehmood, N.Q., Culmone, R., Mostarda, L.: Modeling temporal aspects of sensor data for MongoDB NoSQL database **4**(1), 8. https://doi.org/10.1186/s40537-017-0068-5
13. Meissner, H., Ilsen, R., Aurich, J.C.: Analysis of control architectures in the context of industry 4.0 **62**, 165–169. https://doi.org/10.1016/j.procir.2016.06.113, https://www.sciencedirect.com/science/article/pii/S2212827117300641

14. Mohammed, L.T., AlHabshy, A.A., ElDahshan, K.A.: Big data visualization: a survey. In: 2022 International Congress on Human-Computer Interaction, Optimization and Robotic Applications (HORA), pp. 1–12 (2022). https://doi.org/10.1109/HORA55278.2022.9799819

15. MongoDB: Aggregation operations - MongoDB manual. https://www.mongodb.com/docs/manual/aggregation/

16. MongoDB: MongoDB: The developer data platform | MongoDB. https://www.mongodb.com/

17. MongoDB: PyMongo - MongoDB drivers. https://www.mongodb.com/docs/drivers/pymongo/

18. Oyekanlu, E.A., et al.: A review of recent advances in automated guided vehicle technologies: integration challenges and research areas for 5g-based smart manufacturing applications **8**, 202312–202353. https://doi.org/10.1109/ACCESS.2020.3035729, conference Name: IEEE Access

19. React, F.O.S.: React - a JavaScript library for building user interfaces. https://reactjs.org/

20. Robotics, U.: Magni documentation. https://learn.ubiquityrobotics.com/

21. Robotics, U.: Robot base magni silver. https://www.ubiquityrobotics.com/product/magni-silver/

22. Robotics, U.: Ubiquity robotics GitHub. https://github.com/UbiquityRobotics

23. Saltzer, J.H.: The origin of the "MIT license" **42**(4), 94–98. https://doi.org/10.1109/MAHC.2020.3020234, conference Name: IEEE Annals of the History of Computing

24. UI, M.: Pricing - MUI. https://mui.com/pricing/

25. Vainikka, J.: Full-stack web development using django REST framework and react

26. Wei, W., Tang, Y.: A generic neural network approach for filling missing data in data mining. In: SMC'03 Conference Proceedings. 2003 IEEE International Conference on Systems, Man and Cybernetics. Conference Theme - System Security and Assurance (Cat. No.03CH37483), vol. 1, pp. 862–867 (2003). https://doi.org/10.1109/ICSMC.2003.1243923, ISSN: 1062-922X

27. Woodburn, L., Yang, Y., Marriott, K.: Interactive visualisation of hierarchical quantitative data: an evaluation. In: 2019 IEEE Visualization Conference (VIS), pp. 96–100. https://doi.org/10.1109/VISUAL.2019.8933545

28. Xunzel: SOLARX^{TM}-8. https://www.xunzel.com/inicio/solarx-8/

Optimization Models for Hydrokinetic Energy Generated Downstream of Hydropower Plants

Nelio Moura de Figueiredo[1] , Maisa Sales GamaTobias[1] ,
Lucio Carlos Pinheiro Campos Filho[1] , and Paulo Afonso[2]([✉])

[1] Faculty of Naval Engineering (FENAV/ITEC/UFPA), Technological Institute, Federal
University of Pará, Belém, PA, Brazil
[2] Department of Production and Systems, School of Engineering, University of Minho,
Guimarães, Portugal
psafonso@dps.uminho.pt

Abstract. The mitigation of the energy crisis necessitates the exploration of alternative sources, including hydrokinetic energy derived from downstream regions of hydroelectric facilities. In this context, harnessing the defluent flow from hydroelectric plants through hydrokinetic turbines has become increasingly vital. This study aims to develop a comprehensive model that furnishes essential parameters for the design of hydrokinetic turbines positioned downstream of dams. The model comprises two key modules: a module for predicting remaining energy and defluent flow, and a module for optimizing reservoir operation. The first module employs a Multi-Layer Perceptron (MLP) model with Backpropagation (MLP-BP) and integrates Autoregressive Integrated Moving Average (ARIMA) models. The second module leverages non-linear programming optimization techniques and advanced process modeling. This module ensures efficient reservoir operation by optimizing generation and defluent flow in hydroelectric plants. It enables sustainable operational simulations, capable of minimizing conflicts arising from periods of flood, drought, and high-energy demands. The results demonstrate the model's fundamental significance in both the design and operation of hydrokinetic turbines installed downstream of hydroelectric plants. It enables the optimization of generation and defluent flow, even during challenging conditions, while facilitating sustainable operational simulations that mitigate conflicts of use. The developed model thus emerges as a crucial tool in enhancing the efficiency and sustainability of hydroelectric power generation.

1 Introduction

Over time, the human perspective on observing the world has undergone significant transformations. The previous mechanistic and Cartesian approach to understanding reality has gradually given way to a more systemic and holistic outlook. The conventional mindset, which historically positioned humans as predators and dominators of nature, is now being supplanted by a new paradigm that recognizes the interconnectedness of natural phenomena [1]. In the context of electricity generation in the Brazilian public service and self-producers power plants, there has been a noteworthy development. In 2020, the total electricity generation reached 621.2 TWh, representing a slight

A. I. Pereira et al. (Eds.): OL2A 2023, CCIS 1982, pp. 294–311, 2024.
https://doi.org/10.1007/978-3-031-53036-4_21

decrease of 0.8% compared to the previous year's figures. Notably, the proportion of electricity generated from non-renewable sources accounted for 15.8% of the national total, marking a decline from 17.7% in 2019. It is worth emphasizing the progress made in the utilization of natural gas over the past decade, as it has gradually displaced fuel oil and diesel in the generation of electricity from non-renewable sources. This shift has played a crucial role in mitigating emissions associated with non-renewable electricity generation [2].

The need to expand the energy infrastructure is evident in various regions of Brazil. However, the construction of hydroelectric plants poses constant environmental challenges. Additionally, many communities residing near these plants do not benefit from the energy generated by them due to the absence of substations. It is common to observe transmission grids passing through towns that rely on diesel generators. On a global scale, continuous efforts are being made to enhance water resource distribution and efficient management [3]. Within this context, one of the major obstacles in water management lies in mitigating conflicts associated with multiple uses, aiming to distribute these resources equitably, sustainably, and ensuring high quality for all purposes [4–6].

The utilization of the remaining energy derived from hydropower plants, particularly in the form of hydrokinetic energy found downstream of hydroelectric power plants (HPPs), is progressively gaining prominence. Hydrokinetic turbines are employed to generate electricity by harnessing the hydraulic potential of outflows from HPPs [7–14]. The management of multiple water uses in reservoir operations of hydroelectric plants often involves the application of optimization models and conflict minimization strategies. These approaches consider various parameters such as flow rates, energy generation, and hydrological scenarios encompassing inflows and outflows. Non-linear programming optimization methodologies are implemented to facilitate the management of multiple water uses, with the objective of optimizing reservoir operations.

These models aim to maximize energy generation while simultaneously addressing consumptive and non-consumptive water demands, maintaining hydrokinetic energy generation conditions, and ensuring downstream flood limits are not exceeded [7–14]. The analysis of water management reveals its crucial significance as a fundamental resource for upholding essential living conditions [15–17]. Inadequate policies that prioritize single-use or neglect proper management directly affect the availability, quality, and demand for various sectors such as hydrokinetic energy generation, withdrawal, industrial applications, and hydropower utilization [18–20]. The effectiveness of decision-making in this realm relies on the implementation of coordinated, strategic, and planned actions that consider the objectives related to strategically vital sectors for both the economy and environmental preservation [21–24]. The decision-making process for water resource management encompasses a broad spectrum of variables, including hydrological factors, political and social interests, cost-benefit analysis, and water availability [25–27].

The primary challenge in managing water resources stems from the fact that multiple water uses inevitably lead to conflicts. To address this issue, Ziogou and Zachariadis emphasize the necessity of public policy instruments to ensure efficient and equitable management and distribution [28]. In the context of Brazil, the Water Law, officially known as Law No. 9,433, holds significant prominence. This legislation established the

National Water Resources Policy, recognizing water as a limited natural resource and a public good. To facilitate this division process, integrated hydrological, hydraulic, and water quality modeling systems [29] are employed to develop methodologies that can allocate resources and satisfy multiple uses, optimizing objectives within the constraints that often arise [30].

Extensive research is currently being conducted on the feasibility of implementing hydrokinetic turbines in downstream areas of hydroelectric dams to harness the energy of the outflow. These turbines offer the advantage of low environmental impact and compatibility with hydrokinetic energy generation. They can be strategically positioned in various locations along rivers and within power plant tailrace channels [31]. The buoyancy of water levels downstream of dams is influenced by several factors, including the power generated, turbine flow, and spill flow. To accurately assess the potential for power generation and turbine engulfment, models are being developed to determine the water levels downstream of the dam [32]. Calculating the kinetic potential of watercourses requires considering multiple factors, with bottom topography and affluent flow serving as essential parameters in each analysis section. Integral methodologies that incorporate flow and bathymetry data are employed to calculate the kinetic potential necessary for the successful operation of hydrokinetic turbines [33]. The application of artificial intelligence models, specifically those utilizing artificial neural networks (ANN), has proven valuable in establishing a robust relationship between hydrological variables. These models employ non-linear functions that consist of adjusted parameters, aiming to achieve optimal performance in their output vectors. This correlation between ANN and hydrological variables has been extensively explored in various studies within the field of hydrological modeling, as referenced by [34–40].

Hydrological modeling has emerged as an essential tool in both research and water resource management within large watersheds. By employing hydrological models, researchers and water resource managers can gain valuable insights into the historical and current state of water resources within a given basin. These models provide valuable alternatives for exploring the potential impacts of management strategies in response to various system-driven changes, such as those induced by climate change [41–43]. Efficient optimization of reservoir operations plays a crucial role in determining and making informed decisions regarding water release and transfer. These decisions aim to ensure a reliable water supply, optimize hydroelectric power generation, harness hydrokinetic energy, and effectively mitigate downstream flooding. To achieve such optimizations, existing literature utilizes operational models that leverage probability theory, nonlinear programming techniques, and flow simulation systems. Notable methodologies described in previous works with showcase the analytical and management approaches employed in this domain [44–46]. The existing analysis methodologies perform the simulation of reservoir systems with the insertion of input variables related to hydrological, operational, and physical parameters that depend on the analyzed enterprise [47–49]. With this insertion of variables, methodological developments based on linear and non-linear programming are carried out [50, 51], which required the use of computational tools or reservoir simulation software [52–57]. With the methodological application, output data are obtained, being able to find the minimum or maximum capacity of reservoirs that provide specific objectives under a given hydrological condition, prioritizing power generation [44], urban supply [51], navigation or other multiple water use [58].

Current methodologies for analyzing reservoir systems involve simulating various parameters, including hydrological, operational, and physical variables, which are specific to the analyzed enterprise [47–49]. These methodologies rely on both linear and non-linear programming approaches, as demonstrated in previous studies [50, 51]. To carry out these analyses, computational tools or specialized reservoir simulation software are utilized, as observed in some works.

In the realm of hydrokinetic generation, predictive models for remaining energy and defluent flow in hydroelectric power plants, as well as for reservoir operation, have become essential tools. This study aims to develop a model that provides parameters for designing hydrokinetic turbines downstream of dams. The model comprises two main modules: a module for forecasting remaining energy and defluent flow and a module for reservoir operation. The first module utilizes a Multi-Layer Perceptron (MLP) model with Backpropagation (MLP-BP) coupled with ARIMA models. The second module employs a model based on non-linear programming optimization methods and processes. The methodology was implemented at the Hydroelectric Power Plant, situated on the São Marcos River in the state of Goiás, Brazil. Input data for the models were sourced from the National Water and Sewage Agency (ANA) and the National Electric System Operator (ONS). The forecasting model for remaining energy and defluent flow yielded an average Nash-Sutcliffe efficiency coefficient (R^2) above 0.95 and a root mean squared error efficiency coefficient (RMSE) below 0.07. These results demonstrate satisfactory capturing of the flow behavior necessary for hydroelectric turbine sizing.

2 Materials and Methods

2.1 Remaining Energy and Defluent Flow Forecasting Model

The assessment of hydrokinetic energy generation potential downstream of the hydroelectric facilities managed by the Brazilian National Electric System Operator (ONS) reveals a promising opportunity for increasing energy supply to the Brazilian market, while minimizing environmental impacts. Hydrokinetic energy conversion, occurring downstream of hydroelectric power plants, is regarded as a low-impact process. In order to accurately determine the hydrokinetic energy potential in these downstream areas, it is imperative to have access to operational data from the respective plants. Essential data includes inflow and outflow rates, generated energy, gross head, and downstream water levels. Obtaining and predicting this information with precision is crucial. Models capable of providing such data enable the sizing of hydrokinetic turbines and facilitate the identification of optimal flow conditions for the installation of hydrokinetic turbine sites. To address this imperative need and motivation, the researchers have devised methodological processes for forecasting the remaining energy and defluent flow, which are detailed in this study.

The analysis of stream currents' potential for hydrokinetic energy generation in each hydroelectric plant should be conducted on a case-by-case basis, considering local parameters and operational conditions. This assessment should consider both economic and environmental factors [59, 60]. Several studies highlight the increasing utilization of stream potential in rivers for hydrokinetic energy generation, which has become a widely adopted alternative for electricity generation [61, 62]. In Brazil, research and projects have been undertaken since the 1980s to evaluate the feasibility of harnessing hydrokinetic energy in small and medium-sized rivers, primarily to provide electricity to remote communities lacking access to conventional power services [63].

To forecast the remaining energy and defluent flow based on water resource management, an optimization model was developed to minimize conflicts through the analysis of various input and output variables specific to the given scenarios. These variables encompassed aspects such as power generation, flood control, and climatic and hydrological inflows. The forecasting system for remaining energy and defluent flow consisted of two modules. The first module employed artificial neural networks and ARIMA-type models, utilizing Multi-Layer Perceptron (MLP) networks with the Backpropagation (MLP-BP) algorithm. The second module relied on an optimization model employing non-linear programming. The development of the analysis incorporated hydrological and operational variables as input vectors and produced output variables such as defluent flow, turbine flow, downstream water level, energy generated, and gross drop. Energy production stands out as the primary utilization aspect tied to a hydroelectric project. Consequently, it was imperative to develop an equation that establishes a relationship between the key variables associated with power generation. These variables encompass the maximum capacity of the turbines, the duration of operation in hours, the average turbine efficiency, and a constant unit conversion factor [64–67]. Equation 1 represents the objective function, characterized by its non-linear nature, and designed to maximize power values [68, 69].

$$Maximise \ \ P_t = \sum \left(\frac{g.\rho.\eta.H_{bt}.Q_{t_t}}{n} \right) \tag{1}$$

where P_t is the power generated in the interval t; η is the average yield; H_{bt} is the average gross head in the interval t; Q_{t_t} is the turbine flow rate in interval t and n is the number of time intervals; g is the acceleration due to gravity; and ρ is the specific weight of water. According to Markowska et al. and Evers et al. [16, 70], the concern with the buoyancy of water levels downstream of dams, both for minimum water levels that harm the environment and maximum water levels that cause flooding and inundation, must be considered in reservoir operation modeling to minimize the associated risks. Concerning the objective function that represents flood control downstream, there are direct relationships with the flow and water level downstream [71–74].

The flowchart outlining the operational and methodological steps of the forecasting model can be observed in Fig. 1, constructed based on several works [25, 75–80]. Due to the large number of variables involved in the simplified methodological development in the flowchart of Fig. 1 and detailed below, a schematic section of a hydroelectric plant (Fig. 2) was elaborated to describe the main variables used in the research.

Where V_t is the volume stored in the reservoir in the interval t; Qa_t is the flow affluent to the HPP reservoir in the interval t; Ev_t is the evaporative loss in the reservoir in the interval t; A_t is the area of the Reservoir in the interval t; Hm_t is the water level of the reservoir running in the interval t; Hs_t is the unevenness between the lower level

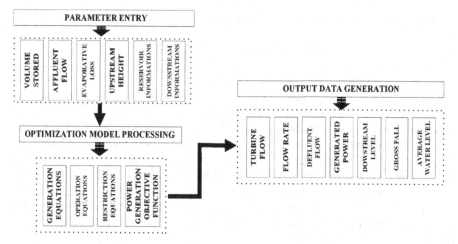

Fig. 1. Methodological development flowchart.

Fig. 2. Variables used in the optimization system.

of the spillway and the water level of the reservoir in the interval t; D_t is the opening of the spillway gate in the t interval; Quc_t is withdrawal by consumptive uses in the interval t; Qt_t is turbine flow rate in the t interval; Qv_t is the flow rate poured in the interval t; Qd_t is the flow rate in the interval t; Hj_t is the water level downstream in the interval t; Hb_t is the average gross head in the t interval; P_t is the energy generated in the interval t. The advancement of optimization models relies on the utilization of objective functions and constraints, both linear and non-linear in nature. Within this context, the modeling of dams and hydro-energy projects, considering multiple water resource uses, necessitates the application of operational rules grounded in objective functions that establish connections between system input and output variables [69–71]. Equation 2 shows the objective function that minimizes the variation in the addition of the water layer in relation to a limit water level downstream, when $Hj_t \geq Hlcij$.

$$Minimise \ \Delta Hcij_t = \sum(H_{jt} - Hlcij) \tag{2}$$

where H_{jt} is the water level downstream in the interval t; $Hlcij$ is the limit water level downstream, where above which floods begin to occur downstream; $\Delta Hcij_t$ is the variation in the increase of the water depth in relation to the Hlj_t in interval t. To mitigate the ecological consequences downstream of hydropower plants, it becomes imperative to establish thresholds for both minimum and maximum flow rates entering and exiting the project [81, 82]. Consequently, it becomes essential to implement a control system that ensures an optimized flow, thereby preserving the environmental flow. In terms of the objective function governing this flow, two scenarios arise:

When $Hj_t \geq Hlaj$, the objective function maximizes the variation of the water depth increase compared to a threshold water level downstream of the HEU as described in Eq. 3.

$$Maximise \ \Delta Haj_t = \sum(H_{jt} - Hlaj) \tag{3}$$

When $Hj_t < Hlaj$, the objective function minimizes the variation in the decrease of the water depth in relation to, as described by Eq. 4.

$$Minimise \ \Delta Haj_t = \sum(Hlaj - H_{jt}) \tag{4}$$

When H_{jt} is the water level at downstream in HPP at the interval t; $Hlcij$ is the limit water level $\Delta Hcij_t$ is the variation in the increase of the water depth in relation to $Hlaj_t$ at the interval t.

In addition to the optics related to power generation and environmental maintenance, there is a need to consider the uses for hydrokinetic energy generation in places where there is hydrokinetic potential downstream [21, 82]. Therefore, it is necessary to consider the maintenance of hydrokinetic potential downstream, which is reflected in the available water depth. Regarding this use, two scenarios are highlighted:

When $Hj_t \geq Hlnj$, the objective function maximizes the variation in the addition of the water depth in relation to a limit water level downstream of the HPP, as described in Eq. 5, where below this there are restrictions on hydrokinetic energy generation. When $Hj_t < Hlnj$, the objective function minimizes the variation in the decrease of the water depth in relation to Hlaj, as described by Eq. 6.

$$Maximise \ \Delta Hnj_t = \sum(H_{jt} - Hlnj) \tag{5}$$

$$Minimise \ \Delta Hnj_t = \sum(Hlnj - H_{jt}) \tag{6}$$

where H_{jt} is the water level downstream at HPP between the interval t; $Hlnj$ it is the limit water level downstream of the HPP, where above which floods begin to occur; ΔHnj_t is the variation in the increase of the water depth in relation to $Hlnj_t$ at the interval t. The development of the "Multiple Use Water Optimization System" was facilitated through the utilization of the GAMS (General Algebraic Modeling System) programming language, alongside the incorporation of a MINOS solver, which specializes in non-linear programming.

The foundation of "Multiple Use Water Optimization System" rested upon the codification of GAMS routines, for constructing models pertaining to water resource management and the administration of water usage in rivers. To address the complexities inherent in optimization problems, a Lagrangian function [83] was introduced. This function incorporates the disparities between non-linear functions and their linear approximations within the objective function. Consequently, the non-linearities are addressed through the integration of linearly constrained Eqs. (7), (8), (9), (10) and (11).

$$minimizex, y : F(x) + \rho^T x + d^T y - \lambda^T (f - f') + \frac{1}{2}\rho(f - f')^T(f - f') \qquad (7)$$

Subject to

$$f(x) + (A_1 y) \sim b_1; \qquad (8)$$

$$A_2 x + A_3 y \sim b_2; \qquad (9)$$

$$l_x \leq x \leq u_x; \qquad (10)$$

$$l_y \leq x \leq u_y. \qquad (11)$$

The objective function in Eqs. (7) is referred to as the augmented *Lagrangian* function, where λ represents the vector of Lagrange multipliers, ρ denotes the penalty parameter, and $(f - f')$ is used instead of the conventional violation of the restriction. The variables u, l, b_1, and b_2 are represented as vectors, while A_1, A_2 and A_3 are matrices with real numbers. The components of x and y represent nonlinear and linear variables, respectively, and $f(x)$ is a vector of continuous or differentiable functions. Additionally, $F(x)$ is a continuous or differentiable scalar function.

To solve the optimization problem defined by Eqs. (7) to (11), which involves a nonlinear objective function and linear constraints, GAMS/MINOS employs the reduced gradient method in conjunction with the quasi-Newton algorithm. The optimization algorithm comprises interior and exterior iterations. In the interior iteration, the reduced gradient method is used to find the optimal solution while keeping the Lagrange multiplier λ and the penalty parameter ρ fixed. The restrictions stated in Eqs. (8) and (9) are converted into equalities by adding vectors of positive auxiliary variables.

The outer iteration involves updating the values of the Lagrange multipliers and the penalty parameter. The penalty parameter is progressively increased and repeated until the outer iteration is completed, either when the problem does not converge or when the violations of nonlinear restrictions substantially increase. The penalty parameter and the Lagrange multipliers approach zero as the problem converges.

2.2 Flow and Water Level Forecasting Model

The prediction of downstream flows from the hydroelectric power plant (HPP) dam relies on a model employing Artificial Neural Networks (ANN) known as Multi-Layer Perceptron (MLP) with Backpropagation (BP) training algorithms. The MLP/BP model is extensively utilized for forecasting variables in hydroelectric power plants (HEP) due to its exceptional capacity to accurately handle non-linear relationships between input and output data. This is particularly relevant given the significant temporal and spatial variations associated with elements of the hydrological cycle [42]. The prediction model implemented for HPP relied on a Multi-Layer Perceptron (MLP) ANN employing the Backpropagation algorithm (MLP-BP). This ANN consisted of three layers, namely an input layer, a hidden layer, and an output layer. Neurons within the hidden layer were equipped with a sigmoid transfer function, while the output layer utilized a linear function. The MLP-BP model was capable of approximating complex functions, thereby facilitating the modeling of intricate relationships between independent and dependent variables.

The mean squared error was adopted as the error measure for training the network, representing the mean squared difference between the correct answers and the network's outputs for all training cases. The calculation of the Mean Squared Error involved comparing the network's output values with the desired output values, assigning a value of 1 for the output corresponding to the correct category and 0 for opposing cases. MATLAB® software, renowned for its high-level language and interactive computing environment, was utilized to operationalize the ANN. The ANN architecture employed in the current research phase corresponds to Fig. 3, forming the basis for each model group specified in Table 1.

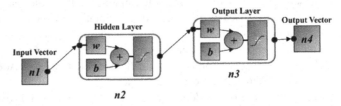

Fig. 3. Architecture of the ANN of the generated energy prediction models

Where n_1 is the number of variables in the input vector; n_2 is the number of neurons in the hidden layer; n_3 is the number of neurons in the output layer; and n_4 is the number of variables in the output vector.

In the process of selecting appropriate architectures, a comprehensive approach was undertaken by dividing the models into five distinct groups based on the characteristics of the variables within the artificial neural network (ANN) input vector. These model groups were specifically designed to capture the intricate relationships between the data derived from the network's input vector and the corresponding output vector. The variables incorporated into the input vector were carefully chosen, drawing upon well-established principles commonly employed in hydrology, which involve the generation of flow values through precipitation and evaporation data.

To ensure the reliability and generalizability of the trained ANNs, a robust cross-validation technique was employed. This method utilizes an independent dataset to determine the optimal breakpoint during the training process, thereby mitigating the risks associated with overfitting. The input dataset was divided into three distinct and independent subsets, each serving a specific purpose. The first subset was allocated for weight adjustment during training, the second sub-set was designated for validation purposes, and the third subset was reserved for the critical verification or testing phase.

During the training phase, a total of 96 input patterns were utilized for each ANN, each pattern carefully constructed to incorporate the relevant characteristics of the input vectors for each specific model. In the subsequent testing phase, 36 input patterns were measured to evaluate the performance of the ANN, effectively assessing its ability to process and predict outcomes based on the input vector characteristics. Finally, in the validation phase, an additional 24 input patterns were meticulously examined, ensuring the ANN's consistency and accuracy by scrutinizing its performance across a range of diverse input vectors.

The development of scenarios played a crucial role in delineating trends and formulating alternative behavioral patterns based on specific water resource demand conditions for multiple applications. The primary objective of scenario definition was to provide essential inputs to the model by projecting plausible situations concerning the prioritization of water resources for a given purpose. At the preprocessing stage, hydrological scenarios were carefully crafted to estimate the monthly flow rates entering the reservoir for different recurrence periods and durations.

With regards to inflow flows, three distinct hydrological scenarios were delineated: dry, medium, and wet. The dry scenario, labeled as H1, ensured that merely 1% of the inflow values fell below each monthly reference, guaranteeing that 99% of the discharge rates remained above the specified threshold. The medium scenario, denoted as H2, aspired to maintain 50% of the inflow values below the monthly reference, consequently ensuring that 50% of the discharge rates surpassed the threshold. Lastly, the humid scenario, designated as H3, aimed to confine 99% of the inflow values below the monthly reference, resulting in a mere 1% of the discharge rates exceeding the threshold. Table 1 provides a comprehensive overview of the affluent flow values corresponding to each of the analyzed scenarios.

In the realm of hydroelectric power generation, the accurate prediction of water levels in reservoir systems plays a vital role in the operationalization of power plants. Understanding the fluctuations in water levels upstream and down-stream of a dam is crucial for maintaining a hydric balance within the system. This research focuses on the operational analysis of the Hydroelectric Power Plant, aiming to predict water levels using an ARIMA (Auto Regressive Integrated Moving Average) stochastic model. The ARIMA model, based on the methodology developed by Box and Jenkins, utilizes past data from fluviometric stations to forecast water levels.

In addition to the above steps, seasonal adjustment was crucial in eliminating the short-term cyclical component from the data. This adjustment aimed to remove any correlation present in periodically lagged seasonal values. To achieve this, a seasonal ARIMA (Auto Regressive Integrated Moving Average) model was employed. The results obtained evinced the remarkable efficiency of ARIMA models in eliminating short-term

Table 1. Hydrologic Scenario (Affluent Flow Scenarios (m³/s))

	Jan	Feb	Mar	Apr	Mai	Jun
H1	7625	10222	17353	15693	9804	6131
H2	16052	21896	26790	25737	17579	9584
H3	29182	39134	39277	38884	30674	14011
	Jul	Aug	Sept	Oct	Nov	Dec
H1	4360	3623	3535	3475	3875	5677
H2	5759	4346	3979	4599	6253	9951
H3	7814	5941	5186	8187	11798	17360

cyclical components within water level and flow series. Through the amalgamation of autoregressive and moving average components, these models rendered cleaner and more appropriate time series for long-term analyses. The accurate application of ARIMA models in eliminating seasonal correlations and short-term cyclical components significantly contributed to a superior comprehension of variations in variables upstream and downstream of the hydroelectric power plant reservoirs. This model specifically addressed serial correlation within the seasonally lagged periods, as indicated by Eq. (12) in this research study.

$$
\begin{aligned}
\left(1 - \phi_1 B - \phi_2 B^2 - .. - \phi_p B^p\right) \cdot \left(1 - \Phi_1 B^s - \Phi_2 B^{2s} - .. - \Phi_P B^{Ps}\right) \\
\cdot (1 - B^s)^D \cdot (1 - B)^d \cdot Y_t = \left(1 - \theta_1 B - \theta_2 B^2 - .. - \theta_q B^q\right) \\
\cdot \left(1 - \Theta_1 B^s - \Theta_2 B^{2s} - .. - \Theta_Q B^{Qs}\right) \cdot a_t
\end{aligned}
\tag{12}
$$

where S is the period of the time series; B is the translation operator; Φ is the parameter of seasonal autoregressive model; ϕ is the parameter of non-seasonal autoregressive model; θ is the parameter of non-seasonal moving average model; Θ is the seasonal moving average model; $\Phi(B^s)$ is the operator of seasonal autoregressive of order "P"; $\Theta(B^s)$ is the operator of seasonal moving average of order "Q"; $\phi(B)$ is the operator of non-seasonal autoregressive of order "p"; $\theta(B)$ is the operator of non-seasonal moving average of order "q". During the verification phase, the model was adjusted and analyzed based on rates obtained for the residuals. The model's calibration was done through the benchmarking of performance criteria of an objective function. Validation verified the suitability of the model obtained in the calibration phase. The coefficients of performance used in the calibration and validation phases of the ARIMA model were: R^2 (Nash and Sutcliffe) and the *RMSE* (root mean square error).

3 Analysis of Results

The suitability and efficacy of the model were assessed through an examination of various hydrological operational scenarios, thus confirming its validity in the São Marcos River basin. Specifically, the proposed methodology was implemented and tested on the Hydroelectric Power Plant, situated within the geographical confines of the São Marcos

River, in the Brazilian state of Goiás. The presented model for forecasting the remaining energy and defluent flow demonstrates excellent predictive performance, as indicated by the average Nash-Sutcliffe efficiency coefficient (R^2) exceeding 0.95 and the root mean squared error efficiency coefficient (RMSE) below 0.07. This model effectively captures the behavior of the flow inputs required for accurate sizing of hydroelectric turbines. To ensure accurate reservoir operation, a non-linear programming approach was employed, yielding highly satisfactory results in simulating water levels downstream of the reservoir and the corresponding energy generation. The model achieved an R^2 value above 0.96 and an RMSE below 0.08, further validating its effectiveness. Accurate predictions of water levels and outflows in the downstream section of the dam hold significant importance in the design and placement of hydrokinetic turbines. Leveraging these model predictions along with the application of altimetric references, a digital elevation model (DEM) was developed to analyze fluctuations in water levels within the downstream segment of the dam.

With the insertion and filling in of the optimization parameters, affluence scenarios, objective functions and their respective constraint equations, the computational tool presented, for the three scenarios related to hydrokinetic energy generation prioritization and power generation prioritization, output data related to the Monthly turbine flow (Qt_t), monthly flow (Qv_t), monthly defluent flow (Qd_t); Monthly generated power (P_t); Monthly downstream level (Hj_t); Gross monthly head (Hb_t) and Average water level of the reservoir (Hm_t). Table 2 shows the monthly values of analyzed variables.

The utilization of an optimization system enabled the acquisition of valuable insights regarding the ramifications of prioritizing a single multiple use at the expense of others. Additionally, a comparative analysis among the various scenarios for each output variable facilitated the observation of the interdependencies between these variables. For instance, the impact of turbine flow on both the generated power values and the other variables could be discerned.

Furthermore, the obtained results offered an opportunity to scrutinize the behavior and fluctuations of the analyzed output variables over the course of a year, specifically during periods characterized by river flooding and ebbing. Notably, elevated water flows were observed during the flooding phase, while reduced water flows were evident during drought periods. These fluctuations necessitate direct interventions in the operation systems of reservoirs. The efficacy of the water level and outflow prediction model played a pivotal role in the reservoir operation model. It served as crucial input data for the development of reservoir operation simulations implemented for the hydroelectric plant. It is apparent that Scenario H1 exhibits diminished turbine flow values, followed by Scenario H2 and H3. Notably, the H3 scenario reaches its peak flow rate of 249 m³/s in the month of December. On the other hand, March registers turbine flow rates of 158 m³/s and 57 m³/s for Scenarios H1 and H2, respectively. Conversely, the minimum flow rates occur in July for both H3 and H2 scenarios, measuring 183 m³/s and 90 m³/s, respectively. The highest power generation values for the H3 scenario are recorded in January, reaching 116.644 MW. In contrast, the H1 and H2 scenarios yield power outputs of 23.561 MW and 68.193 MW, respectively, in January and October. Conversely, the minimum power generation values are observed in June, January, and February for the H3, H2, and H1 scenarios, respectively, measuring 87.746 m^3/s, 36.259 m^3/s, and 12.013 m^3/s.

The analysis reveals that the two scenarios exhibit remarkably similar values, indicating a negligible depletion in the reservoir's amplitude. The gross head represents the disparity between the water level upstream and downstream. Consequently, optimizing energy generation necessitates considering the generated power's objective function, which is directly influenced by the turbine flow. By optimizing the power generation function, the turbine flow increases, leading to a higher flow rate and water level downstream. As a result, elevated downstream water levels contribute to a reduction in the monthly gross head values. Furthermore, it is noteworthy that the gross head values tend to be lower during the period from February to April, coinciding with the flood season in the hydrological scenario. During this period, the affluent flow attains higher magnitudes, consequently increasing the turbine flow and subsequently raising the water level downstream. Consequently, the gross head experiences a decline within this specific timeframe. It is worth reiterating that this trend of reduced gross head values between February and April corresponds to the flood season in the hydrological scenario.

Table 2. Output Data Results

Output	Scen.	Jan	Feb	Mar	Apr	May	Jun	Jul	Aug	Sept	Oct	Nov	Dec
Affluent Flow(m³/s)	H1	48	65	80	74	47	53	40	37	35	28	40	64
	H2	126	121	135	177	161	122	101	76	50	54	75	98
	H3	363	486	377	525	293	165	144	150	130	126	114	148
Turbine Flow(m³/s)	H1	53	55	37	48	30	30	3	33	36	32	57	56
	H2	111	91	94	89	87	89	90	94	96	135	158	135
	H3	227	228	245	201	195	213	183	184	217	240	235	249
Spill Flow (m³/s)	H1	0	0	0	0	0	0	0	0	0	0	0	0
	H2	0	0	0	0	0	0	0	0	0	0	0	0
	H3	0	114	136	31	77	0	0	0	0	0	0	0
Deffluent Flow (m³/s)	H1	60	65	48	59	42	42	20	45	47	43	63	62
	H2	112	93	94	89	87	89	91	95	96	135	158	135
	H3	228	342	381	202	259	213	183	185	217	240	235	249
Generate Power (MW)	H1	23.5	14.45	19.79	12.0	12.35	12.78	13.5	14.7	12.687	23.0	21.96	22.04
	H2	36.2	34.9	36.8	35.9	37.42	39.92	42.5	43.58	62.351	68.1	53.64	48.4
	H3	116.6	116.1	100.	97.4	102.5	87.74	89.9	95.99	102.941	105.	102.0	111.4
Downstream Water Level (m)	H1	674	674	674	674	674	674	674	674	674	674	674	674
	H2	675	675	675	675	675	675	675	675	675	675	675	675
	H3	675	676	675	675	675	675	675	675	675	676	675	675
Reservoir Water Level (m)	H1	737	737	738	739	740	741	741	741	741	740	740	739
	H2	742	742	743	743	744	747	747	747	745	744	742	741
	H3	751	754	755	755	756	756	756	756	755	754	753	751
Gross Head (m)	H1	62	62	63	64	66	66	67	66	66	66	65	64
	H2	67	67	68	68	70	72	72	72	70	69	67	66
	H3	76	79	79	80	81	81	81	81	81	79	78	76

4 Conclusions

The reservoir management model employed hydroelectric plant entailed the representation and modeling of a power generation system. This involved a comprehensive set of mathematical equations established based on operation-related parameters. Non-linear programming was utilized to define power generation functions, enabling the model to simulate various variables, including downstream elevation, upstream and downstream water levels, defluent flow, turbine flow, and generated power. By leveraging these model predictions and incorporating digital elevation models, multiple variational models of downstream flow and water levels were created, facilitating the identification of suitable locations for hydrokinetic turbines. Through comprehensive discussions and result analyses, it can be concluded that the implemented models serve as effective platforms for modeling and optimizing input and locational data essential for the development of hydrokinetic turbine projects. These models effectively minimize conflicts arising from the diverse water uses within watersheds. Within the realm of reservoir operation and its application as a supportive instrument for hydrokinetic turbine design downstream of dams, the scrutinized models have proven to be efficacious tools. These models have displayed commendable outcomes, contributing to the amelioration of environmental repercussions and the resolution of water usage disputes. Overall, it can be deduced that the models have exhibited satisfactory performance in alignment with the research objectives.

Acknowledgments. This work has been supported by FCT – Fundação para a Ciência e Tecnologia within the R&D Units Project Scope: UIDB/00319/2020 and CNPQ - National Council for Scientific and Technological Development to support the research within Call 15/2022/MCTI-FNDCT.

References

1. Cheng, C., Shen, J., Wu, X., Chau, K.: Short-term hydroscheduling with discrepant objectives using multi-step progressive optimality algorithm1. JAWRA J. Am. Water Resour. Assoc. **48**, 464–479 (2012)
2. EPE. Brazilian Energy Balance 2021 Year 2020. Empresa de Pesquisa Energética (2021)
3. Tortajada, C., González-Gómez, F., Biswas, A.K., Buurman, J.: Water demand management strategies for water-scarce cities: the case of Spain. Sust. Cities Soc. **45**, 649–656 (2019)
4. UN. Transforming our world: The 2030 Agenda for Sustainable Development. Sustainable Development Knowledge Platform (2015). https://sustainabledevelopment.un.org/post2015/transformingourworld. Accessed 6 Aug 2019
5. Geressu, R.T., Harou, J.J.: Reservoir system expansion scheduling under conflicting interests. Environ Model Softw. **118**, 201–210 (2019)
6. Tilmant, A., Pina, J., Salman, M., Casarotto, C., Ledbi, F., Pek, E.: Probabilistic trade-off assessment between competing and vulnerable water users – the case of the Senegal River basin. J. Hydrol. **587**, 124915 (2020)
7. McIvor, R., Humphreys, P., Wall, A., McKittrick, A. (eds.): A Study of Performance Measurement in the Outsourcing Decision. Elsevier/CIMA, Amsterdam (2009)

8. Etkin, D., Kirshen, P., Watkins, D., Roncoli, C., Sanon, M., Some, L., et al.: Stochastic programming for improved multiuse reservoir operation in Burkina Faso, West Africa. J. Water Resour. Plann. Manage. **141**, 04014056 (2015)

9. Ahmadebrahimpour, E.: Optimal operation of reservoir systems using the Wolf Search Algorithm (WSA). Water Supply **19**, 1396–1404 (2019)

10. Mohammadi, M., Farzin, S., Mousavi, S., Karami, H.: Investigation of a new hybrid optimization algorithm performance in the optimal operation of multi-reservoir benchmark systems. Water Resour. Manag. **33**, 4767–4782 (2019)

11. Zarei, A., Mousavi, S.-F., Eshaghi Gordji, M., Karami, H.: Optimal reservoir operation using bat and particle swarm algorithm and game theory based on optimal water allocation among consumers. Water Resour. Manage. **33**, 3071–3093 (2019)

12. Chen, H., Wang, W., Chen, X., Qiu, L.: Multi-objective reservoir operation using particle swarm optimization with adaptive random inertia weights. Water Sci. Eng. **13**, 136–144 (2020)

13. Yuce, M.I., Muratoglu, A.: Hydrokinetic energy conversion systems: a technology status review. Renew. Sustain. Energy Rev. **43**, 72–82 (2015)

14. Work, P., Haas, K., Defne, Z.: Tidal stream energy site assessment via three-dimensional model and measurements (2012)

15. Darbandsari, P., Kerachian, R., Malakpour-Estalaki, S., Khorasani, H.: An agent-based conflict resolution model for urban water resources management. Sustain. Cities Soc. **57**, 102112 (2020)

16. Markowska, J., Szalińska, W., Dąbrowska, J., Brząkała, M.: The concept of a participatory approach to water management on a reservoir in response to wicked problems. J. Environ. Manage. **259**, 109626 (2020)

17. Kročová, Š, Kavan, Š: Cooperation in the Czech Republic border area on water management sustainability. Land Use Policy **86**, 351–356 (2019)

18. Chini, C.M., Schreiber, K.L., Barker, Z.A., Stillwell, A.S.: Quantifying energy and water savings in the U.S. residential sector. Environ. Sci. Technol. **50**, 9003–9012 (2016)

19. Xiong, W., Li, Y., Pfister, S., Zhang, W., Wang, C., Wang, P.: Improving water ecosystem sustainability of urban water system by management strategies optimization. J. Environ. Manage. **254**, 109766 (2020)

20. Agrawal, N., Ahiduzzaman, M., Kumar, A.: The development of an integrated model for the assessment of water and GHG footprints for the power generation sector. Appl. Energy **216**, 558–575 (2018)

21. Branche, E.: The multipurpose water uses of hydropower reservoir: the SHARE concept. C. R. Phys. **18**, 469–478 (2017)

22. Hajkowicz, S., Collins, K.: A review of multiple criteria analysis for water resource planning and management. Water Resour. Manage. **21**, 1553–1566 (2007)

23. De Silva, M.T., Hornberger, G.M.: Assessing water management alternatives in a multipurpose reservoir cascade system in Sri Lanka. J. Hydrol. Reg. Stud. **25**, 100624 (2019)

24. Yin, X.-A., Yang, Z.-F., Petts, G.E., Kondolf, G.M.: A reservoir operating method for riverine ecosystem protection, reservoir sedimentation control and water supply. J. Hydrol. **512**, 379–387 (2014)

25. Loch, A., Adamson, D., Mallawaarachchi, T.: Role of hydrology and economics in water management policy under increasing uncertainty. J. Hydrol. **518**, 5–16 (2014)

26. Lu, H., Huang, G., He, L.: Inexact rough-interval two-stage stochastic programming for conjunctive water allocation problems. J. Environ. Manag. **91**, 261–269 (2009)

27. Arunkumar, R., Jothiprakash, V.: Optimal reservoir operation for hydropower generation using non-linear programming model. J. Inst. Eng. India Ser. A **93**, 111–120 (2012)

28. Ziogou, I., Zachariadis, T.: Quantifying the water–energy nexus in Greece. Int. J. Sustain. Energ. **36**, 972–982 (2017)

29. Gourbesville, P., Du, M., Zavattero, E., Ma, Q.: DSS architecture for water uses management. Procedia Eng. **154**, 928–935 (2016)
30. Ren, L., He, L., Lu, H., Chen, Y.: Monte Carlo-based interval transformation analysis for multicriteria decision analysis of groundwater management strategies under uncertain naphthalene concentrations and health risks. J. Hydrol. **539**, 468–477 (2016)
31. dos Santos, I.F.S., Camacho, R.G.R., Tiago Filho, G.L., Botan, A.C.B., Vinent, B.A.: Energy potential and economic analysis of hydrokinetic turbines implementation in rivers: an approach using numerical predictions (CFD) and experimental data. Renew. Energy **143**, 648–662 (2019)
32. Partal, T., Kişi, Ö.: Wavelet and neuro-fuzzy conjunction model for precipitation forecasting. J. Hydrol. **342**, 199–212 (2007)
33. Partal, T., Cigizoglu, H.K.: Prediction of daily precipitation using wavelet—neural networks. Hydrol. Sci. J. **54**, 234–246 (2009)
34. Kisi, O., Shiri, J.: Precipitation forecasting using wavelet-genetic programming and wavelet-neuro-fuzzy conjunction models. Water Resour. Manage. **25**, 3135–3152 (2011)
35. Nourani, V.: An Emotional ANN (EANN) approach to modeling rainfall-runoff process. J. Hydrol. **544**, 267–277 (2017)
36. Honorato, A.G.D.S.M., Silva, G.B.L.D., Guimarães Santos, C.A.: Monthly streamflow forecasting using neuro-wavelet techniques and input analysis. Hydrol. Sci. J. **63**, 2060–2075 (2018)
37. Shoaib, M., Shamseldin, A.Y., Khan, S., Khan, M.M., Khan, Z.M., Sultan, T., et al.: A comparative study of various hybrid wavelet feedforward neural network models for runoff forecasting. Water Resour. Manage. **32**, 83–103 (2018)
38. Elsanabary, M.H., Gan, T.Y.: Weekly streamflow forecasting using a statistical disaggregation model for the upper Blue Nile Basin, Ethiopia. J. Hydrol. Eng. **20**, 04014064 (2015)
39. Lohani, A.K., Kumar, R., Singh, R.D.: Hydrological time series modeling: a comparison between adaptive neuro-fuzzy, neural network and autoregressive techniques. J. Hydrol. **442**, 23–35 (2012)
40. Johnston, R., Smakhtin, V.: Hydrological modeling of large river basins: how much is enough? Water Resour. Manage. **28**, 2695–2730 (2014)
41. Figueiredo, N.M., Blanco, C.J.C., Moraes, H.B.: Forecasting navigability conditions of the Tapajós waterway—Amazon—Brazil. Mar. Technol. Eng. (2014)
42. Li, Z., Kan, G., Yao, C., Liu, Z., Li, Q., Yu, S.: Improved neural network model and its application in hydrological simulation. J. Hydrol. Eng. **19**, 04014019 (2014)
43. Li, L., Diallo, I., Xu, C.-Y., Stordal, F.: Hydrological projections under climate change in the near future by RegCM4 in Southern Africa using a large-scale hydrological model. J. Hydrol. **528**, 1–16 (2015)
44. Dobson, B., Wagener, T., Pianosi, F.: An argument-driven classification and comparison of reservoir operation optimization methods. Adv. Water Resour. **128**, 74–86 (2019)
45. Giuliani, M., Herman, J.D.: Modeling the behavior of water reservoir operators via eigenbehavior analysis. Adv. Water Resour. **122**, 228–237 (2018)
46. Seifollahi-Aghmiuni, S., Bozorg Haddad, O., Mariño, M.A.: Generalized mathematical simulation formulation for reservoir systems. J. Water Resour. Plann. Manage. **142**, 04016004 (2016)
47. Nagesh Kumar, D., Janga, R.M.: Multipurpose reservoir operation using particle swarm optimization. J. Water Resour. Plann. Manage. **133**, 192–201 (2007)
48. Moeini, R., Afshar, A., Afshar, M.H.: Fuzzy rule-based model for hydropower reservoirs operation. Int. J. Electr. Power Energy Syst. **33**, 171–178 (2011)
49. Stanzel, P., Kling, H., Nicholson, K.: Trade-offs of water use for hydropower generation and biofuel production in the Zambezi basin in Mozambique. Energy Procedia **59**, 330–335 (2014)

50. Matrosov, E.S., Harou, J.J., Loucks, D.P.: A computationally efficient open-source water resource system simulator – application to London and the Thames Basin. Environ Model Softw. **26**, 1599–1610 (2011)

51. Celeste, A.B., Billib, M.: Evaluation of stochastic reservoir operation optimization models. Adv. Water Resour. **32**, 1429–1443 (2009)

52. Liu, X., Chen, L., Zhu, Y., Singh, V.P., Qu, G., Guo, X.: Multi-objective reservoir operation during flood season considering spillway optimization. J. Hydrol. **552**, 554–563 (2017)

53. Wang, K., Shi, H., Chen, J., Li, T.: An improved operation-based reservoir scheme integrated with Variable Infiltration Capacity model for multiyear and multipurpose reservoirs. J. Hydrol. **571**, 365–375 (2019)

54. Wurbs, R.A.: Reservoir-system simulation and optimization models. J. Water Resour. Plan. Manag. **119**, 455–472 (1993)

55. Liu, D., Guo, S., Liu, P., Xiong, L., Zou, H., Tian, J., et al.: Optimisation of water-energy nexus based on its diagram in cascade reservoir system. J. Hydrol. **569**, 347–358 (2019)

56. Feng, M., Liu, P., Guo, S., Yu, D.J., Cheng, L., Yang, G., et al.: Adapting reservoir operations to the nexus across water supply, power generation, and environment systems: an explanatory tool for policy makers. J. Hydrol. **574**, 257–275 (2019)

57. Srinivasan, K., Kumar, K.: Multi-objective simulation-optimization model for long-term reservoir operation using piecewise linear hedging rule. Water Resour. Manage. **32**, 1901–1911 (2018)

58. Ahmad, A., El-Shafie, A., Razali, S.F.M., Mohamad, Z.S.: Reservoir optimization in water resources: a review. Water Resour. Manage. **28**, 3391–3405 (2014)

59. Holanda, P.D.S., Blanco, C.J.C., Mesquita, A.L.A., Brasil Junior, A.C.P., de Figueiredo, N.M., Macêdo, E.N., et al.: Assessment of hydrokinetic energy resources downstream of hydropower plants. Renew. Energy **101**, 1203–1214 (2017)

60. Laws, N.D., Epps, B.P.: Hydrokinetic energy conversion: technology, research, and outlook. Renew. Sustain. Energy Rev. **57**, 1245–1259 (2016)

61. Khan, M.J., Bhuyan, G., Iqbal, M.T., Quaicoe, J.E.: Hydrokinetic energy conversion systems and assessment of horizontal and vertical axis turbines for river and tidal applications: a technology status review. Appl. Energy **86**, 1823–1835 (2009)

62. Kumar, D., Sarkar, S.: A review on the technology, performance, design optimization, reliability, techno-economics and environmental impacts of hydrokinetic energy conversion systems. Renew. Sustain. Energy Rev. **58**, 796–813 (2016)

63. van Els, R.H., Junior, A.C.P.B.: The Brazilian experience with hydrokinetic turbines. Energy Procedia **75**, 259–264 (2015)

64. Castelletti, A., Pianosi, F., Soncini-Sessa, R.: Water reservoir control under economic, social and environmental constraints. Automatica **44**, 1595–1607 (2008)

65. Vieira, J., Cunha, M.C., Nunes, L., Monteiro, J.P., Ribeiro, L., Stigter, T., et al.: Optimization of the operation of large-scale multisource water-supply systems. J. Water Resour. Plann. Manage. **137**, 150–161 (2011)

66. Asadieh, B., Afshar, A.: Optimization of water-supply and hydropower reservoir operation using the charged system search algorithm. Hydrology **6**, 5 (2019)

67. Sorachampa, P., Tippayawong, N., Ngamsanroaj, K.: Optimizing multiple reservoir system operation for maximum hydroelectric power generation. Energy Rep. **6**, 67–75 (2020)

68. Loucks, D.P., Stedinger, J.R., Haith, D.A.: Water Resource Systems Planning and Analysis. Prentice-Hall, Englewood Cliffs (1981)

69. Vedula, S., Mujumdar, P.P.: Water Resources Systems: Modelling Techniques and Analysis. Tata McGraw-Hill, New Delhi (2005)

70. Evers, M., Jonoski, A., Almoradie, A., Lange, L.: Collaborative decision making in sustainable flood risk management: a socio-technical approach and tools for participatory governance. Environ Sci Policy **55**, 335–344 (2016)

71. Heydari, M., Othman, F., Qaderi, K.: Developing optimal reservoir operation for multiple and multipurpose reservoirs using mathematical programming. Math. Probl. Eng. **2015**, 1–11 (2015)
72. Shim, K.-C., Fontane, D.G., Labadie, J.W.: Spatial decision support system for integrated river basin flood control. J. Water Resour. Plann. Manage. **128**, 190–201 (2002)
73. Hsu, N.-S., Huang, C.-L., Wei, C.-C.: Multi-phase intelligent decision model for reservoir real-time flood control during typhoons. J. Hydrol. **522**, 11–34 (2015)
74. Wei, C.-C., Hsu, N.-S.: Multireservoir real-time operations for flood control using balanced water level index method. J. Environ. Manage. **88**, 1624–1639 (2008)
75. Elabd, S., El-Ghandour, H.A.: Multiobjective optimization of bigge reservoir operation in dry seasons. J. Hydrol. Eng. **19**, 05014008 (2014)
76. Suzuki, A.H., Zambon, R.C., Yeh, W.W.-G.: Water Supply Planning and Operation in the Metropolitan Region of São Paulo: Worst Drought in History, Conflicts, Response, and Resilience. World Environmental and Water Resources Congress 2015. American Society of Civil Engineers, Austin, pp. 2226–2235 (2015). http://ascelibrary.org/doi/10.1061/978078 4479162.219. Accessed 21 Mar 2020
77. Rheinheimer, D.E., Null, S.E., Lund, J.R.: Optimizing selective withdrawal from reservoirs to manage downstream temperatures with climate warming. J. Water Resour. Plann. Manage. **141**, 04014063 (2015)
78. Wang, J., Liu, S., Zhang, Y.: Quarter-hourly operation of large-scale hydropower reservoir systems with prioritized constraints. J. Water Resour. Plann. Manage. **141**, 04014047 (2015)
79. Côrtes, R.S., Zambon, R.C.: Reservoir Operation with Robust Optimization for Hydropower Production. World Environmental and Water Resources Congress 2012. American Society of Civil Engineers, Albuquerque, New Mexico, United States, pp. 2395–2405 (2012). http://asc elibrary.org/doi/10.1061/9780784412312.242. Accessed 21 Mar 2020
80. Mendes, L.A., de Barros, M.T.L., Zambon, R.C., Yeh, W.W.-G.: Trade-off analysis among multiple water uses in a hydropower system: case of São Francisco River Basin, Brazil. J. Water Resour. Plann. Manage. **141**, 04015014 (2015)
81. Dhar, A., Datta, B.: Optimal operation of reservoirs for downstream water quality control using linked simulation optimization. Hydrol. Process. **22**, 842–853 (2008)
82. Fayaed, S.S., El-Shafie, A., Jaafar, O.: Reservoir-system simulation and optimization techniques. Stoch Environ Res Risk Assess. **27**, 1751–1772 (2013)
83. Chu, W.S., Yeh, W.W.-G.: A nonlinear programming algorithm for real-time hourly reservoir operations. J. Am. Water Resour. Assoc. **14**, 1048–1063 (1978)

Vehicle Industry Big Data Analysis Using Clustering Approaches

Lenon Diniz Seixas[1] , Fernanda Cristina Corrêa[1] , Hugo Valadares Siqueira[1] ,
Flavio Trojan[1] , and Paulo Afonso[2(✉)]

[1] Federal University of Technology – Paraná – UTFPR, R. Doctor Washington Subtil Chueire,
330 – Jardim Carvalho, Ponta Grossa, PR 84017-220, Brazil
[2] Department of Production and Systems, School of Engineering, University of Minho,
Guimarães, Portugal
psafonso@dps.uminho.pt

Abstract. Considering a globalized world economy and industry, data analysis
and visualization offer enlightening information for decision-making and strategic
planning. Data science provides diverse statistical and scientific methods to extract
the most value possible from a data set, covering all data preparation, cleaning,
aggregation, and manipulation. Machine learning (ML) and Artificial Intelligence
(AI) come with it to learn and explore the data, uncovering patterns that cannot
be seen with only the analyst experience. This work performs a study exploring
clustering methods in a trucks data set of logged inclinations on the roadway, a Big
Data problem. With a good clustering, the data becomes key to improve product
development and fuel efficiency, since different environment of truck usage can be
identified. Knowledge discovery and data mining methods were used, namely the
K-means and Fuzzy C-means (FCM) algorithms and compared to a rule-based
method called GTA. The evaluation metrics addressed are the sum of squares
within clusters, the sum of squares between clusters, and the silhouette index. The
proposed approach showed satisfactory results and demonstrated how the ML
application could benefit this real world problem, especially the FCM.

Keywords: Clustering · K-means · Fuzzy C-means · Trucks · Slope

1 Introduction

Data analysis and visualization become crucial components within the new globalized
models of economy and industry, offering comprehensive information for decision-
making and strategic planning in several contexts [1, 2].

The interest in this subject increasingly makes data one of the most valuable
organizational resources. Working with big data transforms businesses, serving as a
cross-functional capacity for aligning strategies and making decisions according to the
demands. Therefore, companies invest heavily, seeking opportunities to apply data analysis and overcome competition [3]. Several studies empirically demonstrate the value
of big data and business analysis to organizational capability, its impact on innovation,
product development, and how it benefits competitive performance [4].

A. I. Pereira et al. (Eds.): OL2A 2023, CCIS 1982, pp. 312–325, 2024.
https://doi.org/10.1007/978-3-031-53036-4_22

Mikalef *et al.* [5] asses the scientific community has increased interest in big data in the last decade, denoting an exponential growth of at least 1,400% from 2010 to 2018 in the number of annual publications. Gandomi and Haider [6] highlight the frequency distribution of documents containing the term "big data" rising from 2010.

Nonetheless, it is necessary to develop the organizational capacity to identify areas within the business where it is possible to derive the proper value from big data. Finding where to benefit from the insights and viewings that data brings is a great challenge to overcome. It provides to strategically plan and execute data analysis projects, combining and pooling resources to turn data into transformative action [7].

Wessel [8] points out that big data allows companies to adapt easily to new environments and more quickly bring disruptive innovations – a term that describes standards-breaking technologies in general – through three principles: low cost, affordability, and a structured business model.

One can resort to Machine Learning (ML) and Artificial Intelligence (AI) algorithms to extract practical value from data sets [9, 10]. ML and AI algorithms present an open field to explore the data, learn from it, and understand things that can be uncovered with only the analyst's experience [11, 12].

The automotive industry has intended to offer personalized products in the last three decades. Various vehicle models efficiently can share several characteristics yet differ from others, but overall, in an optimized way for the client's needs [13]. This community has been improving several data science methods for predictive maintenance, new product development, industrial processes, and many others [14].

The digitalization of the automotive industry can enable the evolution of business-to-business approaches to a business-to-consumer model by engaging customers and partnerships with suppliers, interacting through data technologies, which means a shift from selling a product to offering value with a focus on the customer experience [15]. Mining, collecting, and using historical data information is the key to this entire process.

Many technologies that track vehicle performance and usage generate large data sets with potential information on the growth of the vehicle industry. However, the data extracted from these data sets should be carefully studied and treated to draw every essential information, removing any undesired data that may come along, such as noise and incorrect values [16].

Countries and enterprises worldwide are investing in automated driving and intelligent vehicles, considering this ever-increasing urban mobility and modern logistics sector demand. According to Li *et al.* [17], advanced artificial intelligence techniques can solve problems such as traffic congestion, traffic accidents for human errors, road safety, and environmental pollution problems. Some of these techniques are based on unsupervised learning, where unlabeled data is provided.

Clustering tools belong to the unsupervised learning field and have an established place. The work presented by Kargari and Sepehri [18] shows that clustering techniques were used for automotive spare-parts distribution to reduce transportation costs, achieving a cost reduction of 32% with the proposed method that used K-means in a 3-year data, considering three factors in the similarity function: Euclidean distance, lot size, order concurrency.

Altintas and Trick [19] present a study of a data mining and classification analysis of forecasting patterns in a supply chain in which auto manufacturers provides forecasts for future orders, and the supplier uses them to plan production. With clustering and pattern recognition analysis, the authors could provide a framework to analyze the forecast performance of the customers.

Analyzing driver behavior characteristics is also an aspect of investigation for automotive control once the driver is the controller and evaluator of the quality of the vehicle path following. It can be made based on specific pattern recognition provided by simulation or field test data. However, the driver's behavior characteristics must be clustered before being identified. For that, clustering algorithms are generally used, such Fuzzy C-means and K-means algorithms [20].

To evaluate whether a driving behavior is fuel-efficient, Hao *et al.* [21] proposed a method that uses K-means clustering combined with DBSCAN to group four characteristic parameters related to fuel consumption into three driving behaviors: low, medium, and high fuel consumption. They proposed a fuel consumption-oriented driving behavior evaluation model that estimates whether the driving behavior is fuel-efficient.

Dahl *et al.* [22] compared customers' behaviors using logged data with vehicle configuration presets to investigate if truck usage might impact longevity, efficiency, and productivity.

The article by Wang and Wang [23] propose a clustering algorithm based on Genetic Fuzzy C-Means (GFCM) to group driving behaviors for hazardous material transportation. The authors collected data from real-time GPS monitoring devices into different categories. They evaluated the clustering results using various criteria, such as within-cluster distance and separation between clusters. They found that GFCM effectively identified similar driving behaviors and reduced the impact of outliers. The authors suggest that the proposed algorithm can be used to identify hazardous driving behaviors and provide feedback to drivers to improve safety.

Qi *et al.* [24] discuss the importance of accurately understanding driving behavior for advanced driving assistant systems. The authors propose using clustering and topic modeling to extract latent driving states from longitudinal driving behavior data collected by instrumented vehicles. They employ data mining techniques, including ensemble clustering using the kernel Fuzzy C-Means and a modified latent Dirichlet allocation model, to handle the extensive data set and extract valuable knowledge. The authors identify three driving states: aggressive, cautious, and moderate, and develop a quantified structure for driving style analysis. Overall, this approach can provide insight into the typical and individual characteristics of driving behavior and improve the development of driving assistant systems.

In this sense, this work presents a study of a vehicle's parameter, in which the goal is to find the best clustering strategy to extract knowledge from it, helping to comprehend the usage of vehicles when crossing this information with other parameters, such as driving speed, gross combination weight and fuel consumption. The present parameter refers to the slope conditions tracked on the roadway by trucks, and informs the amount of time the vehicle has spent in each percentage of inclination. For each different type of usage, is expected a different slope environment. The data set used throughout the work comprehends several years of extensive truck usage in the Latin American environment.

A classification method based on data engineers' experience, called here GTA, is compared with K-means and Fuzzy C-means, facing the data set with different approaches. This work aims to contribute with a real-world application in the truck industry, showing how ML methods can over perform a non-ML method and how unsupervised learning can be applied to track different driving environments.

This paper contains Methodology in Sect. 2, discussing the data preprocessing, K-means, and Fuzzy C-Means. The results are discussed in Sect. 3, and Sect. 4 presents the conclusions about this work.

2 Methodology

Alam *et al.* [25] call Knowledge Discovery and Data mining (KDD) the process of automatically searching large volumes of data for previously unknown but exciting and informative patterns using modern information exploration techniques, statistics, machine learning, and pattern recognition. Analyzing the data from various angles, categorizing, and summarizing it are the basic principles of data mining [26].

The KDD process starts with data selection, specifying the scope of the data. Then it is analyzed and preprocessed to enhance its reliability, remove irrelevant data, handle missing values, and often remove outliers' observations. The third phase is trans-formed, including sampling and feature selection. The transformed data is then exploited by data mining methods and post-processed, extracting informative patterns, such as clusters, classification, association rules, sequential patterns, or prediction models. Finally, the interpretation and evaluation of the results are made [27].

Before starting to build any ML models, it is recommended to understand the data entirely, the goals of the project, and how it will be deployed, considering any limitations that need to be addressed and what has already been done in the research field. Discussing with domain experts, surveying the literature, and exploring the data can be helpful. Looking at the data is also crucial since it can give insights. Also, the data scientist should avoid looking closely at any test data in the initial exploratory stage because, consciously or unconsciously, these assumptions can limit the model's generality [28].

2.1 Data Preprocessing

Real-world data are primarily dirty, incomplete, and noisy. They may be incomplete in terms of lacking attributes, values, or attributes of interest; may contain noise, errors, outliers, and inconsistencies on names or values; may have hardware, software or human errors, as data entry errors may occur. Missing values, impossible data combinations, and range values are problems that can produce misleading results.

Data preprocessing is the way to solve some of those problems with cleaning, normalization, transformation, feature extraction, feature selection, etc., delivering a more suitable training set. Notably, preprocessing can be very helpful in image processing, despite the extra computational complexity cost. It can alleviate the deteriorating effects of inherent artifacts [29].

Data preprocessing can be divided into a few steps: cleaning, integration, transformation, and reduction. Cleaning is removing incorrect values and checking the consistency of the data. With the dirt removed, data integration is the step to combining the data from databases, files, and different sources. Then, the data is modified to fit the output system in the transformation step. Finally, the last step is to reduce the data to a smaller size with the same analytical results. Discretization is another step in data reduction that can be mentioned. It refers to converting or partitioning continuous attributes into discretized ones. It is useful when creating probability mass functions.

Considering certain independent variables with small or zero effects on the dependent variables, removing them from the model is wise as it is bound to increase the cost of data collection observation and model application. Applying feature extraction can bring cost efficiency, paying with a decline in the accuracy of estimation and prediction [30].

According to Han *et al.* [31], data normalization attempts to give equal weight to attributes from a feature. It is handy for classification algorithms involving neural networks or distance measurements like clustering and nearest-neighbor classification. In practice, the normalization process on distance-based methods can help prevent attributes that have initially large ranges from outweighing those with smaller ranges. Normalization is an essential data mining process and is very useful when there is no prior knowledge of the data [32].

Some normalization techniques are linear normalization (also called linear scaling or Min-Max), which is used when the feature is close to a uniform distribution across a fixed range; clipping, which is suitable to remove extreme outliers; log scaling or decimal scaling when the feature is conformed to power-law; Z-Score, useful when the distribution does not contain extreme outliers [33].

The data set has 32 features, which represent the number of kilometers spent on each range of inclination, that varies from the range $[-\infty, -20\%]$, in dimension 1, to $[-1, 0\%]$, in dimension 16; and from $[0, 1\%]$, in dimension 17, to $[20\%, \infty]$, in dimension 32. This data set was cleaned, normalized with the linear scaling and transformed into 16 dimensions by summing the mirrored ranges, reducing the curse of dimensionality.

2.2 K-Means

K-means clustering divides the data set creating convex clusters, which are straight lines between data points when it lies within the cluster. The data is divided into pre-defined K clusters with a distance measure calculation. The cluster centers are as far as possible, and each data point within a cluster is most similar to each other as possible. The algorithm starts by assigning each data to a particularly close cluster centroid. Then, new centers are calculated considering the samples that belong to them. This process repeats until the centroids remain unchanged in successive iterations or a stop condition is reached, the number of iterations, time, or limitation imposed.

However, it is essential to note that the first cluster centroid is positioned randomly and updated successively after the distance calculation to each data point. Partitional approaches are efficient, but the randomness of the initialization and the need to specify the number of clusters in advance may affect the quality of the solution [25]. Significant factors can impact the algorithm's performance [34].

K-means is well known for converging fast to local optimum, having its results de-pending even more on the initialization process (the positioning of the centers). To overcome this drawback, the algorithm should be initialized with different sets of centers for multiple iterations [35].

The algorithm, for a given data set $X \subset \mathbb{R}^d$, aims to minimize the objective function Φ, called the Sum of Squared Error or inertia, shown in Eq. (1), where $X(z) = \left\{ x \in X : z = argmin_{\hat{z} \in Z} \|x - \hat{z}\|^2 \right\}$, and produce a set of cluster centers $Z = \{z1,..., zk\}$. After initializing, each center $z \in Z$ is updated following Eq. (2), and then each $X(z)$ assignment is updated using the proximity or similarity method defined [36].

$$\Phi = \sum_{z \in Z} \sum_{x \in X(z)} \|x - z\|^2 \tag{1}$$

$$\forall z \subset Z : \left\{ z := \frac{1}{|X(Z)|} \sum_{x \in X(z)} x \right\} \tag{2}$$

The algorithm convergence towards a minimum point is proven by the fact that $c \in \mathbb{R}^d$ minimizing $\sum_{x \in C} \|x - c\|^2$ is the center of cluster C, for any subset that $C \subset X$. When the algorithm is uniformly randomly initialized, there is no guarantee of closeness to the global optimum, given the objective function [36].

To deal with the initialization problem of falling into local minima, K-means were executed 20 times with different centroid seeds. The best output for the objective function result, which is the distance between each data point to its centroid, was picked as the solution for the run. A single iteration of K-means has a time complexity equal to $O(dNK)$, where N is the number of samples, K is the number of clusters, and d is the number of dimensions [37].

2.3 Fuzzy C-Means

Not have very defined boundaries. They might be fuzzy, requiring a more nuanced analysis of the object's affinity to the clusters [38].

The Fuzzy C-Means (FCM) algorithm was first introduced by Dunn [39], who highlights that the boundaries can be significantly less prone to data's "cluster-splitting" and can deviate less easily to uninteresting locally optimal partitions.

Fuzzy sets are defined by indicator functions called membership functions. On hard clustering, it can be said that the data is assigned to the cluster with a degree of membership equal to one, as presented on the indicator of Eq. (3), which shows the fuzzy partition matrix. On Fuzzy C-Means, that indicator can have continuous values in the interval [0,1]. Each data point can belong to more than one cluster with a given membership degree [40].

$$I_{z_j}(x) = \begin{cases} 1, & \text{if } x \subset Z_j \\ 0, & \text{if } x \not\subset Z_j \end{cases} \tag{3}$$

According to Gath and Geva [41], there are three significant difficulties during fuzzy clustering of real data:

- The clusters number cannot always be pre-defined, being necessary to find a cluster validity criterion to determine the optimal number.

- Initial guesses must be made, as the character and location of centroids are not necessarily known a priori.
- There is much variability in cluster shapes, sizes, and variations in densities in each cluster.

The algorithm, given a data set $X \subset \mathbb{R}^d$, with some centers $K \in \mathbb{N}$ and a hyperparameter $m > 1$, $m \in \mathbb{R}$, tries to minimize the objective function (4), producing a set of centers $Z = \{z_1, ..., z_k\}$ with corresponding membership functions $\mu_1, ..., \mu_k$ [36].

$$\Phi(\mu_1, \ldots, \mu_K, z_1, \ldots, z_K) = \sum_{x \in X} \sum_{j=1}^{K} \mu_j(x)^m \|x - z_j\|^2 \tag{4}$$

Knowing that there is the condition $\sum \mu_j = 1$ and applying a Lagrange multiplier, it is found that repeating the redefinition (5), which updates each $z_j, j \in \{1,..., K\}$ to become the μ_j-weighted center of X, and (6), that updates each $\mu_j, j \in \{1,..., K\}$, provides a local minimum of Φ as an output [36].

$$\forall j \in \{1, ..., K\} : \left\{ z_j := \frac{\sum_{x \in X} \mu_j(x)^m x}{\sum_{x \in X} \mu_j(x)^m} \right\} \tag{5}$$

$$\mu_j(x) ::= \left[\sum_{k=1}^{K} \left(\frac{\|x - z_j\|}{\|x - z_k\|} \right)^{\frac{2}{m-1}} \right]^{-1} \tag{6}$$

The hyperparameter m can be called a fuzzifier since it controls how fuzzy the clustering will be. From that, it can be assumed the asymptotic results that for $m \to \infty$, the fuzziest state, all μ_j are equal, and the representatives coincide at the center of X. For $m \to 1$, the FCM returns into a K-Means, where the membership function is the same as Eq. (3). The useful range of m seems to be close to [1, 30]. For most data, $1.5 \leq m \leq 3.0$ gives good results [36]. In this study, it was set $m = 2$. A single iteration of FCM has a time complexity equal to $O(dNK2)$, where N is the number of samples, K is the number of clusters, and d is the number of dimensions [42, 43].

3   Results and Discussion

The GTA classification is a rule-based classification created with extensive experience of engineers on the subject, which classifies the slope conditions, based on percentages of time spent on each range of inclination, into four groups: Flat, Predominantly Flat, Hilly, Very Hilly. This method is compared with the ML methods presented. Some metrics were used to evaluate each algorithm's performance to choose the best number of clusters that describe the data set. The first metric, SSW (Sum of Squares Within Clusters), is presented in Fig. 1.

The elbow curve method is addressed considering the number of clusters from 2 clusters to 10 clusters [16].

The lowest value is supposed to be the best result, the tightest cluster. However, in this analysis, it is sought for the inflection point. This point means that increasing the

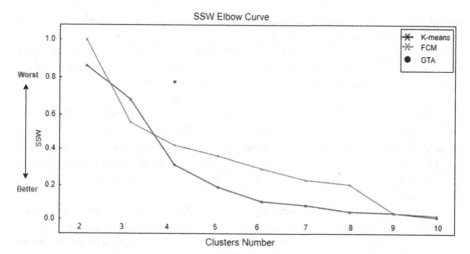

Fig. 1. SSW behavior

number of clusters does not bring huge gains on the current metric further from this point. Crossing that information with the other metrics can give a better view of the best number of clusters for the problem.

The second evaluation metric is the SSB (Sum of Squares Between Clusters), which measures how far cluster centers are from each other, so the highest value is the best result. A good SSB value says that the clusters are well defined. As in the SSW analysis, two lines help indicate the best number of clusters. The results are shown in Fig. 2.

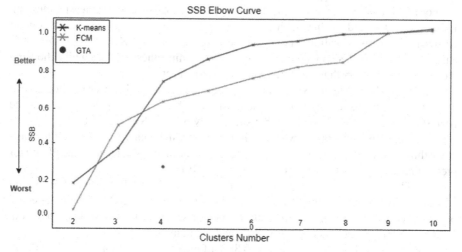

Fig. 2. SSB behavior

Compared with the other algorithms, the K-Means methodology (blue line) returns the best result for every cluster number K. FCM (red line) has a close result to K-Means overall. Still, the GTA classification (cyan dot), which only classifies with $K = 4$, is far from the machine learning methodologies.

Sometimes it is not easy to get a clear elbow point. To facilitate that process, two trend lines help indicate this value, in which the inflection is the crossing point of these lines. The first is a straight line drawn from the first point of the elbow curve, following the curve as closely as possible for at least three periods. The second trend line comes oppositely from the last point in the elbow curve, following backward the elbow curve for at least three periods until it crosses the first line. With that, we can locate the virtual elbow point, the tendency's inflection point. Through that method, the elbow point could be considered $K = 4$ for K-Means. For FCM, the elbow point is also $K = 4$, although there is no significant trend change since it continuously improves as the number of clusters increases.

This study's third and most important metric, Silhouette Index (SI), is an internal validation measurement. It is a normalized score, from -1.0 to 1.0, which the closer to 1, the better the data is classified. Figure 3 illustrates the results considering the average SI score of the data set for each number of clusters K. For this index, SI values from 0.5 to 1.0 are considered a good result (the green region in the Fig. 3), from 0.2 to 0.5 a fair result (yellow region), and from -1.0 to 0.2 a poor clustering (red region) [44]. We chose this metric to be easier to interpret than Calinski-Harabasz, with a normalized score from -1 to 1, and one of the most used for clustering.

When comparing all the algorithms, FCM returns the best result for most cluster numbers except for $K = 3$. In this case, K-Means returns a better result. FCM for every K has SI above 0.5, which is a good result. K-Means algorithm results from $K = 2$ to $K = 7$ present good results, higher than 0.5, but from $K = 8$ to $K = 10$ the SI value fell to consider a fair result, from 0.2 to 0.5. For GTA, with $K = 4$, the SI value lies between 0.2 and 0.5, a reasonable performance.

For FCM, the SSW and SSB presented a good performance with at least 4 clusters. Using the SI to validate that, with $K = 4$ or higher, the algorithm can return a good clustering in terms of validity, being the best for this method $K = 4$. That way, it is ensured to have good SSB (separation) and SSW (compactness) values while choosing the number of clusters that can better classify the data set.

Analyzing the K-Means, SSW and SSB presented that a good clustering should have at least 4 clusters. Validating with SI, the most profitable K is $K = 4$ since it returns the best Silhouette result with the least, but sufficiently better, SSW and SSB.

Analyzing all the samples, we show in Fig. 4 how the data set is clustered for each algorithm. The methods with 4 clusters are presented using the terms Flat, PFlat (for predominantly flat), Hilly, and VHilly (for very hilly).

The GTA classification comprises 3.2% Flat vehicles, 15.4% PFlat, 66.2% Hilly, and 15.2% VHilly. Notice that the Flat classification is very restrictive. A few vehicles could be classified as Flat, while the Hilly cluster comprises more than half the population. PFlat and VHilly are clusters of very close and medium size.

K-Means with 4 clusters classified 10.88% of the samples as Flat, 40.76% as PFlat, 45.48% as Hilly, and 2.89% as VHilly. There is a significant difference when comparing with GTA results, decreasing the population of VHilly vehicles, increasing the Flat

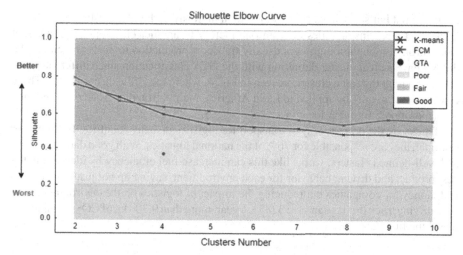

Fig. 3. SI behavior (Color figure online)

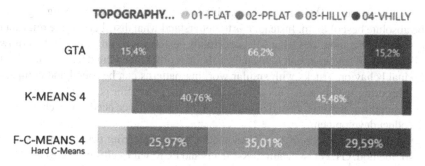

Fig. 4. Slope clusters data set distribution

cluster slice, and maintaining the PFlat and Hilly clusters with somewhat compact sizes and more extensive than the other clusters.

For the FCM, for calculation reasons, only the cluster with the highest membership degree was considered for each vehicle. The results for $K = 4$ showed that the clusters have the closest size to the other algorithms, with Flat being at 9.43% of the samples, PFlat at 25.97%, Hilly at 35.01% and VHilly at 29.59%. Of course, it has to do with how FCM works as a non-binary clustering that everyone has a membership degree for every cluster, which means that every data point takes a percentage share in each cluster. However, that information is lost when transforming into a complex clustering result.

Analyzing average cases and some outliers, we observed that the clustering process made by the proposed methods, in general, is more suitable, especially concerning the Flat and Very Hilly clusters. A very hilly cluster becomes a cluster of trucks that works mainly in mines and environments with more than 8% of inclination. The hilly cluster includes trucks that spend more time in the range of 3% to 6% of inclination, which is "mountain highways". Predominantly Flat is a cluster that describes an environment that is mainly flat but sometimes crosses mountain highways. The Flat cluster has included trucks that work inside cities or from one factory to another close one. Vehicles that work through mountain highways usually transport production to ports and cities. We did not have a clear cluster definition with the GTA classification since different applications were in the same cluster, as seen in Fig. 4, where the Hilly cluster is vast. These conclusions can only be applied to Latin America, mainly Brazilian, roadways and may be inappropriate for other locations.

Trucks are the primary way of transport for logistics in many countries. In China, for example, they are responsible for 76% of the national logistics. With good data extraction and well-defined clusters, works like this can increase fuel efficiency by identifying the best product and driving behavior for each environment, saving up not just liters of fuel and money for companies but reducing the impact of logistics on the environment. The best-driving truck drivers can save 3285 L a year, more than 9.300 kg of CO_2, considering diesel the fuel [21].

4 Conclusions

The machine learning (ML) research goal is not to seek a universal learning algorithm or the absolute best of them. Instead, it is to understand what distributions are relevant to real-world applications and what ML algorithms perform well on essential data-drawn distributions. ML methods can help analysts better comprehend big data sets and clarify individual behavior. Trucks with similar working patterns can be found and compared using clustering techniques. This comparison can help to offer personalized products, fuel consumption analysis, an understanding of the maintenance needs for each behavior, and product development.

Overall, the ML methods have presented a better clustering performance than the non-ML method, GTA classification. K-Means and FCM with 4 clusters were considered to have a "good" classification, while GTA was considered to have a "fair" performance, with a SI score of 0.58, 0.62, 0.39 respectively. The fact that FCM generally performed better than K-Means indicates a highly overlapping data set, which the soft-clustering aspect of FCM could read better. We also could search the elbow point and find the best SI score to choose the number of clusters.

For future works, other clustering methodologies and metrics could be implemented and used to compare with the present methods. This work can also be extended to different vehicle data sets, making a more precise comparison when crossing the data.

Acknowledgments. This work has been supported by FCT – Fundação para a Ciência e Tecnologia within the R&D Units Project Scope: UIDB/00319/2020.

References

1. Katz, Y.A., Biem, A.: Time-resolved topological data analysis of market instabilities. Physica A **571**, 125816 (2021). https://doi.org/10.1016/j.physa.2021.125816

2. Ma, S., Zhang, Y., Lv, J., Ge, Y., Yang, H., Li, L.: Big data-driven predictive production planning for energy-intensive manufacturing industries. Energy **211**, 118320 (2020). https://doi.org/10.1016/j.energy.2020.118320

3. Johnson, J.S., Friend, S.B., Lee, H.S.: Big data facilitation, utilization, and monetization: exploring the 3Vs in a new product development process: BIG DATA VOLUME, VARIETY, AND VELOCITY. J. Prod. Innov. Manag. **34**, 640–658 (2017). https://doi.org/10.1111/jpim.12397

4. Côrte-Real, N., Ruivo, P., Oliveira, T.: Leveraging internet of things and big data analytics initiatives in European and American firms: is data quality a way to extract business value? Inf. Manag. **57**, 1–16 (2020). https://doi.org/10.1016/j.im.2019.01.003

5. Mikalef, P., Pappas, I.O., Krogstie, J., Pavlou, P.A.: Big data and business analytics: a research agenda for realizing business value. Inf. Manag. **57**, 103237 (2020). https://doi.org/10.1016/j.im.2019.103237

6. Gandomi, A., Haider, M.: Beyond the hype: Big data concepts, methods, and analytics. Int. J. Inf. Manage. **35**, 137–144 (2015). https://doi.org/10.1016/j.ijinfomgt.2014.10.007

7. Vidgen, R., Shaw, S., Grant, D.B.: Management challenges in creating value from business analytics. Eur. J. Oper. Res. **261**, 626–639 (2017). https://doi.org/10.1016/j.ejor.2017.02.023

8. Wessel, M.: How Big Data Is Changing Disruptive Innovation. Harvard Business Review 2016. Section: Disruptive innovation

9. Neto, P.S.D.M., et al.: Neural-based ensembles for particulate matter forecasting. IEEE Access **9**, 14470–14490 (2021)

10. Siqueira, H., Luna, I.: Performance comparison of feedforward neural networks applied to streamflow series forecasting. Math. Eng. Sci. Aerosp. (MESA) **10** (2019)

11. Siqueira, H., Boccato, L., Attux, R., Filho, C.L.: Echo state networks for seasonal streamflow series forecasting. In: Yin, H., Costa, J.A.F., Barreto, G. (eds.) IDEAL 2012. LNCS, vol. 7435, pp. 226–236. Springer, Heidelberg (2012). https://doi.org/10.1007/978-3-642-32639-4_28

12. de Souza Tadano, Y., Siqueira, H.V., Alves, T.A.: Unorganized machines to predict hospital admissions for respiratory diseases. In: Proceedings of the 2016 IEEE Latin American Conference on Computational Intelligence (LA-CCI), pp. 1–6. IEEE (2016)

13. Bersch, C.V., Akkerman, R., Kolisch, R.: Strategic planning of new product introductions: Integrated planning of products and modules in the automotive industry. Omega **105**, 102515 (2021). https://doi.org/10.1016/j.omega.2021.102515

14. Theissler, A., Pérez-Velázquez, J., Kettelgerdes, M., Elger, G.: Predictive maintenance enabled by machine learning: use cases and challenges in the automotive industry. Reliab. Eng. Syst. Saf. **215**, 107864 (2021). https://doi.org/10.1016/j.ress.2021.107864

15. Hoffmann, M., Zayer, E., Strempel, K.: A Survival Guide for Europe's Car Dealers (2019). https://www.bain.com/insights/a-survival-guide-for-europes-car-dealers. Accessed 01 Feb 2022

16. Guerreiro, M.T., et al.: Anomaly detection in automotive industry using clustering methods—a case study. Appl. Sci. **11**, 9868 (2021)

17. Li, J., Cheng, H., Guo, H., Qiu, S.: Survey on artificial intelligence for vehicles. Automot. Innov. **1**, 2–14 (2018)

18. Kargari, M., Sepehri, M.M.: Stores clustering using a data mining approach for distributing automotive spare-parts to reduce transportation costs. Expert Syst. Appl. **39**, 4740–4748 (2012). https://doi.org/10.1016/j.eswa.2011.09.121

19. Altintas, N., Trick, M.: A data mining approach to forecast behavior. Ann. Oper. Res. **216**, 3–22 (2014). https://doi.org/10.1007/s10479-012-1236-9

20. Lin, N., Zong, C., Tomizuka, M., Song, P., Zhang, Z., Li, G.: An overview on study of identification of driver behavior characteristics for automotive control. Math. Probl. Eng. **2014**, e569109 (2014). https://doi.org/10.1155/2014/569109

21. Hao, R., Yang, H., Zhou, Z.: Driving behavior evaluation model base on big data from internet of vehicles. Int. J. Ambient Comput. Intell. (IJACI) **10**, 78–95 (2019). https://doi.org/10.4018/IJACI.2019100105

22. Dahl, O., Johansson, F., Khoshkangini, R., Pashami, S., Nowaczyk, S., Claes, P.: Understanding association between logged vehicle data and vehicle marketing parameters: using clustering and rule-based machine learning, IMMS 2020, pp. 13–22. Association for Computing Machinery, New York (2020). https://doi.org/10.1145/3416028.3417215

23. Wang, X., Wang, H.: Driving behavior clustering for hazardous material transportation based on genetic fuzzy c-means algorithm. IEEE Access **8**, 11289–11296 (2020). https://doi.org/10.1109/ACCESS.2020.2964648

24. Qi, G., Du, Y., Wu, J., Xu, M.: Leveraging longitudinal driving behaviour data with data mining techniques for driving style analysis. IET Intel. Transport Syst. **9**, 792–801 (2015)

25. Alam, S., Dobbie, G., Koh, Y.S., Riddle, P., Ur Rehman, S.: Research on particle swarm optimization based clustering: a systematic review of literature and techniques. Swarm Evol. Comput. **17**, 1–13 (2014). https://doi.org/10.1016/j.swevo.2014.02.001

26. Singhal, S., Jena, M.: A study on WEKA tool for data preprocessing, classification and clustering. Classif. Clust. **2**, 4 (2013)

27. Figueiredo, E., Macedo, M., Siqueira, H.V., Santana, C.J., Jr., Gokhale, A., Bastos-Filho, C.J.: Swarm intelligence for clustering—a systematic review with new perspectives on data mining. Eng. Appl. Artif. Intell. **82**, 313–329 (2019)

28. Lones, M.A.: How to avoid machine learning pitfalls: a guide for academic researchers. arXiv: 2108.02497 (2021)

29. Joseph, S., Olugbara, O.O.: Preprocessing effects on performance of skin lesion saliency segmentation. Diagnostics **12**, 344 (2022). https://doi.org/10.3390/diagnostics12020344

30. Yang, L., Ban, X., Chen, Z., Guo, H.: A new data preprocessing technique based on feature extraction and clustering for complex discrete temperature data. Procedia Comput. Sci. **129**, 78–80 (2018). https://doi.org/10.1016/j.procs.2018.03.050

31. Han, J., Kamber, M., Pei, J.: 3 - Data preprocessing. In: Han, J., Kamber, M., Pei, J. (eds.) Data Mining, 3rd edn. The Morgan Kaufmann Series in Data Management Systems, pp. 83–124. Morgan Kaufmann, Boston (2012). https://doi.org/10.1016/B978-0-12-381479-1.00003-4

32. Gavali, P., Banu, J.S.: Chapter 6 - Deep convolutional neural network for image classification on CUDA platform. In: Sangaiah, A.K. (ed.) Deep Learning and Parallel Computing Environment for Bioengineering Systems, pp. 99–122. Academic Press (2019). https://doi.org/10.1016/B978-0-12-816718-2.00013-0

33. Google for Developers. Machine Learning Crash Course (2021)

34. Reddy, C.K., Vinzamuri, B.: A survey of partitional and hierarchical clustering algorithms. In: Aggarwal, C.C., Reddy, C.K. (eds.) Data Clustering, 1 edn, pp. 87–110. Chapman and Hall/CRC (2018). https://doi.org/10.1201/9781315373515-4

35. Celebi, M.E., Kingravi, H.A.: Linear, deterministic, and order-invariant initialization methods for the k-means clustering algorithm. In: Celebi, M.E. (ed.) Partitional Clustering Algorithms, pp. 79–98. Springer, Cham (2015). https://doi.org/10.1007/978-3-319-09259-1_3

36. Malle, J.: Fuzzy clustering: an application to distributional reinforcement learning. Ph.D. thesis (2021)

37. Dinler, D., Tural, M.K.: A survey of constrained clustering. In: Celebi, M.E., Aydin, K. (eds.) Unsupervised Learning Algorithms, pp. 207–235. Springer, Cham (2016). https://doi.org/10.1007/978-3-319-24211-8_9

38. Santos, P., et al.: Application of PSO-based clustering algorithms on educational databases. In: Proceedings of the 2017 IEEE Latin American Conference on Computational Intelligence (LA-CCI), pp. 1–6. IEEE (2017)

39. Dunn, J.C.: A fuzzy relative of the ISODATA process and its use in detecting compact well-separated clusters. J. Cybern. **3**, 32–57 (1973). https://doi.org/10.1080/01969727308546046

40. Bezdek, J.: Pattern Recognition With Fuzzy Objective Function Algorithms. Springer, New York (1981). https://doi.org/10.1007/978-1-4757-0450-1
41. Gath, I., Geva, A.: Unsupervised optimal fuzzy clustering. IEEE Trans. Pattern Anal. Mach. Intell. **11**, 773–780 (1989). https://doi.org/10.1109/34.192473
42. Kumar, P., Sirohi, D.: Comparative Analysis of FCM and HCM Algorithm on Iris Data Set (2010)
43. Kolen, J., Hutcheson, T.: Reducing the time complexity of the fuzzy c-means algorithm. IEEE Trans. Fuzzy Syst. **10**, 263–267 (2002). https://doi.org/10.1109/91.995126
44. Kaufman, L., Rousseeuw, P.J.: Finding Groups in Data: An Introduction to Cluster Analysis. Wiley, Hoboken (2009). Google-Books-ID: YeFQHiikNo0C

Multi-objective Optimal Sizing of an AC/DC Grid Connected Microgrid System

Yahia Amoura[1,3], André Pedroso[1,4], Ângela Ferreira[1], José Lima[1,2], Santiago Torres[3], and Ana I. Pereira[1(✉)]

[1] Research Centre in Digitalization and Intelligent Robotics (CeDRI), Instituto Politécnico de Bragança, Bragança, Portugal
{yahia,andre.pedroso,apf,jllima,apereira}@ipb.pt
[2] INESC TEC - INESC Technology and Science, Porto, Portugal
[3] University of Laguna, San Cristbal de La Laguna, Spain
storres@ull.es
[4] Federal University of Technology - Paraná, Curitiba, Brazil

Abstract. Considering the rising energy needs and the depletion of conventional energy sources, microgrid systems combining wind energy and solar photovoltaic power with diesel generators are promising and considered economically viable for usage. To evaluate system cost and dependability, optimizing the size of microgrid system elements, including energy storage systems connected with the principal network, is crucial. In this line, a study has already been performed using a uni-objective optimization approach for the techno-economic sizing of a microgrid. It was noted that, despite the economic criterion, the environmental criterion can have a considerable impact on the elements constructing the microgrid system. In this paper, two multi-objective optimization approaches are proposed, including a non-dominated sorting genetic algorithm (NSGA-II) and the Pareto Search algorithm (PS) for the eco-environmental design of a microgrid system. The k-means clustering of the non-dominated point on the Pareto front has delivered three categories of scenarios: best economic, best environmental, and trade-off. Energy management, considering the three cases, has been applied to the microgrid over a period of 24 h to evaluate the impact of system design on the energy production system's behavior.

Keywords: Microgrid · Renewable energy · Optimization · Clustering · Sizing

1 Introduction

Renewable energies are the main substitute for fossil fuels responsible for greenhouse gas (GHG) emissions [1], with investments totaling 350 billion euros in 2021. Solar and wind energy supply more than 10% of the world's electricity, predicted to have a 15-18% share by 2050 [2]. The need for a sustainable energy system is increasing due to overpopulation, industrialization, and urbanization.

© The Author(s) 2024
A. I. Pereira et al. (Eds.): OL2A 2023, CCIS 1982, pp. 326–342, 2024.
https://doi.org/10.1007/978-3-031-53036-4_23

Renewable energy sources must be pursued due to rising costs and energy security issues [3,4]. Microgrid systems powered by renewable energy are the best option for remote communities [5]. The worldwide microgrid market exceeded 14.3 billion dollars in 2021 and is expected to reach 43.9 billion US dollars in 2028 [6]. Microgrid systems provide electricity in a reliable, secure, flexible, cost-effective, and sustainable manner, but must be well-sized and monitored to maintain reliability and keep costs low [7].

The use of optimization to design a microgrid system has been widely explained by researchers. Recently, meta-heuristic approaches have been frequently used as a single and a multi-objective approach for the optimal design of a microgrid hybrid renewable power plant in a clean energy production system, including several types of distributed generators arranged in Direct Current (DC bus), Alternative Current (AC bus), or hybrid DC/AC busses configurations, considering the whole system as a standalone or grid-connected system. However, in terms of constraints consideration, the economic and environmental implications are the main criterion, despite other technical considerations such as power losses. On [8,9], several single-objective approaches have been studied. Nevertheless, some multi-objective techniques have been employed in the literature in accordance with this work. For instance, a Multiobjective Particle Swarm Optimization (MOPSO) has been applied to minimize cost, carbon emissions, energy use, and power use in [10]. The same approach has been used by Sellami et al. [11], to reduce network losses and increase efficiency. Non-dominated Sorting Genetic Algorithm II (NSGA-II) [18], has been used on [12,13] to optimize both cost of operation and the rate of consumption of renewable energy, and the same optimization method has been used on [14] to increase the rate of oxygen production, short payback time and lower overall cost inside a microgrid system. An enhanced Differential Evolution (DE) have been used in [15] for the multi-objective optimal sizing of a hybrid micro-grid system considering technical-economic and social factors. In a Stand-Alone Marine Context, a microgrid has been sized by Zhu et al. [16] using an improved multi-objective grey wolf optimizer based on the Halton Sequence and Social Motivation Strategy (HSMGWO).

The study described in this paper is a continuation of [8], in which uni-evolutionary optimization methods, including the Genetic Algorithm (GA) and Particle Swarm Optimization (PSO), were used to achieve the optimal size of a hybrid energy system based on renewable energy. In addition to the technical-economic objective function, the environmental criterion describing the carbon emissions during the manufacture of microgrid components has been taken into account in this work. As a result, a multi-objective optimization problem emerges from the situation. The case study has been applied to the campus de Santa Apolónia, located in Bragança, Portugal.

The main contributions of this paper are organized as the following:

1. Optimal allocation of micro-grid elements subject to technical-economic end environmental consideration.

2. Application of two Multi-optimization approaches including, the non-dominated sorting genetic algorithm (NSGA-II) and the Pareto Search algorithm (PS).
3. Identification of configurations scenario as best economic, best environmental, and trade-off by using the k-means clustering approach.
4. Identification of the microgrid power flow behavior considering all identified scenarios.

The rest of the paper is organized as follows: Sect. 2 describes the adopted configuration of the microgrid system. In Sect. 3, the meteorological and consumption data of microgrid users are presented. The generators used to constitute the microgrid system are defined in Sect. 4. The optimal sizing of the microgrid is formulated as result of multi-objective functions in Sect. 5. The adopted sizing methodology is explained in Sect. 6. The results of the simulation and their discussion are presented in Sect. 7. Section 8 summarises the findings of the paper and proposes guidelines for future work.

2   Microgrid Arrangement

The microgrid configuration proposed in this study is the AC/DC architecture shown in Fig. 1.

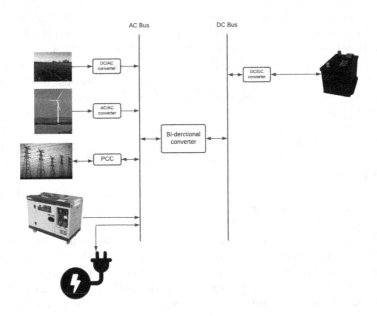

Fig. 1. Microgrid configuration.

The microgrid configuration includes two renewable resources: photovoltaic and wind turbines. Through a common coupling point, the microgrid is connected to the main grid, which acts as a buffer. In the event of a blackout, the diesel group connected to the AC bus is employed as a last-resort solution. The battery system connects to the DC bus in a bidirectional manner, and a bi-directional converter allows energy to flow between the two buses in both directions. Control and energy management technologies are used to ensure the flow of energy and supervision of the microgrid power quality. Microgrids that combine AC and DC power provide harmonic control, economic viability, and voltage transformation, but have drawbacks such as safety and unit coordination [9].

3   Study Data Description

Weather data is essential for sizing a microgrid, as weather mistakes can lead to errors in real operations and larger initial investments. In this study, the Polytechnic Institute of Bragança (IPB), located in the north region of Portugal (Latitude: 41.8072, Longitude: −6.75919 41º 48' 26" North, 6º 45' 33" West, with an elevation of $690\,m$), was the location of the study case. A sequence of measurement series, including average solar irradiation, wind speed, and temperature data for one year (from January 1, 2019, to December 31, 2019), as well as the average load data, have been gathered. Figure 2 represents the profile of data mentioned above. Table 1 describes the critical values of the weather data set, including the minimal value, maximal value, average value, and standard deviation.

Table 1. Data summary.

Parameters	Measurement tool	Max	Min	Mean	Std
Temperature	Thermocouple K-Type	20.06	8	13.42	0.7620
Wind speed (m/s)	Anemometer	5.78	3.19	4.46	4.26
Solar irradiation	Pyranometer	830.73	54.44	279	328.71
Load	Energy meter	9.50	5.50	6.49	1.28

4   System Modeling

The work [8] is the main inspiration of this study that describes the rationale behind the concepts and technology selected. For this reason, the equipment modeling of photovoltaic systems, wind turbines, battery systems, and diesel generators is assumed the same as in [8]. The new contribution of this work is the connection of the microgrid to the main grid which is presented in the following sections.

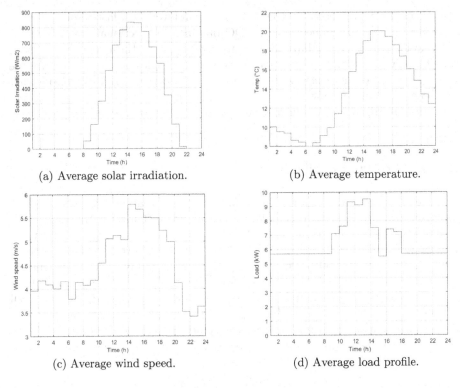

(a) Average solar irradiation. (b) Average temperature.

(c) Average wind speed. (d) Average load profile.

Fig. 2. Study data.

4.1 Main Grid

The main grid with microgrid can operate bi-directionally according to three scenarios as follow, where P_{pv}^t, P_{wt}^t are the total active power output of photovoltaic panels, and wind turbines. $E(t)$, is the energy delivered from/to the energy storage system in an hour t and P_{load} is the total load power, Δ_t is the step time between two periods in this case it is considered 1 h. All defined parameters are widely explained on [15].

- The first scenario occurs when the power verifies the following relation:

$$P_{pv}^t(t) + P_{wt}^t(t) + \frac{E(t)}{\Delta_t} = P_{load}(t) \tag{1}$$

In this case, the main grid has no interaction with the microgrid in terms of reception or feeding.
- The second scenario occurs when the following relationship is verified:

$$P_{pv}^t(t) + P_{wt}^t(t) + \frac{E(t)}{\Delta_t} < P_{load}(t) \tag{2}$$

$$P_{grid}(t) = P_{load}(t) - \left(P_{pv}^t(t) + P_{wt}^t(t) + \frac{E(t)}{\Delta_t} \right) \tag{3}$$

In this case, the main grid will inject the required power noted $P_{grid}(t)$ to balance the energy inside the microgrid by covering all the needed power.
- The third scenario occurs when the following relationship is verified:

$$P_{pv}^t(t) + P_{wt}^t(t) + \frac{E(t)}{\Delta_t} > P_{load}(t) \tag{4}$$

In this case, the microgrid will inject extra power into the main grid.

In this study, the power converters are considered to work in ideal conditions, which means that it will not take into account the losses provided; however, the converters are presented by their theoretical efficiency in the technical study, and they are not subject to optimization. The characteristics of the components for the microgrid presented in this study are described in Table 2.

Table 2. Components technical specifications.

Equipment	Rated power (W)	Rated voltage (V)	Efficiency (%)	Life time (years)
PV Panel	340	44.52	17.12	20
Wind Turbine	3000	240	59	20
Diesel Group	10000	230	5 h in max capacity	20
Battery	2.5 kWh (Capacity)	48	90	5
DC/AC inverter	4000	48DC/220AC	95	4
DC/DC converter	310	48 VDC	80	4

5   Problem Formulation

The problem of optimal sizing the microgrid system is formulated as a multi-objective optimization approach, taking into account two cost functions characterizing the economical and environmental criteria, respectively, subjected to constraints that are defined to satisfy the correct microgrid operation.

5.1   Objective Functions

Objective 1: Installation Cost Minimization. The economic criteria, including the system's component purchase price, maintenance expenses, and component replacement prices, are taken into account by the economic objective function. The objective function aims to satisfy the necessary technical constraints while getting the ideal number of microgrid components. For a system lifespan of T equal to 20 years, the microgrid system cost, in euros, is provided by [8]:

$$C_t(N_{pv}, N_{wt}, N_b) = N_{pv}(C_{pv} + C_{pv}K_{pv} + TM_{pv}) + N_{wt}(C_{wt} + C_{wt}K_{wt} + TM_{wt})$$
$$+N_b(C_b + C_bK_b + (T - K_b - 1)M_b) + C_{die} + C_{conv}$$

where, N_{pv}, N_{wt}, N_b are, respectively, the number of units of photovoltaic modules, wind turbines and batteries, C_{pv}, C_{wt}, C_b, C_{die}, C_{conv} are respectively the purchase costs of renewable units (photovoltaic and wind), battery unit, diesel group and overall converters, M_{pv}, M_{wt}, M_b are the maintenance costs for the renewable energy systems (photovoltaic and wind systems) and also battery bank. Finally, K_{pv}, K_{wt}, K_b are, respectively, the number of equipment replacements during the system lifetime.

The optimization model for microgrid installation cost can be written as follow:

$$\min f_1 = \min\left(C_t(N_{pv}, N_{wt}, N_b)\right) \tag{5}$$

The optimization model will lead to finding N_{pv}, N_{wt}, and N_b, i.e., the optimum set points that define the optimal number of microgrid components: wind turbines, photovoltaics, and batteries, at the lowest price while respecting the constraint that will be defined in the rest of the paper.

Objective 2: Environmental Function. Nitrous oxide (N_2O), carbon dioxide (CO_2), and methane (CH_4) are the main components of GHG emissions. In most cases, carbon dioxide (CO_2), or its equivalent (CO_2eq), is used as the measurement unit for GHG emissions. The overall carbon footprint estimation for the microgrid system set-up represents the emissions released during its manufacturing process [17]. However, the total (CO_2eq) emission function is given as follows:

$$E_t(N_{pv}, N_{wt}, N_b) = GHG_{PV}^{CO2eq} + GHG_{WT}^{CO2eq} + GHG_b^{CO2eq}$$

where, GHG_{PV}^{CO2eq}, GHG_{WT}^{CO2eq}, GHG_b^{CO2eq} are, respectively, the GHG emissions of the photovoltaic, wind turbine, and battery released during the manufacturing process of the units represented on carbon dioxide (CO_2) and expressed on (CO_{2eq}).

$$E_t(N_{pv}, N_{wt}, N_b) = N_{pv}(138.3 \times S_{pv} - 2.54) + N_{wt}(156 \times S_{WT})$$
$$+N_b(1.99 \times C^n + 27.2)$$

where, S_{pv} is the photovoltaic surface panel, S_{WT} is the swept area by the blades of the wind turbine, and C^n is battery nominal capacity [17].

The optimization model for the microgrid environmental model can be written as follows:

$$\min f_2 = \min\left(E_t(N_{pv}, N_{wt}, N_b)\right) \tag{6}$$

5.2   Constraints

Power Balance Constraint. The total amount of power generated must be sufficient to meet the overall demand (including storage) and transmission losses. In terms of frequency stability, the active power balance is a requirement for steady operation. Since the transmission losses are thought to be numerically insignificant, they are neglected in this work. The power balance's state takes on the following form:

$$P_{pv}(t)N_{pv} + P_{wt}(t)N_{WT} + P_b(t)N_b \geq P_{load}(t) \tag{7}$$

being $P_{load}(t)$, the total electrical load demand at hour t. Moreover, the power of the energy storage system $P_b(t)$ can be positive in the case of discharging or negative in the case of charging, and $P_{pv}(t)$ and $P_{pv}(t)$ are the power delivered by the photovoltaic and wind turbine generators at hour t.

Limit Generators Number Constraint. The limited number of generators in terms of setup surface must be considered during the optimization procedure as follows:

$$0 \leq N_{pv} \leq N_{pv}^{max} \tag{8}$$
$$0 \leq N_{wt} \leq N_{wt}^{max} \tag{9}$$
$$0 \leq N_b \leq N_b^{max} \tag{10}$$

where, N_{pv}^{max}, N_{pv}^{max} and N_{pv}^{max} is the maximal permitted numbers of photovoltaic, wind turbines, and batteries, respectively, to be installed.

6   Methodology

In this paper, two multiobjective optimization methods are used to define the optimal configuration of the microgrid: the Non-dominated Sorting Genetic Algorithm II (NSGA-II) and the Pareto Search algorithm. The results will be presented on a set of Pareto fronts, including the non-dominated points that reflect the scenarios proposed by the optimization process according to the constraints defined above, to ensure technical satisfaction for the secure and reliable operation of the microgrid system. Given the clustering of the non-dominated points using the k-means approach, an informed choice of scenarios will be determined. On the reverse side, the effectiveness of scenarios will be investigated through the microgrid operating system's behavior. However, the proposed microgrid system can operate both in isolated mode and/or grid-connected mode. The power distribution approach is simplified into the following situations:

1. The power generated by renewable sources must meet the load demand in order for the system to operate safely. Additionally, excessive amounts of power produced by renewable resources require that batteries be charged first before any extra power is put onto the main grid.

2. Renewable energy sources cannot produce enough power to fulfill demand; an energy storage system will satisfy the shortage. In the event that this latter is insufficient, the main network compensates for the energy imbalance.
3. The electricity produced by the diesel group is regarded as the last resort and a highly polluting source that will only be used in the event of a complete blackout within the main grid.

7   Results and Discussions

This section presents the results of the optimization strategies. After the optimal number of units is reached, a technical study is done to evaluate the installation's dependability given the number of microgrid units. Additionally, a lifetime cost estimate of the system is given, taking into account every scenario that has been suggested. The optimization problem and microgrid operation were programmed and simulated using the MATLAB programming language.

7.1   Optimization Results and Scenarios Identification

The study's microgrid sizing problem has been solved using two multi-objective optimization techniques, NSGA-II and Pareto search algorithms. The Pareto front of non-dominated points is displayed in Fig. 3.

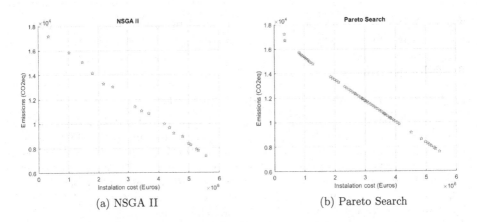

(a) NSGA II   (b) Pareto Search

Fig. 3. Pareto front of microgrid optimization sizing scenarios.

A cluster evaluation using the "silhouette" approach has been carried out in order to determine scenarios that exist in accordance with the optimization results achieved. The silhouette plot reveals that the data are separated into three clusters. Each of the three clusters has a substantial silhouette value determined by the Euclidean distance metric, as illustrated in Fig. 4.

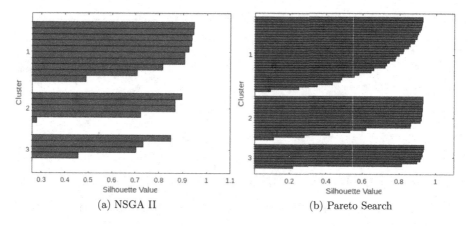

(a) NSGA II (b) Pareto Search

Fig. 4. Silhouette values.

The clustering has been performed using the k-means approach with ($k = 3$), the results are presented in Fig. 5.

According to the clusters, three sets of scenarios can be identified, including the best economic scenarios (**Cluster 03**), best environmental scenarios (**Cluster 02**), and traded-off scenarios (**Cluster 01**). The distinct scenario that represents each cluster has been chosen from the extreme of each recognized set of situations, except for the trade-off case, in which the centroid has been selected as a cluster-representative scenario. Table 3 displays the microgrid sizing scenarios that were selected based on the previously addressed device characteristics.

Table 3. Microgrid sizing scenarios.

Scenario	N_{PV}	N_{WT}	N_{Batt}	Installation Cost (€)	Total Emissions ($KgCO_{2eq}$)
Best Economical	50	3	13	157755.87	17071,00
Trade-off	55	2	7	2351703.20	17302
Best environmental	46	1	44	5623707.70	7468,52

The optimal configurations illustrate three microgrids from different perspectives. However, the first scenario takes into consideration adopting a combination of elements that gives an optimal installation cost; the outcomes of this case were similar compared to the results obtained in [8], in which installation cost minimization was the objective of the study. The second scenario represents a balance between the two criteria, economic and environmental, respectively. The third scenario gives priority to installing sources that emit less CO_2 during their

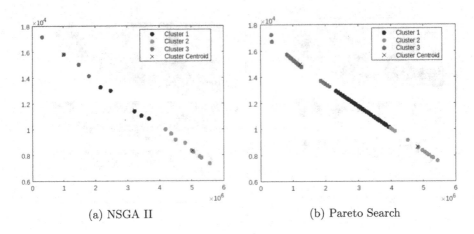

(a) NSGA II   (b) Pareto Search

Fig. 5. Results obtained by k-means ($k = 3$) with the pareto front solutions.

manufacturing process. According to Sect. 5.1, it can be noted that the batteries are the least emissive, which justifies the high number of these devices employed in this scenario.

7.2 Scenarios Technical Evaluation

The effectiveness of the scenario has been evaluated using a 24-hour operation analysis of each microgrid configuration.

Best Economical Scenario. In this case, the microgrid was established via 50 photovoltaic panels, 3 wind turbines, and an energy storage system consisting of 13 batteries, along with the diesel group and connection to the main grid. As shown in Fig. 6b by a 24-hour operation taking into account the presence of all RE sources, it can be seen that under these circumstances, the microgrid is capable of operating in a stable condition in which the load is continuously fed and the excess energy has been used to charge the energy storage system during peak production, when the set of batteries reached nearly the SOC_{max} as Fig. 6a illustrate.

Furthermore, the microgrid was able to feed the user continuously for 24 h in the absence of all RES, reaching SOC_{min} in the last hours of the day, as illustrated in Fig. 7a.

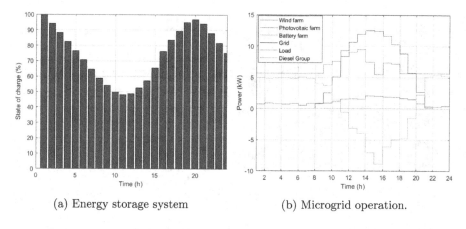

(a) Energy storage system   (b) Microgrid operation.

Fig. 6. Scenario 1: Presence of all RES.

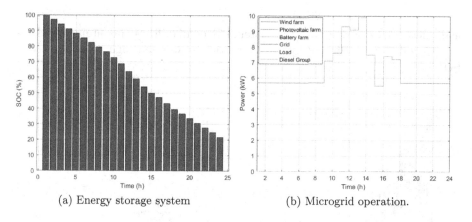

(a) Energy storage system   (b) Microgrid operation.

Fig. 7. Scenario 1: Absence of RES

Trade-Off Scenario. This setup consists of 55 photovoltaic panels, 2 wind turbines, 7 batteries, and a diesel generator that serves as a backup system in the event of a microgrid failure or a main grid blackout. As seen in Fig. 8a the batteries were able to feed the microgrid at night in normal operation. The microgrid users were able to meet their energy needs during the day owing to the photovoltaic park and the wind turbine. In addition, the battery was fully charged at 16 o'clock, when both the wind and the sun's potential were still present, and the excess energy was injected into the main grid between 17 o'clock and 20 o'clock, as shown in Fig. 8b. Practically, the microgrid was producing more energy than was required to supply the load while simultaneously charging the energy storage system to its fullest capacity.

In the absence of all renewable energy sources, the batteries fed the microgrid up to the point of minimal charge before feeding the consumer directly from the

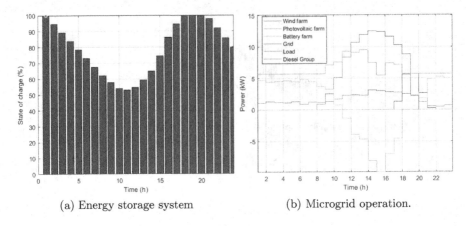

(a) Energy storage system   (b) Microgrid operation.

Fig. 8. Scenario 2: Presence of all RES.

main network, ensuring that the system's dependability is maintained and the user's comfort is unaffected by the microgrid's power shortage, as illustrated in Fig. 9.

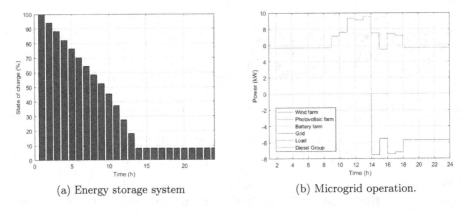

(a) Energy storage system   (b) Microgrid operation.

Fig. 9. Scenario 2: Absence of RES

Best Environmental Scenario. In this instance, the diesel group and the main grid were connected to the microgrid, which included 46 photovoltaic panels, 1 wind turbine, and a system of 44 batteries for energy storage. An abusive number of batteries made the microgrid able to work permanently even in the absence of all renewable features As presented in Fig. 11a. This case brings a very high cost of installation that will not ensure the gain on the investment during the lifetime of the installation ($T = 20$ years) mainly because the batteries have to be changed every 4 years as required to ensure their reliability inside the microgrid system. This set of changes will undoubtedly bring a huge cost of replacement.

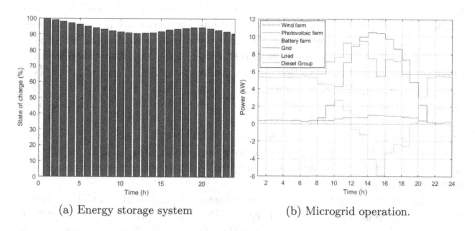

(a) Energy storage system   (b) Microgrid operation.

Fig. 10. Scenario 3: Presence of all RES.

Without ignoring the duration of charging and the high energy flow that must be fully supplied for reaching the SOC_{max} of the energy storage system, the microgrid's local energy sources are insufficient, necessitating an assortment of energy compensations from the main grid.

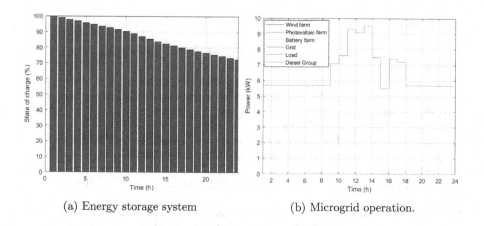

(a) Energy storage system   (b) Microgrid operation.

Fig. 11. Scenario 3: Absence of all RES.

8   Conclusions and Future Work

This study is a continuation of [8] and focuses on the sizing and optimization of an AC/DC microgrid composed of a set of distributed generators, including a park of photovoltaic panels, a wind turbine farm, and a set of electrochemical batteries. The microgrid is connected to the main grid through a common coupling point (PCC). A diesel generator has been used as a backup system in the event of a microgrid failure or main grid blackout. A data set of solar potential, wind speed, and temperature has been analyzed. Two multi-objective optimization algorithms have been used to solve the problem, including the Non-dominated Sorting Genetic Algorithm (NSGA II) and the Pareto Search (PS) algorithm. The results delivered a Pareto front of non-dominated points consisting of two objectives: total installation cost, and total GHG emissions. Three groups of scenarios have been identified by clustering the points of the Pareto front using the k-means method: economic, environmental, and traded-off. The best scenarios for each cluster are analyzed in 24-hour microgrid operation to identify its reliability.

In the future, the authors will extend this paper by including a third objective function representing embodied energy (EE), which represents the quantity of non-renewable energy consumed during the life cycle of different elements of the microgrid with an economic analysis of the microgrid investment costs taking into account all potential outcomes. Additionally, the authors are studying the sizing of the system in a DC configuration.

Acknowledgements. This work has been supported by FCT - Fundação para a Ciência e Tecnologia within the R&D Units Project Scope: UIDB/05757/2020, UIDP/05757/2020.

References

1. Amoura, Y., Torres, S., Lima, J., Pereira, A.I.: Hybrid optimisation and machine learning models for wind and solar data prediction. Int. J. Hybrid Intell. Syst. **19**(7875), 1–16 (2023). https://doi.org/10.3233/his-230004
2. Christopher, S.: Renewable energy potential towards attainment of net-zero energy buildings status - a critical review. J. Clean. Prod. **405**, 136942 (2023). https://doi.org/10.1016/j.jclepro.2023.136942
3. Tvaronavičienė, M.: Towards renewable energy: opportunities and challenges. Energies **16**(5), 2269 (2023). https://doi.org/10.3390/en16052269
4. Li, C., Umair, M.: Does green finance development goals affects renewable energy in China. Renewable Energy **203**, 898–905 (2023). https://doi.org/10.1016/j.renene.2022.12.066
5. Hossain, J., et al.: A review on optimal energy management in commercial buildings. Energies **16**(4), 1609 (2023). https://doi.org/10.3390/en16041609
6. Statista Research Department. Global Microgrid Market Value 2017–2028. Statista (2023). https://www.statista.com/statistics/1313998/global-microgrid-market-size/. Accessed 29 Apr 2023

7. Mustafa Kamal, M., Ashraf, I.: Evaluation of a hybrid power system based on renewable and energy storage for reliable rural electrification. Renewable Energy Focus **45**, 179–191 (2023). https://doi.org/10.1016/j.ref.2023.04.002

8. Amoura, Y., Ferreira, Â.P., Lima, J., Pereira, A.I.: Optimal sizing of a hybrid energy system based on renewable energy using evolutionary optimization algorithms. In: Pereira, A.I., et al. (eds.) OL2A 2021. CCIS, vol. 1488, pp. 153–168. Springer, Cham (2021). https://doi.org/10.1007/978-3-030-91885-9_12

9. Amoura, Y., Pereira, A.I., Lima, J.: Optimization methods for energy management in a microgrid system considering wind uncertainty data. In: Kumar, S., Purohit, S.D., Hiranwal, S., Prasad, M. (eds.) Proceedings of International Conference on Communication and Computational Technologies. AIS, pp. 117–141. Springer, Singapore (2021). https://doi.org/10.1007/978-981-16-3246-4_10

10. Zhang, J., Cho, H., Mago, P.J., Zhang, H., Yang, F.: Multi-objective particle swarm optimization (MOPSO) for a distributed energy system integrated with energy storage. J. Therm. Sci. **28**(6), 1221–1235 (2019). https://doi.org/10.1007/s11630-019-1133-5

11. Sellami, R., Sher, F., Neji, R.: An improved MOPSO algorithm for optimal sizing amp; placement of distributed generation: a case study of the Tunisian offshore distribution network (ASHTART). Energy Rep. **8**, 6960–6975 (2022). https://doi.org/10.1016/j.egyr.2022.05.049

12. Yusuf, A., Bayhan, N., Tiryaki, H., Hamawandi, B., Toprak, M.S., Ballikaya, S.: Multi-objective optimization of concentrated photovoltaic-thermoelectric hybrid system via non-dominated sorting genetic algorithm (NSGA II). Energy Convers. Manage. **236**, 114065 (2021). https://doi.org/10.1016/j.enconman.2021.114065

13. Bora, T.C., Mariani, V.C., dos Santos Coelho, L.: Multi-objective optimization of the environmental-economic dispatch with reinforcement learning based on non-dominated sorting genetic algorithm. Appl. Therm. Eng. **146**, 688–700 (2019). https://doi.org/10.1016/j.applthermaleng.2018.10.020

14. Fathima, A.H., Palanisamy, K.: Optimization in microgrids with hybrid energy systems - a review. Renew. Sustain. Energy Rev. **45**, 431–446 (2015). https://doi.org/10.1016/j.rser.2015.01.059

15. Singh, P., Pandit, M., Srivastava, L.: Multi-objective optimal sizing of hybrid micro-grid system using an integrated intelligent technique. Energy **269**, 126756 (2023). https://doi.org/10.1016/j.energy.2023.126756

16. Zhu, W., Guo, J., Zhao, G.: Multi-objective sizing optimization of hybrid renewable energy microgrid in a stand-alone marine context. Electronics **10**(2), 174 (2021). https://doi.org/10.3390/electronics10020174

17. Khlifi, F., Cherif, H., Belhadj, J.: Environmental and economic optimization and sizing of a micro-grid with battery storage for an industrial application. Energies **14**(18), 5913 (2021). https://doi.org/10.3390/en14185913

18. Deb, K., Pratap, A., Agarwal, S., Meyarivan, T.: A fast and elitist multiobjective genetic algorithm: NSGA-II. IEEE Trans. Evol. Comput. **6**(2), 182–197 (2002). https://doi.org/10.1109/4235.996017

Deep Conditional Measure Quantization

Gabriel Turinici$^{(\boxtimes)}$

CEREMADE, Université Paris Dauphine - PSL, Paris, France
`gabriel.turinici@dauphine.fr`
`https://turinici.com`

Abstract. Quantization of a probability measure means representing it with a finite set of Dirac masses that approximates the input distribution well enough (in some metric space of probability measures). Various methods exists to do so, but the situation of quantizing a conditional law has been less explored. We propose a method, called DCMQ, involving a Huber-energy kernel-based approach coupled with a deep neural network architecture. The method is tested on several examples and obtains promising results.

Keywords: conditional generative algorithms · optimization · conditional quantization · stochastic optimization · vector quantization

1 Introduction

1.1 Conditional Measure Quantization: Motivation

In general terms, quantization is the process of replacing a set of values (possibly an infinity of them) with a finite number chosen to be the most representative according to some metric. This is related to vector quantization [10,14] that operate on objects in a high dimensional space. Applications range from signal processing [11,12,35] to finance [19,23,24], statistics [16,27]. We will be concerned with a particular instance of this question, namely the quantization of probability measures[1]; in this case we want to represent the knowledge encoded into a probability measure μ with support in $\mathcal{Y}$ by a sum of Q Dirac masses $\delta_{\mathbf{y}}^{\beta} = \sum_{q=1}^{Q} \beta_q \delta_{y_q}$, where $y_q \in \mathcal{Y}$ are chosen such that the distance between μ and $\delta_{\mathbf{y}}^{\beta}$ is as small as possible (we will come back later to the definition of the distance); here β are some weight parameters (see Sect. 2).

But, there are times when μ is depending itself on another parameter $\mu = \mu_x$ or μ can be a conditional law. The main question treated in this paper is how to compute efficiently the quantization μ_x of the law μ conditional to x. Our proposal is to involve a deep neural network that minimizes the Huber-energy statistical distance (see [33] for a definition) and outputs the quantized version of the conditional law.

---

[1] We only consider here probability measures, but the extension to signed measures can be done directly following the prescriptions in [33].

© The Author(s), under exclusive license to Springer Nature Switzerland AG 2024
A. I. Pereira et al. (Eds.): OL2A 2023, CCIS 1982, pp. 343–354, 2024.
https://doi.org/10.1007/978-3-031-53036-4_24

The outline of the paper is the following: in the rest of this section we recall some related works from the literature; we present some theoretical information in Sect. 2; the practical implementation of the method is described in Sects. 3 and 4 together with numerical results. Concluding remarks are the object of Sect. 5.

1.2 Brief Literature Review on Measure Quantization, Conditional Sampling and Conditional Quantization

In the general area of (non-conditional) measure quantization, a related proposal [9] investigates the Nystrom mean embeddings, that constructs the quantization based on the exploitation of a small random subset of the dataset. See also [18,37] for non-conditional deep learning vector quantization approach. The literature on general conditional quantization is very scarce, but some papers (see [4] and related works) investigate the 'conditional L^1 median[2]; our approach is similar to that one, with the difference that we look for a general quantization, not only a quantization with a single ($Q = 1$) point and we are not attached to the first order moment. See also [40] for a proposal involving neural network computations of conditional quantiles.

In a related work, Zhou et al. [42] propose a generative approach to sample from a conditional distribution by learning a conditional generator. They exploit a Kullbak-Liebler (KL) divergence formulation (in [30] a 'energy' approach is used instead) but the generator itself is not quantized.

On the contrary, Vuong et al. [38] learn a deep discrete representation using the Wasserstein distance but their approach is not targeted towards conditional distribution representation; in another contribution, [21] introduce a Quantised-Variational AutoEncoder (VQ-VAE) that use vector quantization techniques to avoid the "collapse" of the posterior distribution.

In signal processing, conditional quantization goes often by the name of conditional vector quantization and has been used e.g. for speech encoding (see [15] and related literature), in [1], see also [15,25,26] for other references in the signal processing area. Our approach differs by choosing to treat the question in a general, not application dependent way which materializes into the choice of the Huber-energy statistical distance and the use of deep neural networks (hereafter called 'DNN') for interpolation.

Natural language processing is also an application domain; for instance, even if neither GPT-3 [7][3] nor its follow-up ChatGPT [22] are designed explicitly as quantizers, in practice ChatGPT will answer based on a user question or previous conversation. Put it otherwise, it selects a small set of possible answers from the conditional probability of any text given previous contents. This is indeed a conditional quantization.

---

[2] The L^1 median of a measure ξ (with finite first order moment) is the point that minimizes, with respect to y, the first order moment of ξ centered at y (the median does so in one dimension and can be extended by this definition to several dimensions.

[3] short for "Generative Pre-training Transformer 3", the large language model developed by OpenAI.

Interpolation by Deep Neural Networks. The conditional quantization, or quantization depending on some parameter, can also be viewed as some kind of interpolation. Given a set of parameters $x_1, ..., x_L$ we can pre-compute the quantized conditional distribution for these parameters and then, for any new choice of the parameter, interpolate using the precomputed data.

Several works explored the use of DNNs for interpolation, for instance in [39] a DNN is trained to learn a mapping from input data points to output data points; then, at the prediction time the DNN can generate an interpolated value for any intermediate input value; the applications range from image processing [39] to audio interpolation [31]; in [41] data interpolation was used in scientific simulations such as weather forecasting and fluid dynamics simulations.

Other approaches to using DNNs for interpolation involve using the DNN to learn a probabilistic model of the data [5], and generate the interpolated values using the learned data distribution (with applications to natural language processing and time series analysis). In NLP the possibility of language models to learn to infill (missing parts of) text [3] can also be considered close to a extrapolation method.

2 The Deep Neural Network Conditional Quantization Method

2.1 Setting and Notations

We follow the usual notation with lowercase letter for values, upper case for random variables and bold face for vectors. Let $\mathcal{X} = \mathbb{R}^{n_x}$, $\mathcal{Y} = \mathbb{R}^{n_y}$ (with n_x, n_y non-null integers)[4] and μ a joint law with support in $\mathcal{X} \times \mathcal{Y}$. Denote μ^X and μ^Y the marginals of the law μ; for instance, if X and Y are two random variable with support in $\mathcal{X}$ and $\mathcal{Y}$ respectively, and if (X, Y) follows the law μ then μ^X is the law of X and μ^Y is the law of Y. We look for a method to quantize the distribution

$$\mu_x = \mu(dy|X = x), \tag{1}$$

of Y conditional to $X = x$. Fixing an integer $Q > 0$, and some weights $\beta \in \mathbb{R}^Q$ (that sum up to one) we look for $\mathbf{y}(x) \in \mathcal{Y}^Q$ such that $\delta_{\beta, \mathbf{y}(x)} = \sum_{q=1}^Q \beta_q \delta_{\mathbf{y}_q(x)}$ is as close as possible to μ_x.

To describe what 'close' means, we need to use a distance d defined on the set of probability measures; the distance we use will be the Huber-energy distance that we define below [32]; given $a \geq 0$ the Huber-energy (negative definite) kernel is defined by $h_{a,r}(z, \tilde{z}) = (a^2 + |z - \tilde{z}|^2)^{r/2} - a^r$ ($a \geq 0$, $r \in]0, 2[$); it is known (see [29,33] and related works) that h induces a distance d: for any two probability laws η, $\tilde{\eta}$ on some space $\mathcal{Z}^5$ with $\int_{\mathcal{Z}} |z|^r \eta(dz) < \infty$, $\int_{\mathcal{Z}} |z|^r \tilde{\eta}(dz) < \infty$, we can write:

$$d(\eta, \tilde{\eta})^2 = -\frac{1}{2} \int_{\mathcal{Z}} \int_{\mathcal{Z}} h_{a,r}(z, \tilde{z})(\eta - \tilde{\eta})(dz)(\eta - \tilde{\eta})(d\tilde{z}). \tag{2}$$

---

[4] What is said here can be extended to the situation when $\mathcal{X}$ or $\mathcal{Y}$ are only open subsets of $\mathbb{R}^{n_x}$ or $\mathbb{R}^{n_y}$.

[5] Here $\mathcal{Z}$ will be either $\mathcal{X} \times \mathcal{Y}$ or $\mathcal{Y}$.

Note that in particular $h_{a,r}(z,\tilde{z}) = d(\delta_z, \delta_{\tilde{z}})^2$ and moreover we have for $\mathbf{z} \in \mathcal{Z}^L, \beta \in \mathbb{R}^L, \tilde{\mathbf{z}} \in \mathcal{Z}^M, \tilde{\beta} \in \mathbb{R}^M$,

$$d(\delta_{\mathbf{z}}^{\beta}, \delta_{\tilde{\mathbf{z}}}^{\tilde{\beta}})^2 = \sum_{i=1}^{L}\sum_{j=1}^{M} \beta_i \tilde{\beta}_j h_{a,r}(z_i, \tilde{z}_j) - \frac{1}{2}\sum_{i,j=1}^{L} \beta_i \beta_j h_{a,r}(z_i, z_j) - \frac{1}{2}\sum_{i,j=1}^{M} \tilde{\beta}_i \tilde{\beta}_j h_{a,r}(\tilde{z}_i, \tilde{z}_j). \quad (3)$$

In this paper we will only be concerned with uniform weights (but what is said here can be extended to arbitrary, but fixed, weights, see [33] for related considerations); in this case we write simply:

$$\delta_{\mathbf{z}} = \frac{1}{L}\sum_{\ell=1}^{L} \delta_{z_\ell}. \quad (4)$$

The conditional quantization of the law μ is defined as follows: for any $x \in \mathcal{X}$ we look for the minimizer of the distance to μ_x i.e., any $\mathbf{y}^{opt}(x) \in \mathcal{Y}^Q$ such that:

$$d(\delta_{\mathbf{y}^{opt}(x)}, \mu_x)^2 \leq d(\delta_{\mathbf{y}}, \mu_x)^2, \quad \forall \mathbf{y} \in \mathcal{Y}^Q. \quad (5)$$

Note that in general the minimum is not unique so $\mathbf{y}^{opt}(x)$ is a set-valued function. Accordingly a first theoretical important question is whether one can find a selection[6] of $\mathbf{y}^{opt}(x)$ with good properties such as measurability, continuity etc. These questions are answered in the rest of this section. Then a practical question is how to find convenient conditional quantizations; this is described in Sects. 3 and 4.

2.2   Existence of a Measurable Conditional Quantization

We investigate whether there exists a proper measurable function (i.e. not a set valued function) that represents the conditional quantization. This question is fundamental for working conveniently with such quantizations (by definition any random variable is required to be measurable !).

Proposition 1. *Suppose that the bi-variate distribution μ is such that for any $x \in \mathcal{X}$ the distribution μ_x has finite r-th order moment. Then there exists a measurable function $\mathbf{y}^{opt} : \mathcal{X} \to \mathcal{Y}^Q$ such that $\mathbf{y}^{opt}(x)$ satisfies equation (5) for any $x \in \mathcal{X}$.*

Remark 1. The hypothesis of existence of the r-th order moment condition can be weakened.

Proof. A general proof can be obtained using the Kuratowski and Ryll-Nardzewski measurable selection theorem [17] (see also [8]) but we will follow the faster route that employs the Corollary 1 in [6, page 904]. Denote the function $f(x,\mathbf{y}) : \mathcal{X} \times \mathcal{Y}^Q$ defined by $f(x,\mathbf{y}) = d(\delta_{\mathbf{y}}, \mu_x)^2$. Then, with the notations of the Corollary, $D = \mathcal{X} \times \mathcal{Y}^Q$ and:

---

[6] A selection of a set-valued function $g : A \to 2^B \setminus \emptyset$ is a function $\tilde{g} : A \to B$ such that $\forall a \in A : \tilde{g}(a) \in g(a)$. Recall that 2^B is the set of all subsets of B.

- f is Borel measurable because of our choice of distance d and the definition of conditional probability distribution; for $a = 0$ one can also use the fact that conditional expectation is Borel measurable and for $a > 0$ similar arguments apply;
- both $\mathcal{X}$ and $\mathcal{Y}^Q$ are σ-compact and $f(x, \cdot)$ is continuous thus lower semi-continuous;
- using the Proposition 13 and Remark 14 in [33] the set $I = \{x \in \mathcal{X} :$ for some $y \in \mathcal{Y}^Q : f(x, y) = \inf f(x, \cdot)\}$ is equal to $\mathcal{X}$;

Then, it follows by the Corollary 1 in [6, page 904] that there exists a measurable function $\mathbf{y}^{opt} : \mathcal{X} \to \mathcal{Y}^Q$ such that $f(x, \mathbf{y}^{opt}(x)) = \inf_{\mathbf{y} \in \mathcal{Y}^Q} f(x, \mathbf{y})$ i.e. the conclusion.

Remark 2. The procedure in [6, pages 906–907] results in a selection compatible with some order relation.

2.3   Existence of a Continuous Conditional Quantization in 1D

We now analyze the continuity of the conditional quantization. We do not have general results but will consider a particular case.

Proposition 2. *Let us take $\mathcal{Y} = \mathbb{R}$, $a = 0$, $r = 1$ (i.e. the kernel is the so-called 'energy' kernel). We work under the assumptions of proposition 1 and suppose in addition that the distribution $\mu(dx, dy)$ is absolutely continuous with respect to the Lebesgue measure and admits a continuous density $\rho(x, y)$ which is strictly positive on $\mathcal{X} \times \mathcal{Y}$. Then the conditional quantization $\mathbf{y}^{opt}(x)$ is unique for any $x \in \mathcal{X}$ and continuous as a function of x.*

Proof. Note first that for any fixed but arbitrary $\alpha \in]0, 1[$, the continuity of the density $\rho(x, y)$ implies by standard arguments, the continuity, with respect to x, of the quantile α of the law μ_x. Using [33, Proposition 21], for any x the optimal quantization $\mathbf{y}^{opt}(x)$ is unique and corresponds to the set of quantiles $\frac{q+1/2}{Q}$, $q = 0, ..., Q - 1$ of the law μ_x. Put together, these facts allow to reach the conclusion.

Remark 3. The absolute continuity of μ and the hypothesis on the density $\rho(x, y)$ can be weakened (see also [13, 20] for alternative hypothesis used in this context).

On the other hand similar results can be proven under more general assumptions; for instance one could check (proof not given here) that under the assumption that $\sup_{x \neq y, x, y \in \mathcal{X}} \frac{d(\mu_x, \mu_y)}{\|x-y\|^\alpha} < \infty$ then a Holder-α continuous selection of quantiles can be performed and therefore a Holder-α continuous conditional quantization too.

Remark 4. Another approach could use interpolation: if a quantization is performed for each member of the set of values x_j resulting in vectors $\mathbf{y}_j$ then interpolation can be used e.g., for $\mathcal{X} = \mathbb{R}$ and supposing x_j ordered increasingly, for $x = vx_i + (1 - v)x_j$ one could combine the vectors $\mathbf{y}_j$ with corresponding weights. For higher dimensional $\mathcal{X}$ trilinear interpolation could be invoked.

3 The Deep Conditional Quantization Algorithm (DCMQ) by Conditional Sampling

Being now comforted by the theoretical results of the previous section, we look for a practical way to compute the conditional quantization. In particular we will use deep neural networks and will check numerically that such methods can indeed provide good results.

The deep conditional quantization algorithm (abbreviated DCMQ) that we introduce here uses a network that transforms an input $x \in \mathcal{X}$ into a vector $\mathbf{y}^{dcmq}(x) \in \mathcal{Y}^Q$ with the goal to have $\mathbf{y}^{dcmq}(x)$ as close as possible to the optimal conditional quantizer $\mathbf{y}^{opt}(x)$ of the law μ_x as in equation (5). The procedure is described in algorithm DCMQ below. We describe first the default version which assumes that a **conditional sampling** is possible, i.e., given $x \in \mathcal{X}$ one can sample from μ_x. This algorithm will be tested in Sects. 3.1, 3.2 and 3.3; then in Sect. 4 we present the variant that samples directly from the joint distribution and use it for the restoration of MNIST images.

Algorithm A1. Deep Conditional Measure Quantization algorithm : DCMQ

1: **procedure** DCMQ
2:    • set batch size B, sampling size J, parameters a (default 10^{-6}), and r (default 1.), minimization algorithm (default = Adam) ; max iterations (default 1000)
3:    • choose a network architecture and initialize layers (default : 5 sequential fully connected layers of size $n_y \times Q$, first input is of size n_x);
4:    **while** (max iteration not reached) **do**
5:       • sample i.i.d $x_1, ..., x_B$ according to the marginal law μ^X of X;
6:       • for each $b \le B$ sample i.i.d J times from μ_{x_b} and denote $\tilde{\mathbf{y}}_b$ the sample as a vector in $\mathcal{Y}^J$;
7:       • propagate $x_1, ..., x_B$ through the network to obtain $\mathbf{y}^{dcmq}(x_b) \in \mathcal{Y}^Q, b \le B$
8:       • compute the loss $\mathcal{L} = \frac{1}{B} \sum_{b=1}^{B} d\left(\delta_{\tilde{\mathbf{y}}_b}, \delta_{\mathbf{y}^{dcmq}(x_b)}\right)^2$;
9:       • update the network as specified by the stochastic optimization algorithm (using backpropagation) to minimize the loss $\mathcal{L}$.
10:    **end while**
11: **end procedure**

The numerical performance of the algorithm is tested below; in all cases when no precision is given the default parameters of the DCMQ algorithm are used.

3.1 Quantization of 2D Gaussian Conditioned on Its Mean

The first test will be a 2D Gaussian that has its mean given by another variable: let X and Y be 2D independent standard Gaussian variables and consider μ to be the distribution of $X + Y$. The implementation of the DCMQ algorithm is available at [34] and the results are presented in Fig. 1. The DCMQ algorithm is shown to converge well and the quantization follows the conditional information (the mean).

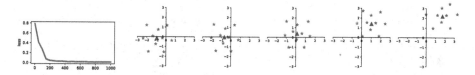

Fig. 1. Conditional quantization with $Q = 10$ points for the test in Sect. 3.1. **Left image:** Convergence of the loss function. **Right images:** Five points $x_1, ..., x_5 \in \mathcal{X} = \mathbb{R}^2$ are sampled from μ^X (plotted as blue triangles); the DNN (after training) is asked to quantize the conditional distribution μ_{x_b} for each $b \leq 5$ (red stars). Recall that μ_{x_b} is a Gaussian shifted by x_b. The quantization points follow precisely the indicated mean.

3.2 Quantization of 2D Gaussian: The Multiplicative Case

We move now to another test case where the condition enters multiplicatively; with the notations above (X and Y 2D independent standard Gaussian variables) μ is taken to be the distribution of $X \cdot Y$. The results are presented in figure 2. The DCMQ algorithms converges well and the quantization follows the conditional information.

Fig. 2. Conditional quantization with $Q = 10$ points for the test in Sect. 3.2. **Left image:** Convergence of the loss function. **Right images :** Five points $x_1, ..., x_5 \in \mathcal{X} = \mathbb{R}^2$ are sampled from μ^X (blue triangles); the DNN (after training) is asked to quantize μ_{x_b} for each $b \leq 5$ (red stars). Here μ_{x_b} is a Gaussian multiplied in each direction by x_b. So, for instance when a point x_b has both component values large, the corresponding quantization will look like the quantization of a bi-variate normal. But when x_b is close to some axis, the quantization will act on a very elliptical form distribution because one of the Gaussian is multiplied by a small constant. This expected behavior is reproduced well by the converged DNN.

3.3 Quantization of a 1D Gaussian Mixture Crossing

We consider now the situation of a parameter X uniform in $[-1, 1]$ and the dependent variable Y will be a even mixture of two 1D Gaussians, centered at $\pm 10X$; the joint density of (X, Y) is plotted in Fig. 3 (background). The DCMQ algorithm converges well and the quantization follows the expected laws.

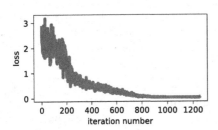 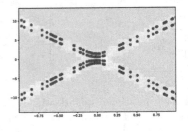

Fig. 3. Conditional quantization with $Q = 4$ points for the test described in Sect. 3.3. **Left image:** Convergence of the loss function. **Right image:** The joint density of (X, Y) is plotted in background (red are low values, blue are high values). The green dots indicate the quantized values. Note that each of the two parts of the mixture is assigned two quantization points that move along the mean.

4 The Deep Conditional Quantization Through Joint Sampling: MNIST Restauration

Conditional sampling from μ_x as in Sect. 3 is not always possible and data presentation can indicate joint sampling as the only way to obtain a couple (X, Y); this arrives especially when X is continuous and it is impossible to ensure that X has a desired value x. We adapt in this section the previous algorithm and test on a image reconstruction task.

The default neural network architecture is as follows: all layers are fully-connected and have as output a tensor of shape $B \times n_y \times Q$ (B is the batch size); the first (input) layer takes data of size $B \times n_x$. All layers act on the output of the previous layer concatenated with the condition (input of the first layer of shape $B \times n_x$). This architecture is akin to a "constant attention" [2,36] U-net [28]. In our tests the default is to use 3 such dense layers with ReLU activations. A graphical description is given in Fig. 4.

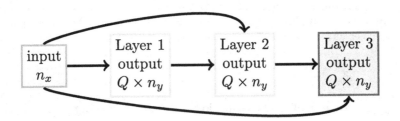

Fig. 4. Default network architecture used in Sect. 4 (batch size $B = 1$).

The algorithm minimizes (by sampling) the following loss functional (with obvious notations)

$$\mathbb{E}_{x \sim \mu^X} \left[d \left(\mu_x, \frac{1}{Q} \sum_{q=1}^{Q} \delta_{x, \mathbf{y}_q^{dcmq}(\mu_x)} \right)^2 \right]. \tag{6}$$

Algorithm A2. Deep Conditional Measure Quantization algorithm through joint sampling : DCMQ-J

1: **procedure** DCMQ-J
2:     • set batch size B, sampling size J, parameters a (default 10^{-6}), and r (default 1.), minimization algorithm (default = Adam); max iterations (default 1000)
3:     • choose a network architecture and initialize layers (default : cf. fig. 4);
4:     **while** (max iteration not reached) **do**
5:         sample i.i.d $(x_1, y_1), ..., (x_B, y_B)$ from the dataset ;
6:         propagate $x_1, ..., x_B$ through the network to obtain $\mathbf{y}^{dcmq}(x_b) \in \mathcal{Y}^Q, b \le B$;
7:         compute the loss $\mathcal{L} = \frac{1}{B} \sum_{b=1}^{B} d \left(\delta_{x_b, y_b}, \frac{\sum_{q=1}^{Q} \delta_{x_b, \mathbf{y}_q^{dcmq}(x_b)}}{Q} \right)^2$;
8:         update the network as specified by the stochastic optimization algorithm (using backpropagation) to minimize the loss $\mathcal{L}$.
9:     **end while**
10: **end procedure**

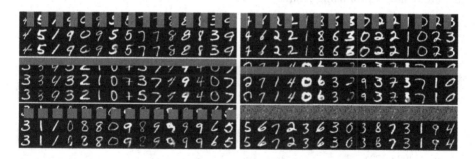

Fig. 5. MNIST reconstruction results as described in Sect. 4.

Remark 5. Note that an alternative formulation can be proposed that employs the following loss functional instead of (6) : $d \left(\mu, \frac{1}{Q} \sum_{q=1}^{Q} \delta_{x, \mathbf{y}_q^{dcmq}(\mu_x)} \right)^2$. This loss has lower variance (gain of order $O(\frac{1}{B})$) but requires more computations per iteration: $O(B^2(1+Q)^2 n_y + B^2 n_x)$ instead of $O(BQ^2 n_y)$. The sampled version used by the algorithm is in this case: $d \left(\frac{\sum_{b=1}^{B} \delta_{x_b, y_b}}{B}, \frac{\sum_{b=1}^{B} \sum_{q=1}^{Q} \delta_{x_b, \mathbf{y}_q^{dcmq}(x_b)}}{B \cdot Q} \right)^2$.

The algorithm was tested on the MNIST dataset for an in-painting (image restoration) task i.e., it was requested to restore the whole image using only a part of it as input; in all cases we considered a part of the image as known corresponding to the condition i.e., the X component (of dimension n_x), and another part as unknown, corresponding to the Y component (of dimension n_y); the $Q = 1$ quantization was learned using the **train** dataset and, at test time, we asked the algorithm to output the quantization for images in the **test** MNIST dataset. Several situations were considered for the unknown part Y depicted in gray in Fig. 5 (the description is consistent with the order of results there): **first line**: right half, left half, **second line**: upper half, lower half, **third line**: lower right $2/3 \times 2/3$ corner, random pixels covering 90% of all 28×28 pixels. The known part, plotted in the first row, was given as input; the true images are in the second row and the guess of the algorithm is in the third row. Good agreement is observed in all test situations as the algorithm manages to reconstruct well the missing parts.

5   Concluding Remarks

In this paper we discuss the quantization of conditional probability laws. We first prove that in general the quantization can be represented as measurable function and then, in a particular case, we give a theoretical result that ensures the quantization points depend continuously on the condition. Then, a deep learning algorithm is introduced using Huber-energy kernels to find numerically the solution of the quantization problem. The procedure is tested on some standard cases and shows promising results.

References

1. Agiomyrgiannakis, Y., Stylianou, Y.: Conditional vector quantization for speech coding. IEEE Trans. Audio Speech Lang. Process. **15**(2), 377–386 (2007). https://doi.org/10.1109/TASL.2006.881702, conference Name: IEEE Transactions on Audio, Speech, and Language Processing
2. Bahdanau, D., et al.: Neural machine translation by jointly learning to align and translate (2014). https://doi.org/10.48550/ARXIV.1409.0473, https://arxiv.org/abs/1409.0473
3. Bavarian, M., et al.: Efficient training of language models to fill in the middle (2022). https://doi.org/10.48550/arXiv.2207.14255, http://arxiv.org/abs/2207.14255, arXiv:2207.14255 [cs]
4. Berlinet, A., Cadre, B., Gannoun, A.: On the conditional L 1-median and its estimation. J. Nonparametric Stat. **13**(5), 631–645 (Jan2001). https://doi.org/10.1080/10485250108832869, publisher: Taylor & Francis
5. Bishop, C.M.: Mixture density networks (1994). https://publications.aston.ac.uk/id/eprint/373/, technical Report, Aston University
6. Brown, L.D., Purves, R.: Measurable selections of extrema. Ann. Stat. **1**(5), 902–912 (1973). http://www.jstor.org/stable/2958290, publisher: Institute of Mathematical Statistics

7. Brown, T., et al.: Language models are few-shot learners. In: Larochelle, H., et al. (eds.) Advances in Neural Information Processing Systems, vol. 33, pp. 1877–1901. Curran Associates, Inc. (2020). https://proceedings.neurips.cc/paper/2020/file/1457c0d6bfcb4967418bfb8ac142f64a-Paper.pdf

8. Cascales, B., Kadets, V., Rodríguez, J.: Measurability and selections of multifunctions in Banach spaces. J. Convex Anal. **17**(1), 229–240 (2010). www.heldermann.de/JCA/JCA17/JCA171/jca17017.htm

9. Chatalic, A., et al.: Nyström kernel mean embeddings. In: Chaudhuri, K., et al. (eds.) Proc. of the 39th ICML. Proceedings of Machine Learning Research, vol. 162, pp. 3006–3024. PMLR (2022). https://proceedings.mlr.press/v162/chatalic22a.html

10. Chazal, F., Levrard, C., Royer, M.: Optimal quantization of the mean measure and applications to statistical learning (2021). https://doi.org/10.48550/arXiv.2002.01216, https://arxiv.org/abs/2002.01216, arXiv:2002.01216

11. Constantinides, A., Lim, J.: Quantization noise in data conversion systems. IEEE Trans. Commun. **32**(10), 1218–1225 (1984)

12. Crochiere, R., Rabiner, L.: Multirate digital signal processing. Proc. IEEE **77**(4), 463–481 (1989)

13. Gannoun, A., Saracco, J., Yu, K.: Nonparametric prediction by conditional median and quantiles. J. Stat. Plann. Inference **117**(2), 207–223 (2003)

14. Graf, S., Luschgy, H.: Foundations of quantization for probability distributions. Springer, Cham (2007)

15. Graham, R.: An efficient algorithm for determining the convex hull of a finite planar set. Inf. Process. Lett. **1**(4), 132–133 (1972)

16. Kreitmeier, W.: Optimal vector quantization in terms of Wasserstein distance. J. Multivariate Anal. **102**(8), 1225–1239 (2011). https://doi.org/10.1016/j.jmva.2011.04.005, https://www.sciencedirect.com/science/article/pii/S0047259X11000613

17. Kuratowski, K., Ryll-Nardzewski, C.: A general theorem on selectors. Bulletin de l'Académie Polonaise des Sciences, Série des Sciences Mathématiques, Astronomiques et Physiques **13**, 397–403 (1965)

18. Lu, X., Wang, H., Dong, W., Wu, F., Zheng, Z., Shi, G.: Learning a deep vector quantization network for image compression. IEEE Access **7**, 118815–118825 (2019). https://doi.org/10.1109/ACCESS.2019.2934731

19. Lyons, T.J.: Cubature on Wiener space. J. Funct. Anal. **129**(2), 483–509 (1995)

20. Mehra, K., Rao, M.S., Upadrasta, S.: A smooth conditional quantile estimator and related applications of conditional empirical processes. J. Multivar. Anal. **37**(2), 151–179 (1991)

21. van den Oord, A., Vinyals, O., Kavukcuoglu, K.: Neural discrete representation learning (2018). https://doi.org/10.48550/arXiv.1711.00937, https://arxiv.org/abs/1711.00937, arXiv:1711.00937

22. OpenAI: ChatGPT: Optimizing Language Models for Dialogue (2022). https://openai.com/blog/chatgpt/, at 2023-01-16

23. Pages, G.: Cubature formulae and gaussian quadrature rules. J. Complex. **31**, 1–29 (2015)

24. Pagès, G.: Optimal quantization methods I: cubatures. In: Pagès, G. (ed.) Numerical Probability: An Introduction with Applications to Finance, pp. 133–173. Springer, Cham (2018). https://doi.org/10.1007/978-3-319-90276-0_5

25. Parks, T., Burrus, C.: Chebyshev-hermite and chebyshev-legendre orthonormal expansions of signals. IEEE Trans. Circuits Syst. **CAS–32**(8), 851–856 (1985)

26. Proakis, J.G.: Digital Communications. McGraw-Hill, New York (1995)
27. Sculley, D., Hinton, G.: Web-scale k-means clustering. In: Proceedings of the 19th International Conference on World Wide Web, pp. 1177–1178. ACM (2010)
28. Shelhamer, E., et al.: Fully convolutional networks for semantic segmentation. IEEE Trans. Pattern Anal. Mach. Intell. **39**(4), 640–651 (2017). https://doi.org/10.1109/TPAMI.2016.2572683
29. Sriperumbudur, B.K., et al.: Hilbert space embeddings and metrics on probability measures. J. Mach. Learn. Res. **11**, 1517–1561 (2010)
30. Strauss, R.R., Oliva, J.B.: Arbitrary conditional distributions with energy (2021). https://doi.org/10.48550/ARXIV.2102.04426, https://arxiv.org/abs/2102.04426
31. Suefusa, K., Nishida, T., Purohit, H., Tanabe, R., Endo, T., Kawaguchi, Y.: Anomalous sound detection based on interpolation deep neural network. In: ICASSP 2020–2020 IEEE International Conference on Acoustics, Speech and Signal Processing (ICASSP), pp. 271–275 (2020). https://doi.org/10.1109/ICASSP40776.2020.9054344
32. Szekely, G.J., Rizzo, M.L., et al.: Hierarchical clustering via joint between-within distances: extending ward's minimum variance method. J. Classif. **22**(2), 151–184 (2005)
33. Turinici, G.: Huber-energy measure quantization (2022). https://doi.org/10.48550/ARXIV.2212.08162, https://arxiv.org/abs/2212.08162, arxiv : 2212.08162
34. Turinici, G.: Huber energy measure quantization repository (2023). https://github.com/gabriel-turinici/Huber-energy-measure-quantization, gitHub repository https://github.com/gabriel-turinici/Huber-energy-measure-quantization
35. Vaidyanathan, P.P.: Multirate Systems and Filterbanks. Prentice Hall Englewood Cliffs, NJ (1993)
36. Vaswani, A., et al.: Attention Is All You Need (2017). https://doi.org/10.48550/ARXIV.1706.03762, https://arxiv.org/abs/1706.03762
37. de Vries, H., Memisevic, R., Courville, A.: Deep learning vector quantization. In: ESANN (ed.) Proceeding of the 24th European Symposium on Artificial Neural Networks ESANN, Bruges, Belgium, April 27–29 2016, vol. ES2016. ESANN (2016). https://www.esann.org/sites/default/files/proceedings/legacy/es2016-112.pdf
38. Vuong, T.L., et al.: Vector Quantized Wasserstein Auto-Encoder (2023). https://doi.org/10.48550/ARXIV.2302.05917
39. Wang, X., Yu, K., Dong, C., Tang, X., Loy, C.C.: Deep network interpolation for continuous imagery effect transition. In: Proceedings of the IEEE/CVF Conference on Computer Vision and Pattern Recognition (CVPR) (2019)
40. White, H.: Nonparametric estimation of conditional quantiles using neural networks. In: Page, C., LePage, R. (eds.) Computing Science and Statistics, pp. 190–199. Springer, New York (1992). https://doi.org/10.1007/978-1-4612-2856-1_25
41. Zhou, Q., Ooka, R.: Comparison of different deep neural network architectures for isothermal indoor airflow prediction. Build. Simul. **13**(6), 1409–1423 (2020)
42. Zhou, X., et al.: A Deep Generative Approach to Conditional Sampling (2021). https://doi.org/10.48550/ARXIV.2110.10277

ECG and sEMG Conditioning and Wireless Transmission with a Biosignal Acquisition Board

Luiz E. Luiz[1,2(✉)] [ID], Fábio R. Coutinho[2] [ID], and João P. Teixeira[1,3] [ID]

[1] Research Centre in Digitalization and Intelligent Robotics (CeDRI) Instituto Politécnico de Bragança, Campus de Santa Apolónia, Bragança 5300-253, Portugal
joaopt@ipb.pt

[2] Universidade Tecnológica Federal do Paraná, Campus Toledo, Paraná 85902-490, Brazil
a52482@alunos.ipb.pt, lluiz@alunos.utfpr.edu.br, fabiocoutinho@utfpr.edu.br

[3] Laboratório para a Sustentabilidade e Tecnologia em Regiões de Montanha (SusTEC), Instituto Politécnico de Bragança, Campus de Santa Apolónia, 5300-253 Bragança, Portugal
https://cedri.ipb.pt/ , https://sustec.ipb.pt/

Abstract. The market for Wearable Health Monitoring Systems (WHMS) has grown together with the demand for devices that offer greater medical reliability and lower cost. This study introduces a wearable system comprising conditioning blocks for electrocardiogram and surface electromyogram signals, an analog-to-digital converter, and wireless data transmission capabilities. These features have been implemented reliably in accordance with the specific requirements of these signals, as well as complying with patient safety directives and ensuring the quality of the resulting signal, allowing it to be used as a data collector for subsequent software implementation. To evaluate its performance, this system is compared against commercially available wearable devices, and the expected outcomes are examined. The obtained results are then presented, showcasing the system's capabilities and leading to a positive conclusion. As future work, there is a focus on enhancing the user interface and implement digital processing in the result for use in pathology recognition software with greater accuracy.

Keywords: Electrocardiogram · ECG · Electromyogram · EMG · Surface Electromyogram · sEMG · Signal Conditioning · Wearable Health Monitoring Systems · WHMS

1 Introduction

The objective of this paper is to present a wearable system that can effectively and affordably acquire, condition, and wirelessly transmit human biosignals. This system aims to collect reliable health data from patients, enabling comprehensive analysis and further investigation.

State-of-the-art devices designed for similar purposes typically incorporate acquisiton features such as electrocardiogram (ECG), electromyogram (EMG) [4,23,35], and electroencephalogram (EEG) [26,27]. Regarding wireless transmission, Wi-Fi technology is commonly employed for transmitting the collected biosignals [32], as well as Bluetooth [10,14,22,29], or even the possibility of both [24]. The signals are acquired from different regions of the body, including the upper body region [24,28], finger [1,31], and the widely used wrist [11,34]. Based on the chosen specifications, the system was developed to acquire electrocardiogram (ECG) and electromyogram (EMG) signals. The system provides the flexibility to select either Wi-Fi or Bluetooth communication for wireless transmission. The sensor is positioned in the torso region of the body.

The versatility of the developed device enable its integration with existing algorithms for the identification of various pathologies. By providing reliable and high-quality biosignal data, the device allows for in-depth analysis of signal characteristics, which can aid in the diagnosis and monitoring of different medical conditions.

Furthermore, the device's integration with existing algorithms and data processing techniques opens up possibilities for real-time monitoring, trend analysis, and long-term data tracking. This can greatly assist healthcare professionals in their decision-making processes and provide patients with a better understanding of their health status [24].

As a starting point, the upcoming section of this paper will introduce the biosignals used, providing a brief explanation of their significance and the reason behind their inclusion. Section 2 will then present the block diagram of the system, along with the hardware developed specifically for conditioning the ECG and EMG signals. Following that, Sect. 3 will compare the system with other commercially available acquisition systems. Finally, Sect. 4 will present the conclusions drawn from the study.

1.1   Electrocardiogram

The electrocardiogram (ECG) is a graphical representation used to analyze the heart's behavior by measuring the variations in electrical potential during cardiac cycles. The utilization of a portable device capable of recording the heart's activity for a duration longer than a day, known as Ambulatory External Electrocardiogram (AECG), enables the analysis of cardiac cycles during various daily activities performed by the patient [21]. This extended monitoring period increases the likelihood of detecting any existing cardiac pathologies [19].

In the acquisition of ECG electric potentials, electrodes, such as Silver/Silver Chloride electrodes, are employed. Under normal heart behavior, the maximum values of electrical potential difference recorded between two electrodes can reach up to 5 mV. The frequency band of the ECG signal typically ranges from 0.5 Hz to 50 Hz [30].

The standard medical ECG acquisition system typically utilizes ten electrodes, with six placed in the precordial region (in front of the heart) and the remaining four positioned on each limb [12]. However, this configuration can be uncomfortable for daily follow-up. Therefore, alternative configurations with only three electrodes have been designed [8]. Figure 1a illustrates the placement of these electrodes, equidistant from the heart. One electrode is positioned on the floating ribs, while the other two are placed at heart height and spread towards the shoulders, forming an Einthoven triangle around the heart [33]. Although patient movement can cause disturbances, it generally does not impact the analysis of the cardiac cycle [13].

The specific amplitudes of each parameter in the ECG signal depend on various factors, including electrode material and placement. However, when using the three-electrode configuration in the Einthoven triangle, voltage values close to 5 mV between the R peak and the S minimum can be expected [30]. This is illustrated in Fig. 1b, which represents an idealized ECG waveform.

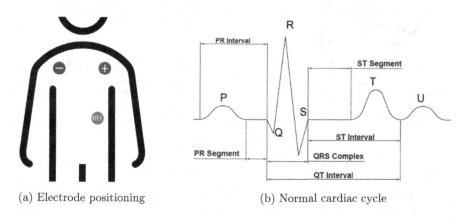

(a) Electrode positioning   (b) Normal cardiac cycle

Fig. 1. ECG configuration

1.2   Electromyogram

The electromyogram (EMG) is a biosignal utilized for the identification and quantification of muscle movements based on the analysis of electrical impulses generated during muscle contractions [33]. Its applications extend beyond medical diagnosis and include muscle rehabilitation and the control of electric prostheses for amputated limbs [15].

Surface electromyogram (sEMG) is a technique used to acquire EMG signals using surface electrodes, typically three in number, which are placed on the skin surface covering the target muscle. This allows for non-intrusive signal acquisition with minimal discomfort to the patient [20].

In this paper, three electrodes are employed for sEMG acquisition. Two potential electrodes are connected to the surface of the biceps muscle with an approximate separation of 2 cm between them, while a third electrode, serving as a reference voltage, is connected to the end of the humerus bone at the elbow [3]. Figure 2a illustrates this electrode placement.

The behavior of the muscle, as captured by sEMG, can be classified into two main states: muscle relaxation and muscle contraction. An idealized representation of an EMG signal is depicted in Fig. 2b, where a higher magnitude signal, modulated by the amplitude of the muscle contraction, is followed by periods of relaxation.

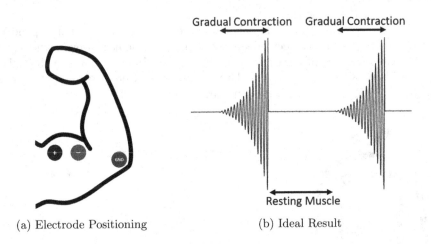

(a) Electrode Positioning   (b) Ideal Result

Fig. 2. sEMG Configuration

When acquiring sEMG signals using Silver/Silver Chloride electrodes with a diameter of 30 mm, it is anticipated that voltage values can reach a maximum of 50 mV. With respect to the mentioned electrode positioning, the frequency band of interest for sEMG signals typically lies between 20 Hz and 500 Hz [15].

2 Development

Regarding the development of the system, the formulation problem to overcome will be presented, followed by the presentation of the hardware developed.

2.1 Problem Formulation

Wearable devices that track vital signs have significantly contributed to making disease diagnosis more affordable and accessible [35]. Moreover, these devices enable independent users to wear them during their daily activities, allowing continuous monitoring of various biological functions. They can detect abnormalities, prompt further examinations, and increase the likelihood of early diagnosis in the presence of any confirmed pathology [24].

When it comes to ensuring patient safety in device connections, regulatory standards play a crucial role in validating medical equipment. Standards such as ISO 13485 and the Medical Device Directive (MDD) - 93/42/EEC have been established for medical use, providing guidelines for compliance [7,9]. Consequently, every connection between the wearable device and the patient's body must exhibit high impedance, ensuring minimal current flow, particularly in the connections responsible for transmitting electrical potentials into the body.

In order to achieve reliable results, several parameters need to be considered for the conditioning of the biosignals. Firstly, a common mode rejection ratio (CMRR) above 100 dB is recommended to effectively reject common mode noise and interference [18]. Additionally, the frequency response of the conditioning system should be designed to respect the specific frequency ranges of interest for each biosignal being measured [2].

In terms of the Analog-to-Digital Converter (ADC), the sampling frequency should respect the Nyquist-Shannon theorem. For this system, a sampling frequency of 1000 samples per second is required, as the highest signal frequency, which is the sEMG, is 500 Hz [25].

Lastly, the system requires a microcontroller responsible for controlling the Analog-to-Digital conversion of the signals, grouping them, and facilitating wireless transmission. These components, along with the necessary conditioning blocks, are integrated into a portable printed circuit board (PCB), as depicted in Fig. 3.

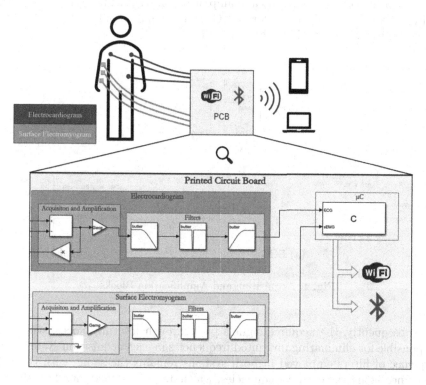

Fig. 3. Block Diagram from the System as a PCB

2.2   Developed Hardware

Following the signal acquisition, the ECG and sEMG conditioning systems starts with a block responsible for correlating the readings from the three electrodes and performing initial signal amplification. In both systems, two of the electrodes serve as opposite point readings of electrical potential. Consequently, the obtained values must be subtracted from each other using an instrumentation amplifier. The resulting signal is then appropriately amplified to optimize the utilization of the ADC operating range. The amplification factor is determined based on the specific area of interest, resulting in a gain of 1000 V/V for ECG and 100 V/V for sEMG.

The treatment of the third electrode differs between the ECG and sEMG acquisition systems [25]. For sEMG, the reference electrode is solely connected to the circuit's ground, effectively reducing the noise at the skin position to a referential zero level. This enhances the common mode rejection capability after the subtraction process. In contrast, for ECG, the third electrode serves as a feedback path for the signal. This technique, known as Right-Leg Drive (RLD) [6], introduces a voltage potential that is opposite to the common mode noise resulting from the subtraction between the other two electrodes. This helps cancel out this component present in the patient's body. The first conditioning block, which involves acquisition and amplification, results in the circuit depicted in Fig. 4a for ECG and Fig. 4b for sEMG. Operational amplifiers U1 and U2 are employed to ensure a CMRR above 100 dB.

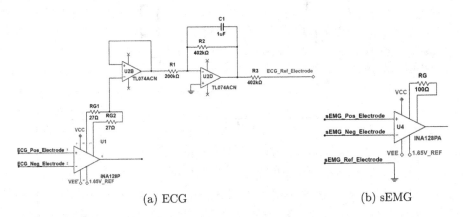

(a) ECG   (b) sEMG

Fig. 4. Acquisition and Amplification Blocks

Subsequently, the acquired signals pass through filtering blocks, which are responsible for eliminating unwanted frequencies in each acquisition system. The sequence of filters employed in both systems remains the same, with the only difference being the cut-off frequencies, which are determined based on the frequency range of interest for each signal [17].

The first filter utilized is a low-pass second-order Sallen-Key filter, primarily aimed at reducing electromagnetic noise. The cut-off frequency for both the ECG and sEMG signals is set according to their respective areas of interest, with an expected value of 50 Hz for ECG and 500 Hz for sEMG. Following this, a Notch filter, also known as a band-stop filter, is employed to attenuate the voltage noise induced in the patient's body by the power source. This filter exhibits a sharp frequency attenuation, typically centered around 50/60 Hz. Finally, the signals pass through a high-pass second-order Sallen-Key filter, which plays a crucial role in eliminating direct current (DC) components and preventing signal saturation in the converter [16,17]. The cut-off frequencies for this filter are set at 0.5 Hz for ECG and 20 Hz for sEMG.

These filters are designed with a Butterworth frequency response, which ensures minimal distortion in the transition regions. A quality factor of approximately 0.707 is employed during the parameterization process. The final circuit configuration for ECG is depicted in Fig. 5a, while the one for sEMG is shown in Fig. 5b.

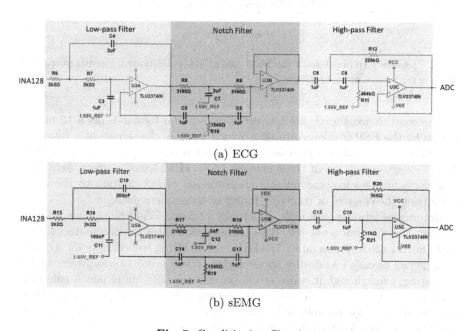

(a) ECG

(b) sEMG

Fig. 5. Conditioning Circuits

The frequency response of the circuits was validated through experimental testing in a real scenario. The resulting frequency response curves are represented by the blue line for ECG and the red line for sEMG, as shown in Fig. 6. These curves demonstrate the performance of the circuits across the frequency range of interest for each signal. Notably, the frequency response curves align with the expected voltage levels and frequency bandwidth, indicated by the blue square for ECG and the red square for sEMG. This alignment confirms that the circuits effectively acquire and amplify the desired signals within the specified frequency range.

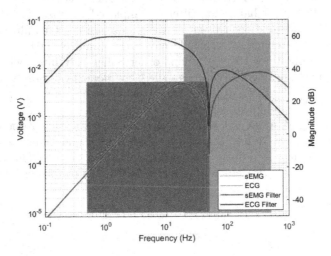

Fig. 6. Frequency response from the ECG and sEMG conditioning circuits overlapped with the respective areas of interest

The conditioned signals are converted into digital format using a 12-bit resolution by the ESP32 microcontroller, which samples the signals at a frequency of 1000 Hz. The converted signals are then organized and grouped into a JSON data package, consisting of three classes: ECG, sEMG, and Timing data. This data packaging ensures the reliable transmission of information to the client, minimizing the chances of receiving faulty or incomplete data.

In terms of wireless protocols, Bluetooth v4.2 and Wi-Fi 802.11 are available options. The maximum one-way data transmission rates for Bluetooth v4.2 and Wi-Fi 802.11 are approximately 784 kb/s and 54 Mb/s, respectively [5]. To mitigate the risk of data loss during transmission, Wi-Fi protocol was preferred during testing, even though it consumes approximately 22% more power compared to Bluetooth [5]. On the client side, the received JSON package is deserialized, and the data is plotted and/or stored, providing the client with the ability to visualize and download all the collected information.

3   Comparative Result Analysis

The data transmission was successfully initiated via Wi-Fi, and the acquired signals were stored for comparison purposes. For the ECG measurement, a Samsung Galaxy Watch 4 smartwatch model was used as a comparative device. To ensure accurate results, the measurements were conducted one after the other, minimizing the introduction of noise from one device to the other.

On the developed device (Fig. 7a), the ECG signal clearly shows the prominent R, T, and S peaks of each cardiac cycle. The heart rate was calculated based on the R peaks, resulting in 84 beats per minute (BPM).

Similarly, on the Samsung Galaxy Watch 4 (Fig. 7b), the positions of the R and T peaks are also evident, although the S peak is not as pronounced. The behavior of the DC segments, with a slight inclination leading to the onset of the peaks, is comparable between the two devices. The heart rate measurement on the smartwatch, based on the grid pattern, approximated to an average of 84 BPM.

These observations demonstrate the capability of the developed device to capture and display the key characteristics of the ECG signal, producing comparable results to a commercial wearable device such as the Samsung Galaxy Watch 4.

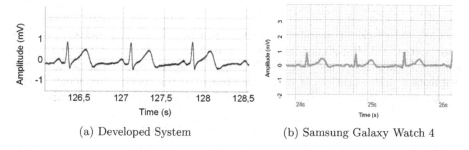

(a) Developed System   (b) Samsung Galaxy Watch 4

Fig. 7. Results obtained with ECG acquisition

For the sEMG measurement, the BITalino [14] device was used as a comparative reference to evaluate the performance of the developed system. A 15-second signal was collected sequentially from each device. After analyzing the results, a specific window with two contractions of the biceps was chosen for comparison.

In Fig. 8a, the sEMG signal collected using the developed system is displayed, while Fig. 8b represents the sEMG signal obtained from the BITalino device.

By examining the signal regions, it is noticeable that both signals exhibit variations in amplitude between the relaxed and contracted muscle states. The intensity of these variations, in relation to the expected ideal result shown in Fig. 2b, can also be observed. In both cases, there is a clear visual correspondence between the rising voltage amplitude and the increased muscle contraction, as well as the low amplitude signals during the resting state.

These observations indicate that the developed system successfully captures and represents the key aspects of the sEMG signal, comparable to the results obtained from the BITalino device.

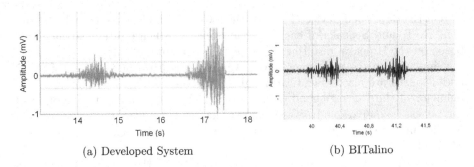

(a) Developed System　　　　　　　　　(b) BITalino

Fig. 8. Results obtained with sEMG acquisition

4　Conclusion and Future Works

In this paper, a comprehensive system for the acquisition, conditioning, processing, and wireless transmission of electrocardiogram (ECG) and surface electromyogram (sEMG) signals was presented. The system was integrated into a single wearable device capable of collecting reliable vital signs. The design of the acquisition and conditioning stages was based on the specific frequency ranges of each biosignal, and the wireless transmission was optimized to minimize data loss.

The obtained results were compared with other devices and the expected ideal results. The ECG signals exhibited all the characteristic waves typically observed in an ECG, demonstrating the accurate acquisition and conditioning of the signal. Similarly, the sEMG signals captured clear indications of muscle contractions and relaxation in both the developed device and the BITalino device. A comparison with the expected sEMG characteristics revealed an increase in voltage amplitude during higher-intensity muscle contractions.

Future work will focus on enhancing the user interface by presenting relevant parameters derived from the acquired biosignals, such as heart rate and identification of specific muscle contractions. Additionally, the utilization of a high-resolution Analog-to-Digital Converter (ADC) will be explored to further improve the system's performance and signal resolution.

Acknowledgements. The authors are grateful to the Foundation for Science and Technology (FCT, Portugal) for financial support through national funds FCT/MCTES (PIDDAC) to CeDRI - Research Centre in Digitalization and Intelligent Robotics (UIDB/05757/2020 and UIDP/05757/2020) and SusTEC - Associate Laboratory for Sustainability and Technology (LA/P/0007/2021).

References

1. Asada, H.H., Shaltis, P., Reisner, A., Rhee, S., Hutchinson, R.C.: Mobile monitoring with wearable photoplethysmographic biosensors. IEEE Eng. Med. Biol. Mag. **22**, 28–40 (2003)

2. Becchetti, C., Neri, A.: Medical Instrument Design and Development: From Requirements to Market Placements. Wiley, New York (2013)

3. Daud, W.M.B.W., Yahya, A.B., Horng, C.S., Sulaima, M.F., Sudirman, R.: Features extraction of electromyography signals in time domain on biceps Brachii muscle. Int. J. Mod. Optim. **3**, 515 (2013)

4. Dias, D., Cunha, J.P.S.: Wearable health devices-vital sign monitoring, systems and technologies. Sensors **18**, 2414 (2018)

5. Eridani, D., Rochim, A.F., Cesara, F.N.: Comparative performance study of ESP-now, Wi-Fi, bluetooth protocols based on range, transmission speed, latency, energy usage and barrier resistance. In: 2021 International Seminar on Application for Technology of Information and Communication (iSemantic), pp. 322–328 (2021)

6. Freeman, D.K., Gatzke, R.D., Mallas, G., Chen, Y., Brouse, C.J.: Saturation of the right-leg drive amplifier in low-voltage ECG monitors. IEEE Trans. Biomed. Eng. **62**, 323–330 (2014)

7. French-Mowat, E., Burnett, J.: How are medical devices regulated in the European union? J. R. Soc. Med. **105**, 22–28 (2012)

8. Jang, Y., Noh, H.W., Lee, I.B., Song, Y., Shin, S., Lee, S.: A basic study for patch type ambulatory 3-electrode ecg monitoring system for the analysis of acceleration signal and the limb leads and augmented unipolar limb leads signal. In: 2010 Annual International Conference of the IEEE Engineering in Medicine and Biology Society, EMBC 2010, pp. 3864–3867 (2010). https://doi.org/10.1109/IEMBS.2010.5627658

9. Jefferys, D.B.: The regulation of medical devices and the role of the medical devices agency. Br. J. Clin. Pharmacol. **52**, 229–235 (2001)

10. Jin, Z., Oresko, J., Huang, S., Cheng, A.C.: Hearttogo: a personalized medicine technology for cardiovascular disease prevention and detection. In: 2009 IEEE/NIH Life Science Systems and Applications Workshop. pp. 80–83 (2009)

11. King, C.E., Sarrafzadeh, M.: A survey of smartwatches in remote health monitoring. J. Healthcare Inf. Res. **2**, 1–24 (2018)

12. Kligfield, P., et al.: Recommendations for the standardization and interpretation of the electrocardiogram: Part I: the electrocardiogram and its technology: a scientific statement from the American heart association electrocardiography and arrhythmias committee, council on clinical cardiology; the American college of cardiology foundation; and the heart rhythm society. Circulation **115**, 1306–1324 (2007). https://doi.org/10.1161/CIRCULATIONAHA.106.180200

13. Kutz, M.: Standard Handbook of Biomedical Engineering and Design. McGraw-Hill, New York (2003)

14. Lazaretti, G., Teixeira, J., Kuhn, E., Borghi, P.: Android-based ecg monitoring system for atrial fibrillation detection using a bitalino® ECG sensor. In: Proceedings of the 15th International Joint Conference on Biomedical Engineering Systems and Technologies, vol. 15, pp. 177–184. SCITEPRESS - Science and Technology Publications (2022). https://doi.org/10.5220/0010905400003123, https://www.scitepress.org/DigitalLibrary/Link.aspx?doi=10.5220/0010905400003123

15. Lopes, V.H.S., Baccarini, L.M.R., Pereira, E.B., Santos, T.M.D.E.O., Galo, D.P.V.: Projeto e desenvolvimento de um sistema portátil de condicionamento e aquisiçao de sinais emg. In: Congresso Brasileiro de Automática-CBA, vol. 1 (2019)
16. Luiz, L.E.: Desenvolvimento de hardware modulado para condicionamento, digitalização e transmissão wireless de biossinais: eletrocardiograma, eletromiograma, saturação da oxigenação sanguíinea e temperatura corporal. Master's thesis, Instituto Politécnico de Bragança (2023)
17. Luiz, L.E., Teixeira, J.P., Coutinho, F.R.: Development of an analog acquisition and conditioning circuit of surface electromyogram and electrocardiogram signals. In: Optimization, Learning Algorithms and Applications: Second International Conference, OL2A 2022, Póvoa de Varzim, Portugal, 24–25 October 2022, Proceedings, pp. 19–34 (2023)
18. Magjarević, R., Badnjević, A.: Inspection and testing of electrocardiographs (ECG) devices. In: Badnjević, A., Cifrek, M., Magjarević, R., Džemić, Z. (eds.) Inspection of Medical Devices. SBE, pp. 59–79. Springer, Singapore (2018). https://doi.org/10.1007/978-981-10-6650-4_4
19. Mclellan, A., Mohamed, U.: Ambulatory electrocardiographic monitoring. Tests and results (2011)
20. Milner-Brown, H.S., Stein, R.B.: The relation between the surface electromyogram and muscular force. J. Physiol. **246**, 549–569 (1975)
21. Mittal, S., Movsowitz, C., Steinberg, J.S.: Ambulatory external electrocardiographic monitoring: Focus on atrial fibrillation. J. Am. Coll. Cardiol. **58**, 1741–1749 (2011). https://doi.org/10.1016/j.jacc.2011.07.026
22. Oliver, N., Flores-Mangas, F.: Healthgear: a real-time wearable system for monitoring and analyzing physiological signals. In: International Workshop on Wearable and Implantable Body Sensor Networks (BSN 2006), p. 4-pp (2006)
23. Pantelopoulos, A., Bourbakis, N.G.: A survey on wearable sensor-based systems for health monitoring and prognosis. IEEE Trans. Syst. Man Cybernet. Part C (Appl. Rev.) **40**, 1–12 (2009)
24. Patel, S., Park, H., Bonato, P., Chan, L., Rodgers, M.: A review of wearable sensors and systems with application in rehabilitation. J. Neuroeng. Rehabil. **9**, 1–17 (2012)
25. Por, E., v Kooten, M., Sarkovic, V.: Nyquist-shannon sampling theorem. Leiden University 1 (2019)
26. Rodrigues, P.M., Bispo, B.C., Garrett, C., Alves, D., Teixeira, J.P., Freitas, D.: Lacsogram: a new EEG tool to diagnose Alzheimer's disease. IEEE J. Biomed. Health Inform. **25**(9), 3384–3395 (2021). https://doi.org/10.1109/JBHI.2021.3069789
27. Rodrigues, P.M., Teixeira, J.P.: Classification of electroencephalogram signals using artificial neural networks. In: 3rd International Conference on Biomedical Engineering and Informatics (BMEI'10). vol. 2, pp. 808–812. IEEE (2010). https://doi.org/10.1109/BMEI.2010.5639941
28. Rutherford, J.J.: Wearable technology. IEEE Eng. Med. Biol. Mag. **29**, 19–24 (2010)
29. Sestrem, L., et al.: Data acquisition, conditioning and processing system for a wearable-based biostimulation. In: Proceedings of the 15th International Joint Conference on Biomedical Engineering Systems and Technologies, pp. 223–230. SCITEPRESS - Science and Technology Publications (2022). https://doi.org/10.5220/0011002300003123, https://www.scitepress.org/DigitalLibrary/Link.aspx?doi=10.5220/0011002300003123
30. Teixeira, J.P., Ferreira, A.: Ambulatory electrocardiogram prototype. Procedia Comput. Sci. **64**, 800–807 (2015). https://doi.org/10.1016/j.procs.2015.08.631

31. Vatavu, R.D., Bilius, L.B.: Gesturing: a web-based tool for designing gesture input with rings, ring-like, and ring-ready devices. In: The 34th Annual ACM Symposium on User Interface Software and Technology, pp. 710–723 (2021)
32. Wang, H., Peng, D., Wang, W., Sharif, H., Hwa Chen, H., Khoynezhad, A.: Resource-aware secure ECG healthcare monitoring through body sensor networks. IEEE Wirel. Commun. **17**, 12–19 (2010)
33. Wilson, F.N., Johnston, F.D., Rosenbaum, F.F., Barker, P.S.: On Einthoven's triangle, the theory of unipolar electrocardiographic leads, and the interpretation of the precordial electrocardiogram. Am. Heart J. **32**, 277–310 (1946)
34. Xu, C., Pathak, P.H., Mohapatra, P.: Finger-writing with smartwatch: a case for finger and hand gesture recognition using smartwatch. In: Proceedings of the 16th International Workshop on Mobile Computing Systems and Applications, pp. 9–14 (2015)
35. Zhang, T., Lu, J., Hu, F., Hao, Q.: Bluetooth low energy for wearable sensor-based healthcare systems. In: 2014 IEEE Healthcare Innovation Conference (HIC), pp. 251–254 (2014)

An Efficient GPU Parallelization of the Jaya Optimization Algorithm and Its Application for Solving Large Systems of Nonlinear Equations

Bruno Silva[1,2] and Luiz Guerreiro Lopes[3(✉)]

[1] Doctoral Program in Informatics Engineering, University of Madeira,
Funchal, Madeira Is., Portugal
bruno.silva@madeira.gov.pt
[2] Regional Secretariat for Education, Science and Technology,
Regional Government of Madeira, Funchal, Portugal
[3] Faculty of Exact Sciences and Engineering, University of Madeira,
9020-105 Funchal, Madeira Is., Portugal
lopes@uma.pt

Abstract. This paper presents a new GPU-accelerated parallel version of Jaya, a simple and efficient population-based optimization algorithm that has attracted increasing interest in different areas of science and engineering. Jaya has recently been demonstrated to be relatively effective at solving nonlinear equation systems, a class of complex, challenging problems that are hard to solve using conventional numerical methods, especially as the size of the systems increases. This class of problems was chosen to illustrate the application of the proposed GPU-based parallel Jaya algorithm and its efficiency in solving difficult large-scale problems. The GPU parallelization of Jaya was implemented and tested on a GeForce RTX 3090 GPU with 10 496 CUDA cores and 24 GB VRAM, using a set of scalable nonlinear equation system problems with dimensions ranging from 500 to 2000. When compared with the Jaya sequential algorithm, the parallel implementation provides significant acceleration, with average speedup factors between 70.4 and 182.9 in computing time for the set of problems considered. This result highlights the efficiency of the proposed GPU-based massively parallel version of Jaya.

Keywords: Metaheuristic optimization · Jaya algorithm · Parallel GPU algorithms · CUDA · Nonlinear equation systems

1 Introduction

Population-based optimization algorithms derived from evolutionary computation, swarm intelligence, and other nature-inspired computational approaches have been increasingly used to solve complex, large-scale, and high-dimensional problems. The quality of the solutions generated by these algorithms is highly dependent on the algorithm chosen, the global and local search strategies employed, and the parameter combinations associated with them [18].

© The Author(s), under exclusive license to Springer Nature Switzerland AG 2024
A. I. Pereira et al. (Eds.): OL2A 2023, CCIS 1982, pp. 368–381, 2024.
https://doi.org/10.1007/978-3-031-53036-4_26

Consequently, their effective application requires a judicious selection of such parameters, strategies, and algorithms, which is neither simple nor obvious. This difficulty has led some parameter-less population-based optimization algorithms like Jaya to gain increasing importance recently.

However, unlike swarm, evolutionary, and nature-inspired algorithms, Jaya is not based on any metaphor. Although the equation defining the Jaya algorithm has a slight resemblance to the equations of the well-known particle swarm optimization (PSO) algorithm, which update the speed and position of the swarm's particles (see, e.g., [3]), the same is based on a rather simple and distinct principle of optimization, which is to try to move away from the worst potential solutions and simultaneously approach the best candidate solutions, while the equations that define the PSO algorithm, proposed by Russell Eberhart and James Kennedy [2,8], are based on a social metaphor inspired by previous computational modeling studies of the movement of organisms within flocks of birds, fish schools and terrestrial animal herds (see, e.g., [13]), simulating in a simplified way the social behavior of fish schools and bird flocks when searching for food [8].

The algorithmic simplicity of Jaya, along with its efficiency and high degree of inherent parallelism, justifies the new GPU acceleration of this algorithm proposed in this paper.

The remainder of this paper is structured as follows: Background information is given in Sect. 2, including a short description of the original Jaya algorithm and references to previous GPU-based accelerations of Jaya that made use of parallelization strategies that are different from those used in this work. The proposed GPU-based parallelization of the Jaya algorithm is presented in Sect. 3, while Sect. 4 describes the experimental setup and test problems used to evaluate the proposed algorithm, and Sect. 5 presents and discusses the main results obtained with it. The conclusion of this work is given in Sect. 6.

2   Backgound

The Jaya optimization algorithm was proposed by Ravipudi Rao in 2016 [11]. Due to its simplicity and efficiency, the Jaya algorithm has received increasing interest and has become a viable alternative to the well-known PSO algorithm in various scientific and engineering disciplines (see, e.g., [12,19]).

Jaya is regarded as a parameter-less algorithm due to its lack of algorithm-specific control parameters aside from the standard control specifications, such as the population size and the maximum number of iterations.

Given the parameters of the problem under consideration, including the number $numVar$ of decision variables, a design variable index v ranging from 1 to $numVar$, a population index p varying from 1 to $popSize$, and the iteration index i ranging from 1 to $maxIter$, the value of the v-th variable of the p-th population's candidate at the i-th iteration is denoted as $X_{v,p,i}$.

The updated value $X_{v,p,i}^{new}$ is calculated according to the following equation:

$$X_{v,p,i}^{new} = X_{v,p,i} + r_{1,v,i}\left(X_{v,best,i} - |X_{v,p,i}|\right) - r_{2,v,i}\left(X_{v,worst,i} - |X_{v,p,i}|\right), \quad (1)$$

where $X_{v,best,i}$ and $X_{v,worst,i}$ are the population candidates with the best and worst fitness values, while $r_{1,v,i}$ and $r_{2,v,i}$ are uniformly distributed random numbers in the interval $[0, 1]$.

The pseudocode of the standard sequential Jaya algorithm is presented in Algorithm 1.

Algorithm 1. Sequential Jaya

1: /* *Initialization* */
2: Initialize $numVar$, $popSize$ and $maxIter$;
3: Generate initial population X;
4: Evaluate fitness value $f(X)$;
5: $i \leftarrow 1$;
6: /* *Main loop* */
7: **while** $i \leq maxIter$ **do**
8:      Determine $X_{v,best,i}$ and $X_{v,worst,i}$;
9:     **for** $p \leftarrow 1, popSize$ **do**
10:         **for** $v \leftarrow 1, numVar$ **do**
11:             Update population $X_{v,p,i}^{new}$ by Eq. (1);
12:         **end for**
13:         Calculate $f(X_{v,p,i}^{new})$;
14:         **if** $f(X_{v,p,i}^{new})$ is better than $f(X_{v,p,i})$ **then**
15:             $X_{v,p,i} \leftarrow X_{v,p,i}^{new}$;
16:             $f(X_{v,p,i}) \leftarrow f(X_{v,p,i}^{new})$;
17:         **else**
18:             Keep $X_{v,p,i}$ and $f(X_{v,p,i})$ values;
19:         **end if**
20:     **end for**
21:     $i \leftarrow i + 1$;
22: **end while**
23: Report best solution found and exit;

Wang et al. [17] presented the first known parallelization of the Jaya optimization algorithm on a GPU. In this parallel algorithm, GPU-Jaya, the data transmission between the host and the GPU is only done at the beginning and end of the algorithm execution, and the update of the candidate solutions, the calculation of the fitness values, and the selection of the best and worst solutions are performed in parallel on the GPU, using both global and shared memories provided by the CUDA (Compute Unified Device Architecture) framework for GPU computing and programming [15]. The algorithm employs a parallel reduction procedure, involving an operator with two inputs and one output that combines all elements of an array into just one, thus accelerating the update of the best and worst candidate solutions.

The GPU-Jaya algorithm was used in [17] to estimate the parameters of a Li-ion battery model. The problem considered involved six variables, relatively small population sizes (between 64 and 512), and up to 20 000 iterations.

The speedup factors obtained with this parallelization on a Tesla K20c GPU with 2496 CUDA cores and 5 GB VRAM ranged from 2.96 to 34.48 for a population of size 500, dropping markedly for lower population sizes.

A different parallelization of the Jaya algorithm on GPU was presented by Jimeno-Morenilla and collaborators [6,14]. In this parallel implementation of Jaya, each algorithm run is conducted in a distinct block of cores, and the rows of a block represent candidate solutions, whereas columns represent design factors. In this parallelization, the core threads exchanged data via the GPU shared memory, which is used to store the population of candidate solutions, the fitness function values, and other data utilized by the algorithm. This algorithm was evaluated on two different GPUs with a set of nonlinear functions containing up to 32 variables and population sizes ranging from 8 to 32. The mean speedup factor obtained in the best case was 53.

The GPU-based parallel version of the Jaya algorithm proposed in this paper takes an entirely different parallelization strategy, as discussed in the next section.

3 A New GPU-Based Parallelization of the Jaya Algorithm

A novel and efficient parallelization of the Jaya optimization algorithm is presented in this section and evaluated on a set of high-dimensional test problems that are challenging to solve with conventional iterative numerical methods. This algorithm leverages the CUDA platform to use the parallel processing capacity of a GPU for general-purpose computing.

CUDA programming enables the development of applications that take advantage of the combined processing power of CPUs and GPUs. The CPU is typically responsible for managing the overall execution of the program, while the computationally intensive portions are offloaded to the GPU. The division of work between the CPU and GPU is also referred to as heterogeneous computing.

In order to abstract the low-level details of the GPU hardware architecture, CUDA provides a programming model for parallel computation based on the concepts of kernel, grid, blocks, and threads. CUDA also provides memory management to manage the data transfers between the CPU (also referred to as the host) and the GPU (also referred to as the device), in addition to providing control over the different memory levels that exist on the GPU. A representation of the CUDA programming model and memory architecture is presented in Fig. 1.

GPU parallelization consists of the creation of one or several CUDA kernels (i.e., a parallel functions that run on the GPU), which are designed in such a way that they can be executed by a large number of threads simultaneously. In order to achieve this, a CUDA kernel is organized into a grid of several blocks, which in turn contain numerous threads (see Fig. 1). This block and thread arrangement can be organized into one-, two-, or three-dimensional grids depending on the parallelization needs of a particular kernel, and is an abstraction of the GPU computational hardware such as Streaming Multiprocessors (a cluster of CUDA cores) and the total available CUDA cores.

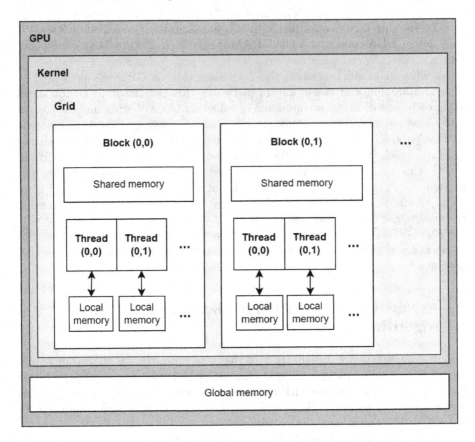

Fig. 1. CUDA programming model and memory architecture.

To have numerous threads running the same kernel and to manage what specific data elements should be accessed by each individual thread to be processed, CUDA uses what is called a thread indexing mechanism. This method specifies that each thread has a specific index within the kernel function that it can use to retrieve the corresponding data elements through the use of integrated variables like `threadIdx.x`, `threadIdx.y`, and `threadIdx.z`, which represent the indices in the x, y, and z dimensions, respectively.

As threads are organized in blocks of threads, CUDA uses a similar indexing method for coordinating the execution of threads within a block using built-in variables such as `blockIdx.x`, `blockIdx.y`, and `blockIdx.z`. In order to differentiate and identify specific threads and blocks within a CUDA kernel, both thread and block indexing are used in conjunction.

GPU hardware occupancy refers to how threads are organized (grid, block, and thread trichotomy). It is an important part of a kernel's performance because it determines how GPU computing resources are used.

Kernel programming also involves explicit data transfer between the host (CPU) and the device (GPU), as both hardware have their own memory spaces. As a result, data transfers are computationally costly tasks that should be avoided in order to hinder performance penalties [5].

Additionally, it is important to leverage the different GPU memory hierarchy effectively when performing CUDA programming, both in terms of performance and computation synchronization. CUDA supports different memory types that can be accessed by a kernel; the most relevant are depicted in Fig. 1, namely global, shared, and local memories. The global memory is the largest but also the slowest memory on the GPU. This memory persists throughout the entire execution of the kernel and is accessible by the host (i.e., it is the recipient of the data transfers from the CPU) and accessible by all threads in the GPU. The shared memory is relatively small, but it is a fast memory that is shared (and therefore accessible) among threads within a block. The local memory is private to each thread and is used to store local variables for thread-local execution, but it is slower than the shared memory.

The Algorithm 2 presents the implementation of a new GPU-based parallelization of the Jaya algorithm that leverages the different characteristics of CUDA programming to achieve considerable speedup gains when compared with the sequential implementation of the same algorithm.

Algorithm 2. GPU-based parallel Jaya

1: /* Initialization */
2: Initialize $numVar$, $popSize$ and $maxIter$;   ▷ CPU
3: $X \leftarrow$ GENERATE_INITIAL_POPULATION_KERNEL();
4: EVALUATE_FITNESS_VALUES_KERNEL(X);
5: $i \leftarrow 1$;   ▷ CPU
6: /* Main loop */
7: **while** $i \leq maxIter$ **do**   ▷ CPU
8:     Determine $X_{v,best,i}$ and $X_{v,worst,i}$;
9:     $X^{new} \leftarrow$ UPDATE_POPULATION_KERNEL(X);
10:     EVALUATE_FITNESS_VALUES_KERNEL(X^{new});
11:     $X \leftarrow$ SELECT_BEST_BETWEEN_KERNEL(X, X^{new});
12:     $i \leftarrow i + 1$;   ▷ CPU
13: **end while**
14: Report solution found and exit;   ▷ CPU and GPU

This implementation employs a heterogeneous computing approach, which uses the CPU and GPU to perform a combination of sequential and parallel computations. All tasks that are performed by the CPU are marked in Algorithm 2, while all function calls that end with the term *kernel* denote a GPU execution. An exception is in line 14 of Algorithm 2, in which the solution is determined by the GPU while the report is handled by the CPU (i.e., the computation is shared by both the CPU and GPU).

Splitting execution across multiple kernels makes it easier to handle thread synchronization. This is because when one kernel finishes executing and the next kernel starts, all processed data is synchronized in GPU global memory.

In order to avoid the performance penalty of data transfers between the host and the device, the generation of the initial population is performed directly in the GPU by the kernel indicated in (line 3 of Algorithm 2).

Such strategy is used throughout the different phases of the implementation of the GPU-based Jaya algorithm, in that the only information exchanged between the host and the device is the algorithm control variables (such as $numVar$ and $popSize$) at the beginning of the algorithm and the solution found at the end of execution.

The implementation of the main function of the Jaya algorithm, where the newly generated candidate solution is obtained, is presented on Algorithm 3.

Algorithm 3. Kernel to update population

1: **function** UPDATE_POPULATION_KERNEL(X)
2:    /* Device code */
3:        Determine row based on the x dimension of the thread and block data;
4:        Determine col based on the y dimension of the thread and block data;
5:        **if** $row \leq popSize$ **and** $col \leq numVar$ **then**
6:            Compute $X^{new}[row, col]$ by Eq. (1);
7:        **end if**
8: **end function**

Algorithm 3 parallelizes both the `for` loops in lines 9 and 10 of the sequential Jaya (Algorithm 1) in a single kernel, meaning that instead of generating a single candidate solution ($X^{new}_{v,p,i}$) for the entire population, it generates all candidate solutions simultaneously. This data parallelism is achieved by employing a two-dimensional block and thread organization that represents a matrix (i.e., a 2D array) with dimensions of $rows = popSize$ and $columns = numVar$, which is used to perform concurrently the computation of all new candidate solutions across multiple threads.

The kernel to handle the selection of the best candidate solution is defined in Algorithm 4. This code is more similar to the one used in the sequential Jaya, with the difference that a variable called $index$ has been added to handle the determination of the best candidate solution throughout the entire population simultaneously in parallel.

The $index$ variable is the result of the one-dimensional block and thread resource allocation chosen for this particular kernel. This symbolizes the allocation of one thread per candidate solution (i.e., a total of threads equal to $popSize$) that in turn handles the determination of the best candidate solution between each element of X and X^{new}.

Compared to other GPU-based Jaya implementations (e.g., [6,16]), this new parallelization uses a heterogeneous computing approach, utilizing both the CPU

Algorithm 4. Kernel to select the best candidate solution

1: **function** SELECT_BEST_BETWEEN_KERNEL(X, X^{new})
2:     /* Device code */
3:     Determine *index* based on the x dimension of the thread and block data;
4:     **if** *index* $<=$ *popSize* **then**
5:         **if** $f(X^{new}[index])$ is better than $f(X[index])$ **then**
6:             $X[index] \leftarrow X^{new}[index]$;
7:             $f(X[index]) \leftarrow f(X^{new}[index])$;
8:         **else**
9:             Keep $X[index]$ and $f(X[index])$ values;
10:        **end if**
11:    **end if**
12: **end function**

---

and GPU efficiently during the computation. In addition, data is generated and stored directly in the GPU, which minimizes data transfers between the host and device, thereby avoiding the associated performance penalties, and data is processed without requiring any kind of additional mapping or conversion.

4   Numerical Experiments

The sequential and parallel versions of the Jaya algorithm were implemented in the Julia programming language (version 1.9.0) using double precision floating-point arithmetic, and both utilized the same parameters.

In the computational experiments carried out, 51 independent executions of each possible combination of algorithm, dimension, and problem were performed, as suggested in [9].

The population size was defined as being 10 times the size of the problem considered, which was 500, 1000, 1500, and 2000, thus corresponding to 2500, 5000, 7500, and 10 000, respectively.

The maximum number of iterations has been set at 1000 since one of the goals of this study is to compare the computational efficiency of the sequential and parallel implementations of Jaya rather than the quality of the resulting approximations (i.e., how well the algorithm minimizes the cost function).

All tests with the sequential version of Jaya were carried out on a computer equipped with an Intel Core i7-5700HQ processor (4 cores, 8 threads, 6 MB cache, 2.70 GHz up to 3.50 GHz) and 16 GB RAM. The parallelization experiments on GPU were performed using an MSI GeForce RTX 3090 GPU with 24 GB VRAM and 10 496 CUDA cores.

The parallelized and sequential versions of Jaya were tested on a set of eight scalable, challenging benchmark problems, each of which with four different dimensions, as previously mentioned, thus totaling 32 distinct problems. The selected test problems are indicated below, along with the problem domain considered for each one of them.

Problem 1. Broyden tridiagonal function [10], $n = 500, 1000, 1500, 2000$.
$$f_1(\mathbf{x}) = (3 - 2x_1)x_1 - 2x_2 + 1$$
$$f_n(\mathbf{x}) = (3 - 2x_n)x_n - x_{n-1} + 1$$
$$f_i(\mathbf{x}) = (3 - 2x_i)x_i - x_{i-1} - 2x_{i+1} + 1, \quad i = 2, \ldots, n - 1$$
$$D = ([-1, 1], \ldots, [-1, 1])^T$$

Problem 2. Discrete boundary value function [10], $n = 500, 1000, 1500, 2000$.
$$f_1(\mathbf{x}) = 2x_1 - x_2 + h^2(x_1 + h + 1)^3/2$$
$$f_n(\mathbf{x}) = 2x_n - x_{n-1} + h^2(x_n + nh + 1)^3/2$$
$$f_i(\mathbf{x}) = 2x_i - x_{i-1} - x_{i+1} + h^2(x_i + t_i + 1)^3/2, \quad i = 2, \ldots, n - 1,$$
where $h = \frac{1}{n+1}$ and $t_i = ih$.
$$D = ([0, 5], \ldots, [0, 5])^T$$

Problem 3. Modified Rosenbrock function [4], $n = 500, 1000, 1500, 2000$.
$$f_{2i-1}(\mathbf{x}) = \frac{1}{1 + \exp(-x_{2i-1})} - 0.73$$
$$f_{2i}(\mathbf{x}) = 10(x_{2i} - x_{2i-1}^2), \quad i = 1, \ldots, \frac{n}{2}$$
$$D = ([-10, 10], \ldots, [-10, 10])^T$$

Problem 4. Powell badly scaled function [4], $n = 500, 1000, 1500, 2000$.
$$f_{2i-1}(\mathbf{x}) = 10^4 x_{2i-1} x_{2i} - 1$$
$$f_{2i}(\mathbf{x}) = \exp(-x_{2i-1}) + \exp(-x_{2i}) - 1.0001, \quad i = 1, \ldots, \frac{n}{2}$$
$$D = ([0, 100], \ldots, [0, 100])^T$$

Problem 5. The beam problem [7], $n = 500, 1000, 1500, 2000$.
$$f_1(\mathbf{x}) = -2x_1 + x_2 + \alpha h^2 \sin(x_1)$$
$$f_n(\mathbf{x}) = x_{n-1} - 2x_n + \alpha h^2 \sin(x_n)$$
$$f_i(\mathbf{x}) = x_{i-1} - 2x_i + x_{i+1} + \alpha h^2 \exp(x_i), \quad i = 2, \ldots, n - 1,$$
where $h = \dfrac{1}{n+1}$ and $\alpha \geq 0$ is a parameter; here $\alpha = 11$.
$$D = ([-100, 100], \ldots, [-100, 100])^T$$

Problem 6. The Bratu problem [7], $n = 500, 1000, 1500, 2000$.
$$f_1(\mathbf{x}) = -2x_1 + x_2 + \alpha h^2 \exp(x_1)$$
$$f_n(\mathbf{x}) = x_{n-1} - 2x_n + \alpha h^2 \exp(x_n)$$
$$f_i(\mathbf{x}) = x_{i-1} - 2x_i + x_{i+1} + \alpha h^2 \exp(x_i), \quad i = 2, \ldots, n - 1,$$
where $\alpha \geq 0$ is a parameter, assuming here $\alpha = 3.5$, and $h = \dfrac{1}{n+1}$.
$$D = ([-100, 100], \ldots, [-100, 100])^T$$

Problem 7. Extended Rosenbrock function [10], $n = 500, 1000, 1500, 2000$.
$$f_{2i-1}(\mathbf{x}) = 10(x_{2i} - x_{2i-1}^2)$$
$$f_{2i}(\mathbf{x}) = 1 - x_{2i-1}, \quad i = 1, \ldots, \frac{n}{2}$$
$$D = ([-100, 100], \ldots, [-100, 100])^T$$

Problem 8. Schubert–Broyden function [1], $n = 500, 1000, 1500, 2000$.
$$f_1(\mathbf{x}) = (3 - x_1)x_1 + 1 - 2x_2$$
$$f_i(\mathbf{x}) = (3 - x_i)x_i + 1 - x_{i-1} - 2x_{i+1}, \quad i = 2, \ldots, n - 1$$
$$f_n(\mathbf{x}) = (3 - x_n)x_n + 1 - x_{n-1}$$
$$D = ([-100, 100], \ldots, [-100, 100])^T$$

5   Results and Discussion

To assess the performance of the GPU-accelerated algorithm against its sequential version, the execution time of both implementations for each test problem, dimension, and population size were measured.

Table 1. Computational results

Test problem	Problem dimension	Population size	Mean CPU time (s)	Mean GPU time (s)	Mean speedup
1	500	5000	97.4952	1.1304	86.25
	1000	10 000	294.5144	2.2590	130.37
	1500	15 000	558.1462	3.7881	147.34
	2000	20 000	948.8058	5.9779	158.72
2	500	5000	101.1668	1.2206	82.88
	1000	10 000	254.9740	2.5754	99.00
	1500	15 000	538.7220	5.0129	107.47
	2000	20 000	840.3786	7.5033	112.00
3	500	5000	108.1746	1.1894	90.95
	1000	10 000	331.1936	2.4839	133.33
	1500	15 000	711.6312	4.5487	156.45
	2000	20 000	1173.8074	7.3193	160.37
4	500	5000	119.8196	1.3993	85.63
	1000	10 000	387.2858	2.9542	131.10
	1500	15 000	882.8966	5.0812	173.76
	2000	20 000	1510.2668	8.2569	182.91
5	500	5000	102.5478	1.2703	80.73
	1000	10 000	309.4632	2.9907	103.48
	1500	15 000	634.3676	5.7055	111.18
	2000	20 000	1028.0264	8.9916	114.33
6	500	5000	103.1358	1.4650	70.40
	1000	10 000	286.9486	2.9412	97.56
	1500	15 000	599.4926	5.5536	107.95
	2000	20 000	1028.6320	9.0365	113.83
7	500	5000	87.1428	1.0113	86.17
	1000	10 000	258.4948	2.0911	123.62
	1500	15 000	532.9252	3.8021	140.17
	2000	20 000	932.9102	5.6747	164.40
8	500	5000	77.3280	0.9808	78.84
	1000	10 000	225.9484	2.0495	110.24
	1500	15 000	461.2750	3.6825	125.26
	2000	20 000	781.9974	5.7397	136.24

The average results for the 51 separate runs are shown in Table 1 along with the relative performance of the two versions of the algorithm (i.e., the obtained speedup).

The results show that the GPU implementation of the Jaya algorithm is significantly and consistently faster than its CPU counterpart. The largest mean speedup gain was $182.91\times$, while the smallest was $70.40\times$.

By averaging the speedup gains by problem dimension, an a average speedup gain of $82.73\times$ was achieved for dimension 500, $116.09\times$ for dimension 1000, $133.70\times$ for dimension 1500, and $142.85\times$ for dimension 2000. This indicates that the GPU implementation makes efficient use of the GPU resources, in particular the block and thread allocations. This is largely the result of the parallelization method used, in which threads are assigned depending on the population size and problem dimension, as explained in Algorithm 3 and the strategies used to minimize data transfers between the CPU and GPU.

By plotting the average execution time to solve each individual problem by the problem dimension, the general performance of each algorithm implementation can be assessed. Figure 2 presents the analysis for the CPU (sequential) implementation, and Fig. 3 the GPU version of the same algorithm.

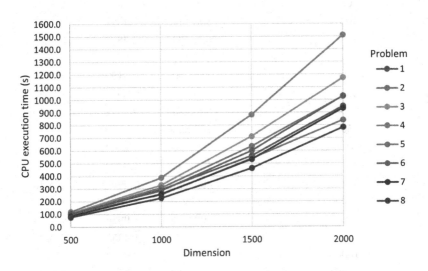

Fig. 2. CPU computation time scaling per problem and dimension.

In the line graph depicted in Fig. 2, all lines exhibit exponential behavior, with the exception of Problem 2, which exhibits a more linear slope after the dimension 1000. This shows that the computation time increases rapidly with increasing dimensionality, indicating that the performance penalty for increasing the problem's dimension is greater than the rate of data growth.

When examining the line graph for the computation time of the GPU parallel algorithm, presented in Fig. 3, it is possible to see that the rate at which the computation time grows is lower than the rate presented by the CPU scaling. This suggests that the time required to compute higher dimensions on the GPU varies at a more constant and predictable rate over equal intervals.

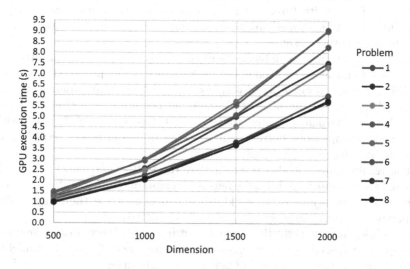

Fig. 3. GPU computation time scaling per problem and dimension.

Figure 4 shows the GPU-accelerated algorithm's response to increased workloads, which in this case correspond to larger problem sizes, and indicates that the GPU implementation can take advantage of available resources efficiently to maintain or improve performance as demand grows.

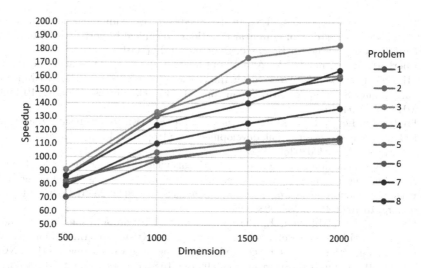

Fig. 4. Mean speedup gains per problem and dimension.

6   Conclusion

Although using GPU technology to accelerate an algorithm might result in noticeable speed gains, there are a number of difficulties involved. The computer platform, GPU architecture, parallel programming ideas, optimization strategies, and method being used, to mention a few, must all be well understood in order to address these problems.

With a set of hard, scalable systems of nonlinear equations converted into nonlinear minimization problems, the performance of the proposed GPU-based parallel implementation of Jaya was tested, and the computation times were compared to those of the sequential version of the same algorithm running on CPU. The results demonstrated that the GPU-based parallel Jaya algorithm performed incomparably better than its sequential equivalent, resulting in a mean speedup factor up to 182.91.

The results obtained also revealed that the GPU-based parallel algorithm proposed scaled quite well. It can achieve and maintain optimal performance even under conditions of increasing workload, and it can handle the computational complexity of solving large systems of nonlinear equations.

In addition to being effective and efficient in terms of increases in computing speedup, the parallelization strategy developed for the GPU-based parallel version of Jaya also has the benefit of being a general implementation. This is due to the fact that the Jaya algorithm's computational capabilities rather than the GPU architecture's limitations are its main emphasis.

Acknowledgement. The authors would like to thank Emiliano Gonçalves for kindly providing access to the GPUs used in the experiments.

References

1. Bodon, E., Del Popolo, A., Lukšan, L., Spedicato, E.: Numerical performance of ABS codes for systems of nonlinear equations. Technical Report DMSIA 01/2001, Universitá degli Studi di Bergamo, Bergamo, Italy (2001)
2. Eberhart, R., Kennedy, J.: A new optimizer using particle swarm theory. In: MHS'95: Proceedings of the Sixth International Symposium on Micro Machine and Human Science, Nagoya, Japan, pp. 39–43 (1995). https://doi.org/10.1109/MHS.1995.494215
3. Freitas, D., Lopes, L.G., Morgado-Dias, F.: Particle swarm optimisation: a historical review up to the current developments. Entropy **22**(3), 362 (2020). https://doi.org/10.3390/e22030362
4. Friedlander, A., Gomes-Ruggiero, M.A., Kozakevich, D.N., Martínez, J.M., Santos, S.A.: Solving nonlinear systems of equations by means of quasi-Newton methods with a nonmonotone strategy. Optim. Methods Softw. **8**(1), 25–51 (1997). https://doi.org/10.1080/10556789708805664
5. Gogolińska, A., Mikulski, Ł, Piątkowski, M.: GPU computations and memory access model based on Petri nets. In: Koutny, M., Kristensen, L.M., Penczek, W. (eds.) Transactions on Petri Nets and Other Models of Concurrency XIII. LNCS, vol. 11090, pp. 136–157. Springer, Heidelberg (2018). https://doi.org/10.1007/978-3-662-58381-4_7

6. Jimeno-Morenilla, A., Sánchez-Romero, J.L., Migallón, H., Mora-Mora, H.: Jaya optimization algorithm with GPU acceleration. J. Supercomput. **75**, 1094–1106 (2019). https://doi.org/10.1007/s11227-018-2316-7

7. Kelley, C.T., Qi, L., Tong, X., Yin, H.: Finding a stable solution of a system of nonlinear equations. J. Ind. Manag. Optim. **7**(2), 497–521 (2011). https://doi.org/10.3934/jimo.2011.7.497

8. Kennedy, J., Eberhart, R.: Particle swarm optimization. In: Proceedings of ICNN'95 - International Conference on Neural Networks, Perth, WA, Australia. vol. 4, pp. 1942–1948 (1995). https://doi.org/10.1109/ICNN.1995.488968

9. Liang, J.J., Qu, B.Y., Suganthan, P.N., Hernández-Díaz, A.G.: Problem definitions and evaluation criteria for the CEC 2013 special session on real-parameter optimization. Technical Report 201212, Computational Intelligence Laboratory, Zhengzhou University, Zhengzhou, China (2013)

10. Moré, J.J., Garbow, B.S., Hillstrom, K.E.: Testing unconstrained optimization software. ACM Trans. Math. Softw. **7**(1), 17–41 (1981). https://doi.org/10.1145/355934.355936

11. Rao, R.V.: Jaya: a simple and new optimization algorithm for solving constrained and unconstrained optimization problems. Int. J. Ind. Eng. Comput. **7**(1), 19–34 (2016). https://doi.org/10.5267/j.ijiec.2015.8.004

12. Rao, R.V.: Jaya: An Advanced Optimization Algorithm and its Engineering Applications. Springer, Cham (2019). https://doi.org/10.1007/978-3-319-78922-4

13. Reynolds, C.W.: Flocks, herds and schools: a distributed behavioral model. ACM SIGGRAPH Comput. Graph. **21**(4), 25–34 (1987). https://doi.org/10.1145/37402.37406

14. Rico-Garcia, H., Sanchez-Romero, J.L., Jimeno-Morenilla, A., Migallon-Gomis, H., Mora-Mora, H., Rao, R.V.: Comparison of high performance parallel implementations of TLBO and Jaya optimization methods on manycore GPU. IEEE Access **7**, 133822–133831 (2019). https://doi.org/10.1109/ACCESS.2019.2941086

15. Soyata, T.: GPU Parallel Program Development Using CUDA. CRS Press, Boca Raton (2018)

16. Wang, C.C., Ho, C.Y., Tu, C.H., Hung, S.H.: CuPSO: GPU parallelization for particle swarm optimization algorithms. In: Proceedings of the 37th ACM/SIGAPP Symposium on Applied Computing, pp. 1183–1189 (2022). https://doi.org/10.1145/3477314.3507142

17. Wang, L., Zhang, Z., Huang, C., Tsui, K.L.: A GPU-accelerated parallel Jaya algorithm for efficiently estimating Li-ion battery model parameters. Appl. Soft Comput. **65**, 12–20 (2018). https://doi.org/10.1016/j.asoc.2017.12.041

18. Wu, G., Mallipeddi, R., Suganthan, P.N.: Ensemble strategies for population-based optimization algorithms - a survey. Swarm Evol. Comput. **44**, 695–711 (2019). https://doi.org/10.1016/j.swevo.2018.08.015

19. Zitar, R.A., Al-Betar, M.A., Awadallah, M.A., Doush, I.A., Assaleh, K.: An intensive and comprehensive overview of JAYA algorithm, its versions and applications. Arch. Comput. Methods Eng. **29**(2), 763–792 (2022). https://doi.org/10.1007/s11831-021-09585-8

Author Index

A. I. Pereira et al. (Eds.): OL2A 2023, CCIS 1982, pp. 383–385, 2024.
https://doi.org/10.1007/978-3-031-53036-4

Printed in the United States
by Baker & Taylor Publisher Services